Politics in

ENGLAND

We live under a system of tacit understandings.
But the understandings are not always understood.

Sidney Low, *The Governance of England*

The Scott, Foresman/Little, Brown Series
in Comparative Politics

Under the Editorship of

GABRIEL A. ALMOND

LUCIAN W. PYE

A COUNTRY STUDY

Politics in
ENGLAND

**CHANGE AND
PERSISTENCE**

Fifth Edition

Richard Rose

*Centre for the Study of Public Policy
University of Strathclyde
Glasgow*

Scott, Foresman/Little, Brown Series in Political Science
SCOTT, FORESMAN AND COMPANY
Glenview, Illinois   Boston   London

TO MY FATHER

LIBRARY OF CONGRESS
Library of Congress Cataloging-in-Publication Data

Rose, Richard, 1933–
    Politics in England : change and persistence / Richard Rose. —
5th ed.
      p. cm. — (Scott, Foresman/Little Brown series in political
science)
  Includes index.
  ISBN 0-673-39892-7
  1. Great Britain—Politics and government.   I. Title.
II. Series.
JN231.R67 1985b
320.941—dc19   88-23998
                                    CIP

1 2 3 4 5 6 7 8 9 10 — KPF — 94 93 92 91 90 89 88

Printed in the United States of America

Acknowledgments

This book sums up the experience of more than three decades of studying politics while moving back and forth between Britain and America. To an American with an English wife and family now living on each side of the Atlantic, the experience has been personally congenial as well as professionally stimulating. It cultivates a point of view in which systems of government are not easily classified as better or worse just because they are different.

In this fifth edition of *Politics in England* each chapter has been revised and updated in the light of events of the 1980s, including Margaret Thatcher's unprecedented third election victory in 1987. In addition, a large amount of material on public policy has been included, resulting from a major program of research on the growth of government that I have conducted under the sponsorship of the British Economic & Social Research Council (E00220001). Drawing on the experience of England under confident Conservative and Labour governments as well as governments that have lost that confidence ensures that generalizations are soundly based as well as up to date.

Much new material is introduced in the freshly written prose, and in newly compiled tables and footnotes; material relevant only to past decades has been removed in order to concentrate upon what is important about politics in England today. Given the enormous expansion of political studies in the past quarter century, there is also a need to synthesize information and ideas. To record events and political debate without interpretation would leave both reader and author suffering from intellectual indigestion. Footnotes guide readers to books and articles that offer additional detail.

The terminology of politics in England is more complicated than most English people realize. While there is no doubt about the identity of England or the Queen of England, in law the government is that of the United Kingdom of Great Britain and Northern Ireland. The United Kingdom Parliament at Westminster is responsible for governing Scotland, Wales, and Northern Ireland as well as England. Yet government is described as "British," not "Ukish." The term Britain has no consistent meaning. To most English people it is interchangeable with the word England. But to most Scots, Welsh, and Ulster people, the term British connotes a loyalty to the United Kingdom as a whole. This complex of identities cannot be dealt with here. Non-English parts of the United Kingdom are treated fully in *The Territorial Dimension in Government: Understanding the United Kingdom* and four other books that I have authored or edited on the subject.

Politics in England is the title of this book because England is central in the United Kingdom. Its people constitute five-sixths of the population; the remainder is divided among three noncontiguous nations. The largest, Scotland, has only 9 per cent of the United Kingdom population. Where differences cause friction, Scots, Welsh, and Ulster people are expected to adapt to English ways. What is important for England will never be overlooked by any United Kingdom government, and politicians who wish to rise in government must accept English norms to do so. One can thus write about British government and English society.

Since the first edition of this book was written, politics in England and the study of politics have changed substantially. Before this book first appeared, most studies of British government devoted little or no attention to parties, elections, or public policy, and references to the past were far more frequent than to contemporary events. Today, there is a danger of leaning too far in the other direction. Government and politics, as these terms are colloquially distinguished, should not be kept separate; here they are treated as two interrelated parts of the practice of representative government.

In addition to data and evidence drawn from published books and articles, unpublished survey data has been courteously made available by the Gallup Poll, the British Election Survey held at the Economic & Social Research Council Archive at Colchester, MORI (Market & Opinion Research International) and NOP (National Opinion Polls).

Acknowledgments vii

Many debts have been accumulated in writing and revising a book as wide-ranging as this. The suggestion that started it all came from Gabriel Almond. In preparing the original study I benefited especially from comments and talks with J. A. T. Douglas and W. J. M. Mackenzie. Dr. P. L. Davies has undertaken computer runs especially for this edition. Ms. Isobel Rogerson and Ms. Anne Shaw have efficiently and cheerfully assisted with various secretarial tasks necessary to move from the author's keystrokes to output ready for computerized typesetting.

Richard Rose

Lady Day, 1988

Contents

Tables and Figures

Only connect . . .

E. M. Forster, *Howards End*

England in Perspective

There is a great difficulty in the way of a writer who attempts to sketch a living Constitution, a Constitution that is in actual work and power. The difficulty is that the object is in constant change.[1]

UNDERSTANDING ENGLAND IS IMPORTANT in the study of politics because England is a deviant case. Violence and revolution are common features of twentieth-century domestic politics in the largest nations of Europe: France, Germany, Italy, Poland, Russia, and Spain. Violence has also intermittently been a feature of American political life. Yet for the past three centuries English people have settled domestic political differences without resort to revolution or civil war. Just as Alexis de Tocqueville traveled to America in 1831 to seek the secrets of democracy, so one might journey to England to seek the secrets of stable representative government.

Modern societies with stable governments are rare in the world today, and many nations where representative government is secure have been much influenced by England. This is especially true of the United States, the first English colony in a distant land and the first colony successfully to revolt against the Crown. Bernard Bailyn, the author of *The Origins of American Politics*, notes: "The pattern of political activity in the colonies was part of a more comprehensive British pattern and cannot be understood in isolation from that larger system."[2]

In order to understand what England is, we must also understand what it is not, by comparison with other advanced industrial societies in Europe, across the Atlantic, and across the Pacific too. In order to understand what England is today, we must also compare the present with the past. England was not made in a day; its Par-

1

liament dates back to the thirteenth century, and it began to experience an Industrial Revolution two centuries ago.

A COMPARATIVE LOOK

Wherever one finds representative institutions of government, there is evidence of the influence of England. The Parliament at Westminster has been a model for institutions of democratic government in places as far-flung as India, Japan, Australia, and Canada. While the United States is today a greater military and economic power than England, the Presidential system of the United States has not been copied by any other stable democracy. The British civil service has served as a model for many developing nations, starting from the days when imperial administrators were sent from London to rule foreign lands. The English tolerance of free speech and freedom of political association is another tradition that is widely admired, especially in countries where individual freedom has often been breached.

The influence of England owes something to history: it was very early in developing a Parliament and a judicial system strong enough to place a check upon the power of the monarchy. Today this sounds obvious, but in the seventeenth century it required a civil war and the beheading of King Charles I to achieve this. The continuity of English institutions has been particularly attractive in nations that are seeking a durable form of government in place of regimes that quickly collapse. The spread of the British Empire and its gradual evolution into a Commonwealth in the twentieth century has made nations on every continent look to London as the standard for representative government.

Comparison implies contrasts too. The distinctiveness of politics in England is evident in the failure of attempts to transplant Westminster institutions to other countries. Dozens of former British colonies were given constitutions modeled on British lines at the time of obtaining independence from Westminster. In the great majority of cases, these institutions have been repudiated or adapted to suit very different circumstances.[3] The distinctiveness of England is even more evident in the failure to export to Northern Ireland political institutions that work well in England.

While England has ties with many different countries, it does not resemble any one. In the days of the British Empire, there were close ties with the Old Dominions of Canada, Australia, New Zealand, Ireland, and South Africa, and with subject colonies. These have not survived the evolution of Empire into Commonwealth. In law the United Kingdom retains a unique relation with the Republic of Ireland, even though the Irish Republic was founded by revolt against the Crown. Britain's closest ties by treaty are with the eleven other member nations of the European Community. While endorsing membership of this common market, most English people do not share a political identity with such European Community nations as France, Germany, Spain, and Greece.

Comparisons and contrasts between England and the United States illustrate the saying that the two nations are separated by a common language. During the Second World War there was unity of purpose in fighting a common enemy. Americans could identify Winston Churchill as a leader in a common cause, and the British government accepted an American general, Dwight D. Eisenhower, as leader of the Allied forces in Europe. For fifteen years after the Second World War, the special relationship of wartime seemed to persist. British politicians reckoned that they had more experience in handling diplomatic problems, and American leaders knew they had greater military and economic resources.

In the early 1960s American models became temporarily popular in England when a youthful John F. Kennedy and an ageing Harold Macmillan were the leaders of the two nations. The difficulties of American domestic and foreign policies—race riots, Vietnam, and Watergate—soon reduced the attractiveness of the American example. When worldwide economic difficulties of the 1970s affected Britain more than most European countries, many American writers gave a new importance to the example of England: it became a country not to imitate. The editor of a state-of-England symposium, *The Future That Doesn't Work*, proclaimed: "The United Kingdom has become the latest version of the Sick Man of Europe."[4] Such remarks prompted a former Labour Cabinet minister, Barbara Castle, to remark, "It is a curious form of special relationship that casts the United States as mourner-in-chief over Britain's corpse."[5]

It is often easier to see the faults of other nations than to see those of one's own. A senior American scholar of British affairs, Samuel Beer of Harvard, can criticize British government for exemplifying "a fragmentation of political life" alleged to create incoherence, immobilism, and pluralistic stagnation. Yet these are just the faults that many Americans attribute to Washington today.[6] Whereas England's economic difficulties are less severe today than a decade ago, today America's dependence upon borrowing abroad to finance public spending and consumption without investment has brought Washington under critical scrutiny from London to Bonn and Tokyo.[7] When Wall Street plummeted in October 1987, Margaret Thatcher had no hesitation in advising the American government to follow Britain's lead and put its fiscal affairs in order.

Criteria for Evaluation. Comparison does not prove the superiority of one society to another. The author has lived too long on each side of the Atlantic to believe that a global evaluation is practicable. As any traveler can verify, the grass is greener on the moister, cooler, and English side of the Atlantic. But the machinery for gardening is more advanced in America, and the sun shines more on American soil. Nor is it practical to live in an ideal-type country, combining the best attributes of many countries, for example, England's political stability, Japanese economic dynamism, French food, and Spanish sunshine. The circumstances of each nation—for better and for worse—must be taken as a package.

Comparison requires the careful specification of the particular object of comparison. In a democracy, popular consent is of first importance, for without the periodic challenge of free elections, a government may be effective but it cannot claim to be representative. Judged against the political experience of major European neighbors, England has an outstanding record of government by consent. Unlike Germany or Italy, England has had no twentieth-century experience of fascist dictatorship; unlike Czechoslovakia, no experience of a communist coup d'état; unlike Spain, no experience of military dictatorship arising from civil war; and unlike France, no experience of military occupation, the collapse of a regime, and the creation of a new constitution by a charismatic general. Representative government is a novelty in Japan, only being firmly established after the Second World War. Domestic violence has been an occasional feature of politics in many industrial societies, not least in resistance to the American civil rights movement.

The durability of representative institutions in England is outstanding in a world perspective (Table Intro.1). The English Constitution has evolved over so many centuries that it cannot be dated with precision; firm foundations back to the seventeenth century make it much older than any other continuing instrument of representative government. Elections have been held in England for many centuries without interruption, and the vote was granted

TABLE INTRO.1 *Government Origins Compared with Other Major Countries*

	England	America	France	Germany	Japan
1. Last foreign invasion	1066	1812	1940	1944	1945
2. Last internal revolution, coup	1688	1861	1958	1933	1940
3. Current constitution dates from	17th cent.	1789	1958	1949	1946
4. Mass suffrage continuous since	1885	1828[b]	1945	1949	1946
5. Deaths in military battle 1816–1980(000)	1,295	664	1,965	5,353	1,371
6. Deaths from internal political violence 1948–77	0[a]	434	164	61	60

Notes: [a] Excludes Northern Ireland, where about 1,500 deaths from political violence occurred in the period to 1977, and more than 2,400 to 1984.

[b] Not allowing for de facto disfranchisement of blacks in the American South until the 1960s.

Sources: Lines 1–4 calculated by the author. Line 5 calculated from Melvin Small and J. David Singer, *Resort to Arms* (Beverly Hills: Sage Publications, 1982), Table 10, Average battle deaths per annum. Line 6 from Charles L. Taylor and David A. Jodice, *World Handbook of Political and Social Indicators*, vol. 2 (New Haven: Yale University Press, 1983), Table II.7.

to a majority of adult males more than a century ago. By contrast, free elections have less than a half century of continuous history in Germany and Japan, and the right to vote was ensured black as well as white Americans only in the 1960s.

The achievements of government are a great source of pride to English people. When the European Values System Study Group asked people in many nations how proud they were of their country, big differences were found (Table Intro.2). Five-sixths or more of English people express pride in their country. Moreover, this very high level of national pride is achieved without the aggressive promotion of patriotism in schools and in the media that occurs in the United States. Pride in England is much higher than in France, Germany, and Japan, countries in which dictatorship and military defeat in the Second World War have left citizens with less cause for pride.

TABLE INTRO.2 *National Pride: A Comparative Analysis (in percentage)*

National pride	Britain	America	France	Germany	Japan
Very proud	55	80	33	21	30
Quite proud	31	16	43	38	32
All proud	(86)	(96)	(76)	(59)	(62)
Not very proud	8	2	8	18	28
Not at all proud	3	1	9	11	3
All not proud	(11)	(3)	(17)	(29)	(31)
Don't know	3	1	7	12	7

Source: See Richard Rose, "National Pride: A Cross-National Perspective," *International Social Science Journal*, 36:1(1985).

Effectiveness is a second criterion for evaluating government; unless a government can make its authority felt, it will collapse or be overthrown. Effectiveness is a requirement of all forms of government, representative or undemocratic. Dictatorships value effectiveness more than consent. The ideal democracy is concerned with achieving both consent and effectiveness. In every advanced industrial nation, one major criterion of effectiveness is success in managing the economy. This is true whether the policies followed are more in accord with classic market principles or involve very active government direction. Economic effectiveness is important for the government's revenue as well as for maintaining the material well-being of citizens.

Member nations of the Organization for Economic Cooperation and Development (OECD) are now more likely to take democracy for granted than to be confident of economic effectiveness, and this is specially true in England. In the 1960s and 1970s the British economy was usually below average in economic effectiveness. Successive Conservative and Labour governments told the electorate that they would secure a high rate of economic growth, but their efforts were not effective. The economy grew, but not as quickly as governments had planned. Domestic and foreign commentators came to describe any nation with a low rate of economic growth as suffering from the "English disease."

As the economies of all advanced industrial nations have accumulated difficulties since the OPEC oil price rises of the 1970s and the world recession of 1975, England can no longer be singled out as the only government that is less effective than its leaders would like. When Britain is compared with other major industrial nations, it is normally neither top nor bottom. Its position depends upon which particular economic indicator is used and which country is the object of comparison. In the 1980s Britain has had a higher growth rate than France or Germany but a lower rate of economic growth than Japan or the United States. Inflation is higher than Germany's but lower than France's. Public expenditure as a proportion of the national product is much higher than in the United States or Japan but lower than in France. Unemployment is the one indicator on which Britain has consistently ranked bottom in the 1980s (Table II.1).

While every nation would like to have the most successful economy in the world, by definition most countries must follow the leader. The British economy has not failed; it is simply not doing as well as those of the nations at the very top. The post–1945 record is best described as absolute progress compared with the past, yet relative decline by comparison with other nations that have achieved higher rates of long-term economic growth. The important point to the average English person is not how the country ranks in an international league table of economic indicators; it is that there has been a perceptible improvement in the standard of living through the years. In 1959 Harold Macmillan successfully campaigned for election with the slogan: "You've Never Had it so Good." In the decades since, the great majority of English people have achieved higher living standards and public benefits than their parents enjoyed three decades ago.

In a mixed-economy welfare state one measure of the effectiveness of the government is how much it can spend on social programs intended to benefit citizens, such as education, the health service, and social security, and also, how much it can afford to spend on defense and other programs intended to promote collective well-being. In order to maintain a relatively high level of benefits, the government's overall macroeconomic policy must contribute to the growth of the national product; the richer the country, the greater the resources that government may be able to spend. A second condition for an effective welfare state is that citizens consent to government taxing and spending a large proportion of the national product. If citizens do not trust government to spend large sums of money on their behalf, then a society can be rich, but the government appears ineffective.

By the standards of advanced industrial nations, England appears about average in its overall effectiveness in mobilizing national resources for public purposes (Table Intro.3). Public spending in total is actually three percent higher than the average for all OECD nations. When attention is directed at specific welfare state programs, then public spending in England is usually a little below the average for advanced industrial nations, but only by a few percent. One reason for this difference is that defense spending is higher.

British government appears more effective than American government, if a government's capacity to win the consent of citizens for taxing and spending is regarded as evidence of effectiveness. In England government mobilizes a much larger share of the national product for public purposes than do public institutions at all levels of the federal system. The United States has a wealthier economy, but Americans are less willing to trust government to make collective provision for their social needs. Americans are more likely to turn to not-for-profit institutions—churches, unions, employers, or the market—to provide for their welfare, than to trust to government. In England government is trusted to make greater provision for health care, education, and other social services than in the United States, and public effort on social security is similar.[8]

England today suffers from the aftereffects of early success. In the late nineteenth century England led the world both politically and economically. Since then it has had nowhere to go but down. Radicals attack what they view as the dead hand of the past and the assumption that past success guarantees future success. In the caus-

TABLE INTRO.3 *Government Spending for Public Purposes*

	Public Spending as a Percentage of National Product		
	OECD Mean	*England*	*America*
Pensions	9.0	7.0	7.2
Health care	5.6	5.3	4.3
Education	5.5	5.3	5.2
Misc. social services	5.1	3.9	1.4
Defense	3.0	5.3	6.5
Other programs	18.4	18.1	10.7
Total public spending	43.7	44.9	35.3

Source: OECD statistics as reported in Richard Rose, "How Big and How Exceptional is American Government?" *Political Science Quarterly* (forthcoming).

tic words of the left-wing historian E. P. Thompson, "We lie upon our heritage like a dunlopillo mattress and hope, in our slumbers, that those good, dead men of history will move us forward."[9] Today, Margaret Thatcher sees herself as a radical, offering a right-wing recipe to secure the country's international standing. Critics regard the slowness of institutions of representative government to change as evidence of political stagnation rather than as a praiseworthy mark of stability. Given that England was one of the first modern nations to create institutions of representative government and industrialization, radicals now argue for the need to "remodernize" England.

Historians view the century-long decline in England's world position more sympathetically. Paul Kennedy declares that credit is due England for sustaining a world role for so long and managing gracefully a gradual decline from its late-nineteenth-century peak.

> In the longer-term perspective—on the fundamental issue of how to preserve a worldwide Empire for as long as possible once the economic and strategic tides had turned—was not this flexible, reasonable, compromise-seeking policy preferable to the assertive "no surrender" one? It was not a bad performance on the whole, not a bad diplomatic juggling-act.[10]

Kennedy goes on to question whether the government of Ronald Reagan has a similar political capacity to adjust American military commitments to the changing economic condition of the United States as a global debtor.

THE BOOK'S OBJECTIVES

The primary object of this book is deceptively simple: to analyze how politics in England works today. In a country with centuries of continuity in government, it is appropriate for Chapter I to focus on the importance of political inertia, a force that encourages persistence from the past, as in the country's unwritten Constitution. It is also necessary to consider the way in which changes gradually occur, whether due to the intentional actions of forceful politicians such as Margaret Thatcher or because of the gradual compounding of pressure from past decisions. Chapter II examines the geographical setting of England; its insular character has historically maintained detachment from Europe while encouraging global political and economic involvement. England is only one part of a multinational United Kingdom of Great Britain and Northern Ireland.

Immigration from New Commonwealth countries has made England a multiracial society too.

The authority of government is symbolized by the Crown, but the length of Chapter III makes evident that the institutions now wielding that authority constitute a complex network including the Prime Minister, Cabinet ministers and ministries, and civil servants in Whitehall. Since each has a substantial influence upon what government does, we should not try to personify authority in a single person or office, such as the Prime Ministership or Cabinet; what is most important is the total influence of the government network. Parliament is less influential, even though the Prime Minister and Cabinet are nominally accountable to it. Chapter IV gives Parliament less space than a study of Washington devotes to Congress, which is an effective check upon actions by the President. The majority of Members of Parliament, whatever doubts they may have about government policy, are bound by party discipline to support the government on votes of confidence at Westminster.

Because the Constitution is unwritten, the informal and nonstatutory norms of the political culture are important in determining whether or not political behavior is consistent with "the rules of the game," such as who should govern and what limits can be placed upon authority. Chapter V compares the relatively limited role of English courts in restricting government with the greater importance of cultural values, beliefs, and emotions in determining the legitimacy of government actions. Norms of the political culture also reflect ideas about who should govern and how. Popular attitudes toward government are formed gradually, by a process of political socialization in the family, at school and in adulthood at work and in other social settings. The socialization process, the subject of Chapter VI, inculcates a few common cultural values; it also differentiates people according to party loyalties and inclinations to become political activists or remain relatively passive voters. The means by which a small minority of people volunteer for or are recruited for public office are examined in Chapter VII. In addition to considering the recruitment of elected politicians, it also examines the recruitment of civil servants and those in leadership positions throughout society.

Political information is disseminated in two different ways. The mass media, analyzed in Chapter VIII, provide the general public with a limited amount of political information. Their activities are complemented by the elite media, which are read or viewed by less than a tenth of the electorate. Whereas Washington has a Freedom of Information Act enshrining the public's right to know about government, the counterpart at Westminster is an Official Secrets Act, protecting the government's right to keep potentially embarrassing information secret. The concentration of authority within the government network encourages pressure groups to discuss their views quietly with government officials with powers of decision, rather than engage in well-publicized debates that could make enemies of government. Chapter IX explains how the capacity of pressure groups to influence British government varies greatly according to differences in group resources and values and the party in office.

Parties are firstly important because the choice that a voter has at a general election is simply a choice between parties nominating candidates in the constituency. Usually, only three candidates contest a seat. Chapter X demonstrates that the choice is even more restricted, for millions of votes are "wasted," being cast for candidates who do not have a chance to enter Parliament. Moreover, the parties for whom people cast their votes tend to exaggerate the differences in policy preferences found in the electorate. The multiple purposes of party organization are analyzed in Chapter XI. Intraparty politics, the struggle for control of their own party, is the immediate concern of many politicians. The need to compete for popular votes produces external cross-pressures, moderating what parties say in hopes of building a winning coalition in the electorate. Once in office, the extra-Westminster institutions of party tend to be superseded by a new authoritative group, the party-in-government. The leaders of the governing party are shown to have more influence over other partisans in the party than they can hope to have in the network of government, for there they face the fact that there are some things stronger than parties.

The production of public policies is a joint concern of party politicians and civil servants in the government network. Party politicians are meant to will the goals of policies, and civil servants to find the means. Chapter XII shows that the resources available to policymakers are multiple—laws, tax revenues, and the services of public employees. The programs produced by government differ in their use of resources: acts of Parliament concerning marriage and divorce are law-intensive; social security acts are money-intensive; and health and education, labor-intensive. The programs of government differ in purpose too: some are about the social welfare of individuals, others directed at the economy, and a third category is concerned with maintaining the authority of government. Chapter XIII shows that the programs approved at Westminster are not delivered there: this requires a network of institutions extending nationwide. Service delivery institutions include locally elected councils accountable to Acts of Parliament and agencies such as the national health service, which are not elected. In a mixed economy, Westminster must try to coordinate its public expenditure and tax revenue through the Treasury and to influence what happens in nationalized industries, the Bank of England, and the national and international economy. The more that government tries to do, the more its influence becomes contingent, not absolute.

Evaluating change, the theme of the concluding chapter, requires an understanding of the dynamic of change, which comes partly from society and partly from the movement of political inertia. Resistance to change is also found within government. Popular evaluations of government are not so much concerned with the problems that worry specialists; they involve an overall judgement about what can realistically be expected from politicians and public policy. The concluding section of the book considers the impact of Margaret Thatcher's long hold on office, which has replaced a search for consensus with a search for direction—yet leaves open the direction of England in the future.

In writing this book, a variety of methods of social science have been used as evidence about different aspects of politics in England. In a democracy, votes count; therefore, we should look at evidence of public opinion. It tells us what the people are thinking far better than the assertions of politicians. While political debate is often cast in terms of absolutes, many questions are actually matters of degree: How much money does government spend on social policies or raise in taxes? What proportion of MPs and of the electorate have a university degree? It is therefore appropriate to complement the interpretation herein with tables and figures showing evidence that the reader can examine.[11]

In scope this book is much broader than old-fashioned histories of kings and queens or studies that concentrate narrowly upon Prime Ministers and Members of Parliament. Important as nationally known politicians are, they are only half the story of politics in England. It is necessary to understand that politics is only part of the life of an individual; instead of speaking of voters it would be more accurate to speak of ordinary people in an electoral role. To analyze politics in its social context follows a tradition that goes back to Bagehot's mid-Victorian study of *The English Constitution*; it is also as modern as social science studies of political behavior. It is appropriate to see politics in its social and economic setting, for the boundaries that divide academics into separate disciplines are not maintained in everyday life. An ordinary person is not just a citizen, consumer, worker, or spouse; each person combines all these roles in his or her life.

Public policy links government with ordinary citizens, for a Cabinet minister depends for office upon popular votes; individual citizens depend upon government for such vital necessities as education, health care, social security, roads, and police protection. To understand the impact of government upon society we must look at what government does as well as what it is. Government is not only about politicians delivering speeches broadcast by the media. It is also about millions of public employees delivering everyday public services nationwide. So accustomed are we to the programs of contemporary big government that we hardly realize how significant they are. A British government that claims two-fifths of the national product in taxes is necessarily committed to providing many services for the mass of the people.[12]

By examining the evolution of politics in England this book seeks to link an understanding of the present with the future. Fifty years ago the distinguished French writer André Siegfried diagnosed England's position thus: "To turn the corner from the nineteenth into the twentieth century, there, in a word, is the whole British problem."[13] Since then England has achieved much. Today it faces a new challenge: to prepare for the twenty-first century. Most of the Cabinet ministers for the year 2001 are already in Parliament; among their number is the Prime Minister at the start of the next century. We are much closer to the year 2000 than to the beginning of the postwar era in 1945. Future historians will not characterize our time by what went before, but by what it is a prelude to.

NOTES

1. The epigraphs in this book are taken from Walter Bagehot's classic, *The English Constitution*, first published in 1867.

2. Bernard Bailyn, *The Origins of American Politics* (New York: Vintage, 1970), p. ix.

3. Cf. J. O. Nwabueze, *Judicialism in Commonwealth Africa* (London: C. Hurst, 1977); S. K. Panter-Brick, "Four Constitutions, Two Models," *Government and Opposition* 14:3 (1979).

4. R. Emmett Tyrrell, Jr., ed. *The Future That Doesn't Work: Social Democracy's Failures in Britain* (Garden City, N.Y.: Doubleday, 1977), p. 2.

5. "Americans Told Britain Still Lives," *The Times* (London), 17 April 1978.

6. Cf. Samuel H. Beer, *Britain Against Itself* (London: Faber and Faber, 1982), pp. 1f; and A. S. King, ed., *Both Ends of the Avenue* (Washington, D.C.: American Enterprise Institute, 1982).

7. Cf. Robert Gilpin, *The Political Economy of International Relations* (Princeton: Princeton University Press, 1987); and Richard Rose, *The Post-Modern President: the World Closes in on the White House Meets the World* (Chatham, N.J.: Chatham House, 1988).

8. To compensate for lower levels of public effort, Americans (and Japanese too) allocate much more of social welfare expenditure through nongovernmental institutions than is the case in England. Cf. Richard Rose, "How Big and How Exceptional is American Government?" *Political Science Quarterly* (1988, forthcoming).

9. E. P. Thompson, "An Open Letter to Leszek Kolakowski," in Ralph Miliband and John Saville, eds., *The Socialist Register, 1973* (London: Merlin Press, 1974), p. 24. Cf. Brian Harrison, *Peaceable Kingdom: Stability and Change in Modern Britain* (Oxford: Clarendon Press, 1982).

10. Paul Kennedy, *Strategy and Diplomacy, 1870–1945* (London: Allen & Unwin, 1983), pp. 217–218. See also Kennedy's comparative study, *The Rise and Fall of the Great Powers* (New York: Random House, 1987).

11. Inconsistencies in the territorial coverage of statistics, which often omit part of the United Kingdom, inevitably must be repeated here. Substantive conclusions are not affected, given that England constitutes five-sixths of the United Kingdom. For data on the non-English parts of the United Kingdom, see Richard Rose and Ian McAllister, *United Kingdom Facts* (London: Macmillan, 1982).

12. On what governments do, see Richard Rose, "The Programme Approach to the Growth of Government," *British Journal of Political Science* 15:1 (1985) 1–28; and Richard Rose, "The Dynamics of the Welfare Mix in Britain," in R. Rose and R. Shiratori, eds., *The Welfare State East and West* (New York: Oxford University Press, 1986) 80–106.

13. *England's Crisis* (London: Jonathan Cape, 1931), p. 11.

CHAPTER I

The Inertia of History

Each generation describes what it sees, but it uses words transmitted from the past. When a great entity like the British Constitution has continued in connected outward sameness, but hidden inner change for many ages, every generation inherits a series of inapt words—of maxims once true, but of which the truth is ceasing or has ceased.

EVERY GOVERNMENT IS CONSTRAINED by its history, for the force of political inertia carries past actions forward, thus limiting present choices.[1] For example, while no politician would choose to have to deal with the conflict in Northern Ireland as it is today, it is part of the inheritance of British government, unfinished business carried forward by political inertia from the Anglo-Irish treaty of 1921 and all that had gone before. The past is also important when it leaves no legacy. In the eighteenth century English traders exported slaves to the New World; since slaves were not imported to England, this avoided racial problems that have subsequently troubled the United States.

To understand politics in England, we must understand the evolution of institutions. Any attempt to explain the subject by a deductive approach drawing inferences from abstract assumptions is doomed to fail, because the political system has developed gradually through the centuries by an accumulation of institutions, values, and conventions. English people have never had to sit down under pressure of military defeat to deduce a constitution from first principles, as has been the fate of France, Germany, Italy, Russia, and the successor states of the Austro-Hungarian and Ottoman empires.

In England government has altered by adapting to changes in the

15

environment about it. Like a well established garden, the major features of the British Constitution today reflect the plantings of many
different proprietors. For example, elections today involve assumptions dating from the seventeenth century and earlier. In apportion-
ing electors into parliamentary constituencies, the Boundary Com-
missioners are not expected to apply mechanically the formula of
one person, one vote, one value. They are expected to make some
allowance for the representation of "communities that are integral,
human entities which have both a history and a very lively sense of
corporate feeling."[2] To prevent the creation of gross anomalies, the
constituency boundaries are reviewed periodically for alterations in
response to the continuous movement of population.

Symbols of continuity often mask great changes in English life.
Much of what we think of as typical of English tradition—the
ceremony of the monarchy, the urbane detachment of a nonparty
civil service, and the global commitments of an empire—reflect
nineteenth-century reforms or the conscious invention of tradition.[3]
The contrast between traditional symbols and practice is particularly great in what Bagehot described as the "undergrowth of irrelevant ideas" enveloping the Constitution.

Institutions, practices, and policies carried forward by the force of
political inertia are central in what we term the present. Nowhere is
this more true than in the politics of England. The heir to an
ancient crown pilots jet planes, and a medievally styled Chancellor
of the Exchequer tries to steer the pound through the deep waters of
the international economy. Former Prime Minister Clement Attlee
summarized the interpenetration of the past in a tribute to Winston
Churchill: "There was a layer of seventeenth century, a layer of
eighteenth century, a layer of nineteenth century and possibly even
a layer of twentieth century. You were never sure which layer would
be uppermost."[4] The first part of this chapter examines how the
unwritten Constitution of contemporary England is a product of a
historical process, the second part reviews the emergence of doubts
about the direction of government and Margaret Thatcher's response, and the conclusion considers how political inertia affects
the "remaking" of England.

WRITING AN UNWRITTEN CONSTITUTION

The conventional way to describe a government is by referring to
its constitution. We cannot do so here, for England has no written
constitution. At no time in the past was there a break with tradition, as in the American Revolution, forcing politicians to think

about the basis of authority and write down how the country should be governed henceforth. The English Constitution has persisted for centuries without ever having been codified on paper or subjected to formal approval. Because it is so identified with the English way of life, the Constitution can only be understood as the product of historical inertia.

The English Constitution is a phenomenon of tradition; it consists of a variety of doctrines, laws, institutions, and practices that have been handed down from one century to the next. It was often argued by defenders of the status quo that traditions were immutable or that changes could not be introduced by conscious choice of ministers or Parliament. In the absence of a written Constitution, changes cannot be made through a public and formal process of amendment. Evolution not revolution is the key to the process of constitutional change in England. It is impossible to date the Constitution. Because it is a jumble of unwritten and written elements from the past, an introduction to a collection of documents about constitutional issues concludes: "It would be foolish to suppose that this mode of systematizing the material gives a complete picture of the British Constitution."[5]

Becoming Modern. Unlike many other nations, England resolved fundamental problems of governance before industrialization. In late medieval times, the Crown was established as the central political authority, and the supremacy of secular power was settled in the sixteenth century, when Henry VIII broke with the Roman Catholic Church to establish a national Church of England. Characteristically, the conflict between Crown and Parliament in the civil war of the 1640s was followed by a restoration; the monarchy returned, but with less power than before. The Constitution prevailing at the start of the Industrial Revolution in the late eighteenth century was a mixed Constitution sharing political authority between the Crown and Parliament.

Industrialization, not political revolution, was the great discontinuity in English history. By the middle of the nineteenth century England was the world's first modern industrial society. The repeal of the Corn Laws in 1846, removing the import duty on a basic food, symbolizes the shift from a self-reliant agrarian society to an industrial economy trading its manufactured goods worldwide. England then claimed to lead the world, both economically and politically.

Social scientists have no agreed means for dating the point at which England gained a modern system of government.[6] A political historian might place the change at 1485, when the Tudors took over the monarchy and Henry VII strengthened the institutions of royal authority. A parliamentary historian might date modern times from the seventeenth century, when Parliament successfully asserted its authority against the King. A specialist in party politics might date the modern era from the grant of the vote to the majority of men in 1884, or to all men and women in 1918. A frustrated radical might proclaim that by his or her values, England hasn't become modern yet.

The simplest way of dating modern government is to say that it came about in Victorian times, for Queen Victoria had a lengthy reign from 1837 to 1901. During this era, the traditional practices of the Old Constitution were altered so that government could cope with the problems of a society that was increasingly urban, literate, and critical of unchanged traditions. The 1832 Reform Act, establishing the principle that constitutional practices could be altered by Act of Parliament, was endorsed by the Prime Minister of the day, Earl Grey, with the argument: "Unless the privileged sections of the community were prepared to adapt and to improve, waves of dangerous and uncontrollable innovation would completely drown the existing social order."[7]

The increase in national wealth due to industrialization gave government more money to spend, as well as confronting it with the problems of an increasingly urban industrial society. Public expenditure per person increased, while simultaneously it fell as a proportion of the national product. In 1800, at the height of England's successful war against Napoleon's France, public expenditure accounted for 22 percent of the national product. By 1850 it had decreased its share of the national product to 11 percent. But because the national product was so much larger, total spending rose by one-quarter in real terms. By 1900, at the time of the Boer War in South Africa, public expenditure accounted for fourteen percent of the national product.[8]

In Victorian times, reform legislation gradually increased the number of people eligible to vote, and party organizations began to develop along recognizably modern lines. Innovations promoted by followers of Jeremy Bentham's rationalistic philosophy led to the development of a civil service capable of organizing everything from the economical saving of candle ends to prototype laws of the modern welfare state.[9] Government grew from a few central institutions around the monarch, supported by a landed gentry and nobility, to an organization capable of delivering major public services nation-wide. In 1837 the Post Office became the first government depart-ment delivering a modern public service; the first minister responsi-ble for health was appointed in 1854, for education in 1857, and for local government in 1871.

Three Challenges. The early creation of a modern political sys-tem did not make the problems of governing disappear. It simply created institutions of representative government that could then respond to challenges confronting England in the twentieth cen-tury. National defense in a war-ravaged world has been the first of these challenges. In the First World War Britain and France held Germany at bay in a trench war of bloody attrition, finally winning in 1918 with American support. In the Second World War Britain stood alone against Nazi Germany until 1941, when the war broad-ened to include Russia, America, and Japan. In 1945 Britain once again was on the winning side.

The second great challenge, the grant of the full rights of citizenship to all subjects of the Crown, was accomplished gradu-ally. A religious test for the right to vote and membership in Par-liament was abolished gradually in the nineteenth century. Within Parliament the supremacy of the elected House of Commons over the aristocratic and hereditary House of Lords was established by legislation in 1911. The right to vote was granted all adults in 1918. The Labour Party, founded in 1900 to secure representation in Par-liament for manual workers, first formed a minority government briefly in 1924. The nonviolent General Strike of 1926 demonstrated the commitment of trade union leaders to constitutional action. When union leaders were confronted with the revolutionary impli-cation of a general strike, the strike collapsed.

Thirdly, government began using Acts of Parliament and taxing powers to distribute the fruits of economic growth to citizens in the form of social programs providing education, security of income, and health services for the majority of citizens. The Liberal government of 1906–14 laid the foundations for the contemporary welfare state by guaranteeing pensions to needy people in old age. Social programs were carried forward by the force of political iner-tia, expanding gradually as demand rose and the nation grew wealthier. The country's national product more than doubled between 1913 and 1938, and public spending on social programs increased from 2.6 percent of the national product in 1900 to 11.3 percent of a much larger national product in 1938.[10]

The Modern Constitution. In a political system that lacks a written Constitution, the Mace is the symbol of political authority. The medieval origin of the Mace is a reminder of the lengthy historical process that created the United Kingdom. In physical form the Mace is a five-foot silver-gilt staff that represented power in the days when kings and knights met in hand-to-hand combat. In the words of Ambrose Bierce: "Its form, that of a heavy club, indicates its original purpose and use in dissuading from dissent."[11]

The Mace represents the consensual as well as the effective force of authority; only when the Mace is in position in the House of Commons is the Commons deemed to be in session. The Mace thus symbolizes the central doctrine of the Constitution: authority rests with the Crown in Parliament. The executive authority represented by the Crown is balanced by popular consent, represented by Parliament. This doctrine leaves vague the identity of those who wield the power of the Mace. At first it might seem easy to find a single locus of authority. But in English usage government was traditionally a plural noun, for the government is an infinity of institutions. *Whitaker's Almanack* devotes seventy-five double-column pages to listing Government and Public Offices, starting with an industrial relations body, the Advisory Conciliation and Arbitration Service, and ending with the White Fish Authority in Edinburgh. Paging through this catalogue of Government and Public Offices is like exploring an endless maze.

In the midst of a maze of institutions, the Mace is the symbol of a single overriding authority, the Crown in Parliament. While many institutions compete for influence within the network of government, the competition is unequal. No group can challenge a decision made by the Prime Minister and Cabinet and endorsed by Act of Parliament; it carries the ultimate authority of the Crown in Parliament. This sets limits to the influence of pressure groups upon government, including local government, nationalized industries and other subordinate public agencies. By creating a final authority to resolve disputes within government, the Mace gives priority to making decisions effective. By contrast, the system of checks and balances in the American Constitution gives priority to preventing any one institution from imposing its will, as a British government can do when wielding the authority of the Crown in Parliament.[12]

The written element of the English Constitution consists of Acts of Parliament, very occasional government statements, or in default of legislation, interpretations of common law. Parliament is deemed sovereign; law courts have no authority to overrule Acts of Parliament by appealing to a written document with the overriding authority of fundamental law. Because the written elements are ordinary Acts of Parliament, the government of the day can alter any laws, institutions, or procedures by a simple majority vote in Parliament. Laws of constitutional status are not entrenched, requiring approval by "more than majority" means, as is normally the case in countries with a written Constitution. The doctrine of parliamentary sovereignty means that as long as it follows the laws that it has enacted, the power of the government is not subject to any judicially enforceable constraints.[13] In the blunt words of a constitutional lawyer: "The constitution is what happens."[14]

The unwritten part of the Constitution consists of a variety of customs and conventions. Customs are the result of what has happened in the past. Sooner or later nearly all customs are subject to change, but the presumption is that they will be followed by the government of the day unless there is a compelling reason, such as wartime, to depart from custom. Conventions are doctrines about how government ought to behave if confronted by a given type of problem. Relations between Cabinet ministers and the House of Commons and between the Prime Minister and Cabinet colleagues are regulated by conventions, not laws. Conventions may be ignored if it is deemed inconvenient by the Prime Minister or Cabinet ministers. Courts normally are not involved in disputes about conventions; these are political issues resolved in Parliament, where the government of the day has a majority of the votes.

The absence of a written Constitution is often said to be a great advantage because it gives flexibility to the government of the day. It can adapt to changing circumstances without the difficulties of amending a written document. But the flexibility of the unwritten Constitution also results in vagueness about what the government of the day can and cannot do. It is able to interpret constitutional doctrines to its own advantage or abandon customs and conventions as it chooses. Because this is usually done in order to achieve an immediate political goal, changes in the practice of the unwritten Constitution often generate a large amount of political controversy. But protests are of no effect because of the restricted role of the courts and the fact that the opposition lacks the votes in Parliament to stop the government from acting as it chooses to do.

Critics of the unwritten Constitution assert that England now needs a written Constitution with judicially enforceable restrictions upon government action and an amendment process that makes it more difficult for the government to change the Constitution at will. Critics also argue that individual citizens should have their liberties protected by a judicially enforceable written Bill of Rights. The virtues of a traditional Constitution are questioned by political groups that find their position weakened by the absence of a judicially enforceable constitution. The weakness of constitutional guarantees is also criticized by many academic commentators. Critics allege that there is a "constitutional wasteland" in the absence of a written document that authoritatively defines the powers and limits of government. Nor is there any charter of citizens' rights enforceable in the courts. So strong is the traditional bias of the Constitution in favor of effective action by government that a leading judge can describe as "a strange idea" proposals "to accommodate the concept of fundamental and inviolable human rights" by ending "the helplessness of the law in face of the legislative sovereignty of Parliament."[15]

Comparing the American and the English Constitutions emphasizes the extent to which an unwritten constitution imposes far fewer constraints upon the government of the day, by contrast with a written constitution (Table I.1). The American Constitution gives the Supreme Court the final power to decide what the government may or may not do. By contrast, Parliament is the final authority in England, and as the government of the day has a disciplined major-

TABLE I.1 *Comparing an Unwritten and a Written Constitution*

	England (unwritten)	*USA (written)*
Origins	Medieval customs	1787: Constitutional convention
Form	Unwritten, indefinite	Written, precise
Final Power to Interpret	Majority in Parliament	Supreme Court
Bill of Individual Rights	No	Yes
Amendment	Ordinary vote in Parliament; unprecedented action by government	More than majority vote in Congress and state legislatures
Centrality in Political Debate	Low	High

ity there, this means that the government itself is effectively the
final interpreter of its own powers. The United States Constitution
includes a Bill of Rights for individuals, so that anyone who
believes his or her personal rights infringed by government can seek
redress through the courts. While British government cannot act
against individuals without authorization by Act of Parliament, an
individual who regards a law as an infringement upon rights has
no effective judicial redress. Amendment of the unwritten Constitution can occur simply by the government taking an unprecedented
action, for the English courts will not enforce customs and conventions, as the American courts enforce written clauses of the Constitution. In the United States, amendment is a cumbersome and
lengthy process that is so difficult that most proposed amendments
are never adopted. American critics of the written Constitution
believe that at the end of the twentieth century the political system
is shackled by "the external forms of an eighteenth-century system
of government."[16]

An English critic has the opposite worry: "The difference
between America and Britain is that their politicians are required to
act within the Constitution, whereas ours make the rules up as they
go."[16]

POSTWAR CONSENSUS AND THE CHALLENGE TO CONSENSUS

The Second World War and its aftermath brought about great
changes within England. In mobilizing the population for total
war, the all-party coalition government of Winston Churchill
sought to provide fair shares for everyone through rationing and
expanded social services. From the wartime coalition came the
Beveridge Report on Social Welfare, Keynes's Full Employment
White Paper of 1944, and the Butler Education Act of 1944. These
three measures—the first two named after Liberals and the third
after a Conservative—remain major landmarks of the contemporary
mixed-economy welfare state.

The wartime fair-shares policy was continued by the Labour
government of Clement Attlee elected in 1945. It maintained
rationing and controls while the economy was being rebuilt. The
National Health Service was established, providing medical care for
all. Coal mines, gas, electricity, the railways, road transport, and the
steel industry were nationalized as part of Labour's program of
increasing government's influence in the economy. By 1951 the
Labour government had accomplished the measures on which there

was agreement within the party; its economic policies had yet to produce prosperity. A much-reformed Conservative Party under Winston Churchill was returned to power by the electorate.

For three decades after the Second World War there was a confident consensus about gradual reform, as Conservative and Labour governments sought to promote economic prosperity, provide generous welfare services, and increase the take-home pay of ordinary citizens. Politicians relied upon the fiscal dividend of economic growth to produce additional public revenues, rising real incomes, and full employment. The 1950s saw a rise in living standards after years of wartime scarcity and postwar austerity. Consumer goods once thought the privilege of a relative few, such as motor cars and refrigerators, became widespread. The Conservatives won general elections with an increase in parliamentary majorities in 1955 and 1959. The Prime Minister, Harold Macmillan,[17] summarized the economic record of the 1950s by saying, "Most of our people have never had it so good." But Macmillan was cautious about the future. When praising prosperity in 1957, he warned:

> What is beginning to worry some of us is "Is it too good to be true?" or perhaps I should say, "Is it too good to last?" Amidst all this prosperity, there is one problem that has troubled us—in one way or another—ever since the war. It's the problem of rising prices.

The political consensus was labeled Butskellism, combining the names of R. A. Butler, a leading Conservative exponent of full employment and government spending on social programs, and Hugh Gaitskell, Labour Party leader from 1955 to 1963, who favored gradual social improvements rather than using the rhetoric of Socialist class war.

Doubts Arise. The 1960s cast doubt upon the government's ability to guarantee continued affluence, for the British economy grew more slowly than the government wished and more slowly than those of foreign competitors. The Macmillan government turned to economic planning in hopes of stimulating steady growth. In opposition, Labour leaders argued that the planning associated with socialism provided a more effective means to develop the economy. In 1964 Labour campaigned with the reform-minded slogan "Let's Go with Labour," an echo of John F. Kennedy's vague 1960 appeal to "get America moving again." The new

Labour Prime Minister, Harold Wilson, won office asserting that Labour would "modernize" the economy and the political system. But Labour became progressively identified with the status quo. The government had no answer to a classic economic dilemma: how to stimulate a domestic economic boom without simultaneously inviting inflation and the devaluation of the pound. It responded by the traditional policy of deflation and devaluing the pound. When Labour left office in 1970, the nation's economy was growing more slowly than at any time since 1945.

The 1960s was also a period of disillusionment with British government. Continuities with the past were attacked as evidence of the dead hand of tradition. In 1963 the fourteenth Earl of Home, then a member of the House of Lords, was chosen as Prime Minister by a small clique of Conservative notables. (When criticized by the Labour leader for his hereditary advantages, the Earl, also known as Sir Alec Douglas-Home, remarked, "I suppose Harold Wilson must be the fourteenth Mr. Wilson.") A new wave of satire on television and in periodicals such as *Private Eye* mocked institutions formerly held in esteem. A series of Royal Commissions and inquiries proposed reforms of the civil service, local government, Parliament, the mass media, industrial relations, and the Constitution. New titles were given to Whitehall offices to signify the desire for change for its own sake. Behind their entrance doors, the same people went through the same administrative routines as before.

The 1970s intensified anxieties about the government (or even the governability) of England.[18] The Conservative government of Edward Heath from 1970 to 1974 demonstrated that the country's difficulties were common to Conservative as well as Labour governments. While promising major changes in policies and institutions of government, the biggest changes were neither intended nor desired. In an effort to limit unprecedented inflation, Edward Heath risked the authority of his office by a confrontation with the National Union of Mineworkers, which had defied the government's pay policy by striking to secure a wage increase. The impasse was broken by the general election of February 28, 1974, called by the Prime Minister to ascertain: Who governs? The electorate returned a vote of no confidence in both major parties. The Conservative share of the vote dropped by 8 percent, and the Labour vote by 6 percent, producing the lowest level of popular support for either party in a generation.

Labour took office in March 1974 under Harold Wilson, whose

party was just short of a majority in the Commons. Labour won a bare parliamentary majority in October with the lowest share of the vote ever to secure a parliamentary majority. Because of by-election defeats and defections by sitting MPs, by 1977 the Labour government under James Callaghan, who replaced Wilson on his retirement, lost its parliamentary majority. A pact with the Liberals was required to guarantee the Labour government a majority in the House of Commons.

The major achievement of the 1974–79 Labour government was to maintain political consensus in the face of economic difficulties. Instead of confrontation with the unions, the Labour government sought a social contract. Initially this was intended to provide higher social welfare benefits and avoid government restrictions upon wage increases. In July 1975 inflation led to the first of a series of measures being enacted to limit wage increases, and real take-home pay fell. In 1976 problems became so great that the government was forced to seek a loan from the International Monetary Fund. In order to reduce inflation, Chancellor Denis Healey abandoned financing high levels of public spending by a large public deficit and imposed strict cash limits, effectively steering the Labour government in a monetarist direction. By the spring of 1979 unemployment stood at the highest since the 1930s, 1.5 million; prices had doubled since 1974, and the economy had contracted instead of growing in two of the preceding four years.

The British general election of May 3, 1979, saw the two major parties reverse their traditional roles. The nominally Conservative Party led by Margaret Thatcher called for a radical change in the country's economic policy. The Conservatives won an absolute majority in Parliament and 44 percent of the popular vote. Labour's share of the popular vote fell below 37 percent, its lowest since 1931. The Liberals won 14 percent of the vote but very few seats in the House of Commons. Margaret Thatcher became the first woman Prime Minister of a major European country.

The Thatcher Response. Margaret Thatcher entered office in 1979 determined to make a break with the past in both style and substance. The economic shortcomings of the previous decades (including those of the Heath and Macmillan governments, as well as of Labour governments) were diagnosed as arising from too much continuity in maintaining Keynesian consensus. Margaret Thatcher rejected the views of traditional Conservatives who favored continuity and had the motto: "Even when I changed [sic], it should be to preserve." Similarly, she rejected the views of such prominent Butskellite politicians as Roy Jenkins, former Labour Chancellor and founder of the Social Democratic Party, who argued: "The test of statesmanship will not be how many trees it pulls up by the roots, but how it fits into a continuous process of adaptation."[19] In place of consensus Margaret Thatcher has offered her convictions to the electorate on a take-it-or-leave-it basis:

> The Old Testament prophets did not say: "Brothers I want a consensus." They said: "This is my faith. This is what I passionately believe. If you believe it too, then come with me."[20]

The 1979 Conservative Party election manifesto described as its substantive goal a fundamental shift in society, claiming: "The balance of our society has been increasingly tilted in favor of the state at the expense of individual freedom." Measures that increase the role of the market in allocating society's resources are, in the eyes of Margaret Thatcher, measures that increase individual freedom. This Prime Minister believes citizens have more freedom of choice in the marketplace than in an election. Just as some Socialists argue that public provision of goods without charge is desirable, so Margaret Thatcher believes in the virtues of the market economy. Just as Socialists believe that equality is desirable, so Margaret Thatcher believes that people who differ in their efforts and abilities should differ in the rewards that they achieve. According to Milton Friedman, a Nobel Prize-winning economist whose monetarist views Margaret Thatcher endorses, she "represents a tradition of the nineteenth century Liberal, of Manchester Liberalism, of free market free trade."[21]

While many advocates of the market as a source of freedom believe in restricting the role of government in noneconomic matters too, Margaret Thatcher believes in strong government. This is most evident in her support for a large defense force and showing undiplomatic toughness in negotiations with other nations. It is also evident in her support for the police and for the claim of the government of the day to act as it thinks best in security matters. Paradoxically, in order to promote policies favoring the market, the Thatcher administration has had to pursue an active legislative policy. Efforts to curb public expenditure lead the government to "interfere" with arrangements sanctioned by the preexisting consensus. The Prime Minister is quick to assert her personal authority against Cabinet ministers and civil servants, and even more than Harold Wilson she is anxious to prevent the media from publishing unauthorized leaks from ministers and ministries.

The contrast between the "libertarian" concern with the market and the "authoritarian" wielding of the Mace is best understood as an indication that many of her policies and principles are developed by instinct and assertion rather than by logical deduction from fixed principles. As political journalist Peter Riddell cautions:

> There has been a tendency, particularly on the left, to make Thatcherism seem more clear-cut than it is—to devise an ideology from what is in practice a series of values and instincts and a political alliance. Both opponents and supporters of the Thatcher Administration have created more of a pattern from the disconnected events and policies than is warranted.[22]

One thing is certain: Margaret Thatcher has enjoyed unprecedented electoral good fortune. Her first term of office, from 1979 to 1983, was particularly difficult. The government was frustrated in its hopes to turn the economy around quickly. Unemployment doubled to 3 million, more than 12 percent of the labor force. Instead of growing faster, the economy slowed down and in some years contracted. One success was a reduction in the rate of inflation. Whereas the cost of living more than doubled from 1974 to 1979, its rise was reduced to 55 percent from 1979 to 1983. The 1982 Argentine invasion of the sparsely populated Falkland Islands, a remote British colony in the South Atlantic, gave the Prime Minister a chance to demonstrate her belief in strong government. Britain went to war to regain the Falklands; the war was brief, virtually bloodless, and immediately successful in its objective. It also helped restore the Prime Minister's domestic political fortunes, which had suffered because of the poor state of the economy.[23]

The Conservatives won a landslide victory at the 1983 general election due to divisions among opponents. The Labour Party found coping with opposition even more difficult than coping with government. Left-wing critics gained control of the party's annual conference and forced through a series of rule changes intended to shift power from the party in Parliament to the extraparliamentary party. When James Callaghan resigned in 1980, he was succeeded by Michael Foot, a veteran left-wing campaigner against nuclear weapons with little experience of government. Labour won only 27 percent of the vote at the 1983 election, its worst showing since 1918.

In protest against the shift left within the Labour Party, four Cabinet ministers in the 1974-79 Labour government—Roy Jenkins, Shirley Williams, David Owen, and William Rodgers—resigned to form a new Social Democratic Party in spring 1981. The SDP then concluded an electoral alliance with the Liberals. The new Alliance proclaimed its goal as "breaking the mold" of the old party system. It differed from the Thatcher government in favoring a more positive role for government in social policy and Keynesian economic measures to combat unemployment; it differed from Labour in rejecting that party's alliance with trade unions and reliance upon planning.[24] At the 1983 election, Alliance candidates won 25 percent of the popular vote but only twenty-three seats in Parliament because its vote was so evenly spread that candidates often came second but rarely first in a constituency. With opponents dividing evenly a majority of the popular vote, the Conservatives gained fifty-eight seats in the House of Commons, even though their share of the vote dropped by 1.5 percent.

Margaret Thatcher won an unprecedented third election victory on June 11, 1987; the Conservative vote held steady at 42 percent, and the party retained a majority of 100 seats in the House of Commons, better than that achieved by any of her predecessors since Clement Attlee in 1945. The Labour Party entered the election campaign with hopes of a big recovery under the leadership of Neil Kinnock, whose "soft left" position was expected to improve the party's popular appeal while also maintaining Labour unity. Labour's vote went up only three percent from 1983; its vote was the second lowest in more than half a century. The Alliance vote fell three percent, and it won twenty-two seats. Disappointment with the results led to an immediate postelection split between the Liberal Party leader, David Steel, and the SDP leader, David Owen. The majority of the SDP then voted to join with the Liberals in a new merged party, the Social & Liberal Democrats, in spring 1988, but Owen and his band of followers remained aloof, claiming that they remained the *true* Social Democrats.

In her tenth year in office, Margaret Thatcher can look back upon a record of achievements, but also frustrations. The Thatcher government has been ready to wield the Mace to break the Butskellite consensus by enacting Acts of Parliament that the opposition parties dislike but must accept as part of the laws of the land. A series of industrial relations acts has reduced the former legal immunities of trade unions and given rights to individual members to ballot on strike action and on the choice of union officers. Legislation has been used to limit local government expenditure, to abolish Labour-controlled metropolitan-area governments in such cities as London, and to replace rates on housing with a community charge or poll tax on each adult living in a local government area. Government legislation has led to the sale of a large number of council houses owned by local authorities. Following reelection in 1987, new legislation was introduced setting central standards for schools and universities and making it possible for some schools to retain public funding while becoming independent of local authorities. Legislation has also authorized new charges for national health service facilities.

In industry, the Thatcher government has expressed its preference for the market, enacting Acts of Parliament to privatize many publicly owned corporations by selling shares to the public. Shares in government-owned British Petroleum were the first to be sold. Some of the industries sold had been regarded as public utilities, providing services in return for monopoly powers, such as British Telecom, running the telephone service, and British Gas. Other institutions sold have been operating in more competitive markets, such as British Airways, Jaguar cars, and the National Freight Company. Privatization is justified on grounds of economic efficiency (the market is deemed to work better than government in determining production, investment and prices); ideology (the power of government is reduced); and short-term financial benefits (the revenue received from the sale of public assets keeps the public deficit and taxation down).

As the force behind political inertia, Acts of Parliament have frustrated the Prime Minister's ambition to bring about a major reduction in the size of government by cutting the proportion of the national product claimed by public expenditure. Because Acts of Parliament are not altered by an election result, in 1979 the Thatcher Administration inherited a host of major spending commitments for social security, health, and education. Each of these programs is costly because the law entitles citizens to receive a free education, a pension in retirement or an income-maintenance grant if in need, and health care on demand. Even though Margaret Thatcher did not like the nonmarket principles underlying these commitments to big-spending welfare state programs, her government had only two choices: to obey the Acts, with all this meant in terms of keeping up public expenditure, or to repeal costly social security, health, and education programs, satisfying market principles at the risk of going down to defeat from an electorate accustomed to publicly financed social benefits. The Thatcher government has usually followed the first alternative.

The acceptance of inertial commitments to finance costly social programs has resulted in public expenditure claiming as high or higher a share of the national product in the Thatcher Administration as under previous Labour governments (Figure I.1). At the start of Mrs. Thatcher's third term of office, public expenditure accounted for 44 percent of the national product, four percent higher than in the final year of Harold Wilson's 1964-70 Labour government. In the Thatcher Administration, public spending as a percentage of the national product has averaged 45.5 percent, the same as under the 1974-79 Labour government, and higher than under either the previous Conservative administration of Edward Heath or the 1964-70 Labour government. If the Thatcher government succeeds in achieving its public expenditure target in 1991—a big *if* in the uncertain world of public finance—public spending as a proportion of the national product will still be higher than at any time in twenty years.[25] The government's inability to cut public spending has led to right-wing criticism that the government is not

FIGURE I.1 *Public Expenditure as a Proportion of the National Product,* 1965-1986

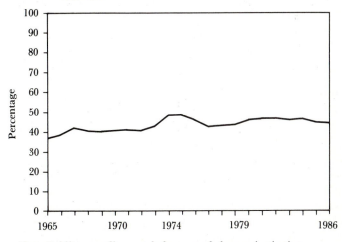

Note: Public expenditure excludes proceeds from privatization.
Source: H. M. Treasury, *The Government's Expenditure Plans 1988-89 to 1990-91* (London: HMSO, Cm. 288-I), Table 5.1.

doing enough to promote the market, and it should extend privatization to education, the health service and pensions. Concurrently, the opposition parties have criticized the government for not spending enough to reduce unemployment and boost the health services and social security benefits.

Difficulties in securing economic growth are a second reason for the frustration of the Thatcher government's ambition to cut the size of government. When the economy is in recession, the national product grows slowly if at all, and public spending grows faster than usual because of the need to spend additional sums on such measures as unemployment benefits. The national product, the single broadest measure of economic activity, actually *contracted* in the first two years of the Thatcher government because of the impact of stringent anti-inflation monetarist policies. By the time of the 1983 election the national product was only slightly higher than when Labour left office in 1979. By 1987 the gross domestic product had increased by 15 percent since 1979, nearly all in the government's second term of office.

Inflation, a second major target of the Thatcher Administration, has been greatly reduced. Whereas the retail price index doubled in the 1974–79 Labour government, it rose by half in the first Thatcher term and at one point was at the lowest for more than two decades. But lower inflation was achieved at the price of increased unemployment. Unemployment more than doubled in the first Thatcher term of office, going above 3 million (that is, above 12 percent of the working population). It then remained virtually constant at this level, before falling below 3 million at the time of the 1987 general election. Just as Margaret Thatcher points with greatest pride to the fall in inflation, so her severest critics concentrate upon the rise in unemployment.

Insofar as freedom is represented by increasing the market power of the ordinary individual, the Thatcher Administration has had just as uneven a record in increasing the take-home pay of the average adult manual workers as that of her predecessors (Figure I.2). Take-home pay—the money that a worker has in hand after deductions of income tax and social security contributions—has gone up in fourteen years since 1964. However, in eight years it has gone down because of low rates of economic growth, a high rate of increase in taxation, or both. The two steps forward, one step backward pattern has resulted in take-home pay increasing by one-quarter in the past two decades. In the first two terms of the Thatcher Administration, take-home pay rose only five percent.

FIGURE I.2 *The Unsteady Course of Take-Home Pay since 1964*

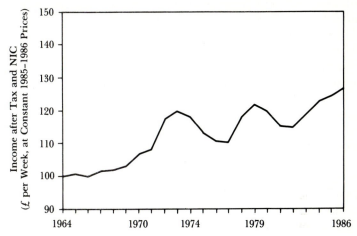

Source: As calculated by the Statistics Division of the Inland Revenue.

The Thatcher Administration demonstrates the difficulties that a strong-willed government has when it confronts the force of inertia, both political and economic. There are some things that a government cannot achieve, however strong the will of its Prime Minister and however big its majority in the House of Commons. Almost every postwar British government has found that the economy has grown less quickly than it would like, and inflation and/or unemployment has grown more quickly than desired. Paradoxically, the longer Margaret Thatcher is in office, the more evidence accumulates of the extent to which political inertia sustains spending commitments, policies, and institutions even in the face of the rhetoric of radical change.

REMAKING AN INHERITANCE

Each newly elected government enters office optimistic about its chances of making big changes and leaves office full of explanations why it was not so easy to change things as it had hoped. It defends its record as the best that could be done, given what was inherited from its predecessors. This is particularly true today, for government is now committed to far more activities than in the nineteenth century. Margaret Thatcher has found that inheriting responsibility for a government already committed to spend more than two-fifths of the national product gives a nominally sovereign government far less room for political maneuver than would have been the case of a government in the 1930s or the 1880s. The momentum is great for spending on such long-established programs as education, the health service, social security, and payment of debt interest.

Political inertia is sustained first of all by legislation. Acts of Parliament remain in force unless repealed. No government has time to scrutinize all the laws for which it is responsible. Even if it did, it would not have time to repeal or amend every law that it found unsatisfactory in whole or part. Of the several thousand Acts of Parliament for which it is responsible, a government will repeal only a few on policy grounds. Laws that are not repealed remain in effect, conferring entitlements upon citizens for social security benefits, health care, education, and other benefits. The statute book is thus a force sustaining big government.[26]

Because government is a set of organizations, the organizations necessary to deliver policies remain in place whatever the result of a general election. The names of Cabinet ministers change, but the ministries continue with the force of inertia. This is even more true of the activities of local authorities, the health service, and all the other public sector agencies outside the direct control of the ministry. Public employees remain in place too; teachers expect to continue teaching, and nurses to treat patients, whatever the outcome of an election. Doctors, soldiers, and tax collectors go about their appointed rounds the same the day after an election as the day before. They look to the law, and to their own professional expertise, for direction about what to do.[27] Political inertia also provides the revenue to pay for these ongoing programs. Politicians do not have to vote for new taxes to meet the rising cost of government: tax laws enacted by their predecessors are a buoyant source of revenue.

Public opinion and popular expectations also sustain programs inherited from the past. A party can in theory propose to the electorate a wholesale transformation of the role of government; for example, a shift left (the nationalization of all basic industries, a wealth tax, government-guaranteed full employment, and so on) or a shift to the right (replacing the National Health Service by private insurance, charging for secondary education, military service for unemployed young people, and so on). But no party has ever put forward such a radical program of change and won office. Voters are prepared to accept some changes with the alternation of parties in office. But even more important, they expect the bulk of government policies to continue as before. The ballot box thus adds to the force of political inertia.

Health and social security programs, the biggest entry in the budget, illustrate the force of inertia. In 1951 Acts of Parliament authorized twenty-five different programs for a wide range of medical and hospital services and income–maintenance grants to the elderly and needy. Three decades later every one of these programs was still in force, after a series of Conservative and Labour governments had come and gone. Programs enacted before the oldest MP had entered Parliament account for more than three-fifths of total spending on health and social security. Of total spending today, only two programs, accounting for 7 percent of health and social security spending, were introduced by the Thatcher government. More than three-quarters of total spending in this field is devoted to programs that have continued in force for nearly four decades.[28]

Whereas prime ministers and parliamentary majorities are transient, government is continuing. Today's commitments of British government are not what any one party or politician has chosen. They are the cumulative inheritance of choices by governments from previous generations. The first Act making education compulsory was enacted in 1870; the first social security Act passed in 1908; and the National Health Service Act dates from 1946. Today, government is not so much about making fresh choices; it is about learning to deal with the consequences of past choices.

Making Changes. Given the difficulty of introducing change, politicians often substitute rhetoric for action. Margaret Thatcher is very good at using rhetoric to convey a sense of change. Opponents as well as supporters are often convinced by her slashing attacks upon "government" and her praise of the market that she has produced big spending cuts and greatly boosted the role of the private sector. In fact, public spending has increased by more than £100 billion since she entered office in 1979. Ironically, Margaret Thatcher is often trapped by her own rhetoric, finding it difficult to take credit for spending more on schools, social security, or the health service when her rhetoric emphasizes the desirability of government spending less.

In order to introduce substantive change, the government of the day must be selective and strategic in the actions that it takes. It must select a few measures that it regards as high priority, and these must have a substantial and continuing impact even after its electoral mandate has expired, if their effect is to be substantial. Where changing Acts of Parliament is practical and sufficient, the Thatcher Administration has been able to introduce measures that are likely to last after it has left office: a legal framework for industrial relations, private ownership of council-built houses, and the privatization of public utilities such as gas and electricity. Similarly, past Labour governments have used their statutory authority to introduce such changes as the introduction of comprehensive secondary schools in place of schools segregating pupils by their examination ability. A government that can introduce a measure that is effective and politically popular can use the force of political inertia to its advantage. An "unrepealable" Act will be in effect after the government that introduced it has passed into history.

Changes are made by a process of expanding existing programs, increasing coverage, or raising the level of benefits. The introduction of a completely new program with no relevance to what government has done before is the exception rather than the rule. While a minister may describe a program as a novelty in hopes of gaining a reputation for being innovative, the actual text of an Act of Parliament is typically full of references to other Acts and measures that have gone before. For example, the first provision for pensions was enacted in 1908. At that time, the government was committed only to pay a minimum sum to persons who would otherwise be destitute at age seventy. At that time an average person without savings for retirement had a life expectancy of only fifty-eight years. In the eighty years since, Acts have been passed to lower the age of entitlement for a pension, increase the level of benefits, and alter the basis of contributions to pay for pensions. The expansion of pensions has meant that a program small in its claim of resources when first introduced is now by far the biggest spending program in the budget.

Measures that initially appear to be only marginal, affecting policy in a single year, can become significant when compounded by the force of inertia. Housing policy illustrates this. When the Conservatives entered office in 1979, the nation's total stock of houses was about 20 million, of which 55 percent were lived in by their owners and 30 percent rented by local councils. The Thatcher Administration has reduced the proportion of new houses being built by local councils from 40 percent to 16 percent, thus introducing a gradual change in the proportion of council house tenants. In addition, it has enacted legislation to make it easy and financially attractive for council tenants to buy their homes. Whereas only 90,000 council houses had been sold in the last four years of the previous Labour government, nearly a million council houses have been sold to their tenants in the first decade of the Thatcher Administration, thus cumulatively leading to a structural shift in home ownership.[29]

Because inertia is a moving force, the actions of the government of the day become part of the legacy for its successors. Upon entering office the Thatcher government inherited programs that represented the accumulation of measures over most of a century. While the authors of these measures are nearly all dead, their programs are kept very much alive by the force of political inertia. The long-term challenge for politicians is not to make big changes in a hurry, but to introduce measures that by compounding through the years grow in effectiveness into the twenty-first century.

NOTES

1. For a discussion of the concept of political inertia, see Richard Rose and Terence Karran, *Taxation by Political Inertia* (London: Allen & Unwin, 1987), especially Chapter 5.

2. Home Secretary Chuter Ede, quoted in Vincent Starzinger, "The British Pattern of Apportionment," *Virginia Quarterly Review*, 41:3 (1965), p. 328.

3. See Eric Hobsbawm and Terence Ranger, eds., *The Invention of Tradition* (Cambridge: Cambridge University Press, 1983).

4. *The Guardian*, 21 April 1963.

5. Leslie Wolf-Phillips, *Constitutions of Modern States* (London: Pall Mall, 1968), p. 182. For another attempt to put down on paper the terms of the Constitution, see S. E. Finer, *Five Constitutions* (Harmondsworth: Penguin, 1979), pp. 33–87.

6. For a much fuller development of points discussed herein, see Richard Rose, "England: A Traditionally Modern Political Culture," in Lucian W. Pye and Sidney Verba, eds., *Political Culture and Political Development* (Princeton, NJ: Princeton University Press, 1965).

7. Cf. G. Kitson Clark, *The Making of Victorian England* (London: Methuen, 1962).

8. See Jindrich Veverka, "The Growth of Government Expenditure in the United Kingdom since 1790," *Scottish Journal of Political Economy* 10:2 (1963); cf. B. R. Mitchell, *European Historical Statistics, 1750–1970* (London: Macmillan, 1975), Table K1.

9. See Henry Parris, *Constitutional Bureaucracy* (London: Allen and Unwin, 1969); and Sir Norman Chester, *The English Administrative System 1780–1870* (Oxford: Clarendon Press, 1981).

10. See Alan T. Peacock and Jack Wiseman, *The Growth of Public Expenditure in the United Kingdom* (Princeton: Princeton University Press, 1961), p. 190.

11. Quoted in Richard Rose, *The Territorial Dimension in Government:*

Understanding the United Kingdom (Chatham, N.J.: Chatham House, 1982), p. 86, which expands on points made here about the Mace.

12. See Richard Rose, "Government Against Sub-Governments: A European Perspective on Washington," in R. Rose and E. Suleiman, eds., *Presidents and Prime Ministers* (Washington, DC: American Enterprise Institute, 1980), pp. 248–347.

13. For a discussion of distinctive English doctrines of a constitution, see Geoffrey Marshall, *Constitutional Theory* (Oxford: Clarendon Press, 1971) and *Constitutional Conventions* (Oxford: Clarendon Press, 1984). For an attempt to specify the fundamentals of statutes and court cases, see Colin Turpin, *British Government and the Constitution* (London: Weidenfeld and Nicolson, 1985).

14. J. A. G. Griffith, quoted by Peter Hennessy, "Raw Politics Decide Procedure in Whitehall," *New Statesman*, 24 October 1986.

15. Nevil Johnson, *In Search of the Constitution* (Oxford: Pergamon, 1977), p. 35; Sir Leslie Scarman, *English Law—the New Dimensions* (London: Stevens, 1974), p. 15. Cf. Philip Norton, *The Constitution in Flux* (Oxford: Martin Robertson, 1982); J. Jowell and D. Oliver, eds., *The Changing Constitution* (Oxford: Clarendon Press, 1985).

16. Peter Kellner, "And if Ollie North were English . . ." *The Independent* (London), 20 July 1987. Cf. Donald L. Robinson, *To the Best of My Ability* (New York: Norton, 1987).

17. Harold Macmillan, *Riding the Storm* (London: Macmillan, 1971) pp. 350–351.

18. On this literature, see Richard Rose, "Ungovernability: Is There Fire behind the Smoke?" *Political Studies*, 27.3 (1979), pp. 351–370; William B. Gwyn, "Jeremiahs and Pragmatists: Perceptions of British Decline," in Gwyn and R. Rose, eds., *Britain: Progress and Decline* (London: Macmillan, 1980), pp. 1–25; and A. H. Birch, "Overload, Ungovernability and Delegitimation," *British Journal of Political Science*, 14:2 (1984) pp. 135–160.

19. Roy Jenkins, "Home Thoughts from Abroad," *The Listener*, 29 November 1979; Lord Hugh Cecil, *Conservatism* (London: Williams and Norgate, c. 1912), p. 243.

20. Quoted in Richard Rose, *Do Parties Make a Difference?* (London: Macmillan, 1984, 2nd ed.) p. 4; see also the preface and epilogue of this edition. Also note Dennis Kavanagh, *Thatcherism and British Politics: the End of Consensus?* (Oxford: Oxford University Press, 1987); Hugo Young and Anne Sloman, *The Thatcher Phenomenon* (London: British Broadcasting Corporation, 1986); Anthony King, "Margaret Thatcher: the Style of a Prime Minister," in A. King, ed., *The British Prime Minister* (London: Macmillan, 1985) pp. 96–140.

21. Quoted in "Thatcher praised by her guru," *The Guardian*, 12 March 1983. For collections of contrasting views on Thatcher's ideology, see e.g., K. Minogue and M. Biddiss, eds., *Thatcherism* (London: Macmillan, 1987); Arthur Seldon, ed., *The New Right Enlightenment* (Sevenoaks: Economic & Literary Books, 1985); Stuart Hall and Martin Jacques, eds., *The Politics of Thatcherism* (London: Lawrence & Wishart with *Marxism Today*, 1983).

22. Peter Riddell, *The Thatcher Government* (Oxford: Martin Robertson, 1983) pp. 15–16.

23. Cf. David Sanders, Hugh Ward, and David Marsh, with Tony Fletcher, "Government Popularity and the Falklands War: a Reassessment," *British Journal of Political Science*, 17:3 (1987), pp. 281–314.

24. For a convenient catalogue of reforms favored by the Alliance, see e.g. Richard Holme, "Better Government," *Parliamentary Affairs* 40:4 (1987) pp. 433–448. For the views of David Owen, SDP leader, 1983–87, see *A United Kingdom* (Harmondsworth: Penguin, 1986).

25. All figures as produced by the Conservative government itself, as cited in source to Figure I.1. The figures exclude privatization proceeds, which are not a reduction in spending but a reduction in the capital assets of government.

26. Richard Rose, "Law as a Resource of Public Policy," *Parliamentary Affairs*, 39:3 (1986) pp. 297–314.

27. See Richard Rose, "Giving Direction to Permanent Officials: Signals from the electorate, the market, laws and expertise," in J. E. Lane, ed., *Bureaucracy and Public Choice* (London: Sage Publications, 1987), pp. 210–229.

28. See Philip L. Davies and Richard Rose, "Are Programme Resources Related to Organizational Change?" *European Journal of Political Research* 16:1 (1988) 73–98.

29. Unless otherwise credited, social statistics are normally calculated from relevant tables in the annual publication *Social Trends* (London: Her Majesty's Stationery Office, HMSO).

CHAPTER II

The Constraints of Place

Are they [the English] not above all nations divided from the rest of the world, insular both in situation and in mind, both for good and for evil?

THE ISLAND POSITION of Great Britain is its most significant geographic feature; insularity is one of its most striking cultural characteristics. London is physically closer to France than to the geographic center of England, but for centuries the English Channel has entrenched the psychological gulf between England and the continent of Europe. A French writer has said, "We might liken England to a ship which, though anchored in European waters, is always ready to sail away."[1]

When Europe was the center of world affairs, England held aloof from commitment there, intervening only when necessary to maintain a balance of power. Notwithstanding many differences between English people and Europeans, the United Kingdom entered the European Community in 1973. The country's military dependence upon America is as meaningful politically as is its geographical nearness to France and Germany. Historic links with Commonwealth countries in other continents further reduce the significance of physical geography. When the Gallup Poll asks people which countries England should work closely with, there is a desire to keep a foot in three worlds: Europe, America, and the Commonwealth. When asked which relationship is most important, 39 percent put Europe first, 26 percent America, and 25 percent put the Commonwealth first.[2]

In an interdependent world no country can be an island complete unto itself. This is most evident in international relations, discussed

in the first section of this chapter. Today domestic economic concerns are just as much a part of international affairs as are diplomacy and military defense. An Empire turned into a multiracial
Commonwealth now poses novel problems, as the immigration to
England of hundreds of thousands of black and brown citizens from
the Commonwealth has challenged a formerly all-white society to
become multiracial. There is also the perennial challenge of governing four nations under one Crown. While the Queen symbolizes the
unity of the United Kingdom, there is no uniformity in the history
of Scotland, Wales, and Northern Ireland, or in political institutions governing the non-English parts of the United Kingdom, the
third example of the constraints of place.

INSULARITY AND INVOLVEMENT

For centuries England's insular position was a great asset, saving
it from military invasions which have cost European countries so
much in the twentieth century. Excluding border wars with Scots,
the last successful foreign invasion of England was the Norman
conquest in 1066; in France it was the German invasion of 1940,
and in Germany, the Allied conquest of 1945. In both world wars of
this century England did not suffer occupation, while the continent
of Europe was a battlefield.

Insularity is not to be confused with isolation. As an island with
a seafaring tradition, Britain has long been a neighbor of every
country accessible by sea. By government actions and by the adven-
turous initiatives of public officials and private traders, Britain
built up an empire that at one time included nearly one-fifth of the
population and land area of the world. The British Empire drew
together territories as scattered and various as India, Nigeria, and
Palestine, as well as the old dominions of Canada, Australia, New
Zealand, and South Africa. At the end of the Second World War the
past achievements of empire-builders left the Crown with political
commitments on every continent.

Imperial Decline. In 1945 the British Empire had more than three
dozen colonies with a population of 800 million people. The end of
empire began with the granting of independence to India and Pakistan in 1947. In the following decades the Westminster government
gradually accepted that it could no longer enforce its authority in
distant lands against colonial peoples demanding independence.

The grant of independence to every major colony and many small colonies meant the end of empire.

The Commonwealth, a free association of forty-nine states, has succeeded the British Empire. The independent status of its chief members is shown by the removal of the word British from the title of the Commonwealth. A number of Afro-Asian nations have exchanged loyalty to the Crown for the status of a republic, and the old dominions of Canada and Australia have symbolically abandoned "God Save the Queen" as their national anthem. Only a miscellany of island colonies and small trading enclaves such as Gibraltar remain from days of Empire. Meetings of Commonwealth countries today emphasize many political and social conflicts among its very heterogeneous membership.[3]

Given the global importance of Britain at the end of the Second World War, the story since 1945 has been that of gradually contracting commitments. Initially Britain was an important partner of America in organizing alliances. In 1947 the Labour government took the lead in organizing a European response to the United States offer of economic aid in the Marshall Plan. In 1949 Britain was important in founding NATO (the North Atlantic Treaty Organization), and after the Korean War broke out in 1950, it took the lead in European rearmament. The United Kingdom remains one of five permanent members of the Security Council of the United Nations. Like France, its influence is of a different and lesser order from that of the three Council superpowers, America, Russia, and China. It is a member of 126 international organizations, but government reports question whether the country today needs such representation or should close down embassies where the economic benefits are not perceived as equal to the cost.[4] In 1962 a leading American diplomat caustically remarked: "Great Britain has lost an empire and has not yet found a role."[5]

Contraction of diplomatic commitments has been paralleled by decline in military strength. The country's inability to pursue an independent foreign policy was made evident in 1956, when Britain, in alliance with France, invaded Egypt with the intent of regaining control of the Suez Canal. The military force was withdrawn in the face of American and Russian opposition. Britain has continued to maintain nuclear weapons, but since 1962 it has depended upon the United States for the sophisticated technology used to deliver these weapons.

In April 1982 Britain showed that it could use military force independently in response to the Argentine invasion of the Falkland Islands, a British colony in the South Atlantic with a population of 1,800. The United Nations Security Council condemned the Argentine invasion and called for a diplomatic resolution of disputed claims to the territory by Britain and Argentina. After negotiations produced no settlement, a British task force landed in the islands; Argentina surrendered on 14 June 1982. The military victory gave evidence of the Conservative government's readiness to meet force with force in defense of British territory.[6]

The Falklands War is atypical of the conduct of British foreign policy. It involved no other major power, and Argentina was led by an unpopular dictatorship without any effective allies. Argentine military forces were badly organized and equipped. The war was very short; it cost 255 British lives, fewer than have died in a bad year of fighting in Northern Ireland. Nor has the Falklands been a precursor of military intervention elsewhere. In 1983 the British government conspicuously held aloof from the troubles of the West Indian island of Grenada, notwithstanding concern by Commonwealth Caribbean nations about Soviet influence there. The United States sent troops to Grenada without consulting the British government.

The United Kingdom's decline as a world power has been readily accepted by most citizens. Before the 1959 general election, 42 percent said that foreign affairs and defense issues were the most important problems facing the country. By the time of the 1987 election, 70 percent put economic issues first, and only 2 percent put defense first. When people are asked whether they would rather Britain was a leading world power or a small neutral country like Sweden or Switzerland, 53 percent endorse the status of the small country as against 33 percent wanting Britain to be a major world power again.[7] The effective choice of government today is not whether England should be a small, rich country like Sweden or Switzerland, but whether it remains a big, rich country or becomes a big and relatively (though not absolutely) poor country.

Into Europe Slowly. Although Europe is the only continent to which England can be said to belong geographically, most English people do not think of themselves as Europeans. However, as England's world position has declined, government has increasingly looked to Europe. Jet aircraft have made the English Channel no barrier to travel; a businessman going from London to Paris,

Brussels, or Frankfurt spends twice as long in journeying to and from the airport as in flight. A tunnel across the English Channel will further ease transport. Television carries entertainment as well as news across national borders, in such programs as the Eurovision song contest and European Football Cup matches. Economic links have grown in response to business and consumer pressures and the activities of multinational corporations such as the Ford Motor Company, which links factories in Britain with factories a few hundred miles away in other European countries, just as it links factories in different American states.

The United Kingdom did not join the European Community when it was established in 1957; the government considered the country's political and economic position superior to that of continental neighbors ravaged by war. In 1961 the Conservative government of Harold Macmillan first unsuccessfully sought entry; the application was reactivated by Harold Wilson's Labour government in 1967. After new negotiations led by Prime Minister Edward Heath, the United Kingdom joined the European Community on 1 January 1973. Entry excited political controversy cutting across party lines. A majority of Conservative MPs (Members of Parliament elected to the House of Commons) and a minority of Labour MPs voted for entry, and a majority of Labour MPs and a minority of Conservative MPs voted against. In 1975 the Labour government took the unprecedented step of calling a national referendum to determine whether or not Britain should remain a member of the European Community. The referendum showed a majority, 67 percent, in favor of Britain remaining in the Community. Membership of the European Community is now an accomplished fact, enshrined in an international treaty approved by Parliament and other nations. It is an obligation that could not easily or lightly be repudiated.

Public opinion continues to be divided about the desirability of Britain's membership in the European Community. Opinion polls show three roughly equal groups: those in favor of the Community, those opposed, and a substantial number who are indifferent. Indifference has been spectacularly registered in the two direct elections held for Britain's representation in the very weak European Parliament. At the first election of Members of the European Parliament in 1979, only 33 percent of the electorate turned out to vote, less than half the number voting at the general election a month before.

In the 1984 European Parliament election, turnout was 32 percent, less than half the turnout in other European Community nations.[8]

Economic arguments were the chief reasons given for Britain entering (or not entering) the European Community, or as English people often refer to it, the Common Market. The British economy was forecast to benefit from the stimulus of wider markets and competition, and exclusion from Continental markets by not joining was depicted as a risk that could not be run. The immediate economic impact of entry to the Community was overshadowed by the October 1973 oil crisis and the world recession that followed. After more than a decade and one-half of membership, it is empirically impossible to argue what the British economy would have become if the country had not joined the Community in 1973. The Community's efforts to encourage free trade among member nations continues with the promulgation of regulations setting common standards for products and commercial practices. Given the diversity in Community nations, completely free trade in goods and services is not expected to be achieved until 1992. The Community also regulates production quotas and subsidies for particular commodities such as agricultural products and steel.

The Act of Parliament approving British membership in the Community introduced a novel principle: it gave the force of law in Britain to regulations made under the terms of the treaty. Moreover, if there were a conflict between Community legislation and an Act of Parliament, the Community law would take precedence. This provision led to protests from MPs that British sovereignty was being breached. Strictly speaking, these complaints were accurate. In practice, the breach has been very slight.[9]

The European Community is governed as a weak confederation. Its powers and finances are limited; important decisions require unanimous consent, thus giving the British government a right to veto measures to which it is opposed. Direction of Community policy is effectively in the hands of the Council of Ministers, which represents the governments of the twelve member states. Prime Ministers attend the important meetings, and other ministers responsible for specific problems such as transport, agriculture, or industry attend when these matters are on the agenda. The Council is shadowed by a Committee of Permanent Representatives (Coreper), in which British civil servants participate as representatives of Whitehall ministries. The European Commission, divided into directorates concerned with major policy issues, constitutes the Cabinet of the Community; its multinational staff are the permanent bureaucracy. The Commission is weak because its members are appointed by the Council of Ministers; they are not accountable to the European Parliament as is the cabinet of a national government. The Commission sits in Brussels, the headquarters of the Parliament is in Luxembourg, and the official meeting place of the Parliament is in Strasbourg, on the border of France and Germany. The European Court of Justice also sits in Luxembourg.[10]

For most British Cabinet ministers, meetings in the European Community are of strictly secondary importance. They are of primary concern only for the Minister of Agriculture. However, agriculture is of little concern to Britain though of great concern in the Community. When ministers are caught up in Community affairs, they can threaten to veto major changes that they oppose strongly—and they can be frustrated when any or all of the eleven other national representatives oppose a British proposal. There is a tendency for British politicians to regard Community affairs as a distraction or a waste of time.

The gradual enlargement of the Community from the six original member states has brought strains. The founder members—France, Germany, Italy, Belgium, the Netherlands, and Luxembourg—had shared common experiences of war and defeat. Britain joined along with two other northern tier countries, Denmark and Ireland. Further enlargement has increased the southern tier, the relatively poor Mediterranean countries of Greece, Portugal, and Spain. As the Community gets larger, the difficulties of achieving unanimous agreement increase, while the risk of being in a minority increases if decisions are made by majority rule.

The limits of the Community's powers are indicated by the small size of its budget. Community revenue is equal to about 1 percent of the gross domestic product of member nations. Its revenue is collected as part of the tax system of national governments. As a major European economy, the United Kingdom is expected to make a substantial contribution to Community funds. But because agricultural subsidies claim the largest portion of the Community budget, it tends to benefit less from Community spending. In annual budget negotiations, the British government has always fought to redirect Community spending and to reduce the claim for revenue from Britain. The British Treasury calculates that its net annual contribution to Community revenue is more than £1 billion.

If a political community is defined as a political system in which all participants share common rights and obligations, then the European Community remains peripheral for the government of the United Kingdom. More than 99 percent of all tax revenues collected by British government are spent by British government. It does not pool its tax revenue with poorer Mediterranean nations such as Greece and Portugal, nor does it benefit from revenues of richer nations such as Germany. The Community budget has virtually no impact upon the biggest spending programs of British government, social security, health, and education. Equally, the Community is not a military alliance, nor are its members bound to pursue a common foreign policy. While the Community does affect national economies, each nation's economy is very much affected by forces outside the Community, from the United States to the Persian Gulf and Japan.

Economic Involvement. Whereas force is used only occasionally, economic transactions are continuous, and today they are increasingly international, for all advanced nations are part of an international economy. The Chancellor of the Exchequer now spends a substantial portion of his time in negotiations with his opposite numbers in foreign countries, so closely is the fate of Britain's domestic economy linked with that of other nations. To protect national interests, the British government must play an active role in global economic institutions. The institutions include the International Monetary Fund and the Bank of International Settlements, both concerned with monetary issues; the World Bank, particularly concerned with developing nations; GATT (the General Agreement on Tariffs and Trade); and OECD (Organization for Economic Cooperation and Development), a forum for advanced industrial nations.

The United Kingdom is a major economic power; its total gross domestic product is the fifth largest among all advanced industrial nations, and much larger than more than 100 member states of the United Nations. Among free nations, only the United States and Japan greatly surpass it in scale. When the value of the national product is related to population and measured in terms of dollars adjusted to achieve a parity of purchasing power across nations, then Britain ranks high on a global standard, though just below the average for OECD nations generally. The reason for this is that the annual growth rate in Britain is also below average (Table II.1).

TABLE II.1 *British Economic Performance in Comparative Perspective*

	UK	USA	France	Germany	Japan	OECD avg.	UK as % OECD avg.
Per capita purchasing power $, 1986	10,882	16,494	11,333	12,158	11,666	12,506	87
Annual growth, Gross Domestic Product, 1980–85 %	1.9	2.4	1.1	1.3	3.9	2.1	90
Annual inflation, 1981–86, %	5.5	3.8	7.4	2.6	5.3	4.9	112
Unemployment, 1986 %	11.6	6.9	10.4	8.0	2.8	7.9	147
Interest rates, avg. % 1980–84	11.6	10.8	13.2	8.4	5.5	9.9	117

Sources: *OECD Observer* No. 145 (April/May 1987); OECD, *Employment Outlook* (September 1987) Table K. Nominal short-term interest rates, *Historical Statistics, 1960–1984* (Paris: OECD) Table 10.7. Per capita purchasing power is after adjusted by OECD Purchasing Power Parity measures.

In the 1980s the performance of the British economy has been around average. The final column in Table II.1 compares each British measure of economic performance with the average for OECD nations. The differences between Britain and other nations are differences of degree, not kind (cf. Table II.1). The growth rate of the economy has been higher than that of Germany or France but lower than that of the United States or Japan. Inflation rates have been lower than in France, higher than in Germany and similar to that of Japan. Unemployment has been relatively high, and interest rates have been relatively high too.

As the world's first industrial nation, Britain has always been an exporter. Since 1846, when the Repeal of the Corn Laws allowed the import of cheap food, it has depended upon imported food. The City of London is one of the world's great financial centers for banking, insurance, investments, and currency exchange, along with New York and Tokyo. By contrast with the United States, Britain has always had to trade internationally. By contrast with countries such as Canada and Ireland, Britain is not dependent upon a single trading partner. Today more than one-fifth of Britain's gross domestic product is exported, and imports are equal to more than one-fifth of the national product too. Thanks to the discovery of oil off the east coast of Scotland, North Sea oil accounts for more than one-fifth of Britain's exports. Much trade is now intra-industry rather than between industries; for example, Britain both imports and exports hundreds of thousands of motor cars.

When the geographical pattern of trade is examined, the European Community is dominant; it now accounts for half Britain's imports and exports (Table II.2). More than four-fifths of United Kingdom trade involves other advanced industrial nations, whether in North America, other parts of Western Europe, or Australia and Japan. Trade with third-world Commonwealth nations is not so important; Britain exports far more manufactured goods and services to oil-producing countries than it imports in return in oil. When the value of imports is not matched by the value of exports, there is a balance of payments problem, and the government takes measures to reduce the demand for imported goods by reducing consumption or raises interest rates to attract foreign lenders. Both steps are politically unpopular. In 1967 and 1976, Labour governments had to go further, borrowing money from the International Monetary Fund to meet balance of payments problems. Conditions attached to the loans required the government to introduce stringent economies that were unpopular with its own supporters.

TABLE II.2 *Worldwide Pattern of Britain's Trade*

	Exports (% total)	Imports (% total)
European Community	49	49
United States & Canada	17	14
Other Western Europe	9	14
Other developed economies	5	8
Developing economies	10	10
Oil producers	8	3
Communist bloc	2	2
Total value, 1985	£78bn	£85bn

Source: *Monthly Digest of Statistics* (June, 1986) Table 15.4.

The Conservative government of Margaret Thatcher faced a novel problem after entering office in 1979: an influx of foreign currency, in response to rising real interest rates and the export of North Sea oil. In consequence, the value of the so-called petro-pound rose against other major currencies. This effectively raised the price of British exports, thus reducing demand for British manufactured goods, and contributing to a rise in unemployment. Since then the value of the pound has fluctuated substantially against the currencies of its major trading partners. Whatever the value of the pound is in foreign exchange markets, the British government must face the policy consequences of a pound that is high (thus making exports difficult), or low (thus making imports costly). Since the pound is traded around the world daily, its value can go up or down against the dollar or the yen in Tokyo while people are sleeping in London.

In an open international economy, the government cannot be insular; it must adapt to fluctuations in international market conditions. Some changes are the responsibility of the government of the day, for example, inflation fueled by a sudden boost in public spending or a recession triggered by austerity policies of the Treasury. Other changes are beyond the control of British government, such as the shock of the 1973 oil price rise, or the abrupt fall in New York's Wall Street in 1987, which triggered off a worldwide fall in stock markets. While Britain remains an island, no British government can insulate the country from the effects of involvement in the world economy.

A MULTIRACIAL ENGLAND

As citizens of a world power, Britons have long been able to move around the world without constraint. For centuries England has also received immigrants from other lands, principally Europe. The Royal Family are the most notable immigrants to England. The Queen is descended from the House of Hanover; George I came from this German princely state to assume the English throne in 1714. German connections were maintained by Queen Victoria's marriage to Albert, Prince of Saxe-Coburg and Gotha, and by their offspring. Until the outbreak of anti-German sentiment in the First World War, the surname of the Royal Family was Saxe-Coburg-Gotha. By royal proclamation, George V changed his name to Windsor in 1917.

As a great port and trading center London has always been accessible to immigrants. Irish, Scots, and Welsh have hardly counted as immigrants because they have also been citizens of the United Kingdom. The chief immigration in the first half of the twentieth century consisted of Jewish refugees from Czarist Russia and then from Nazi Germany, and immediately after 1945 Poles fleeing from Stalinism. By the standards of America, Canada, or Australia, immigration has been slight. The English use of the word *race* refers not only to differences of skin color (for example, West Indians) but also religion (for example, Jews) and nationality (for example, Irish); it thus emphasizes several ways in which cultural differences are defined as salient.[11]

New Commonwealth Immigration. In the late 1950s a few British subjects began migrating to England from populous parts of the new Commonwealth, especially the West Indies, Pakistan, and India. The prospect of a job, whether as a factory worker or shopkeeper, a doctor or hospital orderly, was the principal attraction. Immigrants who disliked England and returned home have been fewer than those who settled here and have sent for their relatives and friends to join them.

Decades of immigration followed by decades in which immigrants settle, marry, and have children have cumulatively increased the nonwhite proportion of the population of Britain from 74,000 (0.2 percent) in 1951 to above 2.5 million today (about 5 percent). Of this total, half come from the Indian subcontinent (India, Pakistan, or Bangladesh), one quarter from the Caribbean, and the remaining quarter from a wide scattering of places, including East and West Africa, Hong Kong and other parts of the Far East, and the Mediterranean.[12]

Immigrants from New Commonwealth nations have had little in common upon arrival. British West Indians came as English speakers, even if some spoke with a calypso accent. The bulk of the early immigrants from India and Pakistan came from alien cultures: the majority were uneducated and unskilled workers. Muslims and Sikhs follow religious practices that have made them especially distinctive. The small number of African immigrants have been divided by tribe and citizenship. Differences among immigrants have made it difficult to establish an American-style political movement, for the immigrants do not share a common black (that is, African) heritage; they share a negative characteristic, that is, all New Commonwealth immigrants are not white.

The entry to England of a relatively small number of nonwhite immigrants has had a significance far out of proportion to number. From the first, public opinion has opposed immigration. In 1958 two-thirds endorsed stricter controls upon immigration, and the proportion rose to 95 per cent by 1968. Since 1962 Conservative and Labour governments have enacted a series of laws intended to limit the number of nonwhite immigrants from the New Commonwealth. In the 1964 general election MPs were shocked out of a complacent belief that their fellow countrymen were free of racial animosity when a racialist candidate, standing as a Conservative, won an upset victory at Smethwick. By 1970 Enoch Powell had become prominent as the proponent of a white England.

Initially control of immigration was difficult because the United Kingdom has never had a clear-cut definition of who is and who is not a British citizen. As part of an imperial legacy, in the 1950s nearly 1 billion residents of the Commonwealth were British subjects, even though most had never come within a thousand miles of Dover. A series of Acts of Parliament progressively reduced the proportion of British subjects in other parts of the Commonwealth who could enter the United Kingdom as of right. The 1981 British Nationality Act limits the right of residence in Britain to persons born in the United Kingdom or having a parent or grandparent born in the United Kingdom, a spouse of a British citizen, or a foreigner lawfully resident in Britain. By an historical anomaly, citizens of the Republic of Ireland are counted as neither British nor foreign, having a right to enter Britain, vote in British elections and sit in the House of Commons while retaining their Irish citizenship.[13]

From Immigration to Integration? Today racial issues are less about immigration and more about the place of nonwhite Britons in English society, for the majority of nonwhite Britons are British-born of immigrant parents.[14] Americans have never doubted that the United States is multiracial; the civil rights movement was about altering relations between blacks and whites in what everyone acknowledged was a multiracial society. By contrast, England has faced the challenge of *creating* race relations in a previously all-white society. The challenge is most evident in London, Birmingham, and other industrial cities where the majority of immigrants have settled.

The leaders of the major parties differ about race relations in degree, not principle. All parties want to keep tight restrictions upon immigration. The critical issue is defined as: How much (or how little) should government do to promote good race relations within England? Politicians who have prided themselves on England's tolerance do not like to admit that racial discrimination exists, nor is there any general agreement about what constitutes discrimination. Laws intended to improve race relations are narrow in scope by comparison with American legislation.[15] The government-sponsored Commission for Racial Equality, established in 1976 to oppose discrimination and promote equality of opportunity and good race relations, relies primarily on investigation and conciliation rather than the courts. The emphasis is upon long-term changes in attitudes rather than laws compelling employers and trade unions to have a quota of nonwhite employees at all levels of an organization from top to bottom.

The electoral impact of nonwhite English people is limited by being in a minority; in a system of majority rule, a party that appealed only for the votes of a minority would be certain to lose. The electoral effect of immigrant voting is further reduced because a fraction do not put their names on the electoral register, especially if not literate in English. Labour has been more active than the Conservatives in promoting policies specially appealing to nonwhite voters, but until 1987 it did not have any nonwhite MPs. Following pressures for separate black sections within the party, four nonwhite candidates were nominated for seats winnable by Labour prior to the 1987 election and demands for black sections rejected as likely to prevent integration of races within Labour ranks. The Conservatives accept this; a 1983 Conservative election advertisement featured a black voter and the slogan: "Labour says he's black; Tories say he's British," inviting all who endorse Conservative policies on social and economic issues to vote Conservative, regardless of race.[16]

Over a period of two decades the British-born offspring of immigrants, and immigrants themselves, have gradually become integrated into electoral politics. Because nonwhite electors tend to be concentrated in about 60 constituencies, parties and pressure groups can organize registration, and turnout is rising to average levels. Residential segregation in cities has the incidental effect of causing parties to nominate more nonwhite candidates for wards where white electors are now in the minority. There are now hundreds of nonwhite local councillors. At the parliamentary level, 28 candidates were nominated by the major parties at the 1987 election, and four, all Labour, were elected. One was born in Guyana, another in Ghana, a third in Aden, and a fourth in London. Nonwhites are more than twice as likely to vote Labour as their white neighbors in a constituency. The Conservative and Alliance parties have sought and succeeded in increasing their share of this group's vote; none of the established parties cultivates a "white backlash" vote.[17]

A minority can gain headlines by street demonstrations. In the summer of 1981 riots in inner-city areas of London and Liverpool spotlighted the problem of young people of immigrant parentage. There was no agreement about the causes or consequences of riots. Diagnoses of the cause ranged from racial discrimination or police misbehavior through youth unemployment to hooliganism. Policing remains a point of friction. Because petty crimes tend to be committed by young people and nonwhite English are disproportionately young, police in cities often question youths who are not white. But because the police forces are almost 100 percent white, there are frequent accusations of police prejudice and failure to treat nonwhite suspects fairly, or to protect nonwhites from harassment by white youths. An Imperial past has made Britain a multiracial society in fact, but it is not yet multiracial in political values.

ONE CROWN AND MANY NATIONS

The English Crown is the oldest and best-known in the world, and English people have had a secure national identity for centuries. The identity is so taken for granted that the government does not think it necessary to put the name of the country on its postage stamps; the head of the Queen is regarded as sufficient. Yet there is no such thing as an English state.[18]

In international law as in the title of the Queen, the state is the United Kingdom of Great Britain and Northern Ireland. The island of Great Britain, the major part of the United Kingdom, is divided into three parts: England, Scotland, and Wales. England, smaller than Alabama or Wisconsin, constitutes 55 percent of the land area of Great Britain. The other part of the United Kingdom, Northern Ireland, consists of six counties of Ulster that have remained under the Crown rather than join an independent Irish Republic ruled from Dublin. Insofar as territorial contiguity is politically significant, a state might occupy an island to itself or a pair of neighboring islands. Irish nationalists have always argued that geography implies the existence of two island states, Ireland and Britain. Unionists long argued for a United Kingdom of the two islands.

As in many other European countries, the boundaries of the United Kingdom are the consequence of centuries of battles won and lost, accidents of dynastic succession, and diplomacy. Wales was joined to England by dynastic inheritance, formalized by legislation in 1536. Scotland was similarly joined in two stages in 1603 and 1707. England has intermittently been sending troops to Ireland from 1169 to the present in efforts to maintain sovereignty in at least part of the island. Although the ancestry of the Crown may be traced back to Alfred the Great in the ninth century, the current boundaries of the United Kingdom date only from 1921.

The people of the United Kingdom differ in their primary identity. When asked how they see themselves, most Welsh people think of themselves as Welsh, and Scottish people think of themselves as Scots. In Northern Ireland there is no agreement about national identity; most Protestants see themselves as British and most Catholics see themselves as Irish (Table II.3). Just as a Texan or a Californian also thinks of himself or herself as an American, so a Scot or a Welsh person is also ready to identify with being British. When asked whether they are proud to be British, 86 percent of the Welsh and Scots give the same answer as 86 percent of English respondents: they are proud of being British. In England, people may call themselves English or British without a conscious sense of the difference between the two, as in the title of a book by a well known journalist, Louis Heren: *Alas, Alas for England: What Went Wrong for Britain.*

TABLE II.3 *National Identity within the United Kingdom (by percentage)*

	England	Scotland	Wales	Northern Ireland Protestant	Northern Ireland Roman Catholic
Think of self as:					
British	38	35	33	67	15
English	57	2	8	—	—
Scottish	2	52	—	—	—
Welsh	1	—	57	—	—
Ulster	—	—	—	20	6
Irish	1	1	—	8	69
Other, don't know	1	10	2	5	10

Source: Richard Rose, *Understanding the United Kingdom: the Territorial Dimension in Government* (London: Longman, 1982), p. 14.

The confusion of England and Britain is justified, for England has a population of 47.1 million, as against 5.1 million in Scotland, 2.8 million in Wales, and 1.5 million in Northern Ireland. In the event of differences of views between parts of the United Kingdom, the voices and votes of the five-sixths of the population that is English is bound to predominate. Except for Ireland (an exception centuries old), it is unusual for political conflicts to arise between the nations of the United Kingdom. Divisions normally occur within each nation; for example, class has been the major dimension of electoral competition. Just as America is a pluralistic society, recognizing major differences among inhabitants of each of its 50 states, so the United Kingdom is a multinational state.[19]

England. While England can be treated as a single unit for purposes of generalization, politics in England stresses divisions within England. These would persist even if the United Kingdom ceased to exist. Divisions are very evident between the industrial North of England and the South of England, which is the center of banking and commerce.

Within England, London is preeminent. With 7 million people, Greater London is seven times larger than Birmingham, the second largest city in the United Kingdom. Whereas New York City is as large as London, it does not similarly dominate American society. The Greater London area contains one-fifth of the population of England. Unlike Washington, London is simultaneously the center of government, finance, the mass media, and the arts. More than two-thirds of people with a biography in *Who's Who* live within a 75-mile radius of the capital. While London is the central city of the United Kingdom, it is not geographically central. Historically it is best described as central to the Crown's medieval claim to the Kingdoms of England, France, and Ireland. As an international center of finance, the media, transport, and tourism, London today depends as much upon contacts with foreign countries as upon links within Britain.

The majority of English people live well beyond daily commuting distance to London. Liverpool or Manchester has far more claim to be central to the geography of the United Kingdom (see the frontispiece map). The term provincial is applied to the regions of England; they have no elected assemblies or major administration institutions. By contrast, all federal systems and many unitary states have administrative and political institutions at the regional level.

The United Kingdom government even lacks a standard definition of a region. Boundaries in use vary from ministry to ministry, thus creating dozens of different regional organizations for nationalized industries, the health service, and so on.[20] There are no English regional parties. Talk about Yorkshire people being different from Londoners, or Geordies from the Northeast of England differing from people from the Midlands is not matched by political differences.[21] England is unique in being the only nation of the United Kingdom without a minister speaking in its name in Cabinet. But given its predominance in population, there is no shortage of English voices there.[22]

Scotland. A number of differences between Scotland and England persist from the centuries when Scotland was a separate kingdom, prior to the Act of Union of 1707, which abolished the Scottish Parliament and created a Parliament of Great Britain at Westminster. The established church is Presbyterian, whereas the Church of England is Episcopal; the Queen worships as a Presbyterian in Scotland and as an Episcopalian in England. Scotland maintains a separate legal system, influenced by the Roman law tradition; the laws enforced are, however, enacted by the Westminster Parliament. The educational system is differently organized; Roman Catholic schools are fully funded by the Scottish Office, and all schools offer a broader, less specialized secondary education. The universities of Scotland were the model for American liberal arts colleges. The industrialized Scottish Lowlands concentrates most of Scotland's population around Glasgow and Edinburgh. The Scottish Highlands is outside industrial civilization. The Highlands has most of Scotland's scenery but less than 5 percent of its population.

Since 1885 there has been a government minister in charge of a Scottish Office; since 1939 the administrative headquarters of the Scottish Office has been in Edinburgh. Within Scotland it is responsible for the administration of health, education, housing, economic development, agriculture, and local government policies of British government. But the actual work of delivering these services is usually in the hands of local government authorities. Political responsibility to Parliament rests with the Secretary of State for Scotland, who is a member of the majority party at Westminster and appointed by the Prime Minister. Like every other Cabinet minister, the Secretary of State for Scotland is accountable to the Westminster Parliament; there is no separate assembly for Scotland.[23]

Wales. Language is the most distinctive feature of Welsh society. The proportion of people speaking Welsh has declined from 53 percent in 1891 to 19 percent in 1981. Many with Welsh ties, such as the Prince of Wales, show a little knowledge of Welsh in tribute to the very different cultural values implied by the gulf between the English and Welsh languages. Whereas Scotland is united in using English, Wales is divided by language, and the language used for education is controversial in parts of Wales. Welsh people are Protestant but often not Episcopal. Welshmen campaigned for generations against the established Episcopal Church of Wales, which was finally disestablished in 1920. Within Wales there are marked contrasts between the English-speaking, industrial, and more populous South and the Welsh-speaking, rural North West.[24]

Since Wales was amalgamated with England in the sixteenth century, it has almost invariably been governed by the same laws as England. In 1746 Parliament declared that the word "England" in an Act of Parliament was deemed to include Wales, a provision not repealed until 1967. In 1907 the first step was taken to treat Wales distinctively for administrative purposes, with the appointment of a Welsh Secretary of Education. In 1964 a separate Welsh Office was established, with its head a Cabinet minister. The laws that the Welsh Office administers are normally Acts of Parliament that apply equally to England and Wales. The Welsh Office is responsible for the administration of a variety of educational, social, and economic infrastructure policies within Wales. Like his Scottish counterpart, the Secretary of States for Wales is an MP of the majority party in Parliament and need not sit for a Welsh constituency. There is no elected assembly for Wales.

Northern Ireland. By wide agreement, Northern Ireland is the most un-English part of the United Kingdom; many generalizations that are true about British politics do not apply in the exceptional circumstances of Northern Ireland.[25] Formally, Northern Ireland is a secular state, but in practice differences between Protestants and Catholics dominate its politics. Protestant loyalty to the Crown rests upon the English monarch's historic status, proclaimed in the Bill of Rights of 1688, as "the glorious instrument of delivering this kingdom from Popery and arbitrary power." Protestants constitute two-thirds of the population of Northern Ireland. Most Catholics in Northern Ireland identify as Irish and express a more or less strong aspiration for their territory to become part of a 32-county Republic of Ireland, with its capital in Dublin. Such a merger would produce a society in which Catholics outnumbered Protestants by three to one. Protestants reject belonging to a United Ireland.

From 1921 to 1972 the government of Northern Ireland was principally the responsibility of a Parliament at Stormont, a suburb of Belfast. Since Protestants were a big majority of the electorate, the Ulster Unionist Party, standing for Northern Ireland remaining within the United Kingdom, won every election; therefore, Catholics were excluded from power. In 1968 Catholic civil rights protesters held street demonstrations demanding full civil rights within Northern Ireland. These protests attracted worldwide attention. In 1969, violence broke out, and in August 1969 the British Army intervened to restore order. The Irish Republican Army (IRA) was revived and in 1971 began a military campaign against the British Army in an effort to break up the United Kingdom.[26] In retaliation, Protestants too organized illegal armed groups. Since August 1969, more than 2,500 people have been killed in political violence in Northern Ireland, the equivalent proportion of population to more than 87,000 killed in Britain, or to more than 400,000 killed in political violence in America. The dead include hundreds of civilian bystanders, as well as hundreds of British soldiers, Ulster policemen, and Irish Republicans and Protestant Loyalists killed on active service with illegal military units.

In 1972 the British government abolished the Stormont government, exercising direct rule through a Cabinet ministry, the Northern Ireland Office. Unlike in Scotland and Wales, the Northern Ireland Secretary has never represented an Ulster constituency; as the British parties ceased contesting seats in Northern Ireland, this minister appears in Ulster like a figure from the Imperial past, ruling without any local support. Neither the British government nor the political parties of Northern Ireland have been satisfied with the institutions of direct rule, which are described as temporary because renewed by an annual Act of Parliament. The Northern Ireland Office has held election for two assemblies and a Constitutional Convention in attempts to secure a locally representative government in which power would be shared between Protestants and Catholics. At each election the collective vote of the Ulster electorate has rejected this proposal; a majority has voted for Unionist candidates (some fighting as Official Unionists and others under the banner of Dr. Ian Paisley's Democratic Unionist Party) opposed to sharing power with politicians favoring a united Ireland. The

Catholic minority has voted for candidates with Irish unity as their aspiration; the antiviolent Social Democratic & Labour Party secures most of the Catholic vote; the pro-IRA Sinn Fein Republicans secure a significant vote too.

Whereas the British government has always upheld the supremacy of Parliament in dealing with nationalists in Scotland and Wales, in Northern Ireland it has consistently been prepared to allow it the right to secede from the United Kingdom, if and when a majority of its population might wish to do so. But this has not happened. There is an impasse between the pro-British and pro-Irish groups within Northern Ireland. When a referendum was held in 1973 about whether Northern Ireland should remain part of the United Kingdom or join with the Republic, 99 percent of those voting favored remaining within the United Kingdom. But the turnout was only 58 percent, because nearly all Catholics abstained from voting.

Exasperated by the impossibility of combining irreconcilable views about Union or Irish unity, in 1985 the British government signed an agreement with the Republic of Ireland intended to promote greater political cooperation and reduce violence. The agreement offered Ulster Catholics symbolic recognition of their aspiration to Irish unity because it accepted that the Republic of Ireland had the right to be consulted about British government actions within the Ulster region of the United Kingdom. It did not establish a new elected body, for that would only reflect existing discord. Instead, it created a joint consultative committee of civil servants and government ministers from Dublin and London, representing constituencies *outside* Northern Ireland. The Catholic Social Democratic & Labour Party welcomed the agreement, because the Dublin government could put forward the views of its supporters. While Unionists were told that the agreement was tacit Dublin recognition of Britain's authority in Northern Ireland, Unionists rejected it as the first step on the road to a united Ireland. The IRA rejected the agreement because it did not promise movement to Irish unity. Killing continues at a level that the British government has considered "an acceptable level of violence,"[27] up to 100 deaths a year, the equivalent of more than 3,500 deaths a year in Britain itself.

Integration Through Cross-Cutting Differences. Politics is about the articulation of conflicting views about government. Nationalism assumes that conflicts unite Scots, Welsh, Irish, and by implication, English people, and divide each nation from the other, thus justifying their claim that each nation should form a separate and independent state. But that is not the only way in which a group of people can divide. Class politics assumes that economic groups are the primary focus of identity; this identity is expected to cut across national boundaries and to create divisions within each of the four nations of the United Kingdom.[28] Constitutional theories assume that whatever differences exist within the United Kingdom should be pursued within a framework of government with a common loyalty to institutions of the Crown.

The relative strength of these competing theories was put to the test in the 1970s by a resurgence of support for nationalist parties in Scotland and Wales, and by violence in Northern Ireland. In Scotland and in Wales the nationalist party has always secured a limited fraction of the votes, but its minority share has fluctuated; so too has the significance of its representation in Parliament. In the four elections of the 1970s the Scottish National Party averaged 20 percent of the Scottish vote (that is, about 2 percent of the United Kingdom vote) and Plaid Cymru, the Welsh Nationalist party, averaged 10 percent of the Welsh vote. From 1974 to 1979 the Labour government was dependent upon the votes of Scottish and Welsh nationalist MPs for a secure majority in the House of Commons; it responded by enacting legislation that proposed the election of separate assemblies for Scotland and for Wales, with the devolution to the assemblies of many domestic responsibilities of the Scottish Office and the Welsh Office.

In response to parliamentary criticism that devolution proposals were an overreaction to nationalist pressures and threatened the continued unity of the United Kingdom, referendums on devolution were held in Scotland and Wales on 1 March 1979. A novel feature of the referendums was the requirement that if 40 percent of eligible voters did not approve, the government would consider repealing the devolution acts. Welsh voters unequivocally rejected devolution; 80 percent voted against, well over two-fifths of the total electorate. A narrow majority of Scots who voted, 51.6 percent, gave approval to devolution. But the proportion of eligible voters endorsing devolution was only 33 percent of the Scottish electorate. In consequence Parliament repealed the Devolution Acts for both Scotland and Wales.

Three general elections since have confirmed Unionist (that is, pro-United Kingdom) sentiments in Scotland and Wales (Table II.4). In 1979 the Scottish Nationalist vote dropped by nearly half, and the party lost nine of its eleven MPs; from being second in the Scottish vote in 1974 it is now fourth. In Wales, the Plaid Cymru vote has been steadier but lower; in 1987 the party took 7 percent of the Welsh vote. In Northern Ireland no British party contests seats, but the majority of votes goes to local parties favoring the maintenance of its link with the United Kingdom.[29]

Paradoxically, the pervasiveness of political divisions within every region and parliamentary constituency of the United Kingdom contributes to unity Britainwide. At the 1987 general election the parties firmly committed to the unity of the United Kingdom— the Conservatives, Labour, and the Alliance parties—together won more than 95 percent of the popular vote. The strength of each party differs as between the nations of Britain. The Conservatives do best in England, and Labour in Scotland and Wales. Differences in electoral support for the Conservative and Labour parties are not due to nationalism but to differences in social structure that have much the same impact throughout Britain. Industrial constituencies in the North and South of England and in Scotland and Wales tend to be Labour and neighboring suburbs or rural areas tend to favor the Conservatives and the Alliance.[30] Whereas nationalist theories imply that everyone within a nation should think and vote alike, each nation is internally divided along social class lines similar in all parts of Britain; thus no party has a majority of votes in England, Scotland, or Wales (Table II.4).

Union without Uniformity. The most important characteristic of United Kingdom government is that it is a union. The inertia of

TABLE II.4 *Voting by Nation within the United Kingdom, 1987*

	Conservative	Labour	Alliance	Nationalist
		(% of vote within nation)		
England	46.2	29.5	23.8	not applicable
Wales	29.5	45.1	17.9	7.3 Plaid Cymru
Scotland	24.0	42.4	19.2	14.0 SNP
N. Ireland	0	0	0	52.0 Unionist
				32.5 Irish Unity
				15.5 Other
United Kingdom	42.3	30.8	22.6	3.5

history explains the lack of uniformity in some of its institutions today. The Union stands for the fundamental unity of political authority. One unintended consequence of the surge in nationalist voting in the 1970s was the demonstration that most Scots, Welsh, and Ulster voters support parties committed to maintain the Union.

The Union is represented in Cabinet by ministers for the Scottish, Welsh, and Northern Ireland offices being chosen according to the party with a majority in the United Kingdom Parliament. In government there is only one source of authority, namely, the Crown in Parliament. Membership in Cabinet constrains territorial ministers to abide by collective decisions; the more important the issue, the narrower the tolerance for territorial variations in policy within the United Kingdom. No Cabinet minister would wish to defend different levels of unemployment benefit or different school-leaving ages or different income tax rates in different parts of the United Kingdom. In a federal system such as the United States all of these policies vary between states.

The great majority of Acts of Parliament apply equally throughout the United Kingdom, whether administration is in the hands of a functional department, such as Trade & Industry, or a territorial department, such as the Scottish, Welsh, or Northern Ireland offices. However, union does not require one hundred percent uniformity. Clauses in an Act can vary in accord with local circumstances, and a small number of Acts are written separately for Scotland or Northern Ireland. While administrative responsibility is in different hands, there is consistency of principle. For example, education acts make distinctive arrangements for each nation in the United Kingdom, but the principles of reading, writing, and arithmetic remain the same. In a few circumstances legislation can be exceptional, for example, about public order in Northern Ireland, the Welsh language, or conditions exclusive to the Scottish Highlands.[31]

The organization of British government is confusing because there is no uniform principle for assigning territorial and functional responsibilities to ministries. Within Whitehall a few ministries such as the Foreign Office and Defence are responsible for the United Kingdom as a whole. Some ministries, such as the Department of Energy, are responsible principally for Great Britain. There are also some ministries whose responsibilities are mostly confined to one part of the United Kingdom, such as the Department of Education and Science (England) or the Scottish Office (exclusively Scotland). Because programs are of primary concern, each territorial ministry is divided internally by function. For example, the Scottish Office is divided into education, health, and agriculture departments that have little in common with each other and much in common with Whitehall counterparts with concurrent responsibilities.

Public expenditure is determined primarily by population, because many programs provide benefits for individuals and families throughout the United Kingdom. Many apparent territorial differences are caused by differences in the composition of population; an area with more children will need more money spent on education, and an area with a greatly dispersed population will need more money spent on roads. Systematic analysis of spending in different parts of the United Kingdom shows that variations in public expenditure for major programs show that most expenditure differences by nation reflect differences in need. Northern Ireland spends more on social services because of greater social needs, and differences in social needs also account for higher expenditure in Scotland. Wales has been unusual in that Welsh Office spending on programs is the same as that of England, when its social needs would appear to justify a higher level of expenditure.[32]

In every political sense territorial ministers are much more part of Whitehall than part of Scotland, Wales, or Northern Ireland. The existence of territorial ministries for Scotland, Wales, and Northern Ireland should not be confused with the degree of political autonomy found in a federal system. A Secretary of State may be looking after affairs in Scotland, but the authority exercised is that of a British, not a Scottish Parliament. There is lots of government in Scotland, Wales, and Northern Ireland, but there is no such thing as a Scottish government or a Welsh government. Decisions affecting the parts of the United Kingdom are the prerogative of British government at Westminster.

NOTES

1. André Siegfried, *England's Crisis* (London: Jonathan Cape, 1931), p. 303.
2. *Gallup Political Index* (London No. 279: November 1983), p.14.
3. See Sir Nicholas Mansergh, *The Commonwealth Experience* (London: Weidenfeld and Nicolson, 1981 edition, 2 vols.).
4. See e.g. the Central Policy Review Staff, *Review of Overseas Representation* (London: HMSO, 1977). Cf. Simon Jenkins and Anne Sloman, *With Respect, Ambassador* (London: BBC Publications, 1985); William Wallace, *Britain's Bilateral Links within Western Europe* (London: Routledge & Kegan Paul, Chatham House Papers No. 23, 1984).
5. Dean Acheson, "Britain's Independent Role About Played Out," *The Times* (London), 6 December 1962.

6. For an official review, see the report of the Falkland Islands Review Committee chaired by Lord Franks (London: HMSO, Cmnd. 8787, 1983), and press comment after it was published on 18 January 1983. For an unofficial review see Sunday Times Insight Team, *The Falklands War* (London: Sphere, 1982). Cf. Walter Little, "The Falklands Affair: A Review of the Literature," Political Studies 32: 2 (1984), pp. 296–310.

7. Gallup Poll Election Release No. 108 (London: Social Surveys, 1959); *Gallup Political Index* No. 323 (July 1987), p. 4; and on small countries, *Gallup Political Index* No. 276 (August 1983), p. 16.

8. See David Butler and Uwe Kitzinger, *The 1975 Referendum* (London: Macmillan, 1976); Anthony King, *Britain Says Yes* (Washington, DC: American Enterprise Institute, 1977); David Butler and Paul Jowett, *Party Strategies in Britain* (London: Macmillan, 1985); and reports in the monthly *Gallup Political Index*.

9. Cf. Colin Turpin, *British Government and the Constitution* (London: Weidenfeld and Nicolson, 1985) Chapter 5.

10. On Community government and politics, see e.g. J. Lodge, ed., *Institutions and Policies of the European Communities* (London: Frances Pinter, 1983); A. Daltrop, *Politics and the European Community* (London: Longman, 1982); William Wallace, *Britain's Bilateral Links within Western Europe* (London: Routledge & Kegan Paul, 1984); and William Wallace, ed., *Britain and Europe* (London: Heinemann, 1980).

11. See R. M. White, "What's in a Name? Problems in Official and Legal Usages of Race," *New Community* 7: 3 (1979), pp. 333–349; and Heather Booth, "Ethnic and Racial Questions in the Census," *New Community* 11, 1/2 (1983), pp. 83–91. See also L. P. Curtis, Jr., *Anglo-Saxons and Celts* (Bridgeport, Conn.: published for the Conference on British Studies by Bridgeport University, 1968).

12. For a careful discussion of what census statistics do and do not show, see Muhammad Anwar, *Race and Politics* (London: Tavistock, 1986), Chapter 1.

13. Vaughan Bevan, *Development of British Immigration Law* (London: Croom Helm, 1986).

14. See *Social Trends* Vol. 17 (London: HMSO, 1987), Table 1.7. More generally, see Z. Layton-Henry and P. Rich, eds., *Race, Government and Politics in Britain* (London: Macmillan, 1986); Nathan Glazer and Ken Young, eds., *Ethnic Pluralism and Public Policy* (London: Heinemann, 1983).

15. See Donley T. Studlar, "Political Culture and Racial Policy in Britain," in R. Rose, ed., *Studies in British Politics* (London: Macmillan, 3rd ed., 1976), pp. 105–114; Z. Layton-Henry, *The Politics of Race in Britain* (London: Allen and Unwin, 1984).

16. Conservatives sometimes draw parallels with the slow assimilation of immigrant Jewish voters to patterns of class politics, after several generations of voting disproportionately Labour because of anti-Semitism. Cf. G. K. Alderman, *The Jewish Community in British Politics* (Oxford: Clarendon Press, 1983).

17. See Muhammad Anwar, *Race and Politics,* and "Ethnic Minorities and the Electoral Process: Some Recent Developments" (London: Commission for Racial Equality, 1987); Donley T. Studlar, "The Ethnic Vote 1983: Problems of Analysis and Interpretation," *New Community* 11, 1/2 (1983) pp. 92–100; C. T. Husbands, *Racial Exclusionism and the City: The Urban Support of the National Front* (London: Allen and Unwin, 1983).

18. For a contrast with Continental Europe, see J. P. Nettl, "The State as a Conceptual Variable," *World Politics*, 22 (1968), pp. 559–581. For an empirical analysis, see Richard Rose, "Is the United Kingdom a State? Northern Ireland as a Test Case," in P. Madgwick and R. Rose, eds., *The Territorial Dimension in United Kingdom Politics* (London: Macmillan, 1982), pp. 100–136.

19. See Richard Rose, *The Territorial Dimension in Government; Understanding the United Kingdom,* Chapter 1. Cf. Richard Rose and Ian McAllister, *United Kingdom Facts;* and Rose, McAllister and Richard Parry, *United Kingdom Rankings* (Glasgow: U. of Strathclyde Studies in Public Policy No. 44, 1979).

20. See Brian W. Hogwood and Michael Keating, eds., *Regional Government in England* (Oxford: Clarendon Press, 1982).

21. See Ian McAllister and Richard Rose, *The Nationwide Competition for Votes* (London: Frances Pinter, 1984), Chapter 5.

22. Richard Rose, *The Territorial Dimension in Government: Understanding the United Kingdom* (Chatham, N.J.: Chatham House, 1982), Chapter 4.

23. See Richard Parry, "The Centralization of the Scottish Office," in Richard Rose, *Ministers and Ministries* (Oxford: Clarendon Press, 1987), pp. 94–141. For studies stressing Scotland's social distinctiveness, see James G. Kellas, *The Scottish Political System* (Cambridge: Cambridge University Press, 3rd ed., 1984); and J. A. Brand, *The National Movement in Scotland* (London: Routledge and Kegan Paul, 1978).

24. For studies of Welsh distinctiveness, see Alan Butt Philip, *The Welsh Question: Nationalism in Welsh Politics, 1945-1970* (Cardiff: University of Wales Press, 1975); Peter Madgwick and Phillip Rawkins, "The Welsh Language in the Policy Process," in P. Madgwick and R. Rose, eds., *The Territorial Dimension in United Kingdom Politics,* pp. 67–99.

25. See Richard Rose, *Governing without Consensus: An Irish Perspective* (London: Faber and Faber, 1971). For a guide to institutions and individuals, see Paul Arthur, *Government and Politics of Northern Ireland* (London: Longmans, 1984); W. D. Flackes, *Northern Ireland: a Political Directory* (London: BBC, 1983).

26. The IRA is also opposed to the Constitution of the Republic of Ireland in Dublin because it accepts the de facto partition of the island of Ireland between two countries. The Republic's Constitution also expresses an aspiration for eventual unification.

27. A phrase casually let slip by a British government minister responsible for Northern Ireland.

28. Until a half century ago, religious differences were also a cross-cutting division that united coreligionists throughout the United Kingdom. Cf. Kenneth Wald, *Crosses on the Ballot* (Princeton: Princeton University Press, 1983).

29. For detailed analyses of voting by nation and by Britain as a whole, see Ian McAllister and Richard Rose, *The Nationwide Competition for Votes* (London: Frances Pinter, 1984).

30. For a cluster analysis grouping constituencies on social rather than geographical lines see McAllister and Rose, *The Nationwide Competition for Votes,* Chapter 10.

31. See Denis Van Mechelen and Richard Rose, *Patterns of Parliamentary Legislation* (Aldershot: Gower, 1986), Table 7.1; and more generally, R. Rose, *The Territorial Dimension in Government,* Chapters 5–7.

32. See the analysis of Treasury figures in R. Rose, *The Territorial Dimension in Government,* Table 6.4.

CHAPTER III

Government as a Network

'On all great subjects,' says Mr. Mill, 'much remains to be said,' and of none is this more true than of the English Constitution. The literature which has accumulated upon it is huge. But an observer who looks at the living reality will wonder at the contrast to the paper description. He will see in the life much which is not in the book; and he will not find in the rough practice many refinements of the literary theory.

IN EVERYDAY CONVERSATION, English people do not talk about the Constitution but about government. The word is used in many senses, as shown by the variety of adjectives that can modify the word. One may speak of the Queen's government, to emphasize its enduring and nonpartisan features. Referring to a Labour or Conservative government emphasizes partisanship. Adding the name of a Prime Minister—the Thatcher government—stresses personal and transitory features. Government officials is a term for referring to civil servants.

Collectively, government departments are often referred to as Whitehall, after the London street in which many ministries are located. Downing Street, the home of the Prime Minister, is a small lane off Whitehall. The Palace of Westminster, home of both the House of Commons and the House of Lords, is at the bottom of Whitehall. The historic clustering of government offices in the Westminster area symbolizes the centralization of government, just as the increasing dispersion of government offices throughout London symbolizes the growing complexity of government.[1]

When British people are asked what first comes to mind in response to the word government, three-fifths reply in terms of the representative institutions of Parliament and parties (Table III.1). Only one-fifth mention Cabinet ministers and civil servants as symbols of their idea of government, and fewer still think first of individual MPs and local councillors. The image of government is impersonal: it is a set of institutions rather than a set of politicians. When people are asked which part of government is most important, Cabinet ministers are recognized as more important than Parliament. This is consistent with the fact that government acts at the direction of Cabinet ministers.

When a constitutional lawyer is asked to describe government, the answer can be, "The Crown represents the sum total of governmental powers."[2] The Crown is a symbol of the institutions of government. Government property is held in the name of the Crown, not in the name of someone as transitory as a Prime Minister, something as abstract as the state, or as diffuse as the people of England. In the law courts, criminal actions are entered as the case of Regina (that is, the Queen) vs. the person accused of offending the Queen's peace. The Crown is a vague term: it has no name; it is an idea to which people are asked to give loyalty. The Crown is a concept of indefinite territorial domain; it does not refer to any particular geographical area or historic community of people. The idea of the Crown intentionally confuses the dignified monarchical parts of the Constitution, which sanctify authority by tradition and myth, with

TABLE III.1 *Public Image of the Term Government*

	First comes to mind %	*Most important* %
Parliament	37	28
Parties	22	9
Total, Parliament and parties	(59)	(37)
Government ministers	18	30
Civil servants	2	7
Total, ministers and civil servants	(20)	(37)
MPs	15	14
Local councillors	4	9
Total, MPs and councillors	(19)	(23)
Don't know, none	(2)	(3)

Source: Louis Moss, *People and Government in 1978: A Survey of Opinion in England and Wales* (London: duplicated Birkbeck College, University of London, 1982), p. 68.

the efficient parts of government. Whereas the President of the United States is both the symbolic head of state and the chief executive of government, the Queen is only the symbolic head of state.

As a dignified part of the Constitution, Queen Elizabeth II does not exercise authority in her own right.[3] The constitutional duties of the Queen are few in relation to what is formally called Her Majesty's Government. The Queen must give formal assent to laws passed by Parliament, but she may not state publicly her own opinion about legislation. The Queen receives major government papers and receives the Prime Minister once a week to discuss current affairs. The Queen has the opportunity to encourage the Prime Minister or to warn privately about points that Cabinet deliberations may have overlooked. No Prime Minister in modern times has suggested that a policy was followed because of the monarch's wishes. The responsibility for government rests with elected politicians. While the Queen is formally the person who invites an MP to become Prime Minister and dissolves Parliament before a general election, in doing this, the Queen is expected to follow the views of Parliament as represented by the leader of the majority party there.[4]

The ceremonial role of the Queen as head of state consumes a substantial portion of royal time and receives a large amount of media publicity. The Queen and other members of the Royal Family appear at many public functions, from horse races and air shows to laying cornerstones for new local government buildings. The Royal Family is also in demand for goodwill tours abroad. Because these time-consuming dignified tasks are performed by the Royal Family, leading elective politicians have more time for the efficient work of government.

Public opinion overwhelmingly favors the monarchy. The Gallup Poll finds that 81 percent of English people prefer a Monarch, as against 10 percent favoring a President.[5] Positive regard for the Queen does not strengthen allegiance to political authority.[6] The Queen is viewed as a nonpolitical figure above the everyday activities of government; the positive emotions inspired by monarchy are not strong. When King Edward VIII abdicated suddenly in 1936 in order to marry an American divorcee, popular support was transferred without difficulty to his hitherto little-known brother, who became King George VI. Respect is for the office. The Royal Family is aware of the limits of its anachronistic office. In the words of Prince Charles, the heir to the throne: "Something as curious as the monarchy won't survive unless you take account of people's attitudes. I think it can be a kind of elective institution; after all, if people don't want it, they won't have it."[7]

To understand government we must understand the institutions that collectively constitute the Crown. This chapter starts by examining the activities of the Prime Minister. It then turns to the role of ministers and ministries, and of the civil servants who advise them. The Cabinet is important as a symbol of collective responsibility as well as a meeting place. Together, these institutions constitute the network that wields the Mace in the name of the Crown in Parliament.

WHAT THE PRIME MINISTER SAYS AND DOES

Within the Cabinet the Prime Minister occupies a unique position, sometimes referred to as *primus inter pares* (first among equals). But as Winston Churchill once wrote, "There can be no comparison between the positions of number one, and numbers two, three or four."[8] Yet the preeminence of the Prime Minister is ambiguous. A politician at the apex of government is remote from what is happening on the ground. The more responsibilities attributed to the Prime Minister, the less time there is to devote to any one task. Like a President, a Prime Minister is the prisoner of the political law of first things first.[9] These are the imperatives of the Prime Minister:

Party Management. A Prime Minister may be self-interested, but she or he is not self-employed. Before becoming Prime Minister, a politician has normally spent more than a quarter-century in party activities and a quarter-century in Parliament. To remain Prime Minister, a politician must retain the confidence of the party as well as of the electorate.

In managing the party in Parliament, the Prime Minister has many resources. Patronage is the most tangible resource that a Prime Minister can use to ensure loyalty. A Prime Minister has the sole power to determine which of several hundred MPs in the governing party will receive an appointment as one of about twenty Cabinet ministers, fifty junior ministers outside Cabinet, or several dozen unpaid parliamentary private secretaries. As the work of government has grown, the number of patronage appointments has grown too.[10] In 1900 Conservative government ministerial jobs were given to one-tenth of MPs; Margaret Thatcher has appointed more than one hundred of her parliamentary supporters to paid posts.

The number of ministerial appointees is augmented by back-bench MPs who eagerly support government policy in hopes that this will gain them promotion to a ministerial post. By giving jobs to MPs or holding up the prospect of future office to back-benchers, a Prime Minister can maintain support of the parliamentary party whatever private doubts MPs may have.

In making ministerial appointments, a Prime Minister can use any of four different criteria: personal loyalty (rewarding friends); co-optation (bribing critics by giving them office and the obligation of collective ministerial responsibility); representativeness (for example, appointing a Scot or a woman); and competence in giving direction to a government department. Of these criteria, loyalty, co-optation and representativeness are meant to maintain the support of the governing party for the Prime Minister; only the last refers to skills relevant in government. While a Prime Minister would like every Cabinet minister to be both loyal and competent, no Prime Minister can risk having insufficient personal support in Cabinet, for in that case the government would no longer be hers or his.

Parliamentary Performance. The Prime Minister speaks only in parliamentary debates that focus upon major foreign or economic issues or questions of confidence in the government. Twice a week the Prime Minister appears in the House of Commons at question time, engaging in rapid-fire repartee with a highly partisan audience. Unprotected by a speechwriter's script or by television's possibility for recording and editing statements, the Prime Minister must show that she or he is a good advocate of the government's actions, or face the demoralization of parliamentary party supporters. Prime Minister's question time is intended to test how well the nation's leader can respond to debating points (more than one-third of questions are not for information but designed to trap the Prime Minister in embarrassing responses) or handle major issues (one-quarter of questions concern economic matters).[11] The departmental policies of more than two-thirds of the Cabinet, including the departments spending the most public money, such as Health and Social Security and Education, are rarely the subject of questions to the Prime Minister.

In the corridors in the Palace of Westminster, a Prime Minister can informally have a quiet word with MPs, flattering their egos, reassuring doubters, or calling their attention to some hard facts of political life. A Prime Minister addresses meetings of MPs in order to encourage back-bench support for government policies and consults frequently with the Chief Whip of the parliamentary party to keep informed about the mood of supporters.

Media Performance. A Prime Minister does not have to seek publicity; attention is thrust upon the incumbent of Downing Street. But a Prime Minister does have to work hard to receive favorable publicity. Unlike the Queen, the Prime Minister is the object of partisan controversy, and Opposition politicians are always trying to put the Prime Minister in a bad light. No matter how hard Downing Street works to project a favorable image, journalists can turn to other politicians for alternative assessments. Because journalists reflect opinion at Westminster, a Prime Minister successful in securing the good opinion of the House of Commons will usually be reported positively in the mass media as well.

Today, television is the favored medium by which a Prime Minister appeals to the ordinary voter. Television enables a politician to cut out the middle man, the newspaper editor, and speak directly through the camera to a mass audience. Television success is affected by personal qualities. A politician may learn to alter personal mannerisms to become more telegenic, but there are limits in the extent to which television advisers can change the personality of a sixty-year-old politician whose profession is the conduct of government, not conducting a TV chat show. Nor can professional television skills hide the message that a Prime Minister has to convey, especially when the news is bad.

Winning Elections. The only election a Prime Minister must win is election as party leader. Five of the nine persons who have held the office since 1945—Winston Churchill, Anthony Eden, Harold Macmillan, Sir Alec Douglas-Home and James Callaghan—first entered Downing Street during the middle of a Parliament. Once in Downing Street, a Prime Minister must look ahead to the next election: Douglas-Home and James Callaghan had short periods in office because they were defeated in their only bid for a general election victory.

The popularity of each Prime Minister with the electorate is measured in frequent opinion polls.[12] While a Prime Minister's personality remains relatively constant, her or his popularity fluctuates considerably, reflecting changes in popular evaluations of the success or failure of the government's policies. On average, less than half the electorate is satisfied with the performance of a Prime Minister, lower than the proportion of Americans satisfied with the President (Table III.2). Only three Prime Ministers have averaged an endorsement by more than half the British electorate during their term of office: Sir Anthony Eden, Winston Churchill, and Harold Macmillan. Margaret Thatcher's average level of popularity, 40 percent, is lower than the average endorsement of any postwar American President. It is also lower than that of any other postwar Prime Minister except for Edward Heath.

The governing party's electoral strength is also tested in by-elections as seats fall vacant through the death or resignation of an MP. A Prime Minister whose party is behind in the opinion polls or losing seats at by-elections can be considered an electoral liability rather than an asset. MPs have a vested interest in the Prime Minister being an election asset, for an unsuccessful government can cause dozens of MPs to be defeated at the next election. In the thirteen general elections since 1945, the Prime Minister has seven times led the governing party to victory and six times to defeat.

Policy Leadership. Leading government is a political rather than a managerial task; the management of public programs is dispersed among twenty Cabinet ministers. The Prime Minister's responsibility is to choose the people who make most of the day-to-day decisions of government; to orchestrate the overall pattern of government by imposing an overall sense of direction and purpose; and upon select occasions to work closely with a few ministers in determining policies that influence the political standing of the government as a whole.

A Prime Minister is ex officio involved in the substance of international affairs. In the course of a year the Prime Minister will spend more days making visits abroad to places ranging from Brussels to Beijing than visiting towns in England. In international affairs, the Prime Minister represents the British government in negotiations with leaders of other countries. The Prime Minister must also balance the diplomatic concerns of the Foreign Office with concerns of the Treasury, with Britain's success in an international economy, and with the domestic political concerns of Parliament and party. The sensitivity of some topics, including intelligence, espionage, and counterespionage, requires Prime Ministerial attention, and the House of Commons will want the Prime Minister to explain every intelligence mistake that occurs. Unlike the White

TABLE III.2 *Popularity of Presidents and British Prime Ministers since 1945 (Slightly revised)*

Leader, years in office	President (% approval)			Prime Minister (% satisfaction)		
	Average	High	Low	Average	High	Low
John F. Kennedy, 1961–1963	71	83	56			
Dwight D. Eisenhower, 1953–1960	65	79	48			
Sir Anthony Eden, 1955–1957				57	73	41
Lyndon B. Johnson, 1963–1968	56	80	35			
Ronald Reagan, 1981–Dec. 1987	52	68	35			
Sir Winston Churchill, 1951–1955				52	56	48
Harold Macmillan, 1957–1963				51	79	30
Richard Nixon, 1969–1974	49	67	24			
Gerald Ford, 1974–1976	47	71	37			
Clement Attlee, 1945–1951				47	66	37
Jimmy Carter, 1977–1980	46	75	21			
Harold Wilson II, 1974–1976				46	53	40
James Callaghan, 1976–1979				46	59	33
Harold Wilson I, 1964–1970				45	69	27
Sir Alec Douglas-Home, 1963–1964				45	48	42
Harry Truman, 1945–1952	43	87	23			
Margaret Thatcher, 1979–Dec. 1987				40	53	25
Edward Heath, 1970–1974				37	45	31
Average	53	76	35	46	60	36

Source: Calculated by the author from publications of the Gallup Poll, Princeton, NJ, and of the British Gallup Poll, London. Two entries are given for Harold Wilson, since his time in office was interrupted by a period in opposition.

House, where the National Security Council is large enough to handle foreign policy issues independently of departments, Downing Street has no foreign policy unit. While the Prime Minister speaks as the ultimate authority for government in foreign affairs, staff work is done by the Foreign Office, the Ministry of Defence, or intelligence agencies.

Because the management of the economy is today the chief political priority of government, a Prime Minister is much concerned with economic success. But a Prime Minister cannot give as much time as half-dozen Cabinet ministers whose departments concern the economy. Nor does Downing Street have a staff that can produce economic policies in competition with the large and sophisticated Treasury staff. As the politician most concerned with the broad aims of government policy, the Prime Minister is uniquely placed to see the interconnections between economic issues and other political objectives. When disputes arise between the Chancellor and spending departments, the Prime Minister can act as the ultimate arbiter. The Prime Minister engages in a continuing dialogue with the Chancellor of the Exchequer, asking questions and giving advice that the Chancellor cannot ignore.

As the spokesperson of British government, the Prime Minister has most political leeway when distant from a Cabinet meeting, for example, at an international meeting of heads of government. At home a Prime Minister can make public speeches that mobilize support for particular policies that may not appeal to every Cabinet colleague. A Prime Minister can pointedly ignore topics or ministers, thus downgrading their influence with their colleagues. However, a Prime Minister cannot normally commit the government to a course of action without checking first with the minister or ministers responsible. Not to consult with responsible ministers risks the Prime Minister making a promise that the government cannot (or will not even try to) deliver.

When the Cabinet faces a difficult or controversial decision, the Prime Minister is in the chair. A Prime Minister can encourage a discussion in which colleagues identify the political elements of greatest importance and indicate their support for conflicting views. If a subject generates great controversy in Cabinet, a Prime Minister may postpone taking a decision. After an issue has been discussed in Cabinet, no vote is taken. The discussion ends with a summing up by the Prime Minister. Prime Minister Clement Attlee described the task thus:

The job of the Prime Minister is to get the general feeling, collect the voices. And then, when everything reasonable has been said, to get on with the job and say, "Well, I think the decision of the Cabinet is this, that or the other. Any objections?" Usually there aren't.[13]

The Importance of Circumstances. Circumstances influence the political priorities of a Prime Minister. This is most evident when international events threaten the nation's security or its economic well-being. The pressures for British rearmament following the creation of NATO and the outbreak of the Korean War in 1950 made Prime Minister Clement Attlee put defense ahead of maintaining Cabinet unity; opponents of rearmament resigned, and a divided Labour Party lost the 1951 election. The OPEC oil price rise of 1973 undercut the economic policies of Prime Minister Edward Heath and led his Labour successors to turn to domestic inflation as a short-term political palliative. The unexpected Argentine invasion of the Falkland Islands in 1982 was a challenge to which Margaret Thatcher responded with military force, and victory in the Falklands War enhanced her status.

The significance of circumstances is specially evident in the actions of persons who have been Prime Minister more than once. When Winston Churchill entered office in 1940 as the wartime leader of a coalition, his immediate task was to give direction to a nation fighting for national survival. When Churchill returned to office in 1951 at the age of 77, he had less energy, and the country was divided about economic matters, which interested him much less. His final years in office were politically lethargic. When Harold Wilson entered office in 1964, he was new to the job and energetic in managing the Labour Party and Cabinet. By the time he returned to office in 1974, Wilson had eleven years as party leader and by his own admission had begun to run out of fresh ideas; two years later he retired voluntarily.

Within a term of office, events will sometimes make a Prime Minister look good—for example, a boom in the economy—and sometimes reduce popularity by a boost in unemployment or inflation. A novice in Downing Street will stress collective leadership upon entering office. This was true of both Harold Wilson and Margaret Thatcher. After winning a second election in 1966, Wilson was far more confident of his authority; Margaret Thatcher has gained in authority too with each election victory. The longer a Prime Minister remains in office, the greater the danger of becoming politically neglectful because of physical exhaustion induced by pressures of office. Toward the end of Harold Macmillan's seven years in Downing Street he passed his political prime, and he resigned after being forced to enter hospital for surgery. Alternatively, a long stay in office can lead to energetic arrogance. After three years as Prime Minister, Edward Heath had become so confident that he called an election on the issue "Who governs"—only to learn that the electorate did not want him.

The Individual Contribution. While the office of Prime Minister is a constant, individual occupants of the office differ in their conception of the job (Figure III.1).[14] Winston Churchill saw his role as that of an inspiring and innovative wartime leader, having taken office when Nazi Germany had overrun Europe and Britain stood alone against a German blitz. By contrast, his immediate successor, Clement Attlee, saw his role as representing the lowest common denominator of agreement within the Labour government, a consensual chairman of a Cabinet with diverse and strong political personalities. Anthony Eden entered office in ill health and had no time to establish a positive role before the debacle of the Suez War led to his resignation. Harold Macmillan had a detached stoic conception, delegating many responsibilities in the style of Attlee, but also ready to give a strategic lead on major matters of policy. His immediate successor, Sir Alec Douglas-Home, had too little support within Cabinet to be more than a weak chairman. Harold Wilson and Edward Heath each assumed office committed to an activist definition of the Prime Minister's job. In the event, Wilson's fondness for maintaining consensus led his critics to describe him as more interested in public relations than in policies. In reaction, Edward Heath stressed action, not words. However, the actions he took were followed by industrial conflict and inflation. The electorate turned to Harold Wilson as a political conciliator. His successor, James Callaghan, also saw himself as a conciliator of diverse interests.

Margaret Thatcher entered office in 1979 with a novel conception of the office. First of all, Mrs. Thatcher is actively concerned with policy making. She is interested in what government does to carry out the convictions that she vigorously espouses in electioneering and on TV. Generalities and symbols are not enough; she wants to see proposals from ministers and civil servants to give effect to her view of government and of Britain's role in the world. While all Prime Ministers necessarily take some interest in policies, Margaret Thatcher's concern with a wide range of policies is unprecedented in postwar Britain.

A second distinctive feature of Margaret Thatcher is her readiness to

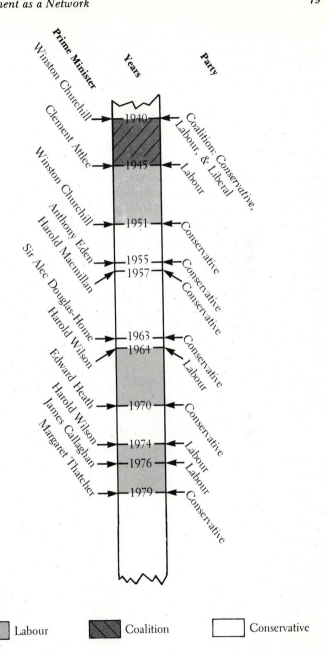

FIGURE III.1 *Prime Ministers and Governments since 1940*

run political risks by following a course of action that is controversial, causes divisions within the governing party, and may fail to show immediate success. By comparison, many of her more cautious or devious predecessors preferred to let other ministers run the risk in presenting new ideas. Because the Prime Minister is ready to speak first in many discussions, occasionally she is defeated by arguments of her Cabinet colleagues. Where other Prime Ministers were ready to make U-turns, reversing direction when a policy did not appear successful in the short run, Margaret Thatcher has as one of her mottos: "The Lady's Not for Turning." Margaret Thatcher accepts the nickname Tina (an acronym for There Is No Alternative, one of the phrases she uses to shut off debate about a proposal that she favors). A less complimentary nickname is Mother (as in Mother knows best). As two biographers note: "There are few discussions in Whitehall in which Number 10 does not make an appearance, if only to be ruled out as a factor for consideration."[15]

A third striking feature of Margaret Thatcher is that she has little regard for conventions of government. She will pursue convictions by whatever means deemed necessary, and change laws or break conventions rather than be thwarted in pursuit of what she believes are the right policies for government. The Westland affair, a relatively minor issue about the purchase of military helicopters, produced a political crisis because the Prime Minister encouraged Whitehall officials and ministers to intrigue against a Cabinet colleague, Michael Heseltine, who resigned in protest. Thatcher's world is not divided along conventional lines of ministers and civil servants, but according to whether people are "one of us," sharing her convictions about government. Ministers and civil servants who pass this test are treated differently from those who do not.

By a combination of political skill and good fortune, Margaret Thatcher has another distinctive characteristic: she is the longest-serving Prime Minister of the twentieth century. Winning three successive elections has given her the opportunity to dominate Cabinet colleagues, for nearly all owe their entry to Cabinet to her patronage and depend immediately upon her favor for promotion. By serving more than twice as long as the average Prime Minister, Margaret Thatcher has been able to multiply her impact, making a mark on economic policy, on industrial policy, and on social policy, and being an active as well as senior statesperson in international affairs.

Whereas individuals come and go, the office of Prime Minister is permanent. The question about the Thatcher Prime Ministership is whether her actions have accomplished a long-term change in the office, in the way that Franklin D. Roosevelt changed the American Presidency. Roosevelt so expanded the responsibilities of the White House that his successors have had to be as active as he was. In only one sense has Margaret Thatcher clearly changed the office of Prime Minister; she has shown what can be done by a determined Prime Minister with a clear policy agenda and a willingness to ignore criticism. But nothing that Margaret Thatcher can do will ensure that her successors have the combination of qualities that explain why she has been far more active in Downing Street than her predecessors. To act as she has done, her successor will need strong policy convictions, the readiness to run risks and accept unpopularity, the assertive determination to override established conventions, and the good fortune to win three elections consecutively. This combination of qualities is rare.

By comparison with the President of the United States, a Prime Minister enjoys less personal authority but more collective authority.[16] In Washington the President is supreme within the executive branch of government; the annual budget and legislative message are made in the name of the President, and the White House dominates important foreign policy issues. The great check upon the President is imposed by Congress. In Westminster Parliament is not a major check upon actions by the government. But the authority vested in a collective institution, the Cabinet, whose authority is derived from a party majority in the Commons, imposes constraints upon the Prime Minister. The budget and the Queen's annual speech on legislation are collective acts, made in the name of the government of the day. Particular ministers are responsible for particular measures: the Chancellor of the Exchequer, not the Prime Minister, is in charge of the budget, and legislative measures are steered through Parliament by the minister whose department sponsors it. Whereas the President is a solo performer, the Prime Minister is the leader of a team.

MINISTERS AND MINISTRIES[17]

Ministries are the building blocks of British government. Organizationally, ministries are important because each program authorized by Act of Parliament becomes the responsibility of a particular ministry; each appropriation of money is assigned to a particular ministry; and each civil servant holds a position within a particular ministry. Government can act effectively only by mobilizing the resources of one or more ministries. War is conducted through the Ministry of Defence, just as social security benefits are administered through the Department of Health and Social Security.

Politically, ministries are important because an ambitious politician normally enters Cabinet by being placed in charge of a ministry (or department, as ministries are sometimes known). Ministries differ greatly in political status, depending upon their publicity value and importance in Cabinet and as stepping stones to senior posts within the Cabinet, such as Foreign Secretary or Chancellor of the Exchequer (Table III.3). An MP entering Cabinet as a minister in a low-status department, such as Agriculture or Education, will seek advancement to a post in a medium-status or high-status department. A minister who is not considered worthy of further promotion will have little influence upon Cabinet colleagues and no political future. A distinctive feature of political status is that it does not depend upon the amount of money or the number of employees that a ministry has; big-spending departments such as Education or Health and Social Security have less political status than ministries spending little money on their own account, such as the Foreign Office or the Treasury (cf. Table III.3 and Table XII.4).

To be judged a political success, a minister must do three things.[18] Firstly, a minister must deal with questions of policy by initiating measures; by selecting between alternative policies brought forward within the department; or, avoiding risks, by minimizing policy decisions. Many ministers prefer to have civil servants identify policies regarded as administratively practicable and then select from this restricted menu. To "make" a policy, a minister must have a point of view clear enough so that civil servants can correctly infer what the minister would like done about matters that cannot be referred to him for lack of time. In default of a clearly defined ministerial viewpoint, civil servants fall back upon the departmental point of view or do nothing.

Secondly, a minister is responsible to Parliament for what is done in his name by thousands of civil servants. Keeping track of what is happening within a ministry is a difficult task, for a ministry is simultaneously concerned with many different activities. The average ministry has more than two dozen different divisions and separate budget lines, each involving matters of consequence to some MPs and pressure groups, for example, the statistics division of Education, responsible for forecasts about future needs for higher education. A minister is not a manager but an overseer of departmental activities, scrutinizing memoranda to ensure that nothing is said or done in his

TABLE III.3 *Political Status of Ministries*

	Publicity value %	Stepping stones %	Chairs cabinet committee %
High status			
Prime Minister	75		37
Treasury	49	12	22
Foreign Office	36	15	4
Trade & Industry	25	15	4
Home Office	12	29	4
Lord Privy Seal & Leader of Commons	8	8	4
Medium status			
Health and Social Security	14	4	0
Employment	16	4	0
Energy	15	3	0
Lord President of Council	3	4	26
Environment & Local Govt.	24	2	0
Defence	22	7	0
Transport	12	2	0
Northern Ireland Office	13	2	0
Scottish Office	3	1	0
Low status			
Education	3	4	0
Agriculture	6	1	0
Lord Chancellor	8	2	0
Welsh Office	1	0	0

(Publicity: Days on page one of *Times* (London); Stepping stones: Post held before highest offices, frequency, Prime Minister, Chancellor of Exchequer, Foreign Secretary or Home Secretary.)

Source: Derived from Richard Rose, *Ministers and Ministries* (Oxford: Clarendon Press, 1987), Table 4.2, Table 4.3.

name that will prove politically embarrassing in Parliament. Answerability for actions is not control. For example, a prison escape will not force the Home Secretary, who is responsible, to resign, for he cannot be expected to watch every prisoner personally. Nonetheless, a minister will face rough questioning from Parliament if a dangerous prisoner escapes.[19]

Even though the convention of ministerial responsibility is largely a constitutional fiction, it is an important fiction. The convention that the department reflects the mind of one individual has a corollary: no one else can speak for the department. Neither junior ministers nor senior civil servants are able to make public statements committing the department to a policy that is not authorized by the minister. The convention of ministerial responsibility appeals to the most important people in government: ministers and civil servants. Ministers do not wish to have news of differences within their department discussed in public prior to making a decision. They are glad to take credit and blame for all that happens, trusting that a well-run department will more often than not make them look good by actions taken in their name.

Thirdly, a minister is ambassador to the "world" outside the ministry, where many compete for influence. A minister is the department's ambassador to the Cabinet, seeking its endorsement for the department's handling of controversial issues, for legislation, and the department's claims for money. A minister is the department's spokesman in the House of Commons, defending its actions from criticism and promoting legislation there. The minister is the department's chief spokesman in consultations with pressure groups, determining which demands are rejected or accepted and seeking group support for departmental initiatives. The minister represents the department in the press and on television, promoting its policies and defending it from critics when things appear to go wrong.

The division of the government's work into ministries is the responsibility of the Prime Minister; it is not fixed by law. Some departments are organized around concerns of client groups such as pensioners or farmers. Other departments are organized according to particular functions, such as the Treasury and Defence. A third principle is organization by territory. In practice, all three principles are followed in part. When Margaret Thatcher formed her third-term Cabinet in June 1987, the departments were organized thus:

Economy and Industry. The Treasury, Trade and Industry, Employment, Energy, Agriculture, Transport.
External Affairs. Foreign and Commonwealth Office, Defence.
Social Services. Health and Social Security, Education and Science.
Territorial and Environmental. Environment (including English Local Government and Housing), Scottish Office, Welsh Office, Northern Ireland Office.
Law. Lord Chancellor's Department, Home Office, the Attorney-General and the Solicitor-General for England and

Wales, the Lord Advocate and the Solicitor-General for Scotland.

Managerial and Nondepartmental. Leader of the House of Commons (job doubled with the nondepartmental portfolio of Privy Seal), Lord President of the Council (and Leader of the House of Lords), Chancellor of the Duchy of Lancaster, Parliamentary Secretary of the Treasury (Chief Whip in the House of Commons).

The compound labels and phrases in parentheses indicate the complexity of ministries, and some ministers have a sinecure office (that is, a post without administrative tasks), such as the Lord Privy Seal, who manages the political business of the government as the Leader of the House of Commons, or the Lord President of the Council, who chairs Cabinet committees. Prime Ministers sometimes cause confusion by putting new labels on established government functions or merging responsibilities in superdepartments with many responsibilities, such as Environment or Trade & Industry.[20]

The limiting consideration in creating a ministry is the political controversy that its work generates. A department cannot be any larger than one minister can answer for in Cabinet and in the House of Commons. The Post Office, a department dealing routinely with a heavy volume of work, required so little ministerial attention that its work was hived off to a separate Post Office Board. By contrast, as troubles in Northern Ireland grew following civil rights demonstrations in 1968, responsibility for monitoring events shifted from a Home Office civil servant to a junior minister, then to the Home Secretary, and finally forced the creation of the Northern Ireland Office.

The ability of a minister to answer for a department also depends upon the coherence of its subject matter. The Department of Education and Science covers a number of interrelated functions, whereas the Home Office is responsible for a very disparate range of policies, from issuing passports to broadcasting and London taxicabs. The smaller and more homogeneous the groups being served by a department, the more focused its work becomes, and the easier it is for a minister to answer for large budgets and staff.

The Treasury and the Home Office illustrate differences between Whitehall departments. The Home Office has a staff of approximately 40,000 and the Treasury less than 4,000. The Home Office has many tasks that can be kept administratively separate: police, fire, electoral law, prisons, broadcasting, drugs, the prevention of cruelty to animals, control of obscene publications, and so forth. By contrast, the Treasury has a few interrelated tasks, all of which affect the economy. Because of the importance of its tasks, the Treasury has more senior civil servants than the Home Office, but because of its greater volume of routine work, the Home Office has more staff at lower levels. The Home Secretary is always vulnerable to adverse publicity, for example, if a television program stirs up concern about drugs. Responsibility for the economy is so diffuse that the Chancellor of the Exchequer has a ministerial colleague, the Chief Secretary, to carry the burden of managing public expenditure.

The two departments vary greatly in procedure and style.[21] The Home Office has a tradition of advice moving slowly up through the civil service hierarchy; recommendations reflect a desire for consistency in handling the details of administration. For example, when the abolition of capital punishment was initially proposed, one senior Home Office official opposed it on the ground that doing so would be manifestly unfair to those who had already been hanged! In the Treasury the Chancellor receives a variety of opinions from civil servants, who can disagree or change their minds as easily as academic economists. Many decisions of a Home Secretary can be readily carried out by departmental officials, whereas whatever a Chancellor decides can easily be upset by international economic trends over which British government has no control.

THE CIVIL SERVICE: SAYING YES AND NO TO MINISTERS

While government could continue for months without ministers speaking in Parliament, it would collapse overnight if hundreds of thousands of civil servants stopped administering prosaic laws about taxes, pensions, health and other responsibilities of the welfare state. Because British government is a big government, even a middle-ranking civil servant may be responsible for a staff of several thousand people or for millions of pounds. The activities of civil servants are the motive force of political inertia. Only if the tasks of civil servants are carried out according to routine will ministers have the time to consider changes in policies.

Defining the Civil Service. While there are legal and theoretical problems making it difficult to define the boundaries of the civil service,[22] public employees working in Whitehall ministries have many things in common: recruitment by examination, a permanent job guaranteed by public funds, preoccupation with paper work, obedience to rules and regulations, and promotion by seniority. Many features of civil service life are characteristic of all large organizations and thus can be found in the private as well as the public sector. However, private sector organizations are far less ridden by bureaucratic rules and procedures, for they are not answerable to Parliament.[23]

The 600,000 civil servants employed by Whitehall constitute less than one tenth of all those working for government (cf. Table XII.3). The civil service is divided into categories unequal in size and political significance. At the base of the pyramid are 90,000 industrial civil servants, principally in defense-related work, and 150,000 clerical staff, whose work is the routine of bureaucracy, typing letters, filing forms, and other tasks allowing little discretion. Responsible posts are of three different types. Specialist and technical staff contribute specific expertise in such fields as public health, highway construction, computing, or tax collection. Executive officers are administrators who carry out policies laid down by their superiors, for example, supervising regional and local offices paying out social security benefits.

The 6,000 senior civil servants in the open structure at the top of the civil service constitute only 1 percent of the total, but in status and political significance they form the "higher" civil service, for 99 percent are beneath them.[24] The motto of the generalists in the higher civil service is: Experts should be on tap but not on top. Prior to reorganization in the late 1960s, this group was known as the administrative class; the word "class" was an apt description of officials who were separately recruited for assignment to work that is primarily political rather than bureaucratic or technical. Ordinary members of the public are most likely to meet clerical staff or technicians. Ministers in Whitehall deal with senior civil servants.

Ambivalent Political Status. Senior civil servants say they are not political; that is, they are not allowed to engage in party politics or in public controversy about issues. But an official publication seeking to recruit bright graduates for the senior civil service declares:

> You will be involved from the outset in matters of major policy or resource allocation and, under the guidance of experienced administrators, encouraged to put forward your own constructive ideas and to take responsible decisions.[25]

Insofar as politics concerns making choices about the policies that government ought to carry out, senior civil servants are very much part of the inherently political process of policy making, advising ministers about issues confronting their department, and dealing with the consequences of ministerial actions. Civil servants are not apolitical; they are bi-partisan, prepared to work for whichever party is the winner of an election.

The immediate responsibility of senior civil servants is to look after the needs of their departmental minister. They are the principal staff to whom a minister can turn for help, and the relationship is intimate. As Headey notes, "In an average week a Cabinet minister is likely to see at least two civil servants—his Permanent Secretary and his Private Secretary—far more frequently than he sees the Prime Minister or any of his party colleagues."[26] A minister is normally glad to accept the help of civil servants because they have expert knowledge about the department of which he is temporarily head.

The first thing a minister wants from civil servants is assistance in formulating and evaluating policies. A minister often enters office with an idea of what he and his party would like to do, but without a clear idea of how this aim might be achieved. Senior civil servants are expected to respond to ministerial initiatives sympathetically but not uncritically, saying Yes to ideas that they think practical, and No to ideas that they believe would not work in practice, but would land the minister and the ministry in political trouble. The idea of expert advice is found in many other professions. For example, a lawyer is expected to advise a client and if requested to advocate his client's case whether or not he believes it.

Secondly, a minister expects senior civil servants to defend him from mistakes. Civil servants spend much time scrutinizing the continuous flow of information that moves through a ministry, trying to spot problems before they can blow up in the minister's face. The civil servant's motto is that it is better to say no or stall a proposal than to stir up unwanted political controversy. If the minister becomes the subject of criticism in Parliament and the press, civil servants are expected to construct arguments that a minister can use to defend actions for which he is formally responsible.

Thirdly, a minister needs the help of civil servants to market policies so that others will also say Yes to them. Marketing begins within Whitehall; the department's position must be defended against other departments fighting their corner in interdepartmental committees. Increasingly, senior civil servants are expected to influence discreetly the climate of opinion about the department, appearing before parliamentary committees, briefing journalists, and talking with pressure groups. When a civil servant advocates a policy, he or she is acting in support of the government rather than the governing party, a distinction not always easy to draw. If a minister wants to undertake activities that will get him favorable publicity or avoid controversy, civil servants are expected to advise on this too.

As officials experienced in working Whitehall, civil servants have ideas about what they do and do not want.[27] They want ministers to respect and listen to their advice so that their decisions will be capable of implementation by the department in ways considered practical. A former permanent head of the civil service, Sir William Armstrong, has argued that the chief danger in government is that "optimism will carry ministers into schemes and policies which will subsequently be seen to fail, failure which attention to the experience and information available from the service might have avoided." Ministers see the advice of civil servants as a mixed blessing. Looking back upon decisions in which his personal preferences differed from civil service advisers, Roy Jenkins regretted some decisions "made with advice, and some made against it."[28]

Secondly, civil servants want their minister to give clear and firm decisions about memoranda that they present and to stick to a decision when it attracts criticism as well as when it is praised. Given a clear lead by their minister, civil servants are willing and able to exercise authority in his name. Civil servants also like a minister to be successful as the department's ambassador, winning battles in Cabinet, defending the department from criticism in Parliament and the press, and securing public recognition and praise for its achievements. A minister who is indecisive when action is imperative makes life difficult for civil servants. A minister who is unsuccessful as an ambassador makes the department a loser in the Cabinet competition for public funds and legislative time, and thus lowers departmental morale.

A third concern is the reputation that each civil servant has with colleagues and superiors, whose assessments influence promotion prospects. What is it that gives a civil servant a good repute? Trustworthiness is essential; one must be scrupulously honest in money matters and not be deceptive in dealing with colleagues in other departments. Be reliable; predictability of actions is important when time is pressing. Coordination occurs best when officials know what their colleagues in other departments expect them to do. Soundness is another cardinal virtue. Be practical: a civil servant who repeatedly voices clever but controversial ideas will become a bore, making more experienced hands explain why a bright idea is not practical politics. Like English university education, Whitehall prizes critical more than constructive intelligence. Intelligence is often demonstrated by finding one more snag than anyone else has found in a proposal for change. A reputation for upholding the Whitehall code is more important than winning a battle about a particular issue. The style of governing is that of the amateur cricketer, not the professional baseball player. English civil servants do not play to win; the important thing is how one plays the game.

The predisposition of civil servants is to minimize conflict; consensus-mongering is a major activity. In the words of Sir William Armstrong, one of the most formidable of postwar civil servants, "There is indeed a great deal of common ground—what I have called ongoing reality—which is properly, necessarily and desirably the concern of a permanent civil service."[29] There usually is limited scope for politicians to make changes within the boundaries of what civil servants define as "ongoing reality." The bias of the senior civil servant is not so much toward any one party as toward the status quo. By definition, the status quo is practicable, because it is already there. This can lead civil servants to challenge Conservative proposals to reduce the size of government as well as Labour proposals to expand it. Before a senior civil servant has completed half a career in Whitehall, he or she will be expert in saying Yes to the inclinations of each party, and also in saying No.

Challenge to the Status Quo. As the responsibilities of government have grown and its activities more and more impinge upon the world outside Whitehall, the success of a minister or ministry can no longer be the skill with which a civil service mandarin drafts a memorandum to a minister or a committee minute.[30]

Difficulties of government have made the senior civil service a target for criticism ever since the publication of the Fulton Committee Report in 1968. Demands for reform have stressed both apolitical management objectives and a desire for more political inputs.[31]

Committed partisans wanting to change government at a faster rate or in a different direction than it has actually gone see senior civil servants as a major obstacle to radical change. According to

Anthony Benn, a left-wing Labour Cabinet minister, civil servants are "always trying to steer incoming governments back to the policy of the outgoing government, minus the mistakes that the civil service thought the outgoing government made."

Sir John Hoskyns, former adviser to Margaret Thatcher, has also attacked the civil service for its caution: "Few, if any, believe that the country can be saved. . . . As each government retires exhausted the service has somehow to continue with the next, persuading itself that the problem was insoluble in order to conserve its self respect."[32] The radical critique of civil servants is also an attack upon party leaders. Critics charge that ministers lack the intelligence or the ideological commitment to do what is willed by the governing party—or that faction to which critics belong. Ministers are said to be "captured" by civil servants or even to surrender without a fight.

One reform favored by partisans of right and left is the introduction of political advisers into Whitehall ministries and 10 Downing Street in the belief that they could provide a partisan influence to set against the outlook of civil servants, who are cloistered in Whitehall. Since 1964 more and more ministers have had at least one partisan appointee in their ministry.[33] One type of partisan appointee is an expert senior policy adviser with a good knowledge of a department's work from academic research or work in a pressure group or business. Senior policy advisers are principally concerned with promoting policies, not personalities. Party links are secondary to the expertise that a professor of economics may contribute while on leave in Whitehall. The second category is a partisan adviser who acts as a personal assistant to a minister. He or she is more concerned with politics and personality than with policies, knowing the party and often committed to a minister, moving with him from department to department. Partisan advisers are expected to maintain contact with the governing party's back-bench MPs, pressure groups, and the press. Rarely do they have any specialist knowledge of the subject matter of the department that their minister heads.

Both types of political advisers have fitted into Whitehall insofar as their work complements that of civil servants. One or two advisers in a department with fifty or one hundred senior civil servants is not a threat to the established civil service. A partisan adviser can assist a department by advocating his minister's (and the department's) case in party circles from which civil servants are barred. A policy adviser who is well informed about the department's subject may create difficulties if advising the minister to take actions contrary to civil service advice. But political advisers make trouble and risk dismissal if they spend most of their time quarreling with civil servants. To get along in Whitehall, transient advisers must come to terms with the permanent civil service. Most ministers welcome having an adviser or two at hand to undertake extradepartmental activities that help promote his reputation in the party and to break the isolation of being in an office surrounded by non-partisan officials. The contribution of political advisers is limited by the attributes that also constitute their comparative advantage.[34] The more novel the perspective brought to Whitehall, the more one must learn in order to operate effectively there. Yet the more an individual learns, the less likely the outside adviser is to have a distinctive contribution to make.

The Thatcher government has introduced a new phenomenon in Whitehall: a Prime Minister predisposed to dislike and distrust the civil service. The distrust is first of all derived from Mrs. Thatcher's ideological belief in the superiority of the market to government and of business practices to civil service procedures. The Prime Minister established in the Cabinet Office an Efficiency Unit under Derek (now Lord) Rayner to recommend savings in the housekeeping activities of government. The number of civil servants has been reduced by 14 percent under her leadership, in part by transferring work to public agencies outside Whitehall, in part by contracting out services to private-sector firms, and in part by cutting staff without reducing the tasks of those remaining in place. The Civil Service Department was abolished and its work divided between the Treasury, strengthening financial control, and the Cabinet Office, bringing it closer to the Prime Minister. Civil service pay has not been allowed to rise in line with the private sector.

In 1982 the Thatcher Administration launched a Financial Management Initiative. It reflected the Prime Minister's belief that principles of managerial efficiency can be translated from the world of profit-making firms to government, even though Whitehall departments do not trade in the marketplace, and most civil servants advise about policies that are delivered by public sector agencies outside Whitehall (see Chapter XIII). Proposals from outside management consultants to make Whitehall more businesslike have run into resistance from ministers and civil servants. The Auditor General noted:

Ministers did not accept all recommendations included in the scrutiny reports. Some were overtaken by events and some regarded as unacceptable, either for administrative reasons or because they conflicted with government policies. In addition, the forecasts of savings from a number of recommendations were inaccurate or substantially over-optimistic.[35]

A second major initiative was announced in 1988: the transformation of some parts of some existing departments into public sector agencies delivering programs outside the ministry but still answerable to the ministry for policy direction. Creating separate agencies is assumed to improve management accountability. The small number of agencies to be subject to this change reflected the Efficiency Unit's loss of influence in interdepartmental battles within Whitehall. The Unit reported wistfully that it still had a long way to go: "There is insufficient sense of urgency in the search for better value for money and steadily improving services." Success "depends heavily on changing the cultural attitudes and behavior of government."[36] The loss of momentum by the Efficiency Unit has come about because of a concentration upon accountancy rather than the microeconomic task of designing incentives to motivate civil servants to become money-saving managers in the Thatcherite mould. Critics argue that the latter task is not difficult; it is said to be impossible.

To alter the direction of departments, Mrs. Thatcher has taken an unusual degree of interest in the promotion of very senior civil servants. The critical question that she asks about individuals is: Is he one of us? The question is not a test of partisanship, but of commitment to Margaret Thatcher's very personal vision of what government ought and ought not to do. Civil servants who show that they are enthusiastic in doing what she wants can expect rapid promotion at a relatively young age. Those who express the traditional scepticism of Whitehall may find themselves on the sidelines when policy advice is sought. Since every very senior civil servant in place after Margaret Thatcher's departure will have had at least one promotion since 1979, her successor cannot dismiss all of them as Thatcherites, and many would vehemently reject this label. A senior civil servant in Whitehall today can claim to be doing exactly what he or she is expected to do: carrying out the instructions of the duly elected government of the day.

The Thatcher approach to the civil service has caused morale to deteriorate. Higher civil servants who have committed twenty or thirty years to working fifty to sixty hours a week in Whitehall for lower pay than in the private sector resent criticisms of the civil service as criticisms of themselves. In the words of Lord Bancroft, prematurely retired as Head of the Civil Service, the Prime Minister's attitude has undermined mutual respect between ministers and their advisers: "The ritual words of praise, forced out of clenched teeth in public, deceive no one if they are accompanied by noisy and obvious cuffs around the ears in semi-private." Another Head of the Civil Service and a trusted Thatcher adviser, Sir Robert Armstrong, sees low morale as creating obstacles to the implementation of the Prime Minister's proposals for change:

> It is difficult to sustain a drive for increased efficiency and reduced numbers, however desirable those changes may be in economic terms, without implying that the service has been inefficient and overlarge. We have paid a price for this in some loss of confidence and self-respect among civil servants.[37]

A few civil servants have challenged the traditional doctrine that the minister knows what is best for British government and that they must support a minister whatever their personal opinion. In one well publicized case, Clive Ponting leaked to the House of Commons evidence questioning the accuracy of the government's public statements about the conduct of the Falklands War. He was indicted for violating the Official Secrets Act. The judge told the jury that the issue was, "Can it then be in the interests of the state to go against the policy of the government of the day?"[38] The jury concluded that this could be the case; Ponting was acquitted.

Most senior civil servants have adapted to the Thatcher era in Whitehall. The knowing, impassive figure of the mandarin is the symbol of the English civil service, just as the Washington counterpart is symbolized by the aggressive athlete, the man with clout. "Why are your officials so passionate?" a British Treasury official asked presidential adviser Richard Neustadt. Neustadt turned the question around, asking why British civil servants are so dispassionate about the outcome of their activities.[39] He concluded that American civil servants care about policies because their careers are wrapped up with success in getting things done for their department. To win a political battle advances an American official personally as well as advancing a government policy.

Political Administration. Ministers and civil servants are both engaged in political administration; together they provide what direction is given to government by Whitehall. Civil servants are usually more expert in government policies and procedures, but they are relatively remote from MPs, political party leaders, and ordinary citizens.[40] Ministers have far more experience in judging the mood of the electorate and of Parliament but political will-power is insufficient to make a policy work. Ministers need help in finding policies that can steer the ship of state toward their desired goals. The classic doctrine of public administration is that ministers and civil servants cooperate at arm's length; ministers are meant to make policy, and civil servants to carry out what elected politicians decide. In fact, ministers and senior civil servants have a symbiotic relationship. Whitehall is a village in which everyone knows every-one else's strengths, weaknesses, and ambitions.[41]

The ship of state has only one tiller, but steering comes from two pairs of hands—ministers and civil servants.[42] Giving direction to government involves both these groups. The difference in their contribution is characterized thus by a leading civil servant, Sir Patrick Nairne:

> If reality—immovable facts, unanswerable argument, uncontrollable pressures—is to be the touchstone, or continuity of policies, and the need to reap what a previous administration has sown, or not to change what the public has come to accept or expect is to be regarded as paramount, then no one is better at fostering and defending the policies to be followed than the average civil servant.

But continuity is only one part of government. Sir Patrick goes on to add:

> The promotion of policy change is the principal challenge of politics. Only when ministers are determined to pursue new and perhaps radical policies—challenging the arguments of reality and continuity in the process—will the politicians exercise real power and be effectively on top.[43]

Sir Patrick tactfully omits mentioning that each virtue is also a weakness. In a changing world, a commitment to the status quo gradually becomes untenable as the moving force of political inertia gradually converts what was yesterday a matter of routine administration into today's political problems. A politician who talks about new and radical policies runs the risk of believing that the rhetoric of change does not require expert assistance in order to become effective government.

THE CABINET: SYMBOL AND REALITY

The Cabinet mobilizes the collective authority of government because its members are the heads of Whitehall departments.[44] It is large enough to include persons with diverse policy responsibilities yet small enough so that every member can sit around a table to participate in its deliberations. The Cabinet was described by Bagehot as the efficient secret of the English Constitution, securing "the close union, the nearly complete fusion of the executive and legislative powers." Fusion is possible because Cabinet ministers represent the majority party in the House of Commons. In the American system of the separation of powers, presidential appointees to Cabinet posts are secretaries for departments, but Congressional committees are in charge of the legislation and appropriations on which the departments depend. Pressures from Congress drive a wedge between Cabinet secretaries and the White House. In Westminster the doctrine of collective Cabinet responsibility requires that ministers resolve differences before measures are debated in Parliament, and vote together there.

Every Cabinet minister has a tendency to bury himself in his department. Within the department he is the chief personage; the limit upon his ability to influence other departments is also a defense against interference by colleagues. Government policy can come to mean no more than the sum of matters that individual ministers will approve or defend departmentally. A study of Cabinet ministers found that half made no mention of their Cabinet role; only one in ten saw himself as in any way a Cabinet minister. Bruce Headey comments, "In so far as the Cabinet is important to ministers, it is seen as an interdepartmental battleground rather than as a forum for collective deliberation on policy."[45]

In order to take major action a minister usually needs the support of other departments in Whitehall. Spending measures require Treasury consent. Legislation requires approval of a Cabinet committee concerned with the government's annual proposals to Parliament. Successful implementation of a policy without friction often requires the cooperation of several ministries concerned with interrelated aspects of a common policy issue. For example, any policy for the inner cities addresses concerns of the departments of

Environment, Education, Employment, Trade & Industry, and the Home Office.

Endorsement by the Cabinet is the strongest sanction that a policy can have; approval by the House of Commons is normally a formality. The Cabinet can delay or frustrate a minister's initiative if it thinks it undesirable on broad political grounds. After a Cabinet decision has been taken, civil servants will be bound by the decision. The doctrine of collective responsibility requires that all ministers must refrain from public criticism of Cabinet decisions once taken. If a minister does not wish to go along with colleagues, he is expected to resign. Such is the political pain of giving up office that even ministers with doubts about a policy rarely take the giant step of resigning from Cabinet. Since 1945 fewer than a dozen Cabinet members have resigned because of political disagreements with their colleagues.

The Cabinet is the court of last resort for the resolution of differences between ministers, but it takes relatively few decisions. One reason is the pressure of time: the Cabinet meets only once or twice a week, and its agenda is extremely crowded by routine business, such as reports on pending legislation and foreign affairs, and by the need to deal with emergencies. A second reason is practical: most Cabinet ministers will not be informed about most of the work of other departments and have little interest in discussing activities for which they are not personally responsible. A third reason is organizational: it is possible to examine issues in formal or informal Cabinet committees.

The Cabinet is a framework within which many decisions can be taken committing the whole of the Cabinet *outside* the formal setting of a full Cabinet meeting. When a crisis requires prompt action, there may not be time to discuss matters with nonexpert ministers, and the full Cabinet may only be told about a decision when it is a *fait accompli*. During the Falklands War, for example, Mrs. Thatcher constituted a small "War Cabinet" to supervise military operations to which the whole of the Cabinet was committed. Actions that give little prospect of political controversy can be taken within a ministry. Measures low in controversy may be settled by bilateral discussions between two ministries, with the object of producing an agreement that will be formally ratified by Cabinet. Ministers who have not been involved in negotiations prefer to let recommendations pass without question, in the expectation that their bargains will similarly be approved when they appear on the Cabinet agenda.

When decisions have an impact upon a number of departments or are political hot potatoes, they are likely to be the subject of a formal Cabinet committee. Because of her desire to be the central driving force in government, Margaret Thatcher chairs the largest number of committees, on matters ranging from the economy and international matters to daily handling of the 1984–1985 miners' strike. Nearly two-thirds of ministers do not chair a single Cabinet committee, and most are not members of committees of major concern to the Prime Minister.[46] In important fields committees often exist at two levels; there is a committee of ministers and a parallel committee of their civil servants clarifying matters of fact and technical matters so that the ministerial committee can concentrate on major political issues. The distinction between matters suitable for civil servants to agree and political issues is easier to talk about than to define. Ministers sometimes feel that their scope for choice is restricted by agreements that their officials make with other departments.

Unofficial networks can be as important as formal committees, especially private discussions between the Prime Minister and the Chancellor of the Exchequer or the Foreign Secretary; other ministers are drawn into these informal committees as appropriate. Margaret Thatcher particularly likes ad hoc committees and informal meetings, in which she can use her position to push ministers to do what she thinks the government ought to be doing, free from many of the restraints of more formal Cabinet meetings. Whereas Harold Wilson saw himself as a team captain taking credit for the goals that ministers scored, Margaret Thatcher sees herself as "playing center forward, and goalkeeper as well, with the referee's whistle clamped between her teeth."[47]

In the process of negotiation that culminates in formal Cabinet approval, ministers clash with each other. While ministers belong to the same party, they often disagree on departmental grounds. (Compare the Washington dictum: Where you stand depends upon where you sit.) Ministers compete for scarce resources of money, skilled manpower, and parliamentary time for legislation. In pursuit of departmental objectives, a minister seeks allies among political friends in Cabinet, among back-bench MPs, and among interest groups. Leaks to the press may be used to affect the climate of opinion. One minister's loyalty to advancing his cause may look like disloyalty to a colleague. Barbara Castle entered the 1964 Labour Cabinet believing "in my innocence" that it would make major policy decisions in collective deliberation. But "I was soon disabused of that . . . I wasn't in a political caucus at all. I was faced by departmental enemies."[48]

In Cabinet deliberations "the one thing that is hardly ever discussed is general policy," that is, underlying political priorities and objectives. "Nothing, indeed, is more calculated to make a Cabinet minister unpopular with his colleagues, to cause him to be regarded by them as Public Enemy No. 1, than a tiresome insistence of discussing general issues."[49]

The Cabinet is not an institution for coordinating policies; it enforces collective responsibility but not collective decision-making. In the words of Colin Seymour-Ure: "The Cabinet seems to have disintegrated in the literal sense of that word. Every member of the Cabinet is important, but his importance depends on functions that are performed almost entirely outside the Cabinet."[50]

In reaction to this problem, Edward Heath established a Central Policy Review Staff (CPRS) within the Cabinet Office in 1970. It was intended to provide a comprehensive review of government strategy, considering how specific policies of different departments related to more general objectives of the government of the day. With a staff of fifteen, less than one person for each government department, the CPRS could not be compared with the Executive Office of the President in Washington. Its creation was evidence of weakness in Downing Street. When asked to name the CPRS's major achievement, its first head, Lord Rothschild, said:

> I don't know that the government is better run as a result of our work. I think the highest compliment I ever got paid was from a Cabinet minister who said: "You make us think from time to time." I thought that was a great achievement, considering how much ministers have to do. They don't have much time to think.[51]

After being neglected by Heath's successors, the CPRS was abolished in 1983. Margaret Thatcher has preferred to have a policy unit half the size of the CPRS but working solely on her own behalf.

The Cabinet's position in British government is part fact and part fiction. It is a fact that the Cabinet meets regularly, and membership in it is an important political asset to a politician. But it is a fiction, insofar as the Cabinet does not take most of the decisions promulgated in its name. Most of the effective work of Cabinet ministers occurs in intradepartmental and interdepartmental settings. The important constitutional fiction symbolized by the Cabinet is that the political decisions of ministers are related because they involve the collective fate of the party in control of government. The most authoritative phrase in Washington is "The President wants this." The equivalent phrase in Whitehall is, "The Cabinet has decided."

GOVERNMENT AS A NETWORK

In an era of big government, power cannot reside within an individual or an office; it is manifest in a network of relations between individuals in institutions. A network need not be a hierarchical pyramid, leading to a single peak, occupied by the Prime Minister or the Cabinet. British government is better conceived as a mountain range with a number of peak individuals and institutions. The politics of government is about the relationship between the different mountains, that is, ministers and ministries. In the network of relationships, some departments and some individuals stand out much more than others, but the range as a whole is greater than any one point.

Prime Ministerial Government? The Prime Minister of the day enjoys a unique eminence, chairing Cabinet meetings, acting as the chief spokesperson for government in Parliament and abroad, and as the object of more publicity than any other member of the government. Because of the Prime Minister's prominence, some writers go so far as to argue that England now has Prime Ministerial government. The complaint has been voiced for more than a century. In the 1840s Gladstone complained about Sir Robert Peel; Labour politicians such as R. H. S. Crossman and Anthony Benn complained about the alleged dictatorship of Harold Wilson, and former members of Margaret Thatcher's Cabinet now voice their complaints about her.[52]

While there is no denying that the Prime Minister is the single most important person in government, it does not follow that the Prime Minister is all-important or the cause of everything that is done in Whitehall. The first weakness in the case for Prime Ministerial government is that the proposition is often vague or tautological. R. H. S. Crossman, a former Labour minister, has argued that "primary decisions" are made by the Prime Minister and "secondary decisions" are made by departmental ministers in consultation

with the Cabinet. Any decision made solely by a minister by definition becomes "not at all important."[53] A professor turned back-
bench Labour MP, John P. Mackintosh, asserted, "The country is
governed by the Prime Minister, who leads, coordinates and maintains a series of ministers."[54] But Mackintosh immediately retracted
the force of this assertion by recognizing that some decisions are
made by the Prime Minister alone, others in consultation with
senior ministers, and still others by the Cabinet, Cabinet committees, ministers, or senior civil servants. Proponents of the theory of
Prime Ministerial government invariably qualify their arguments
by admitting limits to what the Prime Minister can do.

Secondly, proponents of Prime Ministerial government often confuse survival in office with dominance of government.[55] To argue
that the Prime Minister's significance is due to remaining in office
is to confuse Downing Street with Buckingham Palace, the home of
the Queen. A Prime Minister can remain part of the network of
government without necessarily exercising influence. At times the
price a Prime Minister pays for retaining office is to give way to
Cabinet and extra-Cabinet pressures. The situation is summed up
in Peter Jenkins's description of Harold Wilson's position in 1969,
when the Prime Minister abandoned a proposal for a major industrial relations bill: "The power of the Prime Minister was thus sufficient for him to remain in office, but insufficient for him to
remain in office and have his way."[56]

A third limitation upon Prime Ministerial government is that one
individual can only deal with a limited number of problems in the
course of a day or a week. Time is scarce: the more attention given
to international affairs and the economy, the less time there is for
all the everyday domestic concerns of Cabinet ministers. A Prime
Minister's political capital (that is, the capacity to influence other
politicians) is also limited. The Cabinet's function is to mobilize
the efforts of a score of leading politicians to govern on behalf of
the majority party in Parliament. Mackintosh portrays the Prime
Minister as "at the apex, supported by and giving point to a widen-
ing series of rings of senior ministers, the Cabinet, its committees,
non-Cabinet ministers and departments."[57] This view from the top
can be remote. What happens at the base of the mountain range of
government can be at least as important as what can be dealt with at
the peak. The more complex the network of government, the
smaller the proportion of activities that the Prime Minister can
address personally.

A fourth limitation on the Prime Minister's influence is the lack of a large personal staff. Since 1964 successive Prime Ministers have had one or more personal policy advisers in Downing Street in addition to a handful of civil service staff; together the two groups number about a dozen. The head of the Cabinet Office is also in a crucial position to assist the Prime Minister. In numbers and political status the staff of a Prime Minister is slight compared with the staff of an American President. In Washington there are hundreds of White House staff. Moreover, senior White House staff members can issue orders to Cabinet secretaries and civil servants in the name of the President. Downing Street staff lack both the constitutional status and the political weight to give direction to departments and ministers. Any influence they exert is indirect, exercised by conveying advice to or from the Prime Minister.

Influence Within a Network. The Prime Minister is in a central position within the network of government. Centrality means that the Prime Minister is informed by the Cabinet Office about activities in Cabinet committees, and about the mood of the House of Commons by participation in twice-weekly question time and by reports from the party's Leader of the House and the Chief Whip. Because the Prime Minister is not responsible for a particular department, she or he has the opportunity to intervene selectively in a variety of issues of importance to the government as a whole.

International affairs take a high proportion of the time of a Prime Minister, representing Britain in a variety of international meetings with heads of governments in the European Community, NATO, and at the annual world summit meeting. Moreover, a stream of national leaders from abroad come to London and expect to visit the Prime Minister in Downing Street. International issues may concern defense, diplomacy, or economic affairs, given the involvement of Britain in the world economy. The Prime Minister receives Foreign Office papers as a matter of course, but not papers from domestic departments. As long ago as 1900 Sir Henry Campbell-Bannerman commented, "It is absolutely impossible for any man who conducts the foreign affairs of the country at the same time to supervise and take charge of the general action of the government."[58] When Britain no longer has the international influence it enjoyed in Queen Victoria's time, the Prime Minister's involvement abroad is a sign of dependence not power.

A Prime Ministerial intervention often takes the form of a question to a minister: What is the government doing about X? Have you considered the risk of a public reaction against your plan for doing Y? A question from Downing Street cannot be ignored, but it allows a minister an opportunity to answer as he thinks best, as the individual immediately responsible for an issue, and with immediate access to civil service expertise on the subject. Margaret Thatcher's personality is more combative: a question from her may sound like a command. With only one Treasury official and one political adviser on the economy, the Prime Minister cannot work out a full-fledged economic policy from Downing Street. A minister who cannot satisfy the Prime Minister about the wisdom of a course of action will be stymied and may be dismissed from Cabinet. But a Prime Minister who does not get the answer that she or he wants is also frustrated, and there is no assurance that changing ministers will make it possible to change policies as desired.

The Prime Minister pays a very high opportunity cost for any action. Her time is limited. To participate in foreign policy negotiations is to forgo the opportunity to discuss issues with other ministers. One person cannot keep abreast of the complexities of foreign affairs, defense, internal security, economic policy, industrial relations, the environment, housing, education, health, social security, and public order—especially when there are other tasks besides. For every Cabinet minister whom the Prime Minister sees often to discuss policy issues, many more will be seen infrequently or only when a crisis unexpectedly erupts about matters for which a middle- or low-status minister is responsible. In the words of one civil servant, transferred from a department directly concerned with programs to 10 Downing Street: "It's like skating over an enormous globe of thin ice. You have to keep moving fast all the time."[59]

Within the network of government, a small number of very senior ministers and civil servants are also important points for clearing policies and politics. The Chancellor of the Exchequer is trebly important. At the Treasury he has immediate responsibility for managing the economy, with all this implies for the government's electoral fortunes; he directs a large number of talented Treasury civil servants; and he is a substantial political figure in the governing party. Very senior Treasury officials are important in formulating economic advice for the Chancellor. The Foreign Secretary is the principal minister concerned with international relations, and

diplomatic staff in more than 100 nations abroad report to the Foreign Office. When the Prime Minister wants information or action,
she or he must turn to the Foreign Secretary and the Foreign Office
for information and advice. Downing Street has nothing equivalent
to the White House's National Security Council, a parallel State
Department. Nor does Downing Street have a Council of Economic
Advisers or an Office of Management and Budget, institutions that
provide the President with advice in competition with his own
Treasury Secretary.

At any one point in time, a few ministers will stand out because
of their personal relationship with the Prime Minister. For example, Lord Whitelaw was important to Margaret Thatcher because he
was a senior Conservative politician who did not threaten her hold
on Downing Street and because he could receive complaints from
Conservative MPs, at times mollifying critics and at times advising
the Prime Minister of the need to change course. Michael Foot was
important to Harold Wilson and James Callaghan in the 1974–79
Labour governments because he had a personal following of left-
wing MPs who could be mobilized in support of the right turn of
the Labour government.

A handful of leading civil servants are also central points in the
network. The Secretary of the Cabinet, Sir Robin Butler, has a staff
that serves all Cabinet committees and is thus briefed upon many
developments there. As the official responsible for recommending
persons for promotion to the highest ranks in the civil service,
ambitious and senior officials will want to keep the Cabinet Secretary informed about their achievements. Taking notes at each
Cabinet meeting and issuing memoranda about actions to follow
from Cabinet decisions is a third important role. Not least, the
Secretary to the Cabinet is in daily contact with the Prime Minister,
providing information and advice and carrying out requests from 10
Downing Street through the informal civil service network.

It is misleading to conceive of the network of government simply
in terms of a few central figures. The whole point of a network is
that it links dozens of ministries with each other and links dozens of
ministers with hundreds of civil servants. Within a network, problems can be dealt with simultaneously by many different officials in
many different places. It is not necessary for one person to be personally responsible for all that is done in the name of British
government. Nor is it possible.

Government as a Collective Product. While the Crown no longer rules, the doctrine of government in the name of the Crown symbolizes the emphasis upon unity in government action. While the Cabinet no longer makes decisions by collective weekly deliberations, it is a practical expression of the doctrine of collective responsibility for actions taken by ministers outside the Cabinet.

Describing the center of government as a network emphasizes relationships among ministers, between ministers and civil servants, and between the ministries that individuals head. Few policies of major importance can be formulated or carried out by a single ministry, let alone a single minister. Information and opinions must be exchanged within this network in order to create a policy that takes into account financial and administrative problems, difficulties within the governing party in Parliament, and often difficulties abroad. Discussion is also helpful in mobilizing the political resources to overcome difficulties. The policy that emerges reflects the imprint of more than one set of hands (cf. Chapter XIII). The collective responsibility of Cabinet gives all the leaders of the governing party a stake in collective success.

NOTES

1. The term "Whitehall" here describes ministers, civil servants, and Cabinet (usually referred to in America as the executive branch of government). "Parliament" usually means the House of Commons, and the term "MP" always refers to a member of the Commons. "Westminster" refers to Whitehall and Parliament combined.

2. E. C. S. Wade and G. G. Phillips, *Constitutional and Administrative Law* (London: Longman, 1970), p. 171.

3. For the best informed account, see Dermot Morrah, Arundel Herald Extraordinary, *The Work of the Queen* (London: William Kimber, 1958).

4. For problems confronting a monarch in the event of the House of Commons lacking a majority party, see David Butler, *Governing Without a Majority* (London: Macmillan, 2nd ed., 1986).

5. *Gallup Political Index* No. 190 (May 1976), p. 12.

6. See Richard Rose and Dennis Kavanagh, "The Monarchy in Contemporary Political Culture," *Comparative Politics*, 8:4 (1976) p. 560ff.

7. Anthony Sampson, *The Changing Anatomy of Britain* (London: Coronet, 1983), p. 14.

8. Winston S. Churchill, *Their Finest Hour* (London: Cassell, 1949), p. 14.

9. See Richard Rose, "British Government: The Job at the Top," in Rose and Suleiman, *Presidents and Prime Ministers* (Washington, D.C.: American Enterprise Institute, 1980), pp. 1–49. For a comparison with the Presidency, see Richard Rose, *The Post-Modern President: The World Closes in on the White House Meets the World* (Chatham, N.J.: Chatham House, 1988) Chapters 1 & 3.

10. See David Butler and Garth Butler, *British Political Facts, 1900–1985* (London: Macmillan, 6th ed., 1988), p. 82.

11. See Rose, "British Government: The Job at the Top," pp. 12ff; G. W. Jones, "The Prime Minister and Parliament," *British Politics Group Newsletter* No. 47 (Winter 1987) pp. 17–22.

12. Cf. Rose, "British Government: The Job at the Top," pp. 7–11. For long-term data, see David Butler and Gareth Butler, *British Political Facts* (London: Macmillan, 6th ed., 1986), pp. 254–264.

13. Quoted in Francis Williams, *A Prime Minister Remembers* (London: Heinemann, 1961), p. 81.

14. For recent accounts of how Downing Street looks from the inside, see Harold Wilson, *The Governance of Britain* (London: Weidenfeld and Nicolson, 1976); cf. Lord Donoughue, *Prime Minister* (London: Jonathan Cape, 1987).

15. Nicholas Wapshott and George Brock, *Thatcher* (London: Futura, 1983), p. 226.

16. See Richard Rose, *The Post-Modern President* (Chatham, N.J.: Chatham House, 1988), especially Chapter 4.

17. For a detailed statement of ideas set out here, with full citations, see Richard Rose, *Ministers and Ministries: A Functional Analysis* (Oxford: Clarendon Press, 1987).

18. See Bruce Headey, *British Cabinet Ministers: The Roles of Politicians in Executive Office* (London: Allen and Unwin, 1974). For junior ministers, see Kevin Theakston, *Junior Ministers in British Government* (Oxford: Blackwell, 1987).

19. Cf. Colin Turpin, "Ministerial Responsibility: Myth or Reality?" in J. Jowell and D. Oliver, eds., *The Changing Constitution* (Oxford: Clarendon Press, 1985), pp. 48–76.

20. C. Pollitt, *Manipulating the Machine: Changing the Pattern of Ministerial Departments, 1960–83* (London: Allen and Unwin, 1984). Cf. C. Hood and A. Dunsire, *Bureaumetrics* (Farnborough U.K.: Gower, 1981).

21. For an insider's view, see Roy Jenkins, "The Reality of Political Power," *Sunday Times* (London), 17 January 1972. More generally, see Hugo Young and Anne Sloman, *But Chancellor: An inquiry into the Treasury* (London: BBC Publications, 1984); and *The Home Office* (London: Royal Institute of Public Administration, 1982).

22. Cf. W. J. M. Mackenzie, "The Civil Service, the State and the Establishment," in Bernard Crick, ed., *Essays on Reform* (London: Oxford University Press, 1967).

23. See David Howells, "Marks and Spencer and the Civil Service: A Comparison of Culture and Methods," *Public Administration* 59 (1981), pp. 337–352.

24. For a fuller discussion of this group, see Richard Rose, "The Political Status of Higher Civil Servants in Britain," in Ezra Suleiman, ed., *Bureaucrats and Policy Making* (New York: Holmes and Meier, 1984), pp. 136–173. See also *Civil Service Statistics* (London: HM Treasury, annual).

25. Quoted in *Careers in the Civil Service—An Alternative View* (London: First Division Association, 1987), p. 12, a publication by the union of higher civil servants.

26. Bruce W. Headey, *British Cabinet Ministers*, p. 153.

27. See Joel D. Aberbach, Robert D. Putnam, and Bert A. Rockman, *Bureaucrats and Politicians in Western Democracies* (Cambridge, Mass: Harvard University Press, 1981); and Hugo Young and Anne Sloman, *No, Minister* (London: BBC, 1982).

28. Cf. Sir William Armstrong, *The Role and Character of the Civil Service* (London: Oxford University Press, 1970) and Roy Jenkins, "The Reality of Political Power."

29. Sir William Armstrong, *The Role and Character of the Civil Service* (1970) pp. 14–15.

30. See Richard Rose, *A House Divided: Political Administration in Britain Today* (Glasgow: U. of Strathclyde Studies in Public Policy No. 158, 1986).

31. See the Fulton Committee, *The Civil Service*, vol. 1 (London: HMSO, Cmnd. 3638, 1968); the *Report of the House of Commons Committee* (London: HC 535-I, HMSO, 1976–77); and *Efficiency and Effectiveness in the Civil Service* (London: HC 236, 2 volumes, 1982; *Civil Servants and Ministers: Duties and Responsibilities* (London: HC 92, 2 volumes, 1986).

32. Cf. Sir John Hoskyns, "Whitehall and Westminster: an Outsider's View," *Parliamentary Affairs* 36:2 (1983), p. 142; for Benn, see Young and Sloman, *No, Minister*, p. 20; and more generally, Anthony Benn, "The Case for a Constitutional Premiership," *Parliamentary Affairs* 33:1 (1980).

33. See Rudolf Klein and Janet Lewis, "Advice and Dissent in British Government: the Case of the Special Advisers," *Policy and Politics*, 5:1 (1977). Cf. Rob Shepherd, "Ministers and Special Advisers," *Public Money* 3: 3 (1983), pp. 33–35.

34. Samuel Brittan, "The Irregulars," in Richard Rose, ed., *Policy-Making in Britain* (London: Macmillan, 1969).

35. Quoted in "Hopes Dashed of Big Savings in Whitehall," *Daily Telegraph*, 5 April 1986. Cf. G. K. Fry, *The Changing Civil Service* (London: Allen and Unwin, 1984); Les Metcalfe, and Sue Richards, *Improving Public Management* (London: Sage Publications, 1987).

36. Kate Jenkins, Karen Caines, and Andrew Jackson, *Improving Management in Government: The Next Steps* (London: HMSO, 1988), p. 1.

37. "Whitehall drive 'knocks morale of civil service,'" *Daily Telegraph*, 5 December 1987.

38. Quoted in Richard Norton-Taylor, *The Ponting Affair* (London: Cecil Woolf, 1985), p. 10.

39. Richard E. Neustadt, "White House and Whitehall," in Richard Rose, ed., *Policy-Making in Britain*, p. 292.

40. See Aberbach, Putnam, and Rockman, *Bureaucrats and Politicians in Western Democracies*, p. 231.

41. Cf. Hugh Heclo, *A Government of Strangers* (Washington, D.C.: Brookings Institution, 1977); and Hugh Heclo and Aaron Wildavsky, *The Private Government of Public Money* (London: Macmillan, 2nd ed., 1981).

42. Richard Rose, "Steering the Ship of State: One Tiller but Two Pairs of Hands," *British Journal of Political Science*, 17:4 (1987), pp. 409–433.

43. Quoted in Young and Sloman, *No, Minister*, p. 110.

44. Cf. Richard Rose, "Government against Sub-Government: A European Perspective on Washington," in Rose and Suleiman, eds., *Presidents and Prime Ministers*, pp. 284–347; and Colin Campbell, *Governments under Stress* (Toronto: U. of Toronto Press, 1983).

45. Bruce Headey, *British Cabinet Ministers*, Chapter 1.

46. See Peter Hennessy, *Cabinet* (Oxford: Basil Blackwell, 1986); Brian Hogwood and T. T. Mackie, "The United Kingdom: Decision Sifting in a Secret Garden," in Mackie and Hogwood, eds., *Unlocking the Cabinet* (London: Sage Publications, 1985), pp. 36–60.

47. Robin Oakley, "Why She Trusts Nobody," *The Times* (London), March 16, 1988.

48. "Mandarin Power," *The Sunday Times* (London), 10 June 1973.

49. L. S. Amery, *Thoughts on the Constitution*, 87.

50. Colin Seymour-Ure, "The 'Disintegration' of the Cabinet," p. 196.

51. "Thinking about the Think Tank," *The Listener,* 28 December 1972.

52. See e.g. Anthony Benn, "The Case for a Constitutional Premiership," *Parliamentary Affairs* 33:1 (1980); and for a catalogue of Conservative complaints, Michael Doherty, "Prime Ministerial Power and Ministerial Responsibility," *Parliamentary Affairs* 41:1 (1988).

53. See R. H. S. Crossman, "Introduction" to an edition of Bagehot's *The English Constitution* (London: Fontana, 1963), pp. 51ff.

54. John P. Mackintosh, *The British Cabinet,* 2nd ed., p. 529.

55. The same confusion is evident in R. T. McKenzie's discussion of the power *(sic)* of party leadership in *British Political Parties* (London: Heinemann, 2nd ed., 1963).

56. Quoted in Peter Jenkins, *The Battle of Downing Street,* p. 163.

57. *The British Cabinet,* 2nd ed., p. 531.

58. Quoted in H. J. Hanham, ed., *The Nineteenth-Century Constitution* (Cambridge: Cambridge University Press, 1969), p. 69.

59. Quoted in Richard Rose, "British Government: The Job at the Top," p. 43.

CHAPTER IV

The Role of Parliament

The main function of the House of Commons is one which we know quite well, though our common constitutional speech does not recognize it. The House of Commons is an electoral chamber.

DEMOCRATIC GOVERNMENT requires not only effectiveness but also responsiveness: the authority of the Crown must be balanced by representative institutions. In theory, parliamentary government guarantees the responsiveness of Whitehall, for the Prime Minister and Cabinet ministers are individually and collectively accountable to Parliament. When the government of Britain really was His Majesty's Government, that is, when ministers served at the pleasure of the monarch of the day and took their directions from the King, then Parliament could be an independent check upon government. But responsiveness has been greatly weakened by the rise of party government.

While the House of Commons is popularly elected, MPs respond first and foremost to the pressures of party. Every MP knows that once every few years he or she must subject to a campaign for reelection. But the rise of party has meant that an MP is first of all accountable to the parliamentary party. Voters cast their ballots in 650 different constituencies of the House of Commons, but they vote primarily along the lines of nationwide political divisions. The personality or activities of an MP is rarely decisive. An individual MP is expected to vote as instructed by the party whips in the House of Commons, reflecting the policy views of the party leaders there. MPs do not need to poll their constituents to find out how to vote, as Congressmen may do; they respond to the party whip. The pressure to follow the party line is strongest when a party is in government, for a revolt by back-bench MPs, responding to their consciences or their constituents, would produce the worst outcome politically: the governing party would lose office because of defections by its own back-bench supporters in the Commons (cf. chapters X and XI).

The British form of parliamentary government is democratic, inasmuch as at each election voters are able to choose, in Schumpeter's phrase, between "teams of competing elites,"[1] who offer a choice between a Conservative and a Labour Prime Minister and Cabinet or in the case of the Social and Liberal Democrats, a coalition government. The House of Commons is an electoral chamber, choosing the cabinet that controls Downing Street and Whitehall. The elite in the party winning the election then become Prime Minister and Cabinet ministers; almost any proposal that is put forward with their collective authority will be endorsed by a Commons majority, for they are the leaders of the majority party there.

In its dignified aspect, Parliament remains very impressive. The Palace of Westminster, the home of the House of Commons and House of Lords, is a worldwide symbol of representative government. Parts of the building date to the eleventh century; the bulk is of Victorian Gothic design, as massive as it is nonutilitarian. Officers of the House emphasize its dignity by wearing elaborate formal dress, including wigs. The late Aneurin Bevan described his first impression of Parliament as a church dedicated to "the most conservative of all religions—ancestor worship."[2]

Comparing Parliament with the United States Congress makes clear the limited political influence of the former. Whereas Westminster is a system in which the responsive element of government is reduced for the sake of effective authority, Congress maximizes responsiveness while reducing the effectiveness of government, because Congress is elected independently of the President. When Congress is in Democratic hands and the Republicans control the White House, party discipline will produce stalemate. The President can make legislative proposals to Congress, but unlike a British Cabinet minister, cannot be sure whether Congress will approve or reject his proposals. The President's budget is a proposal that Congress disposes of as it sees fit, whereas the Chancellor of the Exchequer's budget speech makes proposals that take effect as he talks. Congress can reject the President's nominees for Cabinet and judicial posts, whereas at Westminster, MPs queue for the prospect of gaining office in Cabinet.

Because the House of Commons endorses but does not make laws, the first section of this chapter examines its nonlegislative as well as legislative functions and the roles it offers individual MPs with careers to make. That active anachronism, the House of Lords, is the subject of the second part of this chapter. The conclusion examines the iron cage of party discipline, which assures that the Prime Minister and Cabinet enjoy the authority of the Crown in Parliament.

A HOUSE BUT NOT A LEGISLATURE

The House of Commons is a talking shop that conducts political discussions in varied ways. A typical day begins with a number of MPs at morning committee meetings, some attending to correspondence or gossip in the Palace of Westminster, and a few pursuing part-time jobs elsewhere.[3] At 2:30 P.M. the House assembles for prayers, followed by an hour of parliamentary questioning of ministers. At 3:30 P.M. ministers, Opposition leaders or back-benchers may briefly raise exceptional or urgent items, such as an international crisis or the threat of a civil service strike. By 3:45 P.M. the House is usually dealing with pending legislation or debating issues, with ministers and front-bench Opposition spokesmen speaking first. By the time the ordinary back-bench MP rises to speak, most members will have left the House for meetings in the Palace of Westminster with other MPs or visitors. The chamber can fill up again for major speeches and a vote at the end of the major debate at 10:00 P.M. The final half hour of each day is reserved for an adjournment debate, in which an individual back-bencher raises an issue of his or her choice and receives a reply from a junior minister. Because the Commons meets for eight hours a day for almost three-quarters of the year, MPs have little time to meet people who do not come to the Palace of Westminster, or to travel to places other than their constituency.

Collectively, the House of Commons has four major institutional functions. Its approval is necessary for legislation; the government must listen to the views expressed by MPs in debates; the government must submit to some scrutiny by committees; and the behavior of individual ministers and MPs is at all times being assessed by parliamentary colleagues.

Legislation in Parliament. The general principles of a bill must be approved by Cabinet; detailed responsibility rests with the minister and ministry sponsoring the bill in Parliament. The actual drafting of legislation is a specialist task assigned to lawyers trained in writing legislation. The questions raised by parliamentary draftsmen often require ministers and civil servants to pause to think about details and difficulties that have been neglected when announcing decisions of principle about a policy.[4] To anticipate criticisms that MPs could make in debate, details of legislation are discussed at length with interest groups before a bill is introduced in the Commons. While the median bill is enacted within eight weeks of being introduced, a year or more of preparatory work is usually required in Whitehall before it is introduced in Parliament. Laws are described as Acts of Parliament, but it would be more accurate if they were stamped: Made in Whitehall.[5]

A bill is introduced without debate for its first reading to the House of Commons. In the second reading general principles of the bill are debated. Major bills are usually referred to the Committee of the Whole House (MPs meeting with special rules of procedure); lesser legislation is considered by standing committees containing a fraction of the House. Party discipline is effective in these committees. A report stage follows, giving all MPs a chance to discuss the bill once again. After a third reading, a bill proceeds to the House of Lords. A finance bill is exceptional; it automatically becomes law within a month after approval by the Commons. When a bill is passed by the Lords in the same form as in the Commons, it receives a formal Royal Assent and thus becomes the law of the land.

Ironically, the one role that an MP will rarely undertake is that of legislator. Each year the government sets aside a small amount of time for MPs whose names are drawn by lot to introduce private members' bills. Because government support is not ensured, fewer than a dozen such bills pass in a session. A number are noncontroversial measures covering such things as litter in the street. A few are issues so controversial that no party will officially take responsibility. Private members' bills secured reform of the laws on abortion and on homosexuality. However, a controversial private member's bill may fail because without party whips to enforce disciplined voting, a small group of MPs opposed to a measure can obstruct its passage.

In a year's parliamentary business the government can secure passage of 100 percent of the bills that it introduces; it has done so eight times since 1945. Since 1945 a government has secured enactment of nearly 97 percent of the bills that it introduces (Table IV.1). Party loyalty explains why the government consistently wins votes in the House of Commons. The government represents the party with a

TABLE IV.1 *Proportion of Government Bills Approved by Parliament*

Parliament (Government)	Bills introduced	Approved	Percent approved
1945–50 Labour	310	307	99.0
1950–51 Labour	99	97	98.0
1951–54 [a]Conservative	167	158	94.6
1955–59 Conservative	229	223	97.4
1959–64 Conservative	251	244	97.2
1964–65 [a]Labour	66	65	98.5
1966–69 [a]Labour	215	210	97.7
1970–73 [a]Conservative	192	189	98.4
1974–79 [a]Labour	260	236	90.8
1979–83 [a]Conservative	177	175	98.9
1983–87 Conservative	201	198	98.5
Total	2,167	2,102	97.0

Note [a]Omits final session of Parliament, interrupted by government calling a general election, voiding all pending bills.

Sources 1945–69: Calculated from Valentine Herman, "What Governments Say and What Governments Do: An Analysis of Post-War Queen's Speeches," *Parliamentary Affairs*, 28:1 (1974), Table 1; and Public Information Office, House of Commons.

majority of the 650 MPs in the Commons, and MPs in the majority party are expected to support Cabinet measures (and vote against motions by the Opposition) in order to keep their party in control of government. A Labour government can thus get its proposals endorsed by a Labour majority in the Commons, and a Conservative government can secure legislation from a Commons with a Conservative majority.

The principal division in British government does not run between Parliament and Whitehall; it is within the House of Commons, separating the majority party in control of both the Commons and Cabinet from the Opposition. A major vote in the House of Commons is treated as a vote of confidence in the government. The MPs of the governing party recognize that only by voting as a disciplined team can their party continue to control government. Rarely is an issue regarded as so important that an MP would want to risk the survival of his party in office by voting against it; defying the whip (that is, the instruction about how to vote) is done only when it will *not* defeat the leadership of the governing party. Defying the whip also usually reduces an MP's chances for promotion to ministerial ranks.

Although party discipline is criticized by independent commentators, most MPs consider it necessary and desirable.

An MP who makes a habit of rebellion to the party's collective damage risks expulsion and almost certain electoral defeat in his or her constituency at the next general election, since an MP is elected because he or she is a party standard-bearer. Prime Minister Harold Wilson threatened Labour MPs thus:

> All I say is "watch it." Every dog is allowed one bite, but a different view is taken of a dog that goes on biting all the time. If there are doubts that the dog is biting not because of the dictates of conscience but because he is considered vicious, then things happen to that dog. He may not get his licence renewed when it falls due.[6]

The Opposition in the House of Commons cannot expect to alter major government decisions; by definition it lacks the votes to win divisions in the House of Commons. The Opposition accepts defeat for each of its proposals for up to five years, the maximum statutory life of a Parliament, because it hopes for victory in the next election. As long as the major parties alternate in winning control of a parliamentary majority, each can expect to enjoy all the powers of British government for part of the time.[7]

During the year the House of Commons spends more time talking about nonlegislative matters than in dealing with bills. The majority of time is devoted to discussing actions that government has the power to take because of long-standing Acts of Parliament, or else debating actions that Cabinet ministers are urged to take. In a typical year 28 percent of Commons's time is devoted to discussing government bills, 3 percent to the budget and other financial measures, 6 percent to statutory instruments promulgated under authority of Acts of Parliament, and 4 percent to private members' bills.

Nonlegislative Functions. The House of Commons is preeminently an assembly for the expression of opinion by 650 politicians of diverse backgrounds and outlooks. Even though MPs may be compelled by the party whip to vote with the party leadership, up to the moment the vote is taken, they can say what they like. Debates on the floor of the House allow MPs to ventilate opinions about how government does (and ought to) manage the economy; conduct foreign policy; improve health, education, and social welfare, and everything else for which ministers in Whitehall are responsible. The views of back-benchers give ministers an idea of support for policies before the Cabinet decides an issue. The average speech by an MP is ignored; only one-sixth of back-bench MPs frequently listen to their colleagues' speeches.[9]

Scrutinizing the activities of government is a second major nonlegislative function of Parliament. Four days a week Cabinet ministers must answer dozens of questions put down on the House of Commons order paper by inquisitive MPs. The most difficult questions are those that appear innocuous—will the Prime Minister consider visiting such and such a place?—because this gives the questioner an opportunity to ask an embarrassing supplementary question: If the Prime Minister makes a visit, will she or he not be shocked by the disgraceful conditions there? An alert minister will be prepared with a reply by civil servants skilled in spotting trick supplementary questions. A great deal of parliamentary question time is now devoted to publicity seeking repartee. Even if it does not alter greatly the course of policy, question time keeps ministers on their toes and tests the skill of Opposition MPs in embarrassing government.

Detailed examination of policies usually takes place in committees.[10] Legislation that is not important enough to merit the attention of the whole House is reviewed by standing committees: ad hoc committees denominated A, B, C, and so on (to avoid being considered subject-matter committees); the Scottish Grand Committee, the Welsh Grand Committee, and the Northern Ireland Committee. The Public Accounts Committee, always chaired by a leading opposition MP, reviews government expenditure after the event, publicizing instances of waste and financial mismanagement. The Statutory Instruments Committee scrutinizes rulings laid down by the executive under powers delegated by Act of Parliament. The Committee on European Legislation acts as a political filter for hundreds of European Community rules issued each year. By calling the attention of the Commons to a limited number of controversial Community proposals, it makes the minister responsible for Britain's position in the Community respond to domestic views of issues determined by multinational bargaining in the Community. Because party lines normally prevail in committee voting, these bodies lack the power of American Congressional committees to rewrite or block government legislation.

Fourteen select committees dealing with subjects ranging from agriculture to Welsh affairs have monitored activities of Whitehall departments since establishment after the 1979 general election. Optimistic reformers hoped that the select committees would enable back-benchers to influence government policy. Pessimists doubted that committees could make a consistent impact upon ministers secure in Cabinet and in the governing party. Select committees have held hundreds of meetings each year, interviewing ministers, civil servants, and outside experts; filling thousands of pages with their reports; and offering an opportunity to back-bench MPs to pursue their interests—and pursue ministers and ministries. Committees have the power of publicity. When partisan controversies arise, a committee is likely to split along party lines and become just another forum for discussing differences of opinion that Whitehall has already discounted. However, the impact of the committees has been slight because it is the Cabinet that decides whether or not government makes any response to committee recommendations.[11]

Since the careers of Cabinet ministers are affected by how they respond to comments from the House of Commons, ministers are kept from becoming introverted, thinking only of their department or of Whitehall. They must also be concerned with presenting to the House of Commons a case for what they are doing. Concentrating upon the presentational aspects of policies has disadvantages too. A department or a minister may become more interested in what is said about its activities in the Commons than about what gets done in the country. A former head of the civil service, Sir William Armstrong relates:

> I happened to be visiting the Welsh Office in Cardiff on the day when there had been an oil slick in the Bristol Channel. So naturally there was a great deal of activity going on, and when I arrived at the office the man in charge there was beginning to get people in to start assessing the situation.
>
> The first question dealt with was: What was to be said in the House? It was not: How much mess was there on the beaches and what damage had been done, and how could progress be made in clearing it up? That came next.[12]

A third nonlegislative function of the Commons is weighing the political reputations of ministers and would-be ministers. Informally and incessantly MPs weigh men and women as well as measures. A minister may win a formal vote of confidence but lose standing with MPs if his arguments are demolished in debate or if he shows little understanding of the case that his civil servants have briefed him to argue. The clublike atmosphere of the Commons permits MPs to judge the personal character of their colleagues in bars and tea rooms as well as in the Commons chamber. In the course of years it separates those who merit personal confidence from those who are unreliable. The judgments of MPs about the character of leading politicians are carefully noted by the Prime Minister and by journalists who write reputations up and down according to changes in the assessments that the Commons makes of each member.

The Role of Individual MPs. A newly elected MP, contemplating his or her role as one individual among 650 MPs, immediately notices the advantages that election brings. As an MP a person will have the opportunity to meet interesting and important people in many walks of life. Remarks that went unnoticed when the MP was a private citizen may now be quoted by the media. An MP can direct inquiries to any branch of British government and expect prompt and very detailed answers. Entering Parliament opens opportunities for free-lance journalism or paid part-time consultancy work. The Palace of Westminster provides the facilities of a good London club; it also has some of the cloistered aspects of a boarding school. The disadvantages of membership slowly dawn upon members—irregular hours, frequent travel, separation from family, a salary ceiling and career uncertainties; few MPs consider the disadvantages so great that they retire from the House voluntarily.[13]

Whereas an individual MP's vote is normally determined by party discipline, behaviour outside the division lobbies is completely open. The variety of roles available to a newly elected MP can be grouped under two broad headings: inner-circle roles oriented toward government and outer-circle roles in which individuals enjoy self-expression without influence in Whitehall.[14]

Among *inner-circle roles* the most important is that of a ministerialist. At any given time about one-sixth of the Commons holds ministerial appointments, and fifty or more Opposition MPs are shadow ministers, expecting office if there is a change of government. A hundred or two hundred more aspire to ministerial positions. To succeed as a ministerialist, an MP must demonstrate that he or she is good at understanding the problems and procedures of Whitehall as well as the tactics of the House of Commons.

Advocating causes and interests is a second role for inner-circle MPs, who can use their privileged position in Parliament to attract the attention of Whitehall and the media to policies that the MP wants to advance. The particular cause of an MP may be partisan (for example, the privatization of industry or protecting trade union interests) or non-partisan (helping the elderly) or a constituency interest (anything from deep sea fishing to inner-city housing). To advocate a cause or interest, an MP will need to do more than make speeches: he or she will also need to work with other MPs and extraparliamentary groups in efforts to influence Whitehall.

Managing party and parliamentary business is a third important role. MPs in the whips' offices have the task of maintaining party discipline in voting and informing party leaders about the objections of back-benchers to actions by the leadership. Organization breeds counterorganization: the Opposition is organized to use parliamentary procedures to exploit government weaknesses. Both government and Opposition have formally or informally organized groups promoting left- or right-wing positions strongly held by some but not all within a party. A small number of MPs contribute to the Commons in nonparty ways, helping to conduct its business by chairing debates or advising about the management of Parliament and its business.

The least conspicuous but most important role of the MP is that of party loyalist. Nearly all MPs are party loyalists when the whips are on. The typical loyalist supports the party position without argument, usually saying little in the Commons and attracting no attention to himself or herself. Loyalists see their role as maintaining party unity. As a former Conservative Prime Minister noted long ago, "An MP may further party ends by his eloquence; he may do so even more effectively perhaps by his silences."[15]

An MP who turns his or her back on government can face in many different directions. Among *outer-circle roles* the most common is that of expressive enthusiast. An enthusiast expresses feelings about an issue regardless of the reaction of Whitehall, whereas an advocate of a cause acts in ways intended to influence Whitehall. An enthusiast believes it important to attract publicity, whereas an advocate would rather listen to a minister announce a change in policy, knowing that it was his or her efforts that helped produce the change. Publicity-seeking roles are always on offer in the Commons; a pointed question to the Prime Minister may enable an MP to grab a headline or be interviewed on television. Questions about topics of popular interest without substantive importance to government, such as the Royal Family or a prison escape, can gain an MP publicity—but it does not gain influence in Whitehall.

The role of constituency representative is increasingly significant to individual MPs, but it is an outer-circle role of no consequence to government. MPs can devote time to looking after the concerns of individual constituents, using their knowledge of bureaucratic procedure to help a disabled person secure a pension or a small business claim a government grant. A good reputation in the constituency can flatter an MP who is a small fish in the big pond of Westminster. It may be prudent, for while few votes are thereby won, there may come a day when a small number of votes makes the difference between winning and losing reelection.[16] An MP cannot gain government favors for a constituency by trading his or her vote in exchange for local benefits; the whip, not constituency interests, determines an MP's vote.

A half-century ago many MPs were extraparliamentary careerists; an elder son of a peer could serve as an MP from a sense of *noblesse oblige,* spending most of his time fox hunting on the landed family's estates. A lawyer could use a seat in the Commons as a means of advancing a career at the bar or of becoming a judge. Today the demands upon an MP's time are such that it is difficult to combine two careers. For example, a teacher must resign his or her job in order to attend the House of Commons.

An individual MP can undertake several of the multiplicity of roles available, for example, being both a party loyalist and a good constituency representative, or an aspiring ministerialist and an advocate of a cause. The work of the Commons requires that collectively MPs are distributed among all the varied roles. A Commons that had nothing but ministerialists would be as limited as a Commons in which everyone was only a publicity seeker. The size and variety of the Commons provides 650 MPs with many opportunities to advance their personal career and to advance political objectives.

THE HOUSE OF LORDS

Among the upper chambers of parliaments in democratic nations, the House of Lords is unique because two-thirds of its 1,200 members belong because of inheriting a peerage. Since 1958, men and women deemed worthy can also be appointed by the Prime Minister of the day to nonhereditary peerages; this gives a seat in the House of Lords for life. Life peers can speak from extraparliamentary experience in varied walks of life: industry, finance, trade unions, education, and the mass media. The Lords also includes in its membership twenty-six bishops of the Church of England, a few people who have had hereditary titles conferred on themselves for public services, and nineteen very senior judges, who sit as law lords.[17] Members of the Royal Family do not sit in the Lords, although they hold titles.

The actual work of the House of Lords is done by a small fraction of its nominal membership; only one in six attends half its meetings in a year, and a third of hereditary peers do not turn up even once a year. Nearly half the peers in regular attendance are life peers. Many active peers are retired members of the House of Commons who find the three-afternoons-a-week pace of the Lords suited to their advancing years.

The Lords have always had a Conservative majority. Before passage of the Life Peerages Act, Conservatives outnumbered Labour peers by about eight to one; since then the Conservative advantage over Labour has dropped to four to one. Liberals and Social Democrats are more numerous in the Lords than in the Commons. As peers are not elected, there is no need for a member of the Lords to belong to a party at all, and hundreds declare no party affiliation. Because peers are not elected, party discipline cannot be as effective as in the Commons. In addition to voting against Labour government measures, Conservative peers are more likely to create difficulties for Conservative government legislation than are back-bench Conservatives in the Commons.[18]

Like the House of Commons, the Lords tests the fitness of its members for ministerial office. Because of the peers' high average age, few expect office. Only in the Conservative ranks are there younger peers seeking to establish themselves politically. Since 1963 the most politically ambitious can disclaim a hereditary peerage and stand for the House of Commons. Because convention requires that every minister be in Parliament, a seat in the Lords can be given to a minister brought in from outside Westminster to contribute expertise to government. The minister will then be able to answer to Parliament by speaking in the House of Lords. The absence of responsibility for a constituency gives a peer an advantage in a post requiring much traveling, such as the Foreign Office, or in which freedom from constituency pressures can be useful, such as race relations.

The Lords's power to reject bills passed by the House of Commons was formidable until the Parliament Act of 1911 abolished its right of vetoing bills; it was left with the power to delay the enactment of legislation and to propose amendments. In the case of disagreement between the two houses, the Commons version of a bill becomes law if it is approved by the Commons in each of two successive annual sessions. Occasionally the Lords have used their powers to delay passage of a major Labour government bill, to oppose a nonparty measure such as abolition of capital punishment, or to harass a Conservative government with a large majority in the Commons. The use of delaying powers is exceptional; the threat of their use occasionally worries a government. The Lords normally avoid rejecting measures from the Commons. The Lords cannot claim to represent the nation because they are neither popularly elected nor are they a cross section of the population.

Because the Lords can initiate or amend legislation, the government often introduces legislation there that deals with technical matters or with nonparty matters such as animal welfare. The government can use the Lords as a revising chamber to incorporate amendments suggested in debate in the Commons. Members of the upper house can also introduce private peers' bills, but these are rarely of political consequence.

Like the Commons, the Lords can discuss public issues without reference to legislation. The government or opposition may initiate a debate on foreign affairs, or individual back-benchers may raise such topics as pornography or the future of hill farming. Peers may scrutinize administration by questioning ministers. Media coverage is slight. A peer who wishes to influence public opinion is more likely to get publicity by making his remarks on a public platform outside the Palace of Westminster than by stating views in the House of Lords itself.

THE IRON CAGE OF PARTY DISCIPLINE

While Parliament is the chief responsive institution of the Crown in Parliament, it is minimally effective. Individual MPs cannot vote in response to their own judgment or pressures from their constituents. An MP soon learns that his or her personal views are subject to the iron cage of party discipline.[19] Because of the iron cage of party discipline, the government does not need to respond to MPs; it is confident of the outcome of votes in the Commons. In the words of a Labour Cabinet minister: "It's carrying democracy too far if you don't know the result of the vote before the meeting." Most MPs accept that placing the collective view of the party above their own judgment is justifiable. In the words of a veteran Labour MP: "When I was young, I always talked a lot about my conscience. When I got older, I learned it was just my blooming conceit."[20]

More Bark Than Bite.[21] The effectiveness of government in securing its legislation is virtually one hundred percent (cf. Table IV.1). It is far higher than what is normal in other democratic countries and qualitatively much greater than what a President achieves in Congress. An individual MP can vote against the party whip, but one bite in the leg does not make a dog dangerous. The average Conservative MP has voted against a Conservative government whip less than once a year, and a Labour MP a little more than once a year. With more than 1,000 divisions in the Commons each year, MPs are thus likely to vote the party whip at least 99.9 percent of the time.

Party discipline is actually stronger today than a century ago. In the overwhelming majority of divisions in the House of Commons, there is one hundred percent cohesion, that is, *all* Conservative MPs vote together, and all Labour MPs vote together. (When MPs do vote against the party whip, they usually do so by Conservatives deviating further to the right and Labour to the left than the party leadership.) This dooms their protest to failure, for right-wing Conservatives cannot make an alliance with Labour MPs, and left-wing Labour MPs cannot make an alliance with Conservatives. The government loses a few votes but still carries its legislation. Government bills are normally approved without any Opposition amendments. In a three-year period the government moved 1,772 amendments to its legislation, and all but two were approved by Parliament. MPs moved 4,198 amendments without government support; of these, only 210 were accepted by the government and approved by Parliament.

The predominance of the government of the day does not make it all-powerful. The procedures of the House of Commons limit the amount of legislation that a government can enact in a year. Only a fraction of the proposals put to the Cabinet annually by ministers succeed in gaining a place in the year's crowded parliamentary timetable. Introducing a major bill is a lengthy and tiring process that can take up to three years from the time a Cabinet decides in principle to promote legislation to a bill receiving the Royal Assent. Members of Parliament can influence government to act by voicing demands that it "do something" about an issue of the moment. If the clamor is widespread and persistent, the government may respond. But it is up to the government to decide whether or not to act, and what it will do.

Within the governing party there are opportunities for back-bench MPs to influence government individually and collectively. The whips' office is expected to listen to complaints from back-benchers and convey their concerns to ministers. In the corridors and clubrooms as well as in the committee rooms of the Commons, back-benchers can tell ministers what they think is wrong with the party's policies. However, individual rebels have little hope of getting the government to respond to their protests. The Opposition is doomed to failure by being in the minority. MPs in the governing party accept the party whip from conviction, and when this is lacking, they usually go along because of party loyalty and because effectiveness is valued more than responsiveness.

Dissatisfaction Without Reform. The limited influence of both Houses of Parliament perennially stimulates demands for reform by back-bench MPs, active peers, and political commentators.[22] Critics of the House of Commons say it does a poor job of reviewing legislation, scrutinizing administration, representing and educating public opinion, and preparing MPs for the job of a minister. Some critics think that the trend to full-time MPs is a bad thing because it isolates MPs from everyday life, whereas others believe it represents a desirable shift from amateurism to professionalism. The remedies prescribed are varied. Since 1964 many minor reforms have been introduced into the work of the Commons, affecting its procedures and improving the pay and facilities of MPs. However, an academic survey of these reforms concludes with "pronounced pessimism" that the changes have been "puny . . . in the extent to which they have failed to grip the essential problem": they need to diminish the power of the government if Parliament is to become more influential upon government.[23]

One reason why reform proposals languish is that critics disagree about the part that the Commons ought to play in government. Some reformers believe that it should have power to prevent Whitehall from taking actions of which many MPs disapprove, whereas others simply wish more opportunities to scrutinize and criticize what government does. The former view implies a transfer of power from Whitehall to the House of Commons; the latter, a strengthening of the Commons's capacity for oversight without giving it teeth with which to bite.

The great obstacle to reform is also the great grievance of critics: powers of decision effectively rest with the leaders of the governing party, the Prime Minister and Cabinet. Whatever MPs say from the back benches or in opposition, once in Cabinet they argue that the present powers of Parliament are all that can be granted it. Back-bench MPs of both parties are sceptical of Cabinet ministers' willingness to give them greater influence; five-sixths think that ministers do not want MPs to be well informed about the work of Whitehall.[24] The result is that Whitehall rather than Parliament is the prime lawmaking institution.

NOTES

1. See Joseph A. Schumpeter, *Capitalism, Socialism and Democracy* (London: Allen and Unwin, 4th ed., 1952), Chapters 11-13; see also Robert T. McKenzie, *British Political Parties* (London: Heinemann, 2nd ed., 1963), Chapter 11.

2. Aneurin Bevan, *In Place of Fear* (London: Heinemann, 1952), p. 6.

3. For a detailed exposition of Commons' procedures and work, see Paul Silk, *How Parliament Works* (London: Longman, 1987). For views of MPs about *whether* they should attend debates on the floor of the House of Commons, see the *Hansard* report of the House of Commons debate of 7 March 1988.

4. See G. C. Thornton, *Legislative Drafting* (London: Butterworths, 2nd ed., 1979).

5. For a detailed political analysis, see David R. Miers and Alan C. Page, *Legislation* (London: Sweet and Maxwell, 1982).

6. Quoted in *The Times* (London), 5 March 1967.

7. See R. M. Punnett, *Front-Bench Opposition* (London: Heinemann, 1973). For the consequences of a Parliament in which no party has a majority, see David Butler, *Governing without a Majority* (London: Macmillan, 2nd ed., 1986).

8. *Sessional Information Digest 1985–86* (London: House of Commons, 1987) pp. 1-2. For additional statistics on legislation, see Denis Van Mechelen and Richard Rose, *Patterns of Parliamentary Legislation* (Farnborough, U.K.: Gower, 1986).

9. See Anthony Barker and Michael Rush, *The Member of Parliament and his Information* (London: Allen and Unwin, 1970).

10. For discussions of various committees, see S. A. Walkland and Michael Ryle, eds., *The Commons Today* (London: Fontana, 1981), and P. Norton, ed., *Parliament in the 1980s* (Oxford: Blackwell, 1985).

11. Cf. Gavin Drewry, ed. *The New Select Committees: A Study of the 1979 Reforms* (Oxford: Oxford University Press, 1985); Ian Marsh, *Policy Making in a Three Party System* (London: Methuen, 1986).

12. Quoted in *The State of the Nation* (London: Granada Television, 1973), p. 30.

13. For a full and varied analysis of the work of individual MPs, see Austin Mitchell, *Westminster Man* (London: Thames Methuen, 1982).

14. For a more detailed discussion of roles of MPs, see Richard Rose, "British MPs: More Bark than Bite?" in Ezra Suleiman, ed., *Parliaments and Parliamentarians in Democratic Politics* (New York: Holmes and Meier, 1986), pp. 8-40.

15. Earl Balfour, *Chapters of an Autobiography* (London: Cassell, 1930), p. 134.

16. Cf. Bruce Cain, John Ferejohn, and Morris Fiorina, *The Personal Vote* (Cambridge, Mass.: Harvard University Press, 1987).

17. For basic data on the Lords see David Butler and Gareth Butler, *British Political Facts, 1900–1985* (London: Macmillan, 1986), pp. 213-221.

18. See Donald R. Shell, "The House of Lords and the Thatcher Government," *Parliamentary Affairs* 38:1 (1985).

19. A term paraphrased from the writings of the German sociologist Max Weber.

20. Eric Varley, quoted in Alistair Michie and Simon Hoggart, *The Pact* (London: Quartet Books, 1978), p. 13. On an MP's conceit, see Earl Attlee, "The Attitudes of MPs and Active Peers," *Political Quarterly* (January 1959) p. 29.

21. For detailed analysis and evidence cited here, see Richard Rose, "British MPs: More Bark than Bite?" pp. 23ff.

22. On reform of the Lords and occasional Labour proposals to abolish the Lords, see e.g., Donald R. Shell, "The House of Lords", in David Judge, ed., *The Politics of Parliamentary Reform* (London: Heinemann, 1983), pp. 96–113.

23. S. A. Walkland, "Whither the Commons?" in Walkland and Ryle, eds., *The Commons Today*, pp. 280, 284. Philip Norton, *The Commons in Perspective* (Oxford: Martin Robertson, 1981), especially Chapters 9 and 10.

24. Barker and Rush, *The Member of Parliament and his Information*, p. 363.

CHAPTER V

Political Culture and Authority

It is the dull traditional habit of mankind that guides most men's actions and it is the steady frame in which each new artist must set the picture that he paints.

THE POLITICAL CULTURE limits the authority of governors as well as affecting the political behavior of citizens. The norms of the culture are more or less clear about the exercise of political authority: what governors are and are not expected to do. The rights and duties of citizens subject to the authority of government are also central to the culture. In a country with an unwritten Constitution, cultural norms are particularly important in setting out the rules of the game, that is, the way in which governors and governed should act. Some actions are out of bounds, for example the suspension of free elections. But because cultural norms are usually concerned with procedure, they do not determine the outcome of elections or dictate what the winning party must do.

Political authority is defined by two characteristics: popular compliance with basic political laws and popular support for the constitutional regime. If citizens support the regime and also comply with its basic political laws, then authority is fully legitimate; this has normally been the case in England. If people comply with basic political laws but refuse to support the regime, then it is coercive; that is the case today in such Eastern European countries as Poland. A system of government that loses both the support and compliance of many citizens, such as the Stormont Parliament in Northern Ireland until 1972, is headed towards collapse.[1] Behavior in compliance with political laws can be coerced by government, but support for the regime is a reflection of attitudes that government can influence but not coerce.

The idea of a political culture appears paradoxical, for a culture emphasizes what people have in common, whereas politics involves the clash of conflicting opinions. The paradox is more apparent than real, for acceptance of common institutions and procedures is necessary to reconcile political differences. The existence of a few common values, beliefs, and symbols does not mean that everyone is of the same political opinion. Only a totalitarian society would expect everyone to think alike about every major decision of government. In England the acceptance of a few common norms is consistent with the expression of different opinions about what government ought to do.

Collectively, the values, beliefs, and emotional symbols that make up the political culture constitute what Sidney Low described as 'a system of tacit understandings' that make government with an unwritten constitution "safe, convenient, effective, and in the main, satisfactory."[2] The understandings are tacit because they are taken for granted. Ordinary citizens do not speak the language of political theorists or political sociologists, or readily articulate thoughts about government. Therefore, in order to depict the political culture of England, this chapter draws upon a variety of sources: public opinion surveys and behavioral data for evidence of mass attitudes and statements by prominent politicians to understand the outlook of governors.

As Bagehot emphasizes, the political culture reflects "the dull traditional habit of mankind." While the cultural outlooks of Englishmen are not biologically inherited, they are transmitted from generation to generation through a process of political socialization. In this way people learn traditions that reflect events long before they were born (see Chapter VI). In the course of a lifetime every citizen learns new ideas from personal and national experience. The extent to which present experience challenges the past is brought out in this chapter by first of all examining different ideas about who should exercise political authority. Subsequent sections concern enforcing laws through cultural norms and institutions, cultural limits upon authority, and support for the constitutional regime.

WHOSE AUTHORITY?

In exercising authority, governors are expected to represent the country as a whole even though they are a very small fraction of the population. In England there are three different sets of cultural norms about representation.[3]

Trusteeship. Traditionally public officials saw themselves as trustees. However, authority was not held by a grant from the people; instead, ministers and civil servants were (and remain) servants of the Crown. According to this doctrine, MPs and the Cabinet are not expected to ask what people want but to use their own judgment about the best interests of society. A trustee's actions are justified by beneficial results. L.S. Amery, a former Conservative Cabinet minister, wrote after the Second World War that England was governed "for the people, with, but not by the people."[4]

Before the introduction of universal suffrage aristocratic trustees justified their position on the grounds that most of the population was unfit by birth, upbringing, and interest to participate in government. Writing in 1867, Walter Bagehot argued that anyone who doubted this had only to go into the kitchen to talk with his cook. Bagehot thought a democratic franchise would work well only if the mass of the electorate showed deference to their betters. Today, only an ageing and very small fraction of English people are prepared to defer to others on grounds of social status.[5]

Education is today the justification for policy makers acting as political trustees. People such as John Maynard Keynes assumed that as the "best and the brightest" of Oxford and Cambridge, they had a right to set out the policies that elected officials ought to follow. Well educated radicals today question the right of a popularly elected government to govern notwithstanding popular endorsement. Radicals assume that they are the trustees of national or class interest. Marsh's survey of *Protest and Political Consciousness* concludes that radicals' criticism of existing leadership has "less to do with altruism and much more to do with their urge to hasten the day when the existing elites have been ousted by themselves."[6]

The trusteeship view of government is summed up in an epigram: The government's job is to govern. The outlook is popular with the party in office, because it justifies government doing whatever it thinks desirable. Civil servants find the doctrine congenial too, because they permanently serve the governing party as trustees of the public interest, ensuring that the Queen's government is carried on.

Collectivism. Both right and left have tended to see the job of government in collectivist terms, in which major socioeconomic groups are the primary units of politics.[7] Collectivists argue that the aggregation of individual preferences by groups is inevitable in decision making in a country with more than 56 million citizens. Political parties and pressure groups, representing class and related economic interests, are regarded as more authoritative than the views of individual voters. The rise of the welfare state has also made government important as the collective provider of education, health services, and income security in old age and unemployment. While these benefits could be sold to individuals in the market, political values and policy commitments result in collective provision by government in the public interest.

The Conservative version of group politics emphasizes harmony between different hierarchically ordered groups. The traditional Conservative conception viewed different groups as organically linked, like the parts of the human body, with the head having a directing role and other parts responding appropriately. Each could make a contribution and receive esteem and benefits. The outlook is summed up in the funeral monument to an eighteenth-century Oxford servant "who, by an exemplary life and behavior, obtained the approbation and esteem of the whole society."

By contrast, the Socialist vision of group politics emphasizes political differences between employers and employees. From this perspective the Labour Party represents the interest of labor as defined by trade union organizations. In the cry of Frank Cousins, formerly leader of the Transport and General Workers, the country's largest trade union: "We represent Britain, we represent the working class of Britain, and they are Britain." Traditional Marxists see authority as a function of class: capitalist power is deemed to make elected governments powerless. British government is said to be an agent of an internationally organized capitalist class. Neo-Marxists give greater emphasis to government's autonomous influence upon class relations. All Marxists postulate irreconcilable political conflicts arising from class divisions within England.[8]

While accepting the linkage of parties and interest groups, corporatist theories emphasize a tripartite structure in which government is an independent force; so too are economic interest groups representing business and trade unions. Policy making is seen as the outcome of discussions among leaders of these groups within formal tripartite institutions. They are called corporatist in order to emphasize the extent to which the different groups are incorporated in a single body that blurs the distinction between what is and is not a part of government. The purpose of corporatism is to reconcile group differences. If the leaders of these groups spend more time accommodating each other than pressing their own sectional demands, they risk repudiation by their supporters because of failing to represent sectional interests strongly. This has frequently happened with attempts to impose wage and price regulations upon unions and business groups.[9]

All collectivist theories agree in assuming that organized interests are far more important than the views of individual citizens. Some recognize government as one among several major organizations in society, but others deny any relevance of government, believing power rests in class-based interests and institutions.

Liberal Individualism. The classic theory of liberalism views society from the perspective of the individual. In politics, authority is derived from individuals, and the direction of government should be determined by the collective preferences of individuals. In the economy decisions are seen as best made by individual consumers. The common element is the sovereignty of the individual as voter or as consumer. This individualist philosophy rejects the idea of pressure group leaders or trustees wielding political authority; it favors the represented rather than representatives.

Liberal individualism sees popular election as the primary justification for authority. Since political authority was established in England for half a millennium before the right to vote was widespread, liberal beliefs have had to be imposed upon predemocratic values of trusteeship. By contrast, in the United States they were embedded in the first words of the American Constitution: "We, the people." Liberal theories have also had to compete with collectivist ideas of class politics, that only by sticking together to bargain collectively can individuals hope to improve their wages and working conditions.

The party victorious in a general election claims that the individuals voting for it have endorsed all of its policies. It then proceeds to exercise authority as the collective representative of interests, simply as trustees for the nation. Many MPs reject the principle of the referendum, believing that it undermines their position as trustees of authority. The late Labour minister R. H. S. Crossman argued that majority opinion is often opposed to many reforms favored by public opinion: "Better the liberal elitism of the statute book than the reactionary populism of the marketplace. Referenda or plebiscites notoriously confirm right-wing acts; they do not voice left-wing opinions."[10]

For half a century the electoral dominance of the Conservative and Labour parties obscured the importance for representative government of liberal values expressed by such philosophers as Jeremy Bentham and John Stuart Mill.[11] The liberal emphasis upon the importance of individuals, freedom to speak and act as one wishes, and the franchise have all become part of the political culture. The revival of the Liberal Party and its merger with the Social Democratic Party to form the Social and Liberal Democrats has sustained a third party promoting the interests of individuals as against such large collective institutions, whether trade unions, business corporations, or public bureaucracies.

A Mixture of Sources. Governors depend upon a mixture of justifications for their authority. When asked directly, almost all MPs say that individual citizens ought to influence government; and 91 percent say that people ought to be allowed to vote even if they cannot do so intelligently. However, more than three-quarters of MPs see their primary role as that of a group representative or a trustee for the nation. A Labour MP says:

> The essential thing in a democracy is a general election in which a government is elected with power to do any damned thing it likes and if the people don't like it, they have the right to chuck it out.

A Conservative MP with an aristocratic background endorses much the same view in a characteristically mock-diffident manner:

> I personally consider myself capable of coming to decisions without having to fight an election once every four or five years, but on the other hand, the people must be allowed to feel that they can exercise some control, even if it's only the control of chucking somebody out that they don't like.[12]

Most individuals see two groups of elected trustees, the Prime Minister and Cabinet, and two collectivist institutions, big business and trade unions, having a lot of influence upon the country. Consistent with the historical evolution of authority from the top down, only 8 percent see people like themselves as having a lot of influence.[13] Many groups are seen as exercising some political influence because the institutions of government are not monolithic. Election victory makes ministers legitimate popular representatives and trustees for the authority of the Mace. Parliament allows MPs to voice individual views or express the collective views of competing parties. Collectivist pressure groups can impose constraints upon what trustees and popular representatives want to do. The sum of votes by individuals determines the outcome of an election.

ENFORCING LAWS AND ORDER

Politics in England encourages people and groups to challenge the law—up to a point. An election invites competing teams of partisans to put forward proposals for new legislation and sometimes the repeal of existing legislation. Debates in Parliament are full of opposition denunciations of "unfair," "unjust," and simply "unwise" laws, and the media daily voice similar criticisms. Compliance is expected only when political opinions are stated as Acts of Parliament; everyone is expected to accept measures enacted by the due process of the law.

The Laws That Count. While all Acts of Parliament have the same formal authority, they are not all equal in political significance. The laws that count most are basic political laws, those few measures that governors deem important for the continuance of the political authority of the regime.[14] For example, inciting a group to refuse military service in time of war is subversive of political authority, whereas encouraging a group of motorists to have one more drink before leaving a pub would be antisocial, encouraging drunken driving but not the collapse of political authority. A political crime is not defined by the amount of violence or the object of attack but by the intent. For example, a Welsh Nationalist's well publicized refusal to license a car because the official form is not printed in Welsh is not an attempt to evade taxation but a political act intended to challenge the authority of government.

National politicians are committed to upholding Westminster's authority even when it is used in pursuit of objectives that they reject, for the Opposition party expects its opponents to obey laws that it will enact when in office. The readiness to comply with basic political laws was made explicit during the Suez War of 1956. The then leader of the Opposition, Hugh Gaitskell, told the House of Commons that the Labour Party would be:

> bound by every constitutional means at our disposal to oppose it. I emphasize the word "constitutional." We shall, of course, make no attempt to dissuade anybody from carrying out the orders of the government, but we shall seek, through the influence of public opinion, to bring every pressure to bear upon the government to withdraw from the impossible situation into which they have put us.[15]

Challenges to authority are often voiced by political activists today. When strikers seek a confrontation with the police or there is a disturbance in an inner city, normally a few MPs will speak up for those who challenge authority. But party leaders remain extremely cautious, for no experienced British politician wants it to be said that he is on the side of rioters against the police, or attacking soldiers or police with words when others attack with rocks, petrol bombs, or even guns. The most that Labour Party leaders will pledge is to review a law that is regarded as unjust, or to repeal it—once the lawful authority of government is in Labour's hands.

At election after election voters have refused to support antisystem parties challenging established authority. This has been demonstrated most strikingly in Scotland and Wales, where Scottish Nationalist and Welsh Nationalist candidates demand independence from Westminster (Table II.4). Moreover, nationalist parties do not reject the idea of parliamentary government; they simply object to authority being in London rather than Edinburgh or Cardiff.

The Communist Party of Great Britain has always polled a derisory vote. Its highest vote was in 1945, when Communists won 0.4 percent of the vote; in October 1974, at a time of high industrial tension, Communist candidates polled less than 0.1 percent of the vote. In 1987 Communist candidates polled less than 0.05 percent of the vote. The British Communist Party has even been described as "overwhelmed by the British political culture and forced to accommodate to the country's political tradition."[16] Today it is split between a group wanting to maintain the party's historic pro-Soviet commitment and those wanting to adapt to contemporary trends.

In reaction against the Communist Party move toward common English cultural norms, a variety of self-styled revolutionary groups such as the Militant Tendency, the Socialist Workers' Party, and the Socialist League have formed, split and re-formed. They avoid testing their popular support at elections. The most significant group is Militant, a Trotskyite organization that greatly multiplies its influence by a policy of "entryism," encouraging its members to join the Labour Party and actively support steps to intensify the class war, leading to the collapse of capitalism and of the Labour Party as it has been known. After a decade of advances in local politics and party organizations, Militant is now under pressure from party headquarters, but it continues to have supporters among Labour MPs and in local parties.[17]

From time to time fascist movements have appeared on the streets

and nominated candidates for parliamentary elections; their popular support is minuscule. In the 1930s the British Union of Fascists,
led by a former Labour MP, Sir Oswald Mosley, failed to gain any
support at a time of high unemployment and the approach of world
war. In the 1970s the National Front sought to stimulate support
for a radical reaction against established parties and institutions.
The National Front occasionally organizes provocative marches in
immigrant areas, but its base of support is very small. When it contested half of the nation's parliamentary constituencies in 1979, it
won only 0.6 percent of the vote. In the 1987 election the National
Front was too disorganized and disillusioned to nominate any
candidates.[18]

The rise of unorthodox extraparliamentary methods of political
activity in the late 1960s—protest marches, rent strikes, sit-ins at
public buildings and occasional violence to property—has had an
effect very different from what was intended by proponents of demonstrations. It has reaffirmed the commitment of the great majority
of English people to compliance with basic political laws. A
nationwide survey of unorthodox political protest finds little support for political action outside the law (Table V.1). A majority
approve signing petitions and lawful demonstrations, but equally
disapprove eight other forms of political protest ranging from boycotts and rent strikes to violence. Support for unorthodox political
behavior drops as the form of protest tends toward violence.

TABLE V.1 *Limits of Support for Unorthodox Political Behaviour*

	Approve %	Believe effective %	Have done %
Sign petitions	86	73	23
Lawful demonstrations	69	60	6
Boycotts	37	48	6
Rent strikes	24	27	2
Unofficial strikes	16	42	5
Occupying buildings	15	29	1
Blocking traffic	15	31	1
Painting slogans on walls	1	6	—
Damaging property	2	10	1
Personal violence	1	11	—

Source: Reprinted from Alan Marsh, *Protest and Political Consciousness*, Sage
Library of Social Research, Vol. 49, Table 2.1, by permission of the publisher, Sage
Publications, Inc. Copyright © 1977 by Sage Publications, Inc.

The commitment of English people to lawful political action reflects values concerning what is and is not appropriate political behavior. It does not reflect pragmatic calculations about what will and will not work, for the minority believing unorthodox measures effective is larger than the proportion approving unlawful measures. For example, 11 percent believe violence is effective, but only 1 percent approve using violence. Because most people disapprove of unorthodox political behavior and do not believe it effective, very few engage in such protest: only 6 percent report involvement in boycotts and 5 percent in unofficial strikes.

The commitment to political authority is shown by popular readiness to support government in taking strong measures if its authority is challenged by violation of basic political laws. Eighty percent approve courts giving severe sentences to protesters who disregard the police, and 73 percent approve police using force against demonstrators. Similarly, a large majority believe that a tough line on law and order is effective. People equally reject the government "bending" the law to repress lawful disagreement. A majority do not endorse the government using troops to break legal strikes, and only one-quarter would infringe on freedom of speech and assembly by making protest demonstrations illegal. The median person takes a middle-of-the-road-position, wanting public officials as well as antigovernment protesters to support the institutions of government and comply with basic laws.[19]

Terrorism is a distinctive form of unorthodox political protest, employing violence as a means to explicitly political ends. While antisocial behavior by football hooligans may occasionally cause death, the violence is not politically motivated. By contrast, when a terrorist group shoots a policeman or a soldier, it argues that this is not murder but a political act. The chief terrorist group operating within Britain, the IRA (Irish Republican Army), does have political ends. It resorts to violence because it has been unable to achieve its aims peacefully and believes that its desired goal of Irish unity justifies the means.

The idea of resorting to violence for political ends is outside the bounds of the English political culture. When people are asked whether there are some circumstances in which political violence can be justified, 84 percent say that it must always be condemned, as against 12 percent believing that somewhere there may be a justification.[20] When people are asked whether organizations such as the IRA should be considered terrorists or freedom fighters, 91 percent consider the IRA as terrorists. By contrast, in Northern Ireland, where political legitimacy is contested, there is a greater readiness to tolerate violence. The IRA has a measure of popular support in the Catholic community for its armed insurrection against the Crown, and the illegal and armed Protestant Ulster Volunteer Force also has a measure of popular acceptance in the opposing community.

The Police. Laws are most effectively enforced when they are drafted so that people voluntarily obey them. Then there is no need for a clumsy and expensive apparatus of police and courts to ensure that everyone does what they are supposed to do. The majority of laws on the statute books avoid political controversy because they are voluntary, that is, the behavior that they regulate is neither compulsory nor prohibited. For example, laws about the purchase of a house do not require everyone to buy a house, and laws about marriage do not compel marriage. A substantial proportion of laws are impersonal, regulating activities of formal organizations or relations between organizations, particularly the activities of government organizations. Only a small fraction of statutes, such as the criminal law, consists of dos and don'ts that everyone is expected to obey.[21]

In every society, and England is no exception, there are always some people who break laws. The typical crimes, unsafe driving, theft, or assault, are nonpolitical in intent. The fact of crime requires institutions of law enforcement. England has no paramilitary security force, nor has it anything like the American national guard for use in the event of domestic political disorder. The internal security forces of England are, in proportion to population, one-third smaller than in America, France, or Italy. The navy is England's premier military service; by its nature the navy cannot be deployed within the country, and the army is hardly ever used to enforce public order within England.

Policing in England is a responsibility of local government; the police are formally accountable to a police authority composed of local councillors and magistrates. The position of the Chief Constable, the local chief of police, is institutionally insulated. The existence of dozens of local police forces prevents the government from directing a national police force from Whitehall. The distinctive identity and professional interests of policemen, reinforced by the police authority not being able to question operational activities, insulates police forces from direction by elected councillors.[22]

Policing in England is based upon trust. The police patrol go about unarmed, and criminals are usually unarmed too. When people are asked how much confidence they have in a variety of major institutions in society, four-fifths express confidence in the police.[23] The importance of trust in police is underscored by the contrast between England and the most disorderly part of the United Kingdom, Northern Ireland. The Westminster Parliament has never been successful in maintaining law and order there because of the absence of popular trust in the police, who are inevitably seen as taking sides by supporting the existing (that is, the United Kingdom) position in the political conflict between Protestants and Catholics. England's rule of law is not for export to all other parts of the United Kingdom.[24]

Today trust between police and the public is subject to erosion on four fronts. First of all, the police are becoming more remote from the people they are meant to protect. A generation ago policemen patrolled on foot or on bicycle; this kept them in close touch with the community. Today, police patrol in cars or keep areas under surveillance electronically and seek an expansion of their formal powers of search and inquisition to replace now-lost informal methods of collecting information. Secondly, illegal acts by the police are increasing. While corruption often involves taking bribes, an antisocial act, increasingly cases arise of the abuse of authority, beating a prisoner, or making a false statement.[25] Thirdly, confrontation policies of some unions in defiance of Acts of Parliament have led to the mobilization of police in strikes, as in the 1984 coal strike. Some Labour Party and trade union leaders have called for workers to "fight, oppose and break unjust and anti-democratic class laws."

The miners' union leader, Arthur Scargill, declared: "We have no intention of abiding by laws either civil or criminal which restrict our ability as a trade union to fight for the rights of our members."[26] Fourthly, in immigrant areas of cities there is ambivalence. Many immigrants desire protection against crime, but there is concern that law-enforcement officials do not enforce the law fairly when immigrants are involved.[27]

As the former Lord Chancellor, Lord Hailsham, has noted: "Law is a confidence trick. Law depends upon *asabia*, that is, a sense of solidarity between people who regarded themselves as the members of a society accepting certain values."[28]

While occasional incidents show that there are a few English people prepared to assault political authority, a Marxist critic concludes: "It is an assault that has taken place without very evident mass support."[29]

Limits on the Courts. Courts have relatively little influence upon Westminster because the role of law is narrowly defined. Whereas in past centuries judges proclaimed the role of law as a means of restraining royal absolutism, twentieth-century English judges do not attempt to decide what Parliament may or may not do; this task is left to Parliament to determine, acting at the direction of the government of the day. English courts claim no power to declare an Act of Parliament unconstitutional. If a statute delegates discretion to a public authority, the courts do not question the motives of the officials exercising discretion. While English judges believe that the unwritten Constitution must be constantly adapted, they want little part of the job. That job is the responsibility of Parliament; the final court of appeal is political rather than judicial.[30]

The government's statutory powers are broad enough to sanction it doing almost anything. In a single day in 1940 Parliament approved an Emergency Powers (Defence) Act that gave the government power to compel persons "to place themselves, their services and their property at the disposal of His Majesty."[31] Even if the courts rule that the executive has acted *ultra vires* (outside its powers), the effect of a judgment can be canceled by a subsequent Act of Parliament retroactively authorizing what the courts ruled should not be done. In 1965 the Burmah Oil Company won a lawsuit claiming government compensation for property damaged in the Second World War. The government promptly passed a law abolishing the grounds for claiming compensation.

The principal activity of the courts is to resolve disputes about the application of the law to particular events or to ascertain facts indicating whether or not a law has been violated. A judge acts as an "interstitial legislator," seeking to fill in minor gaps in the law revealed by awkward cases, or to remove ambiguities, or to determine whether a public agency has acted within the broad limits of its statutory authority. By comparison with a quarter century ago, judges are a little more inclined to rule that government has acted outside its powers, but government remains the final arbiter of what the law says.[32]

Because of the relative insignificance of the courts in the conduct of government,[33] problems that may be dealt with through the courts in other societies are often handled by administrative routines in England. For example, government action to protect the environment from pollution is a common problem of all advanced industrial societies. By comparison with the United States, England is distinctive because it relies primarily upon cooperative negotiation between officials in Whitehall ministries and representatives of polluters to arrive at "enforceable standards," that is, regulations that government regards as preventing the worst pollution and that affected firms believe can be obeyed without suffering greatly economically or in production. In the United States, the process of setting standards, assessing performance, and adjudicating disputes tends to be conducted in an adversarial political and judicial framework.[34]

When an individual citizen has a grievance against government, it is much more likely to involve a specific administrative action, such as a claim for a welfare benefit or planning permission for a house, than a major constitutional issue. There are a variety of specialized administrative tribunals that individuals can use to seek redress for their grievances. If there appears to be gross unfairness or maladministration, a citizen can turn to his MP, who may raise the issue in the House of Commons or refer it for investigation to the Parliamentary Commissioner for Administration, a weaker version of the Scandinavian ombudsman. The mass media will take up sensational cases of maladministration, and a combination of media and parliamentary pressures can cause the government to authorize a special inquiry.[35]

LIMITING AUTHORITY

In theory Parliament can enact any law that the government of the day recommends; in practice the actions of government are limited by what people will stand for. The legitimacy of government does not give a blanket endorsement for it to do anything and everything. The norms of the political culture identify things that are not done. In the words of Bernard Crick:

> The only restraints are political. Governments are restrained by what they think the country will stand for come the general election, and they adhere to things like general elections because they prefer (whether out of ethics, habit or prudence, or all three) to settle disputes politically rather than despotically and coercively.[36]

Characteristic of most English writers on the left, Crick treats courts as coercive institutions enforcing authority rather than as defenders

of individuals against authority. This view is challenged by proponents of a written constitution with a judicially enforceable bill of
rights. However, the existence of a campaign for a bill of rights is
tacit admission that the courts at present set no effective limit on the
power of government.[37]

Freedom of speech is a traditional norm, predating the introduction of the right to vote. Remarks that would constitute crimes
against the state in authoritarian European regimes have been part
of the cut and thrust of political debate for centuries. Freedom of
association largely predates the grant of the right to vote too. Just as
there are no laws requiring the formal registration of political parties, so there are no laws forbidding particular types of parties. Any
organization, even an organization challenging fundamental cultural norms, as does Sinn Fein, the electoral wing of the IRA, can
nominate candidates at a general election.

In the past generation the limits upon government legislation
have been increased by pressures for a more permissive society. This
has led to the repeal of laws that formerly regulated private morality
in the name of public standards. Legislation on pornography and
obscenity has effectively been set aside, leading to the publication of
books, plays, and television programs that would have been literally
unprintable or unviewable in 1960. Writers and media communicators have been far readier to take advantage of changing cultural
values in addition to changes in statutes to introduce explicit sex
and other once-forbidden topics into their work.

Laws prohibiting abortion and homosexuality have also been
repealed. Whereas abortion was once illegal, today abortion is legal-
ized, and it can be a prescribed treatment in the national health
service. The 1967 Sexual Offences Act decriminalized homosexuality
between consenting male adults; lesbian behavior had never been
explicitly illegal. Homosexual groups can now organize politically
to advance their claims and have succeeded in securing special facilities from some Labour-controlled local authorities. There remain
political disputes about exactly where the line should be drawn in
permitting abortion (for example, up to what stage in pregnancy)
or homosexual relationships (for example, the age at which a young
person can consent to homosexual sex), but government now does
not claim that it has the right to forbid on principle actions that it
once deemed illegal and immoral. The unwillingness of the
Thatcher government to reintroduce legislation prohibiting abortion and homosexuality confirms the scale and strength of the shift

in cultural norms. The Prime Minister personally endorses Victorian values about morality but accepts that government no longer has the authority to legislate such morality.[38]

Controversy About the Limits. Although people agree about many things that government ought to do (for example, provide schools and police services) and many things it ought not to do (regulate tastes in food and reading matter), at any point in time there is political controversy about the boundaries of government intervention. Today the greatest controversy is about the limits of government action in a mixed-economy welfare state. While there is widespread agreement about the need for some government direction of the economy and substantial public provision for welfare, within this broadly defined area there is much scope for specific disagreement.[39]

Trade unions argue that they should be able to organize their affairs without any regulation by statute and bargain for wages without any legal constraints or liability for contracts signed with employers. The claim of British unions for freedom from regulation by industrial relations laws is unique in Western nations. Unions do not want a Labour government to give them statutory benefits, preferring to secure these through industrial bargaining. The unions view any Acts of Parliament or judicial intervention as limiting their activities; the unions want to be free to pursue their own interests in the marketplace. In the words of the former general secretary of the Trade Union Congress, Len Murray:

> If it's a free-for-all then we are part of the all. We will do our thing like other people will do their thing. If we take the view that the way in which the government is operating through its impact on employment or prices or the social wage or whatever is against the interests of our members, then we shall get up and say so, and if necessary we'll go and walk up and down the streets to say so.[40]

Union leaders have consistently opposed industrial relations legislation by the Thatcher Administration, including laws giving rights to members to vote on leadership and policy within their union.

Businessmen argue that the laws of the market are, and should be, most important. Acts of Parliament are seen as necessary to guarantee standards but should not compel business firms to act in accord with economic plans of the government of the day. Because capital and trade are mobile, if Whitehall seeks to promulgate regulations that fly in the face of international markets, for example regarding the foreign exchange rate of the pound or prices and wages, then foreign currency dealers, importers, and exporters will refuse cooperation. Britain's membership in the European Community enlarges the influence of international markets. So too has the action of the Thatcher government in repealing control on the export of British capital abroad. Firms that dislike British economic policies can now invest abroad. As a part-time director of the government-owned Bank of England said when advising a private client to speculate against the pound: "This is anti-British and derogatory to sterling but on balance, if one is free to do so, it makes sense to me."[41]

Repeated attempts by government to fix wages and prices illustrate practical and normative constraints upon what government can do. Unions can engage in shop-floor bargaining that exploits local autonomy to negotiate increases above lawfully prescribed limits. Employers can cooperate in getting around the law if this is viewed as useful in retaining a skilled and cooperative work force at wages that the firm can afford to pay. Effective price controls result in some goods becoming hard to find in shops because it no longer pays firms to sell them, and some goods may be supplied on terms circumventing price controls. The lack of normative agreement about what is a fair wage creates differences between unions, which have historically paid much attention to wage differentials between workers. Such is the normative dissensus about wages that government attempts to define and enforce wage standards in the absence of consensus "would carry the very real threat of extending economic into political instability."[42] Recognizing this, the Thatcher Administration has not sought to legislate a wages policy; rising unemployment has instead reduced the bargaining power of unions.

The social policies of the mixed-economy welfare state reflect a very high level of consensus in favor of positive actions by government. Regardless of party preference, nearly everybody believes that government ought to provide education, health services, and social security in old age. While the Thatcher government has been active in promoting the privatization of nationalized industries, it has not withdrawn government commitments to these major social programs. To propose the removal of benefits to which people are now entitled by Act of Parliament would be to court electoral disaster. However, differences of opinion about social policies are sufficient to sustain a continuing debate about social policies. Disagreement about which service should have priority; how much money should be spent; the terms for organizing, delivering, and redistributing benefits; and the role of the nonpublic sector are reflections of everyday political differences of opinion; they do not challenge basic principles.[43]

The importance of cultural norms is brought out clearly by comparing British expectations of government social policy with American expectations (Table V.2). In Britain, the proportion saying that government should deal with particular social problems is on average 34 percent higher than in the United States. The difference is greatest about health care and social security for the elderly. More than three-quarters of Britons believe that government should take positive measures in these fields, whereas in America only a minority endorse such views. The surveys document disagreements in Britain about some areas of government action, for example providing help to industry and reducing income differences between rich and poor. Here again cross-cultural differences are significant, for these are just the areas where Americans register a consensus in favor of government *not* taking such actions.

SUPPORT FOR THE SYSTEM

If a political system is to be fully legitimate, citizens must give it support as well as compliance. The rules of the game are bounda-

TABLE V.2 *Cultural Differences about Government's Social Role*

Government should:	Britain	America (% favoring)	Difference
Provide health care for sick	86	35	51
Provide decent standard for the old	78	40	38
Keep prices under control	60	29	31
Provide help to industry to grow	53	16	37
Reduce income differences between rich and poor	45	16	29
Provide decent standard for the unemployed	43	15	28
Provide a job for everyone who wants one	37	13	24
Average	57	24	34

Source: Calculcated from nationwide British and American surveys reported by James A. Davis, "British and American Attitudes," in R. Jowell, S. Witherspoon, and L. Brook, eds., *British Social Attitudes: the 1986 Report* (Aldershot: Gower, 1986), p. 102.

ries within which controversial political choices are made. Because people support the system, they will comply with laws with which they disagree and accept that a government unsuccessful in handling the economy remains nonetheless the legitimate political authority. As Bagehot noted, a "steady frame" of government is needed to set the picture that each new political artist paints.

Two Cheers for the System. Surveys of popular attitudes toward the political system face methodological and evaluative difficulties. Methodologically, it is hard to get some people to conceive of something as abstract as a political system, and the absence of a written constitution compounds the problem. A second and related difficulty is that judgments may be affected by partisan bias: people tend to confuse judgments about the partisan government of the day, which many vote against, with the Queen's government, which carries on with the support of the electorate as a whole. A third difficulty is the identification of a desirable level of popular support. Not every element of the political system requires (or by some lights, deserves) popular endorsement. Support for a system is consistent with a desire to reform or adapt its parts.

When the public is asked to evaluate government by elected representatives, 94 percent support it as very good or fairly good; only 3 percent consider it a bad way to run the country. Politicians almost unanimously support the established system of representative government too; only 2 percent of MPs say there should be big changes in the way England is governed. The idea of a revolution overthrowing representative parliamentary institutions is inconceivable to the great bulk of English people; only 7 percent say they think it is likely that government might be overthrown in the next decade.[44]

When a survey in Europe and America asked for evaluations of a wide range of major institutions, the confidence expressed by British people was average. Americans and Germans showed more confidence in national institutions, and Spaniards showed less. Overall the French showed much the same level of confidence as the British (Table V.3).

Institutions central to the maintenance of political authority have the highest level of popular confidence in Britain. More than three-quarters express confidence in the police and armed forces, the most authoritative and coercive institutions of governance. It is particularly striking that popular confidence in these institutions is much

TABLE V.3 *Popular Confidence in Major Institutions*

Institution	Percent Expressing a Great Deal or Some Confidence				
	Britain	*America*	*France*	*Germany*	*Spain*
Police	80	88	72	80	44
Armed forces	79	86	59	69	36
Judicial system	56	77	62	72	35
Education system	53	82	82	82	59
Church	56	85	53	66	38
Business community	55	84	30	44	84
Parliament/Congress	52	83	55	64	30
Media: press, TV	38	69	48	41	46
Trade unions	29	52	36	43	26
Average	55	76	55	62	44

Source: Laurence Parisot, "Attitudes about the Media: a Five-Country Comparison" *Public Opinion* 10,5 (1988), Table 1, based on data for surveys by Louis Harris & Associates, Inc.

higher in Britain than in France and Spain, which have had reason at times in the postwar era to doubt the loyalty of these institutions to democratic government. The legal system and the church rank next in popular confidence. Confidence is lowest in extragovernmental institutions that voice demands upon government, such as trade unions and the press, and it is also below average for Parliament, which is the arena in which party political conflicts are articulated.[45] Diverse institutions of authority mobilize support in a multiplicity of ways; most support is given to institutions central in the exercise of political authority.

Confidence in the system does not imply an unthinking and uncritical attitude toward the constitutional regime. People often support political authority while favoring specific reforms. When asked about the prospects for change, only one-quarter emphasize the importance of defending the status quo against change. By contrast, two-thirds favor gradual improvements through the reform of existing institutions. Only 5 percent say that they think society should be radically changed by revolutionary action. The endorsement of gradual change is important in maintaining the political system, because this is necessary for a political system to survive in a changing national and international environment.[46]

Support for the system does not imply agreement about every-

thing that government does. Even though consensus and controversy are logically opposed, in politics they are complementary. MPs
and electors simultaneously disagree about what government ought
to do, yet agree about the rules of the game by which disputes
should be settled. Words written a year after the 1926 General Strike
by a former Prime Minister, the Earl of Balfour, remain relevant in
an era in which three parties contest for the office of government—
and the two losers accept that the third has the right to exercise the
authority thus won: "Our whole political machinery presupposes a
people so fundamentally at one that they can safely afford to bicker:
and so sure of their own moderation that they are not dangerously
disturbed by the never-ending din of political conflict."[47]

Why Support the System? For two reasons the great books of political philosophy cannot provide a satisfactory explanation for contemporary allegiance to authority. First of all, English philosophers
have disagreed fundamentally. In the seventeenth century Thomas
Hobbes disagreed with John Locke; at the end of the eighteenth
century Edmund Burke disagreed with Jeremy Bentham, and John
Stuart Mill disagreed with his Victorian contemporary in London,
Karl Marx. Secondly, even after a century of compulsory education,
the great books of political philosophy are read by only a very small
minority of the electorate. Popular political outlooks are derived
primarily from experience, not books.

Past traditions are often cited as an explanation of the unreflec-
tive, even unconscious, English acceptance of political authority.
But the events of a thousand years of English history offer prece-
dents to justify political revolt. Regicide is an older tradition than
parliamentary government. High-status Englishmen have been
committing treason against the Crown since the time of Thomas à
Becket in the twelfth century. Lowly Englishmen have been revolt-
ing against the Crown since Wat Tyler's peasant rising of 1381.
Traditional symbols such as the monarchy are a consequence, not a
cause, of political authority. The Queen is respected because she
and her predecessors have remained remote from political controversy. Nothing is compelling about the symbols in themselves.
Where there is no consensus about authority, as in Northern Ireland, such symbols of British government as the monarchy and the
Union Jack stimulate a defiant reaction from Irish Republicans.[48]

Support for authority is not the result of carefully calculated policies pursued by politicians. Politicians try to avoid raising consti-

tutional issues because they are so difficult to resolve, especially without a written constitution. Hugo Young comments, "Preserving constitutional order could be called the highest task of politics. Yet the effort applied to it has been derisory. Virtually none of Whitehall has been concerned with the Constitution. To almost all concerned, constitutional issues exist in order to be denied, circumvented or reduced to an administrative inconvenience."[49]

The trust that English people show is not derived from a belief in the effectiveness or competence of government. In the 1970s a number of political economists theorized that the government's failure to maintain a steadily expanding economy was likely to lead to the breakdown of representative government.[50] Notwithstanding severe economic difficulties, such as several years of a falling gross national product and a sixfold increase in unemployment, the system of representative government has continued. People have adapted their political expectations and behavior to less favorable economic circumstances.

Ordinary people can continue to support a political system that does not deliver more and more benefits because most people do not look to government for their primary satisfaction in life or to better their material condition. When people are asked whether they think the actions of government help make their position better or worse, nearly half (47 percent) say that government does not have much effect. The remainder divide into three groups, 24 percent seeing government making their lives better, 18 percent seeing it making their lives worse, and the remainder who see its impact as mixed. Avoiding the abuse of power rather than substantive economic achievement is the guarantee of support for government in England.[51]

When people are asked to evaluate reasons for giving allegiance to authority, the view most often endorsed is pragmatic: 77 percent believe "it's the best form of government we know." Such a judgment does not regard government as perfect or trouble-free. Government is regarded as good enough, or simply as the least of many possible evils. "It's the kind of government the people want" is also thought a good reason for support by 66 percent. A majority (65 percent) also recognize the inevitability of government: "We've got to accept it whatever we think." The effectiveness of government in providing the right things for people is considered less important; 49 percent think it is a good reason for accepting authority. Contrary to the argument sometimes offered by economic determinists, popular allegiance is not bought by providing public benefits. A government that is ineffective in managing a mixed-economy welfare state can still enjoy authority if people consider it the best form of government that they know. The legitimacy of government in England was secured long before it became a great provider of welfare benefits.[52]

NOTES

1. For a fuller discussion of legitimacy, see Richard Rose, *Governing without Consensus* (Boston, Mass.: Beacon Press, 1971), Chapter 1. On contemporary culture, see Dennis Kavanagh, "Political Culture in Britain: The Decline of the Civic Culture," in Gabriel Almond and Sidney Verba, eds., *The Civic Culture Revisited* (Boston: Little, Brown, 1980), pp. 124–176, and for a historical approach, Richard Rose, "England: A Traditionally Modern Culture," in Lucian Pye and Sidney Verba, eds., *Political Culture and Political Development* (Princeton: Princeton University Press, 1965), pp. 83–129.

2. Sidney Low, *The Governance of England*, rev. ed. (London: Ernest Benn, 1914), p. 12.

3. For a wide-ranging review of these theories, see A. H. Birch, *Representative and Responsible Government* (London: Allen and Unwin, 1964).

4. L. S. Amery, *Thoughts on the Constitution*, 2nd ed. (London: Oxford University Press, 1953), p. 21. The term trustee is used by A. L. Lowell, *The Government of England*, Vol. 2 (London: Macmillan, 1908), p. 508.

5. Cf. Bagehot, *The English Constitution*, and evidence reviewed in Dennis Kavanagh, "The Deferential English: A Comparative Critique," *Government and Opposition*, 6:3 (1971).

6. Alan C. Marsh, *Protest and Political Consciousness*, (London: Sage, 1977), p. 197.

7. See Samuel H. Beer, *Modern British Politics: Parties and Pressure Groups in the Collectivist Age*, 3rd ed. (London: Faber and Faber, 1982).

8. See, e.g., Ralph Miliband, *Capitalist Democracy in Britain* (London: Oxford University Press, 1982). For Cousins, quote, see Labour Party *Conference Report* (1962), p. 182.

9. Cf. Keith Middlemas, *Politics in Industrial Society* (London: Andre Deutsch, 1979); Peter Hall, *Governing the Economy* (London: Polity, 1986), p. 268ff; and British contributions to Wolfgang Streeck and Philippe C. Schmitter, eds. *Private Interest Government* (London: Sage Publications, 1985).

10. *New Statesman*, 7 August 1970. Cf. Vernon Bogdanor, *The People and the Party System* (Cambridge: Cambridge University Press, 1981).

11. For an exception, see Birch, *Representative and Responsible Government*, especially chapters 5 and 6; and W. H. Greenleaf, *The British Political Tradition: The Ideological Heritage*, Vol. 2, (London: Methuen, 1983).

12. Quoted from Robert D. Putnam, *The Beliefs of Politicians* (New Haven: Yale University Press, 1973).

13. See Gallup Political Index No. 268 (December 1982), p. 11.

14. See Richard Rose, "Dynamic Tendencies in the Authority of Regimes," *World Politics*, 21:4 (1969), p. 605ff. For a broader sociological analysis, see Ralf Dahrendorf, *Law and Order* (London: Stevens, 1985).

15. House of Commons, *Debates*, 5th series, Vol. 558, Col. 1462 (31 October 1956).

16. Robert Kilroy-Silk, in a book review in *Political Studies*, 18:4 (1970).

17. Cf. Blake Baker, *The Far Left* (London: Weidenfeld and Nicolson, 1981); David Kogan and Maurice Kogan, *The Battle for the Labour Party* (London: Fontana, 1982); Jens-Peter Steffen, "Imprint of the Militant Tendency on the Labour Party," *West European Politics* 10:3 (1987), pp. 420–433. For a discussion of trends from within the left see, for example, the *New Left Review* and *Marxism Today*.

18. Stan Taylor, *The National Front in English Politics* (London: Macmillan, 1982).

19. See Alan C. Marsh, *Protest and Political Consciousness* (London: Sage Publications, 1977), Table 2.1. See also Louis Moss, *People and Government* (London: Birkbeck College, 1982), p. 124ff.

20. *Gallup Political Index* No. 269 (January 1983), p. 13.

21. Van Mechelen and Rose, *Patterns of Parliamentary Legislation* (Farnborough: Gower, 1986), Chapter 6.

22. Cf. L. Lustgarten, *The Governance of Police* (London: Sweet & Maxwell, 1986).

23. *Gallup Political Index* No. 295 (March, 1985), p. 22.

24. Cf. Richard Rose, "On the Priorities of Citizenship in the Deep South and Northern Ireland," *Journal of Politics*, 38: 2 (1976), pp. 247–291.

25. The public regards individual policemen indicted for crimes as uncharacteristic of the force. When asked to rate the honesty of different professions, 55 percent rate the police high and an additional 31 percent rate it average, a far better rating than 12 other professions such as government ministers, civil servants, businessmen, trade union leaders, journalists, and university teachers. See *Gallup Political Index* No. 295 (March 1985), p. 21.

26. Scargill quoted in "'MPs' Motion Attacks 'Above Law' Scargill," *Daily Telegraph*, 22 June 1984; Eric Heffer, quoted in "Traditional to Break Bad Laws," *ibid.*, 7 April 1984. Cf. Hugo Young, "A Jury of Courage That Put the Valleys to the Test," *The Guardian*, 28 May 1985, on the conviction for murder of two striking miners whose actions had killed a man.

27. For critical accounts of policing, see e.g. John Benyon and Colin Bourn, eds., *The Police: Powers, Procedures and Proprieties* (Oxford: Pergamon, 1986); Maurice Punch, *Conduct Unbecoming* (London: Tavistock, 1985); and Robert Reiner, *The Politics of the Police* (Brighton: Wheatsheaf, 1985).

28. Lord Hailsham, quoted in Terry Coleman, "His Lordship in the City of Destruction," *The Guardian*, 25 May 1984.

29. Martin Kettle, "The Police," in H. Drucker et al., *Developments in British Politics* (London: Macmillan, 1983), p. 28.

30. For useful Anglo-American comparisons, see Louis L. Jaffe, *English and American Judges as Lawmakers* (Oxford: Clarendon Press, 1969); and Richard Hodder-Williams, "Courts of Last Resort," in Hodder-Williams and James Ceaser, eds., *Politics in Britain and the United States* (Durham, NC: Duke University Press, 1986), pp. 142–172.

31. Quoted in G. H. L. LeMay, *British Government, 1914–53: Select Documents* (London: Methuen, 1955).

32. See John Bell, *Policy Arguments in Judicial Decisions* (Oxford: Clarendon Press, 1983); Michael Zander, *The Law-Making Process* 2nd ed., (London: Weidenfeld and Nicolson, 1985); and for a review of the literature, Gavin Drewry, "Judiciary and Government," in D. Engelfield and G. Drewry, eds., *Information Sources in Political Science* (London: Butterworths, 1984) pp. 209–225.

33. A meaningful outline of the different courts, chronicling those with initial and final jurisdiction for civil actions, lesser and greater criminal charges, etc., can be obtained in a standard legal textbook. See e.g. R. M. Jackson, *The Machinery of Justice in England*, 7th ed. (Cambridge: Cambridge University Press, 1977).

34. David Vogel, *National Styles of Regulation: Environmental Policy in Great Britain and the United States* (Ithaca: Cornell University Press, 1986).

35. For an overview, see F. F. Ridley, "British Approaches to the Redress of Grievances," *Parliamentary Affairs*, 37:1 (1984), p. 32, and Geoffrey Marshall, "Parliament and the Redress of Grievances: The Role of the Parliamentary Commissioner," in Walkland and Ryle, eds., *The Commons Today*, (London: Fontana, 1981),pp. 260-278.

36. Bernard Crick, *The Reform of Parliament*, revised 2nd ed. (London: Weidenfeld and Nicolson, 1970), p. 16; see also J. A. G. Griffith, *The Politics of the Judiciary*, 3rd ed. (London: Fontana, 1985).

37. See e.g. Anthony Lester, "The Constitution—Decline and Renewal," in Jowell and Oliver, eds., *The Changing Constitution*, (Oxford: Clarendon Press, 1985), pp. 273-296; and Philip Norton, *The Constitution in Flux*, (Oxford: Martin Robertson, 1982), chapters 7, 13.

38. For studies arguing in favour of broadening the scope of private action and narrowing the scope of government actions, see e.g. Harry Street, *Freedom, the Individual and the Law*, 5th ed. (Harmondsworth: Penguin, 1982); and Patricia Hewitt, *The Abuse of Power: Civil Liberties in the United Kingdom* (Oxford: Martin Robertson, 1982).

39. Cf. Richard Rose, "Two and One-Half Cheers for the Market in Britain," *Public Opinion*, Washington DC, 6:3 (1983); Peter Taylor-Gooby, *Public Opinion, Ideology and State Welfare* (London: Routledge & Kegan Paul, 1985).

40. Brian Connell, "Len Murray: A Life in the Movement," *The Times* (London), 22 August 1977.

41. Quoted in W. J. M. Mackenzie, "Models of English Politics," in R. Rose, ed., *Studies in British Politics*, 3rd ed. (London: Macmillan, 1976), p. 13.

42. J. H. Goldthorpe, "Social Inequality and Social Integration in Modern Britain," in R. Rose, ed., *Studies in British Politics*, 3rd ed.

43. See e.g. Richard Rose and Ian McAllister, *Voters Begin to Choose* (London: Sage Publications, 1986) chapters 7-8; Peter Taylor-Gooby, "Citizenship and Welfare" in R. Jowell, S. Witherspoon, and L. Brook, eds., *British Social Attitudes: The 1987 Report* (Aldershot: Gower, 1987), pp. 1-28.

44. See R. Jowell and C. Airey, eds., *British Social Attitudes: The 1984 Report* (Aldershot: Gower, 1984), p. 31. Cf. Committee on the Management of Local Government, Vol. 3, *The Local Government Elector* (London: HMSO, 1967), pp. 60ff; and Putnam, *The Beliefs of Politicians*.

45. The expression of confidence is also persisting. See *Gallup Political Index* No. 295 (March 1985), p. 22.

46. See *Eurobarometer* (Brussels: Commission of the European Community No. 28, December 1987), p. B-34. These survey results have been stable for years.

47. "Introduction" to Walter Bagehot, *The English Constitution*, p.xxiv.

48. See Richard Rose, *Governing Without Consensus*, p. 244.

49. "Into the Golden Future," *Sunday Times* (London), 7 August 1977.

50. See e.g. Samuel Brittan, "The Economic Contradictions of Democracy," *British Journal of Political Science*, 5:2, pp. 129-159; Anthony King, ed., *Why Is Britain Becoming Harder to Govern?* (London: BBC Publications, 1976).

51. Louis Moss, *People and Government*, p. 23. See also Richard Rose, "Ordinary People in Extraordinary Economic Circumstances," in Rose, ed., *Challenge to Governance* (London: Sage Publications, 1980), pp. 151-174.

52. Richard Rose and Harve Mossawir, "Voting and Elections: A Functional Analysis," *Political Studies* 15:2 (1967), pp. 173-201.

CHAPTER VI

Mass Political Socialization

People who learn slowly learn only what they must. The best security for a people doing their duty is that they should not know anything else to do.

POLITICAL SOCIALIZATION IS the process by which the values and beliefs of the political culture are transmitted from one generation to the next through experiences in the family, at school, and at work. The socialization process influences the antisystem views of the youthful radical as well as the positive allegiance of the ordinary adult. Because of the continuity of English institutions, many values transmitted through political socialization antedate the birth of an individual.

Political socialization is a continuing process. In childhood, the effects are conservative, inasmuch as a new generation learns from elders about the political system. By the time a person is 18, the minimum age for voting, a number of political values and beliefs have been developed. Adulthood offers many opportunities to think again; it may reinforce childhood learning or cause people to act differently from their parents' generation. Political events are also an important force for change. For example, war has a major impact on the mass of the population. In peacetime such events as the split or merger of parties presents voters with a choice that previously was not available. Individuals are always open to learning new ideas or altering old ones—but as people become older, the weight of prior experience becomes greater, and older adults are less likely to change established political outlooks.

Everyone in English society has a multiplicity of roles, such as spouse and parent, worker and consumer, and taxpayer and beneficiary of public services. Most people do not view their lives in terms of what can be achieved in politics. Instead of speaking of people as voters, it is more accurate to speak of the behavior of ordinary individuals in electoral situations. Many institutions can influence political outlooks even though they are not explicitly political in intent. Very few parents have children for the good of the party. Schools are established to teach children reading, writing, and other skills valued in nonpolitical contexts. Neighbors may influence political outlooks, but a house is rarely chosen for political reasons. Parties are the major social institution primarily concerned with political socialization.

What a person learns about politics more directly affects behavior than does how an outlook is acquired. In England a history of legitimate government emphasizes support for authority and compliance with basic political laws; as Bagehot said, people hardly "know anything else to do." By contrast, in Northern Ireland youths are socialized into conflict. The political division of labor is also influenced by socialization. Children learn early that people differ from each other, and these differences gradually become relevant politically. A young person learns to identify differences between political parties and between roles in the political system.

The socialization of the mass of the population is so different from that of active politicians that the two groups are best examined in separate chapters. This chapter concentrates upon mass political socialization. As the first section emphasizes, the great majority of adults are only voters; they are more likely to participate in politics by receiving benefits from the welfare state than by actively voicing demands through party politics. Succeeding sections consider in turn the influence of socialization experiences: family and generation, gender, schooling, and class. The concluding section assesses the combined effect of all these influences upon political attitudes and behavior.

LIMITS OF PARTICIPATION

When the majority of English influence government they are likely to use actions, not words. Popular sayings about voting with your feet or voting with your pocketbook have real meaning in the economy, for actions by consumers affect price levels, and actions by businessmen affect investment for economic growth. Citizens often voice demands for public services by actions taken without political intent. When people who formerly relied upon public transportation buy cars, the extra traffic they add to the roads constitutes a demand that something be done about the road network that they overload. When people have larger families, the increase in the number of children is a pressure to increase the number of teachers and schools.

If all activities of citizens are defined as political behavior, then everyone is involved in politics as both a subject of government and as a recipient of public services. Everyone is expected to obey laws and to pay taxes. Government provides a wide variety of benefits for individuals and families: health care from birth to old age, education in youth, a pension in old age, and a host of other social services. So taken for granted are these familiar programs of the welfare state that they are often thought of as nonpolitical. A child at school or an elderly person visiting a doctor does not think of himself or herself as participating in politics. Yet in both instances the services consumed are authorized, organized, and paid for by government.

Nearly nine-tenths of families are currently receiving at least one benefit of major importance from government, benefits that would cost weeks or months of wages if purchased in the market (Table VI.1). The average household receives 2.3 welfare benefits, for example, having a council house and using subsidized public transport, or drawing a pension and receiving National Health Service treatment. No one service is of concern to a majority of families at one point in time, but in the course of a lifetime nearly everyone

TABLE VI.1 *Families Receiving a Major Social Benefit*

	Receive %	Do not receive %
Dependent on public transport	38	62
Pension	36	64
Regular treatment doctor	35	65
Education	34	66
Housing	30	70
Hospital care in past year	29	71
Unemployment benefit	23	77
Personal social services	5	95
% of all families	89	11

Source: Calculated by the author from data reported in *Gallup Political Index* No. 285 (May, 1984) pp. 22-35.

draws upon many major services of government. Independence of major state benefits is a temporary phase in the life cycle. The small minority not currently benefiting from a major public service—for example a young single person with good health and a car, living in a privately rented flat—is likely to marry, start a family, and rely upon public education, health services, and eventually upon a pension in old age.[1]

Three ways in which individuals can participate in politics are examined here: voting, membership in an organization that can act as a pressure group, and standing as a candidate at an election. Given the small number of elected offices, mass participation in politics is limited.

Voting. The opportunity for one individual to exercise influence in an electorate of 43 million is very limited; nonetheless, voting in a parliamentary election is the one way in which the great majority of people actively participate in national politics. Almost every British citizen eighteen years old or over is eligible to vote. Registration is undertaken by local government officials, and the register is revised annually, thus avoiding the American situation of a large fraction of the electorate being unable to vote because they have not registered.[2] Election day is not a legal holiday, but widely dispersed polling stations, compact territory, and the individual citizen's sense of duty bring a high turnout of voters by American although not by European standards.

In the twelve general elections since 1950, turnout has averaged nearly 77 percent of the electoral register; in 1987 the turnout was 75 percent of the electorate. Many who do not vote are prevented from doing so by temporary illness or holidays. There is no substantial group of people who persistently refuse to vote because of apathy or disaffection. Englishmen are well advised to vote when a parliamentary election is held. Casting a vote for one candidate for one seat in the House of Commons is the only chance there is to participate in a nationwide ballot.[3]

For more than three-quarters of the population, voting is the maximum expression of political interest. Only 6 percent say they are very interested in politics, and 11 percent discuss politics frequently. The majority of the electorate has no interest in politics and discusses politics only occasionally if at all.[4]

Local government elections offer individuals a second opportunity to vote. Unlike in the United States, in England local electors are not allowed to vote on a host of tax and bond issues or referendum questions, or for a mayor or city manager. Since most councillors are nominated by parties, a voter has a choice between competing teams of local partisans. Participation in local election is very limited. Only two in five voters turn out to vote in local elections. In 1979, when district council elections were held the same day as a parliamentary election, the turnout was abnormally high, 77 percent; the following year, when there was no national election, turnout fell to 40 percent.[5]

Local government offers unique opportunities for political participation because it is near at hand. A person does not need to give up a full-time job or travel in order to be a member of the local council. Furthermore, local government delivers services that are immediately and visibly of concern, such as education, housing, roads, refuse collection, and social services. About one person in twenty tells a survey interviewer that he or she has thought of becoming a candidate for the local council. But the number of people who are actually councillors at any one time is about 0.06 percent of the electorate. People who have thought about standing for the council say they do not follow through because they do not have the time or good health to do so; they lack the self-confidence and temperament; have insufficient knowledge and interest in local politics.[6]

Group Membership. As well as representation through MPs and councillors, an individual can be represented by organizations that act as pressure groups, presenting demands for government action in the name of their members. Tens of thousands of British organizations have a total membership covering 61 percent of the electorate. But most organizations do not recruit members on political grounds, nor would they describe themselves as political institutions. The most common type of organization is a leisure, social, or sports club. About one in five voters sees himself or herself as a member of an organization concerned with public issues. One elector in seven reports holding an office or belonging to the local committee of an organization that has the potential to act as a political pressure group.[7]

Political parties provide another means by which individuals can participate in national politics. The Conservative and Labour parties have long maintained constituency associations throughout England, and the Social and Liberal Democrats seek to do so. Parties seek as many members as are willing to join. With a little effort, a person can become a ward secretary of a local party or a member of its general management committee. Political parties define membership by dues paid to constituency organizations. The majority of English people identify with a political party, but not so strongly that they become dues-paying members. In the Labour Party, only 5 percent of the party's 6 million nominal members join the party themselves. (The great bulk of Labour Party members are affiliated by trade unions, who give a portion of union dues to the party, unless an individual takes the trouble to contract out of the union's wholesale affiliation of members.) The Conservatives do not know how many members they have; estimates are that the party has about a million dues-payers. The membership of the Alliance parties has been less than the individual membership of the Labour Party. Only 3 percent or 4 percent of the electorate belongs to a political party, and for most party members, paying annual dues is the extent of their participation.[8]

Local politics is kept alive by the efforts of a small number of political activists for whom politics is an avocation. A survey by Market and Opinion Research International (MORI) classifies 7 percent of the electorate as activists taking part in at least five of ten common political activities such as voting, helping in fund-raising efforts, urging people to vote, holding office in an organization, advising people to contact their MP, making public talks, and presenting their views to an MP. The activists are almost evenly divided among the parties. While not an exact social cross-section of the population, activists do include substantial numbers from all ages, classes, and educational backgrounds.[9]

Ad hoc protest groups appear sporadically in local and national politics. Many of the problems that cause concern are such municipal services as housing, education, social services, and planning. In addition, some people may be temporarily activated by an issue that concerns them directly, for example, a road problem on their housing estate, a problem at the local primary school, or the prospect of an unwelcome building being constructed near their house. Once the issue is resolved, they again become politically inactive.[10]

The concentration of politics in London allows London-based protest groups to appear as nationwide organizations. In a metropolitan area of more than 10 million inhabitants, it is not difficult to attract hundreds of people to a protest meeting on almost any issue. One requires a cause, a speaker with a name or status, and money to hire a hall and advertise the meeting. Overall, only 6 percent of the electorate say they have taken part in a lawful street demonstration, and even fewer in illegal protests.[11] The effect of this relatively small percentage is much multiplied insofar as demonstrations become media events, reported nationwide.

The great majority of English people participate in national politics by voting and by belonging to an organization which may or may not act as a pressure group (Table VI.2). The proportion regularly involved in politics is 3 percent to 14 percent, depending upon the indicator selected.[12] The evidence can be interpreted in two contrasting ways. One can emphasize that as many as 2 million or 3 million people are political activists or one can say that about 40 million people are not political activists. Whichever emphasis is used, for the mass of citizens political socialization need only provide sufficient knowledge and motivation to vote.

INFLUENCE OF FAMILY AND GENERATION

The family's influence comes first in chronological order; political attitudes learned within the family become intertwined with primary family loyalties. A child may learn little of what the Labour or Conservative Party stands for except that it is the party of Mom and Dad. Family circumstances also determine the class milieu in which a child grows up.

Parental Influence. While family upbringing can influence political outlooks, politics is not important in most families. A MORI survey during the 1983 general election found that among married

TABLE VI.2 *Involvement in National Politics*

	Estimated	% Adults
Eligible to vote	43,000,000	98
Voters, 1983	32,500,000	75
Organization members	26,000,000	61
Officer of organization	5,500,000	14
Political activists	2,800,000	7
Very interested in politics	2,500,000	6
Protest demonstrators	2,500,000	6
Individual party members	1,500,000	3

Sources: As cited in text; official statistics.

couples, only 55 percent said that their spouse voted for the same party, 34 percent did not know how their spouse voted, and 10 percent reported that their spouse voted for a competing party.

In studies of voting in the 1960s, David Butler and Donald Stokes argued that the central importance of family made it natural for a large proportion of the electorate to identify in youth with the party that their parents favored and to continue voting for the same party throughout their adult life. Insofar as parents also transmit their class identification to their children and class is also an influence upon voting, the importance of parents is reinforced. Voters brought up in middle-class Conservative homes would be expected to become middle-class Conservatives, and those in working-class Labour homes to identify with Labour.[13]

A family-oriented theory of political socialization must be rejected, for more than half the electorate do *not* vote as their parents did.[14] A third of the electorate say they do not know how both parents voted or that their parents identified with different parties. There is also a tendency for some people to misremember their parents' views, altering their recollections so that parents are said to favor their current party preference.[15] Only 38 percent of the electorate say they know how both parents voted and vote the same, and another 5 percent know how one parent voted and follow in his or her steps. Because less than half the support that a party needs to win an election is delivered at birth, each party has an incentive to seek floating voters who are not lifelong supporters.

A religious identification will also be acquired from parents, and until 1918 this was a substantial influence upon voting. Families attached to the state-established Church of England tended to be Conservative, and nonconformist Protestants to favor the Liberals. The Labour Party took over from the Liberal Party the support of nonconformists and Irish Roman Catholics, who disliked Conservative opposition to a united Ireland. The political importance of religion has waned with the decline of church attendance. Today a quarter of the electorate say that they do not belong to any religion, more than half have only a weak religious attachment, and one-fifth attend church at least once a month. Only half of Britons raised in churchgoing homes continue to be regular churchgoers themselves.

Notwithstanding the decline in religion, it retains a little influence on party loyalties. After controlling for the effect of class, Conservatives do disproportionately well among Anglicans, and Labour does relatively well among Roman Catholics. The Alliance parties have tended to do a little better than average among nonconformists. While consistent with historical alignments, the overall effect of religion upon voting is minor today.[16]

Age and Generations. Every citizen goes through a series of stages in the life cycle from childhood through adulthood to old age. Politically, youth is the most malleable, because young people have yet to form firm political attitudes, lacking the experience of older adults. Young people are readier to support new parties, such as the nationalist parties in Scotland and Wales or the Alliance parties. Moreover, younger people are readier to be influenced by temporary movements of opinion between established parties. In the 1987 general election, when Labour fought a good campaign, young voters were 5 percent more Labour than average and older voters 3 percent more Conservative.[17] Younger people are also more predisposed to engage in unconventional or unorthodox forms of political protest.

Whereas life-cycle influences are temporary, generational differences that result from the impact of distinctive historical events are lifelong. Elderly voters can remember the interwar depression clearly, and also the Second World War. By contrast, middle-aged voters are likely to have had their political ideas first formed in a period of peace and prosperity. Voters in their twenties have formed initial political outlooks in a period of economic recession and uncertainty. The median voter at the 1987 general election was born just after the Second World War and started work when the Beatles and Harold Wilson first became popular in the early 1960s. By the time of the first general election of the 1990s, more than a third of the electorate will have cast its first vote after the world recession hit Britain hard in 1974 and the party system had become a system of multiparty competition.

Extrapolating the political future from generational differences is very risky.[18] Age-related differences are matters of degree, not kind, and are often small. Parties and pressure groups normally draw support from people of every age. Pressure groups specific to one age bracket, such as the National Union of Students, represent minorities and suffer from a rapid turnover of members. Because a given generation of eighteen- to twenty-one-year-old students changes every four years, its political character can also change rapidly. Moreover, such is the conserving effect of intergenerational socialization that the political attitudes of young people differ by only a few percent from the political views of their elders (see Table XIV.1).

GENDER: SIMILARITIES AND DIFFERENCES

In law the rights of men and women to participate in politics were made equal by the grant of the vote to women age 30 or above in 1918 and at the same age as men in 1928. Most women voting today grew up in a home in which their mother as well as father had the right to vote. Politicians too have spent all their lives appealing for the support of an electorate that contains 2.8 percent more women than men because women live longer.

All political parties actively seek the votes of both women and men, making their primary appeal to the electorate by stressing such issues as the economy without regard to gender. At the 1987 general election, the Conservative Party and the Alliance had no section of their manifesto specifically directed at women; Labour had a three-paragraph section. When a party addresses an issue such as education or foreign policy, it emphasizes concerns of both men and women.

At each general election, women divide their votes between parties in much the same way as men. From 1950 until 1979 women were slightly more inclined than men to favor the Conservatives, but the differences of a few percent could easily reflect the fact that women are disproportionately elderly and churchgoing, two pro-Conservative categories. In 1983 and 1987 the Gallup Poll found women slightly less likely to favor the Conservatives, even though the party had a woman as a leader, and slightly more likely to favor the Alliance.[19] Margaret Thatcher's leadership confounds conventional thinking about gender issues in politics, for feminists assume that gender issues predispose women to vote left. Margaret Thatcher is indubitably a woman and indubitably rejects the left and feminist politics.

When the political attitudes of men and women are compared, similarity is also the rule. Women divide in their opinions about a wide range of topics, and divide in almost the same proportions as men (Table VI.3). For a range of twenty different questions on subjects from inflation and unemployment to nuclear weapons and abortion, there is an average difference of only 5 percent between men and women. Three-quarters of the differences are statistically insignificant.

TABLE VI.3 *Similarity of Views of Men and Women about Issues*

	Men	Women	Differences (Women–Men)
		(Percent endorsing)	
Increase public spending to reduce unemployment	80	80	0
Take Britain out of Common Market	34	34	0
Withdraw troops from Northern Ireland now	48	49	1
Send coloured immigrants home	47	46	−1
Spend more money on health service	96	94	−2
Tenants have right to buy council house	75	75	2
Government influencing wages and prices	74	76	2
Shift power from London to regions, local govt	56	54	−2
Re-establish selective grammar schools	48	46	−2
Spend more to combat pollution	86	83	−3
Make abortion more widely available	44	40	−4
Spend whatever needed to defend Falklands	41	37	−4
Redistribute wealth to poorer people	65	70	5
Do more to promote equal opportunities for women	72	78	6
Cut public spending to reduce inflation	43	49	6
Unilateral nuclear disarmament	28	35	7
Bring back death penalty	70	62	−8
Give more aid to poor Afro–Asian countries	48	57	9
Introduce stricter laws to regulate unions	42	53	11
Reduce sex and nudity on TV, films, magazines	40	64	24
Average difference			5

Source: Calculated by the author from Gallup Poll survey, 12–17 November 1986.

Similarities between the opinions of men and women occur on issues that might be thought of as feminist issues, such as abortion, as well as for such socioeconomic issues as council housing. The views of men and women are virtually identical on so-called tough proposals such as sending colored immigrants to their countries of origin as well as for so-called tender proposals such as spending more to combat unemployment. The greatest difference of opinion—about the amount of sex and nudity in the media—is a limited difference. There is no mass base in political attitudes for a feminist political party.[20]

Women and men differ much more in their attitudes toward work than in views of politics. When women are asked their views about work, the majority state that a career is less important than the home. An NOP (National Opinion Poll) survey found that 89 percent of women of working age considered a woman's first duty should be to children, as against 10 percent saying it should be equally to a job and to children. Housewives thinking of returning to work are more likely to be looking for a part-time job than a full-time job.[21] Women predominate in public employment; women are 47 percent of public sector workers as against 42 percent of the total labor force. Women are 89 percent of employees in social services, 78 percent in the National Health Service, and 72 percent in education. Only in the armed services and in nationalized industries are women underrepresented. Women are much less likely to be employed at managerial levels in the health service, in local government, or in Whitehall.[22]

EDUCATION

Although there is no formal educational requirement to vote or hold public office, education has the potential to influence political outlooks, for young people are in school for more than a decade before they first become eligible to vote. Moreover, schools teach young people about adult roles, including that of the citizen. Since the Constitution and national identity are taken for granted, there is little pressure to make education for citizenship a major goal of education, as has been the case in the United States.

Education has always assumed inequality, for students differ greatly in their performance on examinations, and the national examination standards are such that half of secondary pupils have not been expected to pass any national examination. Speaking as the Conservative Minister of Education, Lord Hailsham argued:

> Equality of opportunity in education or life does not mean either equality of performance or ability or uniformity of character. The object of education is to bring out differences just as much as to impose standards, and the democracy of the future will not be a drab mass of second-rate people in which distinction of intellect or character is

described as eggheadness. It will be a society governed by its graduates—science and arts and social sciences—and largely run by people who put public service in front of enjoyment, profit or leisure.[23]

By contrast, Socialists have viewed schools as institutions for changing society by reducing social differences.

For more than two decades after the 1944 Education Act made secondary schooling free and compulsory, pupils were segregated according to academic ability by an examination at age 11-plus. About one-quarter attended academic grammar schools, which concentrated upon educating pupils to pass external examinations up to the standard of university entrance. The remainder were said to have failed, attending secondary modern schools giving an education for manual work or routine white-collar jobs. In 1965 a Labour government circular requested that all local authorities reorganize secondary education, abolishing the selective 11-plus examination. Gradually the policy became effective throughout the country; today only 3 percent of secondary pupils were in selective state grammar schools. The comprehensive school is now the norm for this generation of youths and young adults.

Secondary schools discriminate by social status as well as intelligence. Today, about 7 percent of young people are in public schools, that is, private, fee-charging schools independent of the state. Most of these schools are chosen by parents in the belief that they offer a better formal academic education than neighboring state schools.[24] Whereas Americans may seek better education for their children by moving house to a superior suburban school district, the limited variation within the state system causes English parents to seek a better education by paying for private education.

Higher education further differentiates young people, for only one in four youths leaving secondary school goes on to further study, and only 8 percent of all young people follow a degree course at a university or polytechnic.[25] In 1956 half of English university students were attending one of three institutions: Oxford, Cambridge, or the University of London. A university degree was not required for entering business, for a commission in the army, or to become a lawyer. In consequence of higher postwar birthrates and a rising demand for higher education, in the 1960s dozens of new universities were created; sixteen of the thirty-four English universities were founded between 1961 and 1967. State-financed scholarships, adjusted according to financial needs of students, have greatly

increased the total number of graduates in English society. Reciprocally, young people who have not attended a university now face
barriers to career advancement, for many jobs formerly open to
those who leave secondary school now recruit only university
graduates.

The stratification of English education has encouraged many
social scientists to study the political effects of educational differences. The hypothesis is that the more education a person has, the
more likely a person is to favor the Conservatives as the party favoring those with the ability to win middle-class jobs; the less education, the more likely a person is to favor Labour as the party identifying with the mass of uneducated voters.[26]

In the 1980s, the Conservative Party has won the largest amount
of support from people at all levels of education, but it has not done
increasingly well as educational attainments rise. Among the majority of the electorate with only a minimum of state education (leaving school at 14, 15, or 16, according to the legal requirement for
compulsory education in their youth), the Conservatives secured 43
percent of the vote in 1987. Among those with a university degree,
Conservative support fell to 33 percent, less than the support for the
Alliance parties.[27]

Because people with more education are likelier to hold middle-
class jobs, it is desirable to control for class difference when examining the relation between level of education and party preference.
This shows that for persons with a minimum education, the likelihood of voting Conservative rather than Labour rises with social
class. In 1987 Labour secured 44 percent of the vote of semiskilled
and unskilled manual workers with a minimum of education and
only 12 percent of the votes of persons with a minimum of education but solid middle-class status. Among Alliance voters, support
was more likely to rise with education than with social class. There
was only a 4 percent difference in support for the Alliance in 1987
between middle-class and working-class voters. However, within the
middle class there was a 10 percent difference between those with a
minimum of education and persons with some further education.
Labour too did better with university graduates than with less educated middle-class voters.

One explanation for well educated voters not being as conservative as their class is that teachers in further education are a left-wing
group. In 1987 a MORI survey of teachers in further education
found only 17 percent favoring the Conservatives, as against 39 per-

cent Labour and the same proportion the Alliance parties. The median lecturer is thus a supporter of a middle-of-the-road anti-Conservative party but not left-wing on principle. The influence of teachers is not determining, for while primary and secondary school teachers are also anti-Conservative, those whose education stops at secondary school tend to favor the Conservatives. In 1987, only 24 percent of school teachers favored the Conservatives, as against 28 percent favoring Labour and 46 percent the Alliance,[28] a pattern very different from their former pupils. The reason for teachers being anti-Conservative in 1987 appears to be ad hoc, a temporary reaction against the perceived government cuts on education spending and further plans for reorganizing education against the recommendations of those running the system.

The major educational and political changes of the postwar era have ended the old presumption that more education caused people to move to the right politically.[29] As access to further education has broadened, more and more young people from working class Labour-voting homes have graduated from university. Concurrently, there has been a national rise in support for third-force parties, such as the Alliance, offering an alternative between the two established parties. The evidence of the 1980s is that the tenth of the electorate with further education are inclined to be floating voters, temporarily favoring the Alliance parties.

CLASS

To speak of class is to invoke an idea as diffuse as it is meant to be pervasive. Sometimes it refers to one of a number of not necessarily related socioeconomic characteristics such as occupation, income, consumption patterns, or education. Sometimes it refers to the cumulative effect of all socialization experiences, which are assumed to provide a clear-cut differentiation between middle-class and manual workers in politics as well as at work. Occupation is the most common indicator of class in England and will be employed henceforth here. But this does not mean that everyone in the same occupational stratum is identical in every other respect. Whereas a farmer usually lives in a community where his occupation is part of a network of social relations with family, friends, and neighbors, most social relationships of a person working in central London but living in a suburb are remote from work.

Nearly every definition of occupational class places more than three-fifths of English people in the working class and a third to two-fifths in the middle class.[30] It is also important to distinguish differences among nonmanual workers. About one-sixth of the electorate is in the solid middle class, which can be divided into two groups, persons in leading positions in the professions, major profit-making and non-profit-making organizations and government, and a larger group holding responsible posts in business and the public sector. The lower middle class hold routine white-collar jobs; this group is larger than the other two sections of the middle class. Within the working class, sociologists often discriminate between skilled workers, who have specialist skills, for example, an electrician, as against semiskilled and unskilled groups.

Class Does Not Equal Party. For most of the twentieth century political behavior and party competition in England have been interpreted in terms of class equals party. The Conservative Party has been perceived as the party of middle-class interests supported by middle-class voters, and the Labour Party as the party of working-class interests supported by working-class voters. The viewpoint was summed up thus by Peter Pulzer: "Class is the basis of British party politics; all else is embellishment and detail."[31]

Party politicians only half accepted the idea of the dominance of class. Labour politicians expected to benefit, as the working class is a large majority of the electorate. But Labour politicians carefully campaigned for middle-class support too; the party constitution describes Labour as a party for all workers by hand and brain, that is, 99 percent of the electorate. The Conservatives have always sought and won a substantial minority of working-class votes; this is a necessary condition of the party winning an election. Political leaders in both parties rejected Marxist ideas of class conflict; class differences have been treated as capable of resolution by political bargaining. Major changes in society have been expected to come from processes of economic growth and social change deemed beneficial by all classes, such as a higher level of education, home ownership, and income security.

A multiplicity of changes have reduced such influence as class had upon voting a generation ago. First of all, the middle class has increased in size as against the working class, and a majority of electors now combine characteristics formerly associated with only one class. Working-class homeowners and middle-class trade unionists are inconsistent with the stereotypes of class politics in England. Secondly, the rise of the Alliance parties has offered voters a third alternative, a party not easily aligned with any class. Thirdly, voters are becoming much more ready to change their party preferences, and floating between parties tends to occur independently of changes in occupational class.

At the 1987 election, there was a weak relationship between occupational class and voting, and it was often negative. Among working-class electors, no party won as much as half the vote. If Labour claims to be the party of unskilled workers because it wins the largest share of the vote of this group, then by the same standard the Conservatives can claim to be the party of skilled manual workers (Table VI.4). The tendency to support a particular party was strongest in the smallest social stratum, the solid middle class; even then only four in seven of this group voted Conservative. The apparent dominance of the Conservative vote there is due to its two opponents dividing the non-Conservative vote. The Alliance parties consistently win a fifth to a quarter of the vote in each class. Altogether, less than half the electorate voted as would be predicted by their class.

The link between class models of politics and party preference is limited for at least three reasons. First of all, awareness of class origins is not translated into an active consciousness of class today. Whereas 96 percent of the electorate can identify their parents' class, when asked to identify their own class, almost half do not think of themselves as being either middle class or working class. Less than one in seven of the electorate conforms to the ideal-type model of a middle-class person (nonmanual occupation, education qualification, homeowner, no trade union membership, and subjective middle-class identification) or its working-class counterpart. Most peo-

TABLE VI.4 *Between and within Class Divisions of the Vote, 1987*

	Con.	Labour (% within row)	Alliance
Middle class	(52)	(20)	(26)
Solid middle (16% of electorate)	56	17	26
Lower middle (23%)	50	23	26
Working class	(37)	(39)	(21)
Skilled (30%)	44	33	21
Semi-, unskilled (31%)	31	45	21

Source: Calculated from 1987 Gallup Poll campaign surveys. (Rows do not add to 100% because of omission of support for other parties.)

ple today have a mixture of middle-class and working-class attributes.[32]

Secondly, class is no longer perceived as very important in social relations. When the 1979 British Election Survey asked people whether or not they thought it would be difficult to have friends in other classes, 67 percent said it would make no difference, and only 6 percent saw it as making a lot of difficulties. Similarly, when the Gallup Poll asks people to describe good things and bad things about each class, most people show a lack of any clearly defined image of class; 55 percent cannot describe any faults in the middle class and 50 percent find no faults in the working class. Similar proportions have nothing good to say about either class, because class is not central to the way in which people are often labeled, favorably or unfavorably.[33]

Thirdly, even when there is an awareness of class differences, they are not normally translated into a sense of class grievances leading to conflict. Only 6 percent told the 1979 British Election Study that they thought that everyone should have much the same wage regardless of their skill or responsibility. More than five-sixths think that people who get ahead in life do so because of their ability. Only one in ten think that social background is of primary importance in a person getting ahead in Britain today, and less than one-tenth of the electorate see politics in terms of opposing class interests.[34]

THE CUMULATIVE EFFECT

The most distinctive feature of political socialization in England is that there are fewer social divisions of political relevance than in many European countries. Language creates a political gulf in Belgium and Canada. Religious differences have divided societies politically into groups of churchgoers and anticlericals or Protestants and Catholics in France, Italy, Austria, the Netherlands, and Belgium, and also in Northern Ireland. Nor is there anything in England comparable to the political division between races in the United States.[35]

The degree of social homogeneity within England is also underscored by comparison with other nations of the United Kingdom. Language socializes Welsh people into two different groups, a bilingual fifth who speak Welsh as well as English and a majority who are simply English-speakers. In Scotland the division of youths into separate state-supported Catholic and non-Catholic schools emphasizes differences of religion. In Northern Ireland differences of religion are compounded by conflicts of national identity. By contrast, nearly everyone in England speaks English and is indifferent to nominal religious differences. Thus, social characteristics that create political divisions in many countries are in England a source of common experiences.

Class differences have been considered important because they are the only substantial division within English society. Like every other industrial society, England has a social structure divided into manual and nonmanual workers. But class differences have not been translated into political differences to the degree implied by many sociological theories and much political rhetoric. The largest group in the electorate—white urban Protestant manual workers—divide their support almost evenly between the Conservatives and Labour, and the Alliance also secures a significant fraction of their vote.

Lifetime Learning. To understand the cumulative effect of political socialization, we need to think of it as a lifetime process of learning. In the course of a lifetime, every person is subject to many experiences, some giving clear cues to party preferences and others without any partisan bias. Politically important influences can be grouped under four headings. Preadult socialization in the family and adult experiences in society come first in time and are central to an individual's life. Sociological theories postulate that these experiences, creating and sustaining class differences, are also central to politics. To test whether or not this is so, it is also necessary to examine the influence of political principles that can be distilled by individuals independently of class and family and what voters learn by observing the current performance of parties and party leaders. Political science theories usually emphasize the importance of explicit and current political learning, whereas sociological theories infer political behavior from socioeconomic characteristics.

The cumulative effect of political socialization is shown in Figure VI.1; it links the different experiences that individuals have, from preadult socialization to exposure to an election campaign. To test the influence that each step in the socialization process has, we can use stepwise multiple regression, which calculates how much (or how little) of the variance in vote between the Conservative and Labour parties is explained by each set of experiences, after taking into account the influence of preceding stages in a lifetime of learn-

FIGURE VI.1 *Cumulative Model of A Voter's Lifetime Learning*

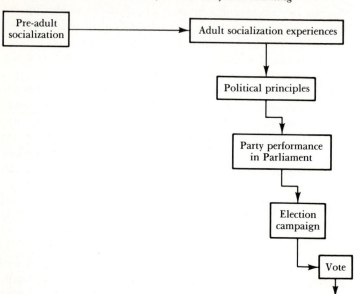

Landmark dates in the life history of a voter

Source: Richard Rose and Ian McAllister, *Voters Begin to Choose* (London: Sage Publications, 1986), p. 127.

ing. Collectively, the whole process accounts for seventy-seven percent of the variance in the vote of the two parties.[36]

Preadult socialization. (Explains 14 percent of the vote.) The party identification of parents is the single most important influence in the home, explaining seven percent of the voting of adults after they have left the family home. Party identification is twice as important as parents' class, which often does not determine party loyalties. Religion and education are each minor secondary influences upon voting.

Socioeconomic interests. (Explains 12 percent of the vote.) When the relative importance of occupational class is tested against cross-class influences, class adds only 2 percent to the explanation of party preference, less than the influence of housing, trade union membership, or living in Scotland or Wales. Housing is consistently the most important current influence, adding 5 percent to the explanation of voting, above and beyond that provided by preadult experiences.[38] The Conservative Party is the party of homeowners, whereas Labour is the party of tenants in municipal council housing that concentrates largely semiskilled and unskilled workers and their families in low status neighborhoods.

Political principles. (Explains 29 percent of the vote.) Political principles are persisting political attitudes relevant to a variety of different day-to-day issues. Principles link experiences and interests more or less remote from politics with a party preference. Unlike attitudes about current issues, principles concerning Socialism, the welfare state, race relations, or traditional morality can persist from decade to decade, and voters' principles have been stable for more than a decade, notwithstanding substantial changes in votes.[39]

Socialism—attitudes toward the nationalization of industries, the power of trade unions, government measures to redistribute wealth, and so on—is the most electorally important political principle, but not in the way that Labour would like. It explains more than one-quarter of the variance between Conservative and Labour voters. Because more voters are anti-Socialist than pro, when socialism is the issue, Labour loses votes in competition with opponents. Attitudes toward the social welfare services of government cannot affect voting much, for nearly the whole of the electorate favors government action to prevent poverty and to maintain the health service. Attitudes toward race relations and traditional morality have no effect upon voting because the parties normally avoid taking official positions on such "hot" issues, treating them as matters of conscience. Moreover, divisions between the tolerant and anti-immigrant and between permissive and conventional moralists split each party's supporters.

Current performance of parties. (Explains 21 percent of the vote.) For the duration of a Parliament the Opposition seeks new ways to attract voters so that it can win office at the next election, and the government seeks to avoid falling out of favor. Parties can change their leaders, a governing party can make an impact by its performance in office and the Opposition by raising hopes for future improvements, unexpected events can influence votes, and an election campaign is meant to force voters to concentrate their attention upon a choice of parties. Altogether, the current performance of the parties explains one-fifth of the vote; this is more than the influence of more remote socialization experiences, but less than that of political principles by which current performance is judged.

While the media treats election campaigns as a competition between leading personalities, only 6 percent in the variance of the Conservative-Labour vote could be thus explained. The Conservatives benefited more from the weakness of the Labour leader, Michael Foot, than from the effect of Margaret Thatcher's personality. The record of the Conservative government in the past four years influenced 7 percent of the electorate, and expectations of what the parties would do in the next Parliament also influenced 7 percent of the vote. An election campaign has very little influence upon voting, because it is an event of a few weeks in the lifetime of a voter.

Understanding political behavior as the cumulative consequence of a lifetime of socialization experiences avoids reducing behavior to a reflex response to a single cause. Every person brings to current events a set of experiences for assessing what the parties say and do. Voters are usually not much moved by a television program featuring a party leader or even by such an event as the Falklands War.[37] What a person has *already* experienced is a better predictor of how a person will act politically than the latest news item or carefully staged political event. Just as political institutions ensure continuity in Westminster, so the combination of political principles, stable economic interests, and preadult experiences gives individuals a firm foundation by which to assess the current performance of parties. When individuals do change their political views and vote, this is not the reflection of a whim of the moment; it is an immediate response grounded in a lifetime of political learning.

NOTES

1. See Richard Rose, "The State's Contribution to the Welfare Mix," in Rose and Shiratori, eds., *The Welfare State East and West* (New York: Oxford University Press, 1986).

2. Legislation proposing the introduction of a community charge or poll tax on every adult is likely to reduce the accuracy of the electoral register, as some people seek to evade the poll tax by leaving their name off the electoral register.

3. See Ivor Crewe, Tony Fox, and Jim Alt, "Non-Voting in British General Elections, 1966-October 1974," in Colin Crouch, ed., *British Political Sociology Yearbook*, Vol. 3, (London: Croom Helm, 1977) pp. 33-109.

4. See David Phillips, "Participation and Political Values," in Mark Abrams, David Gerard, and Noel Timms, eds., *Values and Social Change in Britain* (London: Macmillan, 1985), Table 6.1.

5. See W. L. Miller, "Local Electoral Behaviour," Committee of Inquiry into the Conduct of Local Authority Business, *The Local Government Elector* (London: HMSO, Cmnd. 9800, Research Vol. 3, 1986), Chapter 3.

6. See Mary Horton, *The Local Government Elector* (London: HMSO, 1967) chapters 5, 6; and Committee of Inquiry into the Conduct of Local Authority Business, *The Local Government Councillor* (London: HMSO, Cmnd. 9799, Vol. 3, 1986).

7. See Mary Horton, *The Local Government Elector,* pp. 113ff.

8. See the report of the Houghton Committee, *Financial Aid to Political Parties* (London: HMSO, Cmnd. 6601, 1976), pp. 31ff. See also *Gallup Political Index* No. 200 (March 1977), pp. 12–15.

9. See Robert M. Worcester, "The Hidden Activists," in Richard Rose, ed., *Studies in British Politics*, 3rd ed., and David Phillips, "Participation and Political Values," p. 153.

10. See, e.g., Robert E. Dowse and J. Hughes, "Sporadic Interventionists," *Political Studies*, 25:1 (1977); Paul E. Peterson and Paul Kantor, "Political Parties and Citizen Participation in English City Politics," *Comparative Politics*, 9:2 (1977); and Ken Young, "Attitudes to Local Government," in Committee of Inquiry into the Conduct of Local Authority Business, *The Local Government Elector*, Vol. 3.

11. See Alan C. Marsh, *Protest and Political Consciousness* (London: Sage, 1977), p. 45.

12. For a thorough statistical analysis of modes of participation supporting this conclusion, see George Moyser, Geraint Parry, and Neil Day, *Political Participation in Britain* (Manchester: University of Manchester Department of Government Research Report 21, 1986).

13. See David Butler and Donald Stokes, *Political Change in Britain*, 2nd ed. (London: Macmillan, 1974).

14. See Richard Rose and Ian McAllister, *Voters Begin to Choose* (London: Sage Publications, 1986), Chapter 6.

15. Cf. Hilde Himmelweit, Marianne Jaeger Biberian, and Janet Stockdale, "Memory for Past Vote; Implications of a Study of Bias in Recall," *British Journal of Political Science* 8:3 (1978), pp. 365–375; and Richard S. Katz, Richard G. Niemi, and David Newman, "Reconstructing Past Partisanship in Britain," *British Journal of Political Science* 10:4 (1980), pp. 505–515.

16. See Rose and McAllister, *Voters Begin to Choose*, Tables 4.7 and 6.7. On church attendance and religious identification, see the 1983 British Election Survey, Question 63. For historical and institutional views, see Kenneth Wald, *Crosses on the Ballot* (Princeton, N.J.: Princeton University Press, 1983); and K. N. Medhurst and G. H. Moyser, *Church and Politics in a Secular Age* (Oxford: Oxford Clarendon Press, 1988).

17. Calculated by the Gallup Poll from its 1987 campaign surveys (10,204 interviews).

18. For efforts to do so, see Butler and Stokes, *Political Change in Britain;* for a caution against doing so, see Rose and McAllister, *Voters Begin to Choose*, especially pp. 66–69 and Chapter 8.

19. See Rose and McAllister, *Voters Begin to Choose*, pp. 46ff, 69ff.

20. Cf. Pippa Norris, "Conservative Attitudes in Recent British Elections: An Emerging Gender Gap?" *Political Studies* 34:1 (1986), pp. 120–128.

21. NOP, *Review* (London: NOP Market Research No 46, February 1984), pp. 14ff; Sharon Witherspoon, "Sex Roles and Gender Issues," *British Social Attitudes: the 1985 Report*, p. 60.

22. See Richard Parry, "Britain: Stable Aggregates, Changing Composition," in R. Rose, *Public Employment in Western Nations* (Cambridge: Cambridge University Press, 1985) pp. 85–87.

23. "A Society Governed by Graduates," *The Times* (London), 24 January 1962. Cf. Raphaella Bilski, "Ideology and the Comprehensive Schools," *Political Quarterly*, 44:2 (1973).

24. See Tessa Blackstone and Irene Fox, "Why People Choose Private Schools," *New Society*, 29 June 1978.

25. For statistics on educational achievement, see the annual HMSO publication *Social Trends*, from which data cited here are taken.

26. For complementary hypotheses about the relationship of education to active participation in politics, see Chapter VII.

27. Calculated by the author from Gallup Poll data for the 1987 election; for 1983, see Rose and McAllister, *Voters Begin to Choose*, pp. 106ff.

28. See "Labour, Alliance Neck-and-Neck," *Times Higher Educational Supplement*, 5 June 1987; "Teacher Vote Goes to the Alliance," *Times* (London) *Educational Supplement*, 29 May 1987.

29. For data on 1970, when the link still held, see Richard Rose, "Britain: Simple Abstractions and Complex Realities," in R. Rose, ed., *Electoral Behavior* (New York: Free Press, 1974), Table 10. For detailed evidence on 1983, see Rose and McAllister, *Voters Begin to Choose*, Tables 6.3, 6.4.

30. The standard method of assigning classes in British voting studies is: groups A, B, the solid middle class; C1, the lower middle class; C2, the skilled working class, and D and E, manual workers. For a review of the suitability or unsuitability of different classification schema, see Rose and McAllister, *Voters Begin to Choose*, Chapter 3.

31. See Peter Pulzer, *Political Representation and Elections in Britain* (London: Allen and Unwin, 1967), p. 98. For a review of evidence showing the limited reality of this generalization see Richard Rose, *Class Does Not Equal Party; the Decline of a Model of British Voting* (Glasgow: U. of Strathclyde Studies in Public Policy No. 74, 1980).

32. Calculated from British Election Survey 1983. See Richard Rose, *Class Does Not Equal Party*, Table 13. Social change has also led sociologists to disagree among themselves about the appropriate classification schema for analyzing voting. Cf. Anthony Heath, Roger Jowell, and John Curtice, *How Britain Votes* (Oxford: Pergamon Press, 1985); and Patrick Dunleavy, "Class Dealignment in Britain Revisited," *West European Politics* 10:3 (1987) pp. 400–419.

33. Cf. *Gallup Political Index* No. 261 (May 1982) pp. 11ff, and NOP, *Bulletin* No. 109 (June 1972), pp. 17–18 for similar findings a decade earlier.

34. Martin Harrop, "Popular Conceptions of Mobility," *Sociology* 14:1 (1980), pp. 88–98; and Butler and Stokes, *Political Change in Britain*, 2nd ed., pp. 90ff.

35. See Richard Rose, "Comparability in Electoral Studies," in Rose, ed. *Electoral Behavior* (New York: Free Press, 1974), Table 1.

36. For full statistical details, see Rose and McAllister, *Voters Begin to Choose*, pp. 127ff.

37. David Sanders et al., "Government Popularity and the Falklands War," *British J. of Political Science* 17:3(1987) pp. 281–314.

38. For a sophisticated analysis of the limits of inferring party preferences from economic interests, see Mark Franklin and Edward Page, "A Critique of the Consumption Cleavage Approach in British Voting Studies," *Political Studies* 32:4 (1984), pp. 521–536.

39. See Rose and McAllister, *Voters Begin to Choose*, pp. 117ff.

CHAPTER VII

Recruiting Political Leaders

> *The principle of popular government is that the supreme power, the determining efficacy in matters political, resides in the people—not necessarily or commonly in the whole people, in the numerical majority, but in a chosen people, a picked and selected people. It is so in England.*

POLITICAL PARTICIPATION REFLECTS both individual aspirations and institutional opportunities. While every adult citizen is formally eligible to participate in politics, no one is compelled to do so, and the institutions of representative government strictly limit the number who can take positions of leadership. Everyone has the right to vote, but only 650 people can be MPs, and elective offices in local government are fewer than the proportion of persons with political aspirations.

The office comes before the individual; the institutions of government define the jobs for which politicians can compete. An individual wanting to be somebody must follow well established career lines that lead to the top in Westminster. The most visible path is to become active in party politics, then to become an MP, and finally to become a Cabinet minister. The less visible route is to enter the higher civil service and gradually rise to a position as a senior adviser to ministers. While political ambitions are not so different on opposite sides of the Atlantic, the offices that people seek and the methods used to win office are different. Americans campaign for Congress and the White House by means that strike English people as excessively energetic and costly. Building a political career in Whitehall while maintaining a stiff-upper-lip approach strikes Americans as odd.

An individual's political career depends upon his or her ability to do what is expected by those already in leadership positions. Expectations reflect institutionalized cultural values and beliefs about what kind of behavior is suitable for a political leader. An individual may enter politics wanting to change the party, the government, or the world. But even an individual with as strong a personality as Margaret Thatcher had no chance of imposing her views on government until after thirty years in party politics.

The recruitment of political leaders involves intensive socialization that differentiates all politicians, whatever their social origins, from nonpoliticians. Socialization in the family, school, or work influences general attitudes, whereas socialization in parties, local government, or Parliament, is on-the-job learning for specific jobs. As people are socialized into more and more important positions, they begin to change their outlook, reflecting what they learn about government and about politics as the art of the possible. As a Labour MP, and former left-wing rebel admitted, "I think instead of me turning this place inside out, they turned me inside out a little."[1]

In order to understand the recruitment of political leaders, we must first focus upon the offices that aspiring politicians can seek. Leadership positions are of two contrasting types, visible and invisible. Members of Parliament are the most visible politicians in the nation, and ministers are the visible leaders of government. Higher civil servants are the invisible influences behind ministerial thrones, advising ministers about the opportunities and pitfalls of leadership. Intermittent public persons are important behind the scenes; they are neither MPs nor civil servants, but act as occasional advisers, either publicly chairing government committees or in private consultations.

The process of political recruitment is inherently discriminatory: less than 0.01 percent of the electorate can hold leading political positions, and only a few hundred are at any one time in top positions in Whitehall.[2] In order to understand political recruitment, the first section of this chapter examines the social factors—family, gender, and education—that predispose a small number of people to seek political office when most do not. The route to the top for an MP or minister as contrasted with that of a civil servant or intermittent public person is the focus of the second section. The conclusion considers the ways in which apprenticeship to a political career creates similarities among political leaders, even of different parties, and also differentiates politicians from leaders in other parts of society.

PRECONDITIONS AND PREDISPOSITIONS

To achieve a position of political leadership, individuals must meet certain preconditions, some firm and formal, such as age and education, and others less firm and informal, such as class and gender. While most political leaders are white middle-class males, it is also true that most white middle-class males do *not* go into political careers. In a sociological sense, all politicians are deviants; that is, they are untypical of successful middle-class professional males. We must thus consider what predisposes people to seek the unusual career of a politician. It is also important to remember that some political leaders do not conform to the normal patterns: for example, the present Conservative Prime Minister Margaret Thatcher is a woman and comes from a lower-middle-class family.

Family. For the deviant minority who enter politics, family influences are often strong. When a person born into a politically active family enters politics, it is the equivalent of following in a father's or mother's footsteps. This is most evident for the eldest son of a hereditary peer, who is guaranteed a seat in the House of Lords on his father's death.

The number of politicians from political families is disproportionately high in every Cabinet. In the Cabinet that Margaret Thatcher named in 1987, of the twenty-one members ten had parents who were actively involved in politics at levels ranging from local government to the House of Lords. In Harold Wilson's first Labour Cabinet, a similar proportion had family involvement in politics, from growing up in the home of a highly politicized mining family to membership in the House of Lords.

Prime Ministers have often had immediate family encouragement to enter politics. Winston Churchill's ancestors had been in the Commons or the Lords since early in the eighteenth century, and his father's failure to become Conservative Party leader left a deep impression upon him. His son and grandson (as well as two sons-in-law) also sat in the Commons. Sir Alec Douglas-Home inherited a seat in the House of Lords, which he resigned to become Prime Minister. Harold Wilson's parents and grandparents, though never in Parliament, were also keenly interested in politics; he claims, "I was born with politics in me."[3] Margaret Thatcher's father was active in local politics as a Liberal.

Gender. Women are much less likely than men to seek or gain nomination for Parliament, to be elected to the House of Commons, or to become a Cabinet minister. Moreover, at each step up the hierarchy of political position, the proportion of women is fewer (Table VII.1).

Women are more likely to enter politics by competing for the higher civil service than by competing for a seat in the House of Commons. One reason is that the higher civil service can be entered directly upon graduating university. Another reason is that these posts are normally sought by arts and social studies graduates rather than science graduates, and more women tend to be arts and social studies graduates. Women constitute nearly half the applicants to the higher civil service and 28 percent of those successfully passing the final selection board and being offered an entry post to the higher civil service. Since women have only recently begun entering in large numbers for the higher civil service, the proportion in very senior posts is much lower but slowly rising.

Women were 13 percent of the candidates at the 1987 general election, more than double the proportion in 1970. Women parliamentary candidates are less likely to be elected than men because they are more likely to be nominated in constituencies that are hopeless for their party. The Alliance parties, with the fewest seats in the Commons, nominated the most women candidates.

Forty-one women MPs, a record number, were elected to the House of Commons in 1987. This was more than double the number of women elected in 1979, albeit far below the goal of the

TABLE VII.1 *Gender of Recruits to Leading Political Positions*

	Women	
	N	%
Entrants, higher civil service	46	28.3
Parliamentary candidates, 1987	243	12.8
MPs	41	6.5
Cabinet	1	4.8

Source: *Civil Service Statistics 1987* (London: HM Treasury, 1987), p. 30; and B. Criddle, "Candidates," in D. Butler and D. Kavanagh, *The British General Election of 1987* (London: Macmillan, 1988), p. 197.

activist 300 Group, which seeks to secure the election of 300 women MPs.[4] In party terms, women divided twenty-one Labour, seventeen Conservative, two Alliance, and one Scottish National Party. Women in Parliament have earned their position through their political activity; they have not inherited a seat from a spouse. At Cabinet level the Prime Minister is expected to appoint at least one woman, a figure in proportion to the number of women in the Commons but not in the population. From 1964 to 1979, four women served in Cabinet—Margaret Thatcher, Barbara Castle, Judith Hart, and Shirley Williams; Margaret Thatcher is the only woman in her Cabinet.

Party, not gender, is the primary influence upon the behavior and attitudes of women in Parliament. Even in the House of Lords, where life peers can be appointed for distinction independent of party politics, most women peers follow a party line rather than espouse a feminist view, nor do women peers address their speeches to issues that are regarded as distinctively women's issues.[5] Women in Cabinet achieve their position by competing with men without regard to gender or the expression of feminist views. For example, Barbara Castle was a Labour Cabinet minister in Transport, Overseas Development, Employment, and Health and Social Security. Margaret Thatcher's election as leader of the Conservative Party in 1975 showed the readiness of MPs to judge women on political grounds, not gender. Both supporters and critics react more strongly to her political views than to her gender.

The difference between numbers of men and women in leading political positions cannot be ascribed to women lacking an interest in politics. The proportion of women who are interested in politics is similar to that of men, according to the British Election Survey. Moreover, there is virtually no difference in political interest or attitudes among boys and girls in secondary schools, and most schools today are coeducational.[6]

Many of the reasons why women are not often found in leading political positions are also causes of the historic underrepresentation of women in British society. In addition, there are specific reasons inhibiting entry to national politics. One particularly important inhibition is that a person aspiring to Parliament often needs to spend many years from the ages of twenty-one to forty cultivating a party position in order to win nomination for a safe parliamentary seat. At this stage of the life cycle many women are occupied rearing children; by the time they seek to reenter employment, opportunities leading to a parliamentary career are often fore-closed.[7] Margaret Thatcher demonstrates that a woman can rise to the top in politics. But as the only woman in her Cabinet, she also shows that it is exceptional for a woman to reach so high a position.

Education. Even though there are no formal educational qualifi-cations for election to Parliament and only a very small minority of university graduates seek a political career, education is an impor-tant precondition for achieving a leading political position. As one rises up the career ladder, educational qualifications become increasingly important. The 5 percent with a university degree con-stitute more than half the MPs, Cabinet ministers, and high-ranking civil servants (Table VII.2).

While education has always been important for the career of poli-ticians, the meaning of education has changed very greatly. Until the 1960s, education said as much about who you were (parents, social status, and income) as it did about what you knew (examina-tion success). A very small proportion of the population went to prestigious public schools, of which Eton, Harrow, and Winchester remain the best known. The primary test for admission was family status and income. Youths without the appropriate family back-ground could achieve an education by passing an examination for a place at a selective grammar school and then winning a place at university. The great mass of the electorate went to state schools that provided neither sound education nor status; they often left at the minimum age without any academic qualifications.

Historically, the Labour Party had cross-class leaders, recruiting

TABLE VII.2 *Educational Qualifications and Political Position (in percentage)*

	University graduate	*Nongraduate*
Higher civil servants	100	0
Cabinet ministers	72	28
MPs	65	35
Local councillors	19	81
Electorate as a whole	5	95

Sources: Derived by the author principally from M. Burch and M. Moran, "The Changing British Political Elite, 1945–83," *Parliamentary Affairs* 38:1 (1985); and Committee of Inquiry into the Conduct of Local Authority Business, *The Local Government Councillor*, vol. 3 (London: HMSO Cmnd. 9799, 1986), p. 24.

both trade unionists, with only an elementary school education, and university graduates, some with public school backgrounds. In the 1945 Labour Cabinet five of the twenty Labour ministers were from high-status public schools with an Oxbridge (that is, Oxford or Cambridge) education; another five had won their way to university through scholarships; and half had had only an elementary education. In the first postwar Conservative Cabinet, formed by Winston Churchill in 1951, three-quarters had been at prestigious public schools, but few more than half had proceeded to university. Churchill himself did badly at Harrow and went into the army. Membership in the House of Commons reflected these distinctions, and leading civil service posts were invariably filled by academically able Oxbridge graduates.[8]

Because it takes half a working lifetime for an individual to reach a leading position in politics, postwar educational changes have taken decades to be registered in Westminster. In 1964 the election of a Labour government brought in a new and younger group of politicians, led by Harold Wilson, a scholarship boy from a grammar school and Oxford. In 1965 the election of Edward Heath as Conservative Party leader symbolized that party's readiness to recruit on merit without regard to social background. Concurrently, students from public schools have become anxious to add a university degree to their high-status secondary education. Political involvement at university does not control what happens afterward. While many Labour Cabinet ministers had been Oxford contemporaries of Prime Minister Harold Wilson, in their student days these Labour ministers had belonged to the Labour, Conservative, Liberal, and Communist parties. Wilson was a Liberal.

Today, most leading political positions are held by people who achieved success at university as a precondition of competing for a major political role. The change has been described as the rise of the meritocracy, that is, persons who get leadership positions by virtue of educational merit at universities new and old, rather than because of family background or wealth. The leaders of both the Conservative and Labour parties, Margaret Thatcher and Neil Kinnock, are examples of meritocrats, for each is a first-generation university graduate. It is characteristic of the way in which old and new values are combined that Michael Young, who coined the term meritocracy in 1961, subsequently entered the House of Lords as a life peer.[9]

The rise of the meritocracy has brought about major changes in the way in which each of the established parties recruits its political leaders; in cricketing terms it is a shift from amateur gentlemen to professional players. As educational qualifications have become more important, the proportion of working-class people who achieve leading positions in the Labour Party has been much reduced. Only a third of Labour councillors are working class, as are a third of Labour MPs. When the last Labour Cabinet left office in 1979, seventeen of its twenty-two members had a university education, including two who had started life as coal miners. While leading Labour politicians come from a wide variety of social and educational backgrounds, they have one characteristic in common: relatively few have been manual workers.[10]

Concurrently, the Conservative Party has opened its leadership ranks to aspiring politicians from very middling middle class backgrounds. Whereas Conservative leaders from 1923 to 1965 had been educated at Eton, Harrow, or Rugby, since 1965 the party has been led by meritocrats. Margaret Thatcher, a shopkeeper's daughter who won a scholarship to Oxford, values people for what they can achieve by their own efforts, not by what their families and schools provided for them. The 1987 Thatcher Cabinet had eighteen of twenty-one graduates, but only a third had been to prestigious public schools.

The higher civil service has changed its recruitment pattern; the expansion in the number of universities has broadened the field from which it recruits. Given that 3,500 take examinations for fewer than 100 places, the great majority of aspirants are likely to be unsuccessful. Among the small group who do succeed, Oxbridge graduates take more than half of the places on offer, but the proportion from other universities shows a marked increase from two decades ago. The major problem facing civil service recruiters today is that relatively few able graduates now want to enter the higher civil service, since prospects of pay, promotion, and prestige now tend to be higher in other fields, such as banking and finance, advertising, television, and journalism. In a period of historically high unemployment, the civil service has had difficulties in securing a sufficient number of able graduates for its posts, and some are left unfilled.[11]

Changes in recruitment are more important for individuals with political aspirations to reach the top than they are to voters. Politicians are viewed as representatives of parties rather than as representing social classes or educational institutions. A National Opinion Polls survey found that a majority rejects the idea that the social characteristics of an MP are important. Voters think it more important that an MP should live in the constituency than that the MP should be of the same class as most of the people who vote for him or her.

CENTRAL POLITICAL ROLES

Within the small world of Westminster, ministers, civil servants, MPs, and intermittent public persons work together. While their roles are complementary, they are recruited to their central political positions in very different ways.

MPs and Ministers. Election to the House of Commons is virtually a condition of becoming a Cabinet minister. Members are self-recruited, in the sense that an individual must decide to take an active part in party politics as a precondition of securing nomination for a seat in Parliament. A young person eager for a central political role does not need to become an MP; entry to the higher civil service provides a more secure post at the political center. MPs are personalities who prefer the promise, the publicity, and the uncertainties of a public life in the Palace of Westminster to a cloistered life in Whitehall.

The motives leading people to seek election to Parliament are multiple, combining public and private interests.[12] Case studies, statistical analyses and novels have been written about the trials to be surmounted to succeed in the House of Commons. An MP and his or her assistant and spouse might each emphasize different motives. One thing is certain; ambition for power is not the only motive; in a multiparty system most parliamentary candidates are sure to be defeated. In the Alliance parties, about 95 percent of candidates could be reasonably confident of defeat. Liberal Party headquarters at one time even discouraged "any potential candidate who indicates he is interested in standing because he hopes to get into Parliament." Ego satisfaction can be derived from electoral victory; more than three-quarters of defeated candidates describe campaigning as satisfying in itself.[13]

Being an MP is now normally a full-time job; once elected, most MPs can count on a career of fifteen years or longer in the Commons, because more than four-fifths of parliamentary seats are safe against electoral tides. This has been true even in the 1980s, when party politics has been much less stable than at any previous time since 1945. It is unusual for a sitting MP not to be renominated to contest a seat. Changes in the Labour Party rules now require each Labour MP to be renominated before each election. In fact, only a handful of Labour MPs were denied renomination in 1987.

MPs form the pool of individuals eligible for a ministerial post when their party has a parliamentary majority.[14] The discretion that a Prime Minister can exercise in recruiting ministers is limited. Many of the party's back-bench MPs are ruled out by parliamentary inexperience, old age, ideological extremism, personal unreliability, or even lack of interest in office. One analysis of Conservative and Labour MPs found that a chief requirement for securing office was survival in the Commons. A majority of MPs elected three times or more achieve a ministerial post. A Prime Minister is likely to spend as much time deciding what posts are to be offered individual MPs as in deciding which MPs are suited to office.

Experience in the Commons does not lead naturally to the work of a minister—as primary school leads to secondary school. The MP's chief business is dealing with people and talking about ideas. A minister must have other skills too: knowing how to analyze policy options and relate political generalizations to technical problems; mastering complex arguments for use in Cabinet committees; and digesting large masses of information. A minister may find the transition from the back-benches to government greater than the shift from being a constituency activist to becoming a back-bench MP.

An MP joining the government is usually appointed first to a junior ministerial post, as an undersecretary of state. This post involves a variety of low-level political tasks; it carries no authority within the department. About half these very junior ministers are promoted to the next highest rank of Minister of State in the same or another department; this involves oversight of a substantial portion of a department's work, for example, housing in the Department of the Environment. A Minister of State may also deputize for the Cabinet minister in charge of the department, who is usually called the Secretary of State for Defense, for Education, or for any other department. A junior minister's power is limited to matters of lesser political significance. The doctrine of individual ministerial responsibility formally fixes the whole responsibility for the department upon its top minister, the Secretary of State. A Cabinet minister will not readily trust a junior minister to make a decision for which he can receive a lot of blame if things go wrong.[15]

Restricting the recruitment of Cabinet ministers to the ranks of MPs ensures that they have had ample experience to meet one important task, handling parliamentary business. But the restriction also prevents a nationwide canvass for persons specially suitable for particular posts. Little more than one-tenth of ministers are appointed to departments where they can claim some specialized knowledge. A Cabinet minister normally relies upon on-the-job learning to come to grips with the problems of a department. Anthony Crosland, a minister with an unusually analytic mind, reckoned, "It takes you six months to get your head properly above water, a year to get the general drift of most of the field, and two years really to master the whole of a department." It can take from two to five years for a policy to be formulated, approved by Cabinet and Parliament, and implemented. Prime Ministers frequently reshuffle ministers from department to department. A minister cannot expect to stay in the same job for more than two years before experiencing a change, moving up in the Cabinet hierarchy, or being pushed out. The turnover rate is one of the highest in Western nations. Nearly every move by a minister takes him to a job in a department where he has no experience, and on-the-job learning must start again.[16]

The closed-shop convention of Parliament makes it unusual for a person to become a Cabinet minister without an apprenticeship in the House of Commons. The convention has been criticized by industrialists arguing the need for more businesslike ministers; economists, the need for more economic expertise; and by academics impressed by the American system of appointing Cabinet secretaries on the basis of previous knowledge in diplomacy, banking, or agriculture. Efforts by Harold Wilson in 1964 and Edward Heath in 1970 to bring in outsiders to prominent Cabinet posts were generally failures because individuals appointed have lacked the necessary knowledge of the House of Commons. In Margaret Thatcher's 1987 Cabinet there is only one member without previous parliamentary experience, Lord Young of Graffham, Secretary of Trade & Industry. His eminence has not so much been due to winning the confidence of Parliament; it reflects his ability to formulate policies that win the confidence of the Prime Minister.

Civil Servants. Whereas MPs come and go from ministerial office with great frequency, civil servants have a job in Whitehall for almost forty years, and the recruitment process makes all civil servants very much aware of the views of their elders. For example, the present head of the civil service, Sir Robin Butler, entered government in 1961, when the head was Sir Norman Brook, who had entered the civil service in 1925, when it was under a head who had entered the service in 1903.

A distinctive feature of higher civil servants in Britain is that they are recruited without any specific professional qualification or training. In commenting upon the qualities required in a civil servant, the historian Lord Macaulay gave a classic justification:

> If, instead of learning Greek, we learned the Cherokee [language], the man who understood the Cherokee best, who made the most correct and melodious Cherokee verses, who comprehended most accurately the effect of the Cherokee particles, would generally be a superior man to him who was destitute of those accomplishments.[17]

Today, 70 percent of successful entrants to the administrative grade have arts degrees, as against 15 percent with a social science degree and 14 percent with a degree in science and technology. The practice of recruiting higher civil servants with a specialized education in Greek, Latin, and medieval or modern history is unparalleled in any other major Western nation.[18]

In reaction against this tradition the Fulton Committee on the civil service recommended that recruits for the higher civil service should have "relevant" knowledge of the work of government, "minds disciplined by the social studies, the mathematical and physical sciences, the biological sciences or in the applied and engineering sciences." It did not explain why scientific or engineering knowledge should be specially relevant to the work of Whitehall administrators, nor could it agree how to test for relevant knowledge.[19] The Civil Service Commission examinations now test candidates for ability to summarize lengthy prose papers, to resolve a problem by fitting specific facts to general regulations, to draw inferences from a simple table of social statistics, and for facility with words on paper and in group discussions.

Because bright young persons enter the civil service with no specialized skill and spend decades before reaching the highest posts, role socialization is especially important. Civil service recruits, whether their fathers were coal miners or members of the aristocracy, are expected to learn what to do by following those senior to them. Very senior civil servants usually determine the promotion of their juniors. An individual gains promotion by knowing how

Whitehall works rather than because of views about policies. A young civil servant is inoculated against deep involvement in subject matter by frequent moves from post to post; the median administrator is 2.8 years in a particular job. Part of the training given cadet civil servants is intended to instruct them how "to write briefs on something you know nothing about."[20]

Like members of other professions, in the course of a life working in Whitehall civil servants become specialists; they are specialists in the difficult task of managing political ministers, and in managing government business. Their knowledge of public administration extends far beyond what can be learned in textbooks. They know how to deal with the Treasury in annual negotiations about departmental estimates, how to remind a minister tactfully that his preferred policy may be a political disaster, how to produce a cover-up answer for an awkward parliamentary question, and how to arrive at a departmental policy when the mind of the minister is blank.

In a typical Whitehall career a senior civil servant will tend to concentrate in a few departments; 48 percent have served in one or two departments, 27 percent in three, and 26 percent in four or more departments.[21] Within a department an individual will frequently be posted from one job to another, for example, from a finance job to a personnel task. Concentrating a career in a few departments enables a higher civil servant to know intimately the habits of immediate colleagues; this greatly facilitates coordination within a ministry. But a civil servant is not meant to become an advocate of a ministry; he or she is expected to serve the Crown, that is, the institutions and ethos of the higher civil service, which continues while Cabinets and Prime Ministers come and go.

The Thatcher era in Whitehall has altered career expectations of higher civil servants. The government's determination to reduce the number of civil servants, including higher civil servants, has significantly reduced promotion prospects for individuals who entered the civil service in the 1970s and early 1980s. The Prime Minister's indifference to protocols about the neutrality of the civil service has put pressure on civil servants to put more emphasis upon measures that reflect what ministers would like to do without regard to the awkward objections that their professional expertise indicates ministers should be made aware of. Activist commitment to policy making can be done from conviction and lead to rapid promotion by identifying a higher civil servant as an individual who brings

Downing Street the solutions it is looking for. In addition, the Prime Minister has sought to make civil servants more conscious about securing value for money in administration, and to think as business managers would be expected to think.[22]

Intermittent Public Persons. Many individuals are involved in public positions, appointed by government or financed by public funds, yet they do not think of themselves as in a political role. If all those holding government appointments were defined as political, then such diverse persons as the Archbishop of Canterbury, the Director-General of the British Broadcasting Corporation, the Regius Professor of Greek at Oxford and the Astronomer Royal could be called politicians. If challenged, each would probably deny being a politician, yet also claim to be carrying out duties in the public interest.

In addition, tens of thousands of people are intermittently public persons, appointed to a committee, commission, or other advisory committee, or to assist law enforcement as lay magistrates. Appointments are normally part time and unpaid. Many members are appointed because of their position in interest groups concerned with the committee's responsibilities. Pressure-group representatives are often balanced by having as a chairman a "lay gent," a person whose amateurism implies neutrality in government. The Treasury keeps a list of "the great and the good" to act as lay representatives of the public on specialist committees.[23] An official tabulation of public boards staffed by intermittent public persons found 310 variously denominated bodies with more than 10,000 full- and part-time members appointed by the Whitehall departments sponsoring the bodies.[24] Most individuals held only one appointment in their field of interest or expertise. Fewer than half the appointments carry a part-time salary or honorarium; appointees may be rewarded by an honor, ranging from the lowly rank of OBE (Order of the British Empire) up to a knighthood.

Intermittent public persons come from a variety of backgrounds. Politicians on the left sometimes criticize these appointees because they are not elected and because they tend to overrepresent the professional middle class. Politicians on the right sometimes criticize the system on the ground that it provides influence and a useful part-time income for protégés of Labour politicians. The varied careers of intermittent public persons indicate as wide a range of viewpoints as are found in the ranks of full-time politicians at Westminster. Consider the following prominent examples:

Lord Goodman. Born 1913. Educated secondary school in London; University of London, and Cambridge. Solicitor. Entered army as enlisted man, 1939; left as major, 1945. Solicitor to Harold Wilson for various personal matters. Chairman, Arts Council of Great Britain, 1965-72. Member, Royal Commission on Working of Tribunals of Inquiry, 1966; Chairman, Committee of Inquiry on Charity Law, 1974. President, National Book League since 1972; Chairman, Observer Newspaper Trust, 1967-76; Member, Industrial Reorganization Corporation, 1969-71. President, Institute of Jewish Affairs since 1975; Chairman, Housing Corporation, 1973-77. Director, Royal Opera House, 1972-83. Master, University College, Oxford, 1976-86. Created Life Peer, 1965.

Lord Rayner. Born 1926. Educated City College, Norwich; Selwyn College, Cambridge. Retailer. Joined Marks & Spencer, 1953; director, 1967; chief executive since 1983. Fellow, Institute of Purchasing and Supply, 1970. Special Adviser to Government, 1970. Chief Executive, Ministry of Defence Procurement 1971-72; deputy Chairman, Civil Service Pay Board, 1978-80; Adviser to Prime Minister on improving efficiency and eliminating waste in government, 1979-83. Member, Design Council, 1973-75; Security Advisory Commission, 1977-80. Created Life Peer, 1983.

Lady Warnock. Born 1926. Educated St. Swithin's, Winchester; Lady Margaret Hall, Oxford. Fellow and tutor in Philosophy, St. Hugh's College, Oxford, 1946-66; Headmistress, Oxford High School, 1966-72; Member, Independent Broadcasting Authority, 1973-81; Member, Royal Commission on Environmental Pollution, 1979-84; Social Science Research Council, 1981-85; United Kingdom Commission for UNESCO, 1981-84. Chair: Committee of Inquiry into Special Education, 1974; Advisory Committee on Animal Experiments, 1979-85; Committee of Enquiry into Human Fertilization, 1982-84; Head, Girton College, Cambridge, since 1985. Created Life Peer 1985.

Different as the careers of these three public persons are, they have two things in common. None has ever been a candidate for elective office or held a post as an established civil servant. But their abstention from conventional public office does not make them any less involved in policy making and public affairs.

POLITICAL LEADERS: MORE ALIKE AND MORE DIFFERENT

While political leaders often differ in their views and official positions, the experience that they have in common creates many similarities in outlook and tends to set political leaders apart from leaders in other fields of national life.

First of all, political leaders are not expected to start at the bottom and work their way to the top. A civil servant does not start out working in local government or in a clerical job at the bottom of a Whitehall ministry. Nor do elected officeholders first make their name in local politics and then seek a seat in Parliament. Of the twenty-one members of the Cabinet appointed by Margaret Thatcher in 1987, only two had ever been active in local government as councillors. Of the twenty-two members of the Labour government when it left office in 1979, only three had been local councillors before becoming a Member of Parliament. Unlike federal systems such as those in the United States and Germany, where local political experience can be a stepping stone to a national political career, in England involvement in local politics is an alternative to a national political career.

A second common feature is that at a young age an individual becomes an apprentice with a foot on the escalator of a political career. The process might be described as working one's way sideways. Starting in a relatively junior position near the top, an individual knows that the reward for accumulated skill, experience, and seniority will be a high-ranking job. The process is most evident in the civil service, for a person winning a place in the higher civil service at the age of twenty-one can expect a career involving close work with a variety of Cabinet ministers, and perhaps a knighthood at the end. In party politics a person seeks to become known as promising before age thirty, in order to win nomination to a safe seat and become an MP before the age of forty, a junior minister in the forties, and a Cabinet minister by the age of fifty.

Geographical propinquity is a third important shared characteristic. Members of Parliament, higher civil servants, and most intermittent public persons spend their working life in London. To get somewhere in public life an individual must first go to London and gain recognition there. Parliamentary candidates are not required to have lived in the constituency that nominates them; even if an MP has a weekend residence in the constituency, the Palace of Westminster remains his or her regular place of work. Individuals in central political roles think in terms of functional, not geographical, representation. Insofar as they share a common sense of place, it is London, which is the least typical of English cities.[25]

Education plays a critical role in enabling aspiring political leaders to launch their career early. By gaining a place at university, an individual exchanges the parochial world of home and school for membership in an institution drawing students from all over the country and abroad. At university an individual is judged on what he or she does, whether it is to compile a brilliant academic record or make a name in student politics, which can be the start of a reputation as a bright young Conservative, Socialist, Liberal, or Social Democrat. Upon leaving university an ambitious individual will seek a position that is an apprenticeship to a leading political post.

Implications of Professionalism. Traditional English leaders were simultaneously important in society and the economy as well as in politics. Aristocrats could claim seats in Parliament by virtue of noble birth and inherited wealth. When the chief tasks of government were traditional tasks, social leaders could easily double in political roles. In an earlier historical era, a wealthy person could buy himself a seat in the House of Commons, or even a peerage. The present division between the roles of minister and civil servant also did not exist. The past half century has seen the rise of the full-time professional politician, just as it has brought professionalization to many other social roles, from sports to scholarship.[26]

As careers become more specialized, a successful professional will have an individual increased understanding of his or her own sphere of society, while becoming increasingly remote from other spheres. Politicians may feel that they are superior to economic leaders because popularly elected, but businessmen, economists, and trade unionists may believe that they have the real jobs of importance in society, and aristocrats with inherited social status may feel superior to both. Television celebrities such as David Frost are "leaders" without any authority in government, the economy, or the traditional social order. The qualities and achievements that confer money, status, and political authority are today very different from each other.

Today, there are substantial difficulties in an individual translating a high position in one arena of society to high political status. Television celebrities cannot easily run for public office, since to do so requires party backing, and the nature of public service broadcasting prevents prominent television personalities from becoming closely identified with a political party. Public policy experts in universities and research institutes cannot be named to high positions in Whitehall ministries because these posts are reserved for the career civil service. Ambitious businessmen are discouraged from a political career because it requires sacrificing high earnings in exchange for the uncertainties of life as a seeker after a seat in Parliament. Senior businessmen and trade union leaders cannot easily move into Cabinet, because these jobs are reserved for MPs with more than a decade of experience in Parliament and as junior ministers.

The careers of Cabinet ministers since 1945 emphasize the distance between political and economic leadership. No leader from the business world has been a senior minister since the end of the Second World War, and only two leading trade union officials have sat in Labour Cabinets. In Harold Wilson's 1964 Cabinet there were seven MPs with experience as trade union officials. In the Labour Cabinet that left office in 1979, no minister had ever held an important post in a trade union. In Margaret Thatcher's 1979 Cabinet few ministers were businessmen, and no leader of the business world sat there. In the 1987 Thatcher Cabinet, the majority of members had been actively seeking a parliamentary career since student days, working as lawyers, journalists, or other jobs consistent with launching a career in Parliament.

Intensive apprenticeship is a prerequisite for success in most aspects of English life today. Just as a Cabinet minister must usually spend years as an MP, so a bishop must serve as a vicar, a general as a lieutenant, a professor as university lecturer, and a managing director of a firm must first work under others. Leadership positions in England today are far more differentiated than they were in 1832, when the local lord might also appoint the local clergy, lead the militia, sit as a magistrate, and send his son to the House of Commons, while himself attending the House of Lords. After years of interviewing people in leading positions in many areas of English life, Anthony Sampson concluded:

> My own fear is not that the Establishment in Britain is too close, but that it is not close enough, that the circles are overlapping less and less

and that one half of the ring has very little contact with the other half.[27]

Selective Recruitment. The extent to which political recruitment is selective depends upon the definition of political participation. Nothing could be more selective than a parliamentary election that makes one person the Prime Minister of a country with 56 million people. Yet nothing is considered more representative, because an election is the one occasion in which every adult can participate in politics. The greater the scope of activities defined as political, the greater the number of positions that are political. Government intervention in the economy has made company directors and trade union shop stewards at least intermittently politicians. Yet their economic position gives them freedom to act independently of government. Workers can vote with their feet by an unofficial strike. Businessmen can vote with their pocketbooks by investing money outside the United Kingdom.

Like success in any sport, success in national politics is ultimately achieved by skill and experience. But the readiness and opportunity and inclination to play a game differ greatly from sport to sport. So too does the disposition to take up a sport. Most English men and women prefer to be political spectators rather than players. This is true of university graduates, successful businessmen, and trade union leaders, too.

The need for recruiting a few thousand people for leading positions in politics is undoubted. Debates about the recruitment of politicians cannot be resolved by stating that competence should be the criterion for selection. This begs the question: Competence in doing what? Efficiency dictates that some people specialize in major political offices. The need for analytic skills justifies selection for civil service posts by criteria that favor university graduates. Yet the need for communication between representatives and the represented—by empathy as well as face-to-face dialogue—favors selecting some politicians because they are socially representative of the electorate. The need for Cabinet ministers to defend their actions in Parliament leads a Prime Minister to promote MPs who show skill in the unusual and demanding arts of parliamentary debate.[28]

The social origins of politicians do not, however, predict the outlooks of individual politicians. Politicians gain promotion because of abilities relevant to Whitehall and Westminster rather than by conforming to the expectations of their parents, a schoolmaster, or university teachers. Among those in full-time political roles, intensive socialization in Westminster tends to be the most important formative experience, and a person's current position is of immediate importance. This is illustrated by what happens when an Opposition party enters office. A newly elected Cabinet can alter policies of government, but accession to office also alters the politicians. Lord Balniel, heir to one of the oldest titles in Britain, has argued that patterns of politics are preserved "not so much by the conscious efforts of the well established, but by the zeal of those who have just won entry, and by the hopes of those who still aspire."[29]

NOTES

1. Quoted by Donald D. Searing, "A Theory of Socialization: Institutional Support and Deradicalization in Britain," *British Journal of Political Science* 16:3 (1986), p. 372.

2. See F. M. G. Willson, "Policy-Making and the Policy-Makers," in R. Rose, ed., *Policy-Making in Britain: A Reader in Government* (London: Macmillan, 1969), pp. 355–368.

3. Quoted from "The Family Background of Harold Wilson," in Richard Rose, ed., *Studies in British Politics* (London: Macmillan, 1976), 3rd ed., p. 192.

4. See Elizabeth Vallance, *Women in the House* (London: Athlone Press, 1979); and Jill Hills, "Candidates, the Impact of Gender," *Parliamentary Affairs* 34:2 (1981), pp. 221–228.

5. See Gavin Drewry and Jenny Brock, *The Impact of Women on the House of Lords* (Glasgow: U. of Strathclyde Studies in Public Policy No. 112, 1983); and survey results reported by Pippa Norris and Joni Lovenduski, "Women Candidates for Parliament: In a Different Voice?" Conference on Women and Parliament, Birkbeck College, London, February 27, 1988.

6. R. E. Dowse and J. A. Hughes, "Girls, Boys and Politics," *British Journal of Sociology*, 22:1 (1971).

7. See Elizabeth Vallance, *Women in the House*, pp. 1ff; Vicky Randall, *Women and Politics* (London: Macmillan, 1982), especially pp. 184ff; Cynthia Cockburn, *Women, Trade Unions and Political Parties* (London: Fabian Research Series No. 349, 1987).

8. All statistics calculated by the author from relevant biographical reference works such as *Who's Who*. For interpretations of the recruitment system prevailing up to the 1960s, see e.g. W. L. Guttsman, *The British Political Elite* (London: Macgibbon & Kee, 1963); R. K. Kelsall, *Higher Civil Servants in Britain* (London: Routledge & Kegan Paul, 1955).

9. See Michael Young, *The Rise of the Meritocracy* (Harmondsworth: Penguin, 1961).

10. Cf. Dennis Kavanagh, "From Gentlemen to Players: Changes in Political Leadership," in Rose and Gwyn, *Britain: Progress and Decline,* (London: Macmillan, 1980), pp. 73–93; Martin Burch and Michael Moran, "The Changing British Political Elite, 1945–83," *Parliamentary Affairs* 38:1 (1985), pp. 1–15.

11. See e.g. Civil Service Commission, *Annual Report 1983*, p. 8.

12. Note the catalogue of motives in Sir Lewis Namier, *The Structure of Politics at the Accession of George III*, 2nd ed. (London: Macmillan, 1957), Chapter 1. Cf. Austin Mitchell, *Westminster Man.*

13. See Dennis Kavanagh, *Constituency Electioneering in Britain* (London: Longman, 1970), pp. 81ff, and Jorgen Rasmussen, *The Liberal Party: a Study of Retrenchment and Revival* (London: Constable, 1965), p. 212.

14. See Richard Rose, *The Problem of Party Government* (London: Macmillan, 1974), Chapter 14, for a detailed discussion of the making of Cabinet ministers.

15. See Kevin Theakston, *Junior Ministers in British Government* (Oxford: Basil Blackwell, 1987).

16. Crosland quoted in Maurice Kogan, *The Politics of Education* (Harmondsworth: Penguin, 1971), pp. 155ff. See also Rose, *Ministers and Ministries*, Chapter 4; Headey, *British Cabinet Ministers*, pp. 90ff.

17. *The Life and Letters of Lord Macaulay*, Vol. 2 (London: Longman, 1923), pp. 585-586. See also Lord Bridges, *The Treasury* (London: Allen and Unwin, 1964) pp. 51-52, 101-102.

18. See Civil Service Commission, *Annual Report 1983* (Basingstoke: Civil Service Commission, 1984), p. 41. Cf. Aberbach, Putnam, and Rockman, *Bureaucrats and Politicians in Western Democracies*, p. 52.

19. See The Fulton Committee, *Report*, Vol. 1, pp. 27ff and Appendix E, especially p. 162. See also *Qualifications* (London: Management and Personnel Office, 1983).

20. Comment by a Civil Service College instructor, quoted in Peter Kellner and Lord Crowther-Hunt, *The Civil Servants* (London: Macdonald, 1980), p. 145.

21. For career data on civil servants, see Richard Rose, "The Political Status of Higher Civil Servants in Britain," and sources cited therein.

22. Cf. Les Metcalfe and Sue Richards, *Improving Public Management;* Anthony Harrison and John Gretton, eds., *Reshaping Central Government* (Oxford: Policy Journals, 1987); *Top Jobs in Whitehall* (London: Royal Institute of Public Administration, 1987).

23. See Peter Hennessy, *The Great and the Good* (London: Policy Studies Institute Research Report No. 654, 1986); K. C. Wheare, *Government by Committee* (Oxford: Clarendon Press, 1955), pp. 15ff.

24. Cf. Cabinet Office, *Public Bodies 1984* (London: HMSO, 1984); Anthony Barker, ed., *Quangos in Britain* (London: Macmillan, 1982); Alan Doig, "Public Bodies and Ministerial Patronage," *Parliamentary Affairs* 31:1 (1978).

25. Scottish, Northern Ireland, and to a lesser extent Welsh MPs and civil servants are a partial exception; see Richard Rose, *Understanding the United Kingdom* (London: Longman, 1982). On the atypical nature of London, see the cluster analysis in Richard Rose and Ian McAllister, *The Nationwide Competition for Votes* (London: Frances Pinter, 1984), chapter 10.

26. Cf. J. M. Lee, *Social Leaders and Public Persons* (Oxford: Clarendon Press, 1963); Henry Parris, *Constitutional Bureaucracy* (London: Allen and Unwin, 1969); and Anthony King, "The Rise of the Career Politician in Britain—and its Consequences," *British Journal of Political Science,* 11:2 (1981), pp. 249-285.

27. Anthony Sampson, *Anatomy of Britain* (London: Hodder and Stoughton, 1962), p. 632 and endpapers.

28. On these criteria, see Robert A. Dahl, *After the Revolution?* (New Haven: Yale University Press, 1970).

29. Lord Balniel, "The Upper Classes," *The Twentieth Century* No. 999 (1960), p. 432. See also Donald D. Searing, "A Theory of Socialization: Institutional Support and Deradicalization in Britain."

CHAPTER VIII

The Media of Communication and Noncommunication

A parliamentary minister is a man trained by elaborate practice not to blurt out crude things.

COMMUNICATION IS A NECESSARY link between parts of the political system. Government wants citizens to know what is expected of them, and it needs information about what citizens are thinking and doing. Citizens want government to know what they would like, or at least what they will not stand for. Noncommunication is also important. If a minister does not know that a problem exists, he cannot act, and a voter cannot react to Whitehall actions that remain an official secret. Because politics is about differences of opinion, communication does not resolve conflicts. With perfect information about the views of every citizen, policy makers would still need to decide between competing opinions.

Channels of communication include public media, such as the press, television and Parliament, and private media, such as conversations in the corridors of Whitehall. The influence of an audience varies inversely with its size: small private meetings are often more important than televised political discussions. Only at election time does a mass audience determine political outcomes. The roles of communicator and audience are often exchanged. Those who speak often, such as MPs, are also expected to listen to those who seek to influence them. Those who usually listen, the voters, speak decisively at elections. After politicians propose a course of action, they are meant to listen for reactions from those affected.

Everyone is part of both horizontal and vertical communication networks. *Horizontal* communication involves people of similar political status, such as Cabinet ministers. *Vertical* communication links individuals differing in their political status. For example, the Employment minister must ensure that his views reach down to the local offices where unemployment benefits are paid. Reciprocally, an unemployed person wants his or her views to reach up to where economic decisions are made. The greater an individual's involvement in politics, the more political information will be received from all sources. But the more information a politician receives, the more he or she must learn to ignore much that is said in order to avoid being buried in an information overload. Most citizens have an information underload, for low levels of interest result in a low level of political knowledge.

In the liberal model of English politics, more information is viewed as making for better government; official secrecy is assumed to be undesirable in itself and harmful in its consequences. The public is deemed to have the right to know what government is doing; the greater the flow of information, the better informed the public can be. A better informed public is also expected to make government better. In Washington this doctrine of the public's right to know is given statutory expression in the Freedom of Information Act; virtually everything that government does is made publicly available.

The Whitehall model takes a very different view of the supply and demand for information. Information is assumed to be a scarce commodity, and "like all scarce commodities, it is not freely exchanged."[1] Publicity is considered costly, because of the time required to carry out an extensive public relations campaign and because public discussion might make private negotiations more difficult. Whitehall conventions assume that publicity is "not in the public interest."[2] David Butler, an academic and media commentator on politics, writes, "Conducting the whole business of advising and policy-forming in public just wouldn't work." A Foreign Office official says more bluntly: "It is no business of any official to allow the government to be embarrassed. That is who we are working for."[3]

Government sometimes faces a dilemma about whether to keep deliberations secret or discuss its business in public. For example, from 1964 to 1967 the Labour government faced a policy choice about devaluing the international exchange rate for the pound. To debate the possibility openly for months would have produced a great deal of speculative pressure in currency markets against the British pound. But avoiding discussion meant that there was no opportunity for senior ministers to consider whether devaluation was appropriate. As a senior economic minister remarked, it was "a very difficult subject to discuss because it was absolutely essential that nobody should know that it was being discussed."[4]

Communication through the mass media is the subject of the first section of this chapter. The media are the principal means by which the ordinary citizen learns about actions of government and sees politicians advocating their case. Both broadcasting and the press are affected by legal and political constraints. Because of the unusual degree of secrecy in British government, the second section examines Whitehall as a source of secrecy rather than information. It explains how government operates by providing a minimum of information. The concluding section examines how cracks are opening in the wall of silence and asks: What price information? Costs and benefits of the existing system are examined along with proposals to increase the public's right to know what government does.

PUBLIC MEDIA

The media of communication are plural, with many differences in form. Radio and television differ from newspapers in that broadcasting requires a government license but newspapers do not. The majority of the media are run as part of profit-making companies; they thus differ from the British Broadcasting Corporation, which is a nonprofit agency dependent upon government as its principal source of funds. Within any media organization, outlooks differ between corporate managers and journalists concerned with the news. There are also major differences between journalists who write about politics and those concerned with the entertainment function of the media. In the production of television and newspapers, technical considerations create opportunities and impose limitations upon what can be done. Each media institution is limited by its audience: a newspaper whose average reader is above average in education writes about politics in a far more sophisticated manner than a mass-circulation tabloid or a pop radio station.

Broadcasting. Television and radio (collectively described as broadcasting) are highly centralized but competitive. The British Broadcasting Corporation maintains two network television services,

BBC-1 and BBC-2; four nationwide radio networks, each providing a distinctive range of programs; and local radio stations. The Independent Broadcasting Authority (IBA) licenses television companies to transmit programs for a particular region; the companies each produce some programs and exchange with each other to create a nationwide Independent Television (ITV) network. Most entertainment and current affairs programs are produced by Thames Television, London Weekend, Granada, and Central Television. Independent Television News provides national and international news for the IBA stations. In 1982 Channel 4 started under IBA sponsorship to offer programs for specialist audiences, ranging from devotees of foreign films to ethnic audiences as well as new audiences that it created for sports such as American football. Channel 4 also devotes more time to minority political opinions. Commercial local radio stations are also widespread.

Both the BBC and independent television companies are subject to government licensing, which affects their conditions of operation. The BBC's Board of Governors is appointed by the Home Secretary, as are the members of the IBA. The Boards contain a variety of individuals, with experience in Parliament, trade unions, the arts, education, and so forth, and individuals from Scotland, Wales, and Northern Ireland. Each body operates under a statutory charter, subject to periodic review and renewal. The BBC does not sell advertising; it depends for much of its revenue upon the license fee required of each household receiving programs. In an era of inflation, the government can exert influence by determining when this fee may rise. The annual profits of independent television companies, derived primarily from advertising, are affected by licensing conditions requiring payment for the use of IBA transmission facilities and by special taxes upon gross revenues and net profits. The license to operate an independent television station is subject to periodic renewal, and if this is not granted, a company suffers a severe financial loss.[5]

The directors and senior staff of the BBC and ITV companies are concerned with balancing four objectives. First of all, audience ratings are important, for television is a medium for mass communication. Even so-called minority programs would prefer a million viewers (2 percent of the total audience) to 500,000 (1 percent). Secondly, critical approval is important, particularly for the BBC, which justifies its noncommercial status by the provision of a range of quality programs. Thirdly, attracting good staff and performers is important to produce good programs and attract big audiences. The most successful television stars and producers can choose between competing companies. Making money is a fourth consideration. Independent companies are by definition profit-making, and the BBC needs revenue from selling programs abroad to meet production costs as well as big audiences to justify a big license fee. The four objectives are sometimes in conflict.

Because broadcasting authorities can never be sure which party will be in office when their license is up for renewal, they have a strong incentive not to take sides between parties, but to maintain a balance between differing points of view expressed in Parliament.[6] In the 1987 general election campaign, broadcasting divided coverage of the parties almost equally among the three main parties—32 percent each for Conservative and Alliance and 33 percent Labour, with 4 percent for other candidates.[7] Parties and candidates are not permitted to purchase time to advertise themselves. The parties are allocated time for party political broadcasts on radio and television roughly in accord with their electoral strength. Within each party there is a running dispute about whether the party's broadcasts should feature leading politicians discussing policies in detail or use commercial advertising techniques to project an appealing image to a mass audience.

Broadcasting staffs do not agree about the best way to treat political news. The BBC still reflects in part the ethos of Lord Reith, director-general during its formative years between the wars, who commented: "It is occasionally indicated to us that we are apparently setting out to give the public what we think they need—and not what they want—but few know what they want and very few what they need." Lord Reith's high-minded ethic, it was alleged, resulted in very few people "at the top of the Corporation knowing, or indeed caring, what the audience makes of the service it receives."[8]

Competition from commercial television has made BBC staff more audience-conscious without completely eliminating its public service ethos. In a study of BBC current affairs election staff, Jay Blumler found two contrasting outlooks: one group had a "sacerdotal" approach, seeing elections as intrinsically important events and the BBC as the quasi-priestly intermediary between politicians and people. By contrast, "pragmatic" producers reflect an outlook that is common among ITV companies, which want to report an election only insofar as events are newsworthy; a crime story could thus be given more prominence than a Cabinet minister's repetition of a familiar campaign theme.[9]

Communicators see themselves as public watchdogs guarding against politicians manipulating the media. In their role as watchdogs for the public, television interviewers can subject leading politicians to cross-examination or run exposés of facts that government has tried to keep quiet. Programs can themselves become a cause of controversy. Labour MPs and left-wing media critics have attacked television for projecting a superficial image of society or being insufficiently critical of society. Conservatives, including Party Chairman Norman Tebbit prior to the 1987 general election, have attacked television, and especially the BBC, for being too critical of society and displaying an alleged left-wing bias.[10]

Most of the audience for television regards it as impartial. After the 1987 election, a substantial majority of the electorate said they thought that television coverage was not biased against any political party (Table VIII.1). Those who did think there was bias disagreed about the direction; the fraction thinking a network was biased against the Conservatives was virtually the same as the proportion thinking it was biased against Labour.[11]

During an election campaign, virtually all of the viewing public is exposed to reporting of the election campaign and statements by politicians. Two-thirds report that they watch a party political broadcast on television, usually a broadcast given by the party that they favor. For most people, television is likely to reinforce established views. People tend to judge political television by their prior party loyalty; they do not choose a party simply in response to a particular television program. Longtime Conservatives like Conservative broadcasts best, and Labour supporters like Labour best, regardless of style. The less well known the personality or the less well known the party—the position of the Alliance parties—the

TABLE VIII.1 *Perceived Fairness of Television Coverage (in percentage)*

	BBC	ITV
Unbiased	61	67
Biased:	26	17
Against Conservatives	(11)	(8)
Against Labour	(13)	(8)
Other	(2)	(1)
No opinion	13	16

Source: *Gallup Political Index* No. 329 (January 1988), p. 17.

more important television is as a means of increasing popular awareness of a political cause.

The long-term influence of television upon mass political attitudes is less clear-cut. Television news and current affairs programs are likely to increase political knowledge for the mass of voters. Insofar as party loyalties have been weakening for reasons independent of the media, television can reinforce this process by providing floating voters with information about all the available alternatives. In the long run, television does not tell voters what to think, but it does give them more food for thought than the typical popular newspaper.[12]

The Press. The press is centralized in London, unlike the press in the United States, Canada, and many European countries. Morning newspapers printed in London circulate throughout England and account for the great bulk of newspaper circulation. Non-London papers concentrate upon local news; politics is treated as an event that happens in London.[13] Centralization reflects the economics of the newspaper industry: many millions of pounds must be invested to start a newspaper; advertisers tend to prefer large-circulation dailies; and economies of scale make it much easier to run a paper at a profit if it has a large circulation.[14]

Centralization is even more evident in the ownership of newspapers, for several publishers own more than one national newspaper. Rupert Murdoch, an Australian, owns the down-market *Sun* and the up-market *Times*, which together account for 31 percent of the readership of national papers. Former Labour MP Robert Maxwell owns the *Daily Mirror*, the country's second most successful tabloid, and an even more successful tabloid published in Scotland, the *Daily Record*; together they have 25 percent of British daily morning press readership. David Stevens's United Newspapers owns both the *Express* and the *Star*, which account for an additional 19 percent of daily readership. Together, the three publishers account for three-quarters of the total daily national newspaper circulation.[15]

National newspapers are sharply divided between the popular and the quality press. England has five quality daily papers: *The Times, The Guardian, The Telegraph, The Independent* (started in 1986), and *The Financial Times*. By contrast, the United States has only three papers that can claim to be quality papers for a national audience: *The New York Times, Washington Post,* and *The Wall Street Journal.* While each paper has a distinctive editorial policy, all are prepared to report major political events in detail and assume a substantial degree of sophistication and knowledge among their readers. One or more of these quality papers is invariably read by MPs and civil servants in Whitehall. While only a handful of the electorate read a serious weekly, such as *The Economist,* these publications are very widely read in Whitehall.

The six popular papers are better described as entertainment media than as papers printing news. Stories about TV celebrities, sports, sex, and crime—or some combination—receive more prominence than the actions of government and Parliament. Anyone who read only the popular press could not be reasonably informed about events in England and abroad. Political stories consist of headlines, photographs and catch-phrases; there is little information. Three popular papers—the *Daily Mail, Today,* and the *Daily Mirror*—make some effort to inform their readers. Two papers—the *Sun* and the *Star*—are best described as vulgar rather than popular, since their brief political reports are usually expressed coarsely. The *Sun* became the biggest selling daily paper in Britain by introducing the practice of depicting bare-breasted models on page three.

While quality and popular papers are nearly equal in number, they differ greatly in circulation. Popular papers account for five-sixths of the total readership of national newspapers (Table VIII.2). The two coarsest tabloids, the *Sun* and the *Star,* together sell more than twice as many copies as the quality dailies. Because their readers are more prosperous, the advertising rates of quality dailies are high and they can make a profit on low circulation. While the level of education has been rising, the information content of the popular press has been falling. England lacks the middle-brow papers common in countries such as the United States.

Readers are usually very clear about the political-party inclination of the paper that they read. A clear majority see five papers as favoring the Conservatives; the *Mirror,* as favoring Labour; *The Guardian* as favoring the Alliance parties; and one quality and two popular dailies as without any clear party leaning. When the circulation of papers is taken into account, 63 percent of readers receive a paper that is Conservative, 20 percent a Labour paper, 3 percent a paper of the Alliance parties, and 13 percent a paper that is viewed as without partisanship (*The Independent*) or that prints too little political news for its readers to be sure of its slant.[16]

The existence of a correlation between the party preferences of readers and a newspaper is *not* proof that newspaper cues determine

TABLE VIII.2 *Politics of National Daily Newspaper Readers (in percentage)*

	Circulation (thousands)	Readers' view of paper's party				Own party preference		
		Con	Lab	Allc	Don't know	Con	Lab	Allc
Popular								
Sun	4,045	63	12	7	18	41	31	19
Daily Mirror	3,128	2	84	8	6	20	55	21
Daily Mail	1,810	78	2	5	15	60	13	19
Daily Express	1,690	87	0	4	9	70	9	18
The Star	1,137	23	16	7	54	28	46	18
Today	340	11	4	18	67	43	17	40
Quality								
Daily Telegraph	1,169	85	0	3	12	80	5	10
Guardian	460	13	30	43	14	22	54	19
Times	447	61	0	33	6	56	12	27
Independent	361	12	6	20	62	34	34	27

Source: Circulation figures from Audit Bureau of Circulation, July-December 1987 (six-monthly average); readers' views from MORI surveys during 1987 general election.

how people vote. First of all, while a paper can only support one party editorially, its readers divide their support among several different parties. The readers of the *Sun*, the *Star*, *Today*, and the *Independent* are so divided that no one party secures the backing of half their readers. Only two papers, the *Telegraph* and the *Express*, have two-thirds of their readers backing a single paper. A second reason why readers do not vote their paper is that the popular press is not marketed on its political appeal, but by its entertainment value. Thirdly, the choice of a newspaper often reflects class and family influences that also affect the choice of party. A manual worker from a Labour voting home is more likely to read the *Mirror* than the more up-market and similarly anti-Tory *Guardian*.[17] The press do not create public opinion; they tend to reinforce the predispositions of their audience.

What's News? Collectively, the media can reinforce or influence perceptions of politics by selecting some types of events as newsworthy and ignoring others as unsuitable for reporting. For example, media headlines about inflation or unemployment are more likely to be seen by ordinary people than official statistics.[18] The high degree of professionalism among journalists, reinforced by a tendency to read each other's work and imitate each other, tends to produce "pack journalism," as the popular press hunts for news in a pack. On any given day the quality press will cover many of the same subjects on their news pages.

The criteria for defining political news are broad. Although ministers complain that bad news is always news, claims of success will be printed if the speaker has high political status. As a Westminster lobby journalist once remarked, "You may not believe what a person is saying, but if it is the Prime Minister, that person has a right to have his or her views known." Activities are deemed newsworthy if they are:

Immediate (the latest economic figures, not trends of a decade)
Novel within a familiar context (a Social and Liberal Democratic party victory in a by-election)
Interesting to lots of people (an increase in pensions)
Concerning a high-status individual (the Prince of Wales)
Close at hand (poor rubbish collection in London, but not in Newcastle upon Tyne)
Occurring when little else is happening (during the holiday season, when news sources such as Parliament are not open)

Journalistic criteria also define how events are reported. A demonstration may be reported because of its potential for disorder rather than because of the issue that the demonstrators are marching about.[19] Sometimes the opportunity to write a major story occurs fortuitously: a slum-property millionaire became newsworthy by being on the fringes of a scandal involving a junior minister, John Profumo. Because the slum landlord was dead, an unfavorable account of his property dealings could be printed without risk of libel. The exposé won a prize, and the publicity led to government legislation.

The parliamentary lobby correspondent is the main figure in a paper's political reporting. The lobby correspondent usually writes the paper's lead political news story each day, because it is assumed that Parliament is the focal point of government. Since a lobby journalist is privileged in mixing daily with ministers and MPs, he or she can write with authority and inside knowledge. The professional role breeds detachment and scepticism about Parliament. One survey of lobby journalists found that they divided their votes into three almost equal groups: Labour, Conservative, and those who voted Liberal or abstained.[20]

A lobby correspondent gets political news by spending fifty hours a week in and around the Palace of Westminster, developing close personal relations with a variety of politicians, and learning how MPs and ministers think. The contact between the lobby and political leaders is thus much greater than in Washington, where journalists do not have easy access to the President. By becoming immersed in the Palace of Westminster a journalist learns to think like a politician and to anticipate how leading politicians are likely to react to particular events. An experienced lobby correspondent can get some stories by mind reading, working out what politicians must be thinking, and when they refuse to deny what both know to be true, printing the statements as confirmed by political sources.

The reporting of what occurs in dining rooms, bars, and party meetings at the Palace of Westminster is subject to the restrictions of the lobby system. The basic rule is: "never to identify an informant without specific permission."[21] A reporter will thus write about what senior ministers are thinking without naming the Cabinet minister who is the source of a story and refer to sources close to the Prime Minister rather than name the Downing Street official to whom he has spoken. Behind the cloak of anonymity, politicians are free to leak stories favorable to themselves or unfavorable to opponents. This passion for anonymity means that the regular meeting between the Prime Minister's press secretary and lobby journalists is treated as a secret; news and opinions are voiced by the Prime Minister's press secretary on a not-for-attribution basis.

The occupational hazard of the lobby correspondent is to become too close to politicians. A journalist who sees and hears much that occurs at all hours of day and night within the Palace of Westminster is unlikely to print everything that he or she learns there. The information would be more suitable for use in a novel about the foibles of human nature. Lobby correspondents develop a view of government like that of back-bench MPs. They have little interest in what happens in Whitehall departments, even important departments such as the Treasury or the Foreign Office, and they depend upon ministers to provide information about government policy. Specialist correspondents in such fields as economics, defense, and education provide supplementary coverage of public affairs. The lobby journalist, a paper's chief political correspondent, cannot act as a watchdog in Whitehall because he "stands guard in the wrong place."[22]

When the press and television are taken together—which is how most people get their news of politics—the electorate appears as part of a multimedia system of political communication. For a growing segment of the electorate, television is the most important source of political information, and it is required by law to present the views of all the established parties. More and more readers are showing a readiness to switch between newspapers, and television provides a less partisan view of public affairs than that of the press. As voters assimilate political news and views from many different sources, they are less likely to be certain that one party is always right. In the long term, this encourages an increase in the proportion of the electorate who are open-minded floating voters (cf. Chapter X).

GOVERNMENT AS A SECRET

In medieval times the government of England was literally the King's business, and this business was regarded as strictly private. The King's advisers were members of the Privy (that is, Private) Council; each took a thirteenth-century oath swearing to "keep secret all matters committed and revealed unto you," and not to reveal any decisions of government "until such time as, by the consent of His or Her Majesty or the Council, publication shall be made." The oath is still in force today; so too is the idea that the activities of government are private unless there is explicit reason for government to make information public.

The Range of Secrets. Every government keeps some information secret; British government is distinctive in the broad range of information kept secret. It covers not only military matters but also deliberations in Whitehall about possible changes in domestic policies. For example, a circular from the health minister to hospital authorities asking them to convey Christmas greetings to all the staff included an instruction that this message was to be kept secret until Christmas Eve.

The Official Secrets Act of 1911 covers the activities of all government departments; it is not confined to national security measures involving the armed forces, the police, and diplomats. The Act makes it a criminal offense for any civil servant to communicate information obtained in the service of the Crown to anyone other than those immediately authorized to receive it. The scope of the Act is so broad that it is not enforced literally, for to do so would be to prohibit much communication that the government of the day regards as in its interest. But the government readily invokes the Act in efforts to prevent the publication of accounts of activities in government by former officeholders.

Formal and informal procedures reinforce the assumption of secrecy in the 1911 Act.[23] The government has the authority to issue D notices to newspapers requesting that they not report matters affecting national security. While the press and broadcasting media are not legally compelled to obey such notices, matters subject to a D notice are usually not reported. In the 1982 Falklands War the Ministry of Defence controlled all communications from the battle zone in the South Atlantic. It prohibited the transmission of what one officer described as "pictures of the sort of realism that the Americans had during the Vietnamese war," because televising the violence of war was reckoned to be bad for military morale.[24]

The practice of Whitehall officials is to assume that everything said within a government ministry is not for discussion or publication outside the department. The outlook is expressed in a Labour government White Paper entitled *Information and the Public Interest.*

It does not follow, of course, that public consultation on tentative proposals is invariably the right course. It may result in slower decisions and slower action when prompt action is essential. Sometimes, too, conflicting views and conflicting interests are already well known. In such cases a prolonged period of consultation will merely impose delay without any compensating advantages. Each individual case has to be considered on its own merits.[25]

The government declares that it favors prior publication of information about policy matters "whenever reasonably possible." Whitehall remains the sole judge of what is reasonable and possible.

Members of Parliament are often frustrated in their inquiries into government policy. Question time in the House of Commons is of limited value in probing Whitehall actions because the minister responsible may refuse to answer. During the Suez crisis Sir Anthony Eden refused to tell Parliament whether or not the country was at war with Egypt![26] Because only a few minutes are allowed to answer each question, a minister can reply evasively. In the opinion of a former civil servant:

The perfect reply to an embarrassing question in the House of Commons is one that is brief, appears to answer the question completely, if challenged can be proved to be accurate in every word, gives no opening for awkward supplementaries and discloses really nothing.[27]

Faced with such constraints, 91 percent of MPs believe that they are not adequately informed about the actions of government and that ministers and senior civil servants want to keep them in the dark. In the view of one back bencher: "The tendency of paternalism toward(s) government back benchers is strong: 'If you knew what I know you'd see I'm right.' Meanwhile, father knows best."[28]

One justification for official secrecy in Whitehall is that no government willingly makes information about its activities available on an unselective basis because knowledge is power.[29] The Whitehall ministers and officials who wield the power of the Mace have no wish to diminish it by being subject to close and informed scrutiny. Where such power is lacking, as in Washington, the government is open to public scrutiny, because neither the White House nor Congress has the authority to keep information private. In England a tradition of civility, that is, trust in private dealings and trust and deference to governors, is said to make it inappropriate or unnecessary to compel all actions of government to be carried out in a goldfish bowl.[30]

A second reason is that secrecy is seen as necessary to maintain collective Cabinet responsibility. The doctrine of collective Cabinet responsibility requires that all ministers defend what is done by their colleagues, and each minister expects to benefit from the public support of colleagues. The doctrine does not deny that ministers often disagree with each other in the deliberations that lead up to a decision taken in the name of the Cabinet as a whole. In the words of a confidential briefing to ministers on the conduct of government business: "It is contrary to the doctrine of collective responsibility to make known the attitude of individual ministers on matters of policy."[31]

A third justification for secrecy in Whitehall is that it protects the confidentiality of the relationship between ministers and civil servants. As long as the advice given by civil servants is an official secret, civil servants can speak frankly, raising doubts about the difficulties of proposals being considered by the government. If the Cabinet nonetheless adopts the measure in question, the doubts of civil servants will not be public information that can be quoted against it in the Commons. If civil servants put forward ideas that a minister adopts, it is the minister who receives the credit or blame for a policy; secrecy insulates civil servants from both public praise and public criticism.

A final argument is that secrecy enables the government to be run to the satisfaction of most people, who have little interest in the minutiae of policy making. As long as the results of government are good, the procedures can be kept private. The view was expressed bluntly by Bernard Ingham, Downing Street press secretary to Margaret Thatcher:

> There is no freedom of information in this country; there's no public right to know. There's a commonsense idea of how to run a country and Britain is full of commonsense people.
> Bugger the public's right to know. The game is the security of the state, not the public's right to know. Don't confuse public interest with media interest.[32]

Operating without Publicity. Communication and noncommunication are complementary and concurrent. There is never enough time to talk to every group about every policy that the government is considering. In theory, representatives of all groups who need to know should be consulted, and those unaffected need not be consulted. Decisions about who should and should not be informed are usually made within Whitehall. Those in the know have a chance to act or react in their own interest. Those not consulted may sometimes consider that what they didn't know has hurt them.

The most economical form of communication is virtual representation based on a silent bond of understanding. When individuals know each other's mind, one person can put himself in another's place and make the decision that the other would have taken. The intensive socialization of politicians in Westminster and Whitehall and the career-long socialization of higher civil servants makes it easy for most policy makers to anticipate how others in their network think. But communication is horizontal. It is deceptively easy for people in Westminster to mistake the echo of their own voices for the views of a much larger public. In an essay on government in wartime, Sir Norman Chester remarked:

> What can come to be important, if one is not careful, is not how decisions affect people, but how they are thought to operate by people in the Whitehall circle. The leader or letter in *The Times* or *Economist* can become the reality by which one's actions are judged.[33]

The habits of wartime persist in peacetime. A study of the way public expenditure is controlled by the Treasury is aptly titled *The Private Government of Public Money*. The authors comment:

> To say that British political administrators care more about themselves than about the country would be wrong; to say that more of their time and attention is devoted to themselves than to outsiders would be closer to the truth.[34]

Concern with secrecy can make it difficult for one part of Whitehall to know what another is doing. Within a department a minister cannot expect to read everything about its work or write every statement issued in his name. Because the media are unable to probe deeply into departments, ministers often have difficulty in receiving warning signals of difficulties until they have erupted into scandals. For example, Conservative Prime Minister Harold Macmillan was politically embarrassed when a sex scandal broke involving a junior minister, John Profumo. Lord Denning's inquiry said that the Prime Minister was not to blame because the security services did not tell him what was going on.[35]

Whitehall officials are skilled in communicating in code, using circumlocutions and oblique references so that only those people who are already in the know will understand what is being said. A report on control of public expenditure by a committee under Lord Plowden, himself a former civil servant, illustrates how communication in code operates. The committee prepared both private memoranda and a formal report for publication. Unusually, W. J. M. Mackenzie, a former classical philologist and wartime civil servant, decoded the report and published his translation. The first paragraph of the official report read:

> For these studies we co-opted the Permanent Secretaries of the departments with whose expenditure we are concerned or who had special experience of the general problems under review. In some cases we sought specialist advice from outside the civil service. We decided, however, not to take evidence from outside bodies: our review was primarily concerned with the inner working of the Treasury and the departments, and was necessarily confidential in character, and we decided that the group itself (except on certain specialist matters) provided a sufficient body of outside opinion to bring to bear on this task.

Mackenzie translated it thus: "We proceeded on two principles: no dirty linen in public: outside critics are bores."[36]

Whitehall ministers and senior civil servants can readily extend horizontal communication by participating in not-for-publication discussions that create an informal marketplace for the exchange of views among public officials, experts, and pressure-group representatives. For example, defense policy involves the feedback of information between government ministers, senior military officers, defense correspondents of serious papers, members of the International Institute for Strategic Studies, the Royal Institute of International Affairs and similar research institutes, a few MPs of each party specifically interested in defense, and present and former military officers, some working for firms producing armaments.[37] While this horizontal network has few contacts with the mass of the population, it is open to a variety of ideas within England and from the United States and Europe.

Most Whitehall departments have few vertical communication links extending to the localities where public services are delivered to citizens. The two most important Whitehall departments, the Treasury and the Foreign Office, have no channels of communication within England. Their listening posts are abroad in Washington, Brussels, Tokyo, and elsewhere. Only through the marketplace can the public and Treasury officials speak to each other about economic policies. Most Whitehall ministries lack any direct contact with the citizens receiving services for which a minister is nominally responsible; local authorities deliver education, housing, police, and the health service. A minister is removed from the "coal face," that is, the place where public services are delivered (see Chapter XIII).

If a government department wishes advice about a major issue of policy, it can establish an ad hoc Royal Commission or departmental committee to consider the problem. A commission or committee can collect information through its own research staff, receive submissions of evidence and opinion from interested groups and experts, and identify and commend a course of action likely to be accepted by the majority of affected interests. The characteristic method of proceeding is described thus, by an experienced committeeman, Andrew Shonfield:

> Just plunge into your subject: collect as many facts as you can; think about them hard as you go along; and at the end, use your commonsense, and above all your feel for the practicable, to select a few good proposals out of the large number of suggestions which will surely come your way.[38]

Appointing a committee is a good way for a government to avoid becoming caught up in a controversial subject, such as gambling or human embryos, that is not central to its own policy concerns. It is also a good way to delay taking a decision about a controversial topic, since a committee usually takes several years before issuing a report. If the report is unanimous, then the government can accept the recommendation without fear of intense opposition. If the report shows widespread differences of opinion, then controversy reflects on the committee, and not on the Cabinet. Unusually among Prime Ministers, Margaret Thatcher does not like to appoint committees; she believes in acting promptly and is not afraid of controversy.

While Whitehall ministers accept that the public has a right to determine who governs, ministers and civil servants remain confident that it is their responsibility to decide what government should do about a particular problem. Thus, little systematic attention is given to ascertaining the views of the general public, even when they are meant to be the principal beneficiaries of a policy. When

Whitehall officials have reason to believe that evidence may be embarrassing, they can explicitly *exclude* information. For example, two academic researchers undertaking a study of the civil service on behalf of the Fulton Committee admitted in the second paragraph of their report, "Enquiry into such matters as political allegiance, religious affiliation, attitudes to career and promotion opportunities was ruled out as too delicate and difficult."[39]

Whether Conservative or Labour, the governing party is invariably the chief defender of official secrecy, because it considers itself the primary beneficiary of it. Opposition parties often call for greater openness in government, but only as long as they are in opposition. The Labour government under Harold Wilson was in office when the misleadingly titled report *Information and the Public Interest* was published in 1969. The Conservative government of Edward Heath did not act upon recommendations of the Franks Committee on updating the Official Secrets Act.[40] A Labour government under James Callaghan approved a 1977 memorandum by the head of the civil service, Lord Croham, which offered as an "initial modest step" to publish "as much as possible" factual and analytical material constituting background to policy debates.[41] Critics found that the most that government would publish was too little for informed discussion, and Margaret Thatcher has respected the value of Whitehall information by making sure that it remains scarce.

CRACKS IN THE WALLS OF WHITEHALL?

The privy nature of government survives because it serves the interest of the government of the day, but when groups find that their interests are no longer served, then cracks emerge in the monolith of Whitehall secrecy, and information can leak or even be given out by government itself.

Interests Opening Cracks. The amassing of large computer data bases containing files of personal information about individuals has generated widespread complaints that it is unfair if individuals do not know what information an organization has about an individual. In 1984 the government enacted a Data Protection Act giving individuals the right to inspect records concerning them and to insist that computer files be corrected if inaccuracies are found. The immediate reason for the Act was the need to conform to a European convention for the exchange of data. It also reflects a more general trend in public opinion in favor of openness about information concerning themselves.[42]

As part of its campaign to alter local authorities, in 1985 the Conservative government enacted the Local Government (Access to Information) Act. The Act required local councils to admit the public to full meetings and committee meetings of local authorities and to give the public access to council records. The chief exclusions were intended to protect the privacy of individuals and to avoid prejudicing the council's position in commercial negotiations with contractors or in legal proceedings. As local authorities were never covered by the Official Secrets Act, mandating public access to their records is no precedent for doing the same in Whitehall. Moreover, it provides central government with more information for use in monitoring the way in which local authorities carry out central government policies.

The opposition of some civil servants to official secrecy presents a fundamental challenge to the conduct of Whitehall as we have known it. The official position is unchanged: civil servants are expected to keep confidential the information that they receive as part of their work and are subject to disciplinary action or prosecution for unauthorized disclosure. In practice, a few civil servants are now ready to leak information without authorization. In 1984 a minor clerk, Sarah Tisdall, went to jail for sending a photocopy of a nuclear weapons memorandum to the press. Following the Falklands War, a senior civil servant in the Ministry of Defence, Clive Ponting, passed to an MP on a Commons committee a memorandum indicating that his minister was misleading the House of Commons about matters of fact. Ponting was indicted for violating the Official Secrets Act. He argued that informing Parliament was not a violation of the law because the interests of the Crown, he asserted, are broader than those of the government of the day. While the judge's charge pointed toward a guilty verdict, the jury acquitted Ponting.[43] When a retired member of the secret service, Peter Wright, published his memoir, *Spycatcher,* in Australia in 1986, the British government sued in Australian courts to stop it. It lost there and in the United States; the book is nominally banned in Britain and thanks to the publicity of the court action, a best-seller elsewhere.

A government that has narrowed its policy options may publish a Green Paper in order to obtain feedback about the alternatives among which it plans to choose. Doing so gives a minister the benefit of criticism before officially committing the department. However, the more controversial the subject, the more difficult it is to issue a Green Paper, for this will leave the government open to attack for abandoning policies that it has not decided to adopt. If it abandons a controversial policy, it appears weak in the face of opposition. For example, the first Thatcher Administration wanted to undertake a fundamental review of the principles of welfare-state policies. However, when a Whitehall document setting out controversial possibilities was leaked, the Prime Minister felt forced to repudiate it, being unwilling to be attacked for policies which the government was considering but had not endorsed.[44]

The costs and benefits of secrecy and publicity differ from issue to issue. The greater the number required to cooperate to make a policy a success, the greater the need to seek information in advance and to publicize the reasons behind the policy in the hope of mobilizing consent. For example, a government effort to encourage exports requires widespread publicity to inform businessmen. The fewer the people involved in carrying out a policy, the less the need to communicate widely in advance of a decision. Many decisions in foreign policy are confined within Whitehall because the principal affected interests are outside the United Kingdom, and prompt and discreet communication with foreign governments is given priority. Every decision involves a trade-off between the speed gained by noncommunication and the risk of lacking widespread understanding and support.

Individual politicians today are increasingly interested in publicizing themselves more than in maintaining secrecy in Whitehall. Every Prime Minister feeds the lobby with stories designed to make the government look good and the Opposition look bad. A distinctive feature of the Thatcher government is that the Prime Minister has often disagreed with colleagues about policy matters and has used her press secretary to brief the lobby anonymously with criticisms of colleagues. In a dispute within Cabinet involving a relatively minor matter, whether or not to purchase helicopters from the Westland Company, documents critical of Defence Secretary Michael Heseltine were leaked, and Heseltine resigned. The finger of suspicion pointed to the Prime Minister's office. A number of former Cabinet ministers have accused the Prime Minister's press secretary, Bernard Ingham, of "using the lobby to raise the cult of personality so far as the Prime Minister is concerned, at the expense of colleagues who have happened to disagree."[45]

The leak is the politician's characteristic way of paying lip service to the doctrine of noncommunication while ensuring that friendly journalists will print his or her version of current political controversies. The distinction between a leak, which is a breach of convention, and a briefing, which is accepted as a way of giving background information to journalists, has been defined by former Prime Minister James Callaghan as: "Briefing is what I do; leaking is what you do." Any determined minister can publish what he or she wishes without judicial punishment, for the rules to be observed are voluntary obligations. Richard Crossman established this point when three volumes of his political diary of six years as a Cabinet minister were published in spite of objections from Whitehall about frequent references to civil servants who had worked with him and accounts of what was purportedly said in Cabinet. Technically, such disclosures are violations of the Official Secrets Act. But as the director-general of the Security Service has complained: "The chances of their being prosecuted are minimal, if they exist at all, because the ministers can always say that they authorized themselves to disclose the information."[46]

Communication as Instrumental. Busy policy makers want help, not information for its own sake. Politicians attend to information if the benefits of doing so are likely to be greater than the costs of ignoring it. A policy maker's attention is not a function of the quality of information but of immediate political requirements. When the costs of inaction are great, as in a political crisis, any kind of information—statistical, literary, or half-baked—will be seized upon for clues of what to do.[47]

"The need to know still dominates the right to know;" this is the conclusion of Colin Bennett's study of political communication in Whitehall, entitled *From the Dark to the Light.*[48] The study would be more aptly entitled *From the Dark to the Shadows.* The Thatcher government has continued to defend the government's right to refuse to communicate information to Parliament and to the public. When a back-bench Conservative MP proposed a bill to liberalize the Official Secrets Act, the government used the whips to defeat the measure. After courts refused to convict civil servants charged with violating the Official Secrets Act, the head of the civil service declared that even if individuals who disclosed information were not convicted on criminal charges, they remained subject to internal civil service discipline. When accused in an Australian court of tell-

ing a lie about the British government's efforts to suppress the memoir *Spycatcher,* the then head of the civil service, Sir Robert Armstrong, said: "It is a misleading impression, not a lie. It was being economical with the truth."[49]

While often urged as a good in itself, freedom of information is but a means to the end of governance. The possession of perfect and complete information cannot by itself resolve political problems, for by definition politics is about conflict. The communication of views of political significance inevitably produces arguments supporting conflicting choices, and controversy without authority can lead to stalemate. A government that is seeking action will therefore favor restricting information to that which supports its case; an opposition trying to sustain an argument will favor the publication of information to embarrass government—as long as it is not in office.

NOTES

1. Samuel Brittan, *Steering the Economy* (London: Secker and Warburg, 1969), p. 29.

2. The title of a book by David Williams (London: Hutchinson, 1965); see also K. G. Robertson, *Public Secrets* (London: Macmillan, 1982); Richard A. Chapman and Michael Hunt, eds., *Open Government* (London: Croom Helm, 1987).

3. Quoted by Anthony Sampson from a 1970 Official Secrets Act trial in *The New Anatomy of Britain* (London: Hodder and Stoughton, 1971), p. 369. See also David Butler, "Cabinet Secrets," *The Listener,* 29 February 1968.

4. George Brown, *In My Way* (Harmondsworth: Penguin, 1972), p. 105. See also Henry Brandon, *In the Red* (London: Deutsch, 1966), p. 43.

5. Developments in technology and in the economics of broadcasting are creating pressures for change in government policy. For a review of opinions, see Sir Alan Peacock's *Report of the Committee on Financing the BBC* (London: HMSO Cmnd. 9824, 1986); and comments by MPs debating the report in the House of Commons, 20 November 1986.

6. Cf. a special issue of *Parliamentary Affairs* 37:3 (1984); and Jean Seaton and Ben Pimlott, eds., *The Media in British Politics* (Aldershot: Avebury, 1987).

7. See Martin Harrison, "Broadcasting," in Butler and Kavanagh, *The British General Election of 1987,* (London: Macmillan, 1988), p. 143.

8. Tom Burns, "Public Service and Private World," in *The Sociology of Mass Media Communicators* (Keele: Sociological Review Monograph No. 13, 1969), p. 71.

9. Jay G. Blumler, "Producers' Attitudes towards Television Coverage of an Election Campaign," in R. Rose, ed., *Studies in British Politics* (London: Macmillan, 1976), 3rd ed.

10. Cf. Glasgow University Media Group, *Bad News* (London: Routledge & Kegan Paul, 1976); *More Bad News* (London: Routledge & Kegan Paul, 1980); Martin Harrison, *TV News: Whose Bias?* (London: Policy Journals 1983); Godfrey Hodgson, *Cut! The BBC and the Politicians* (London: Macmillan, 1988).

11. Cf. *Attitudes to Broadcasting in 1987* (London: IBA, 1988).

12. See the argument of Martin Harrop, "Voters," in Seaton and Pimlott, *The Media in British Politics*, pp. 45–63.

13. What follows explicitly excludes the media in Scotland and Northern Ireland, which offer a different mixture of news than London-based papers. Cf. Richard Rose and Ian McAllister, *United Kingdom Facts*, Chapter 7.

14. The economics of newspaper production has been revolutionized in the 1980s by the introduction of electronic typesetting and the ending of restrictive labor practices imposed by printing unions to generate high wages and bonuses.

15. Cf. James Curran and Jean Seaton, *Power without Responsibility* (London: Methuen, 1985).

16. If Scotland were included, the pro-Conservative bias would be reduced by the importance of the *Daily Record*, the Glasgow-based cousin of the pro-Labour *Daily Mirror*.

17. For detailed evidence and discussion, see Butler and Stokes, *Political Change in Britain* 2nd ed. (London: Macmillan, 1974), pp. 114ff; W. L. Miller, J. Brand, and M. Jordan, "On the Power or Vulnerability of the British Press: A Dynamic Analysis," *British Journal of Political Science* 12:3 (1982), pp. 357–373.

18. See Paul Mosley, "Popularity Functions and the Role of the Media," *British Journal of Political Science* 14:1 (1984), pp. 117–128.

19. See James Halloran, Philip Elliott, and Graham Murdock, *Demonstrations and Communication* (Harmondsworth: Penguin, 1970).

20. For details, see Jeremy Tunstall, *The Westminster Lobby Correspondents* (London: Routledge & Kegan Paul, 1970) pp. 20, 35, and 59ff.

21. See Michael Cockerell, Peter Hennessy, and David Walker, *Sources Close to the Prime Minister* (London: Macmillan, 1984), pp. 240–244, for the code of lobby practice.

22. Cf. Colin Seymour-Ure, *The Press, Politics and the Public* (London: Methuen, 1968), p. 176ff, 311; Jeremy Tunstall, *Journalists at Work* (London: Constable, 1971); M. Cockerell, P. Hennessy and D. Walker, *Sources Close to the Prime Minister.*

23. For a convenient catalogue and examples of the use of such restrictions, see Harry Street, *Freedom, the Individual and the Law*, 5th ed., (Harmondsworth: Penguin, 1982), Chapter 9.

24. See Select Committee on Defence, *Handling of Press and Public Information During the Falklands Conflict* (London: HMSO, 1st report, sesion 1982/83 HC 17-1, 1982).

25. *Information and the Public Interest* (London: HMSO, Cmnd. 4089, 1969), pp. 6–7.

26. See House of Commons *Debates*, Vol. 558, Cols. 1452–4 (31 October 1956) and Cols. 1620ff. (1 November 1956).

27. H. E. Dale, *The Higher Civil Service of Great Britain* (London: Oxford University Press, 1941), p. 105.

28. Or in the case of Margaret Thatcher, mother knows best. Anthony Barker and Michael Rush, *The Member of Parliament and His Information*, pp. 150, 363ff.

29. See Colin Bennett, "From the Dark to the Light: The Open Government Debate in Britain," *Journal of Public Policy* 5:2 (1985), pp. 192ff.

30. Cf. Edward Shils, *The Torment of Secrecy* (London: Heinemann, 1956).

31. For the full text, see Clive Ponting, "Hopeless Hypocrisy of Propriety Rules," *New Statesman*, 21 February 1986, p. 14.

32. Quoted from an off-the-record briefing. See John Lloyd, "The Ferret," *New Statesman*, 30 January 1987, p. 12.

33. "The Central Machinery for Economic Policy," in D. N. Chester, ed., *Lessons of the British War Economy* (Cambridge University Press, 1951), p. 30.

34. Hugh Heclo and Aaron Wildavsky, *The Private Government of Public Money*, 2nd ed. (London: Macmillan, 1981), p. 9.

35. Lord Denning's Report (London: HMSO, Cmnd. 2152, 1963).

36. Cf. W. J. M. Mackenzie, "The Plowden Report, a translation," in Richard Rose, ed., *Studies in British Politics*, and the original, *Control of Public Expenditure* (London: HMSO, Cmnd. 1432, 1961).

37. See L. W. Martin, "The Market for Strategic Ideas," *American Political Science Review*, 56:1 (1962).

38. "In the course of investigation," *New Society*, 24 July 1969. See also K. C. Wheare, *Government by Committee* (Oxford: Clarendon Press, 1955); and Martin Bulmer, ed., *Social Research and Royal Commissions* (London: Allen and Unwin, 1980).

39. A. H. Halsey and I. M. Crewe, "Social Survey of Civil Servants," The Fulton Committee Report, p. 1.

40. See the report of Lord Franks's *Departmental Committee on Section 2 of the Official Secrets Act, 1911* (London: HMSO, Cmnd. 5104, 1972).

41. See *Open Government* (London: HMSO, 1979).

42. For opinion poll evidence, see Chapman and Hunt, *Open Government*, p. 23.

43. See Richard Norton-Taylor, *The Ponting Affair* (London: Cecil Woolf, 1985); Clive Ponting, *The Right to Know* (London: Sphere, 1985).

44. Cf. Hugo Young, "Come the Revolution," *Sunday Times*, 10 February 1983; Michael Cockerell et al., *Sources Close to the Prime Minister*, p. 130ff.

45. Sir John Nott, quoted by Nicholas Wood, "Ingham Lobby against Ministers," *The Sunday Times*, 5 January 1988. For a review of the inconclusive evidence on Westland, see Defence Committee, *Westland Plc: the Government's Decision-Making* (London: HMSO, 4th report, HC 519, 1986).

46. Quoted in Rudolf Klein's note in *New Society*, 5 October 1972. Ironically, colleagues and friends always regarded Crossman as a notoriously misleading reporter of events and discussions. Cf. "The Crossman Diaries Reconsidered," *Contemporary Record* 1:2 (1987), pp. 22–30.

47. See Richard Rose, "The Market for Policy Indicators," in Shonfield and Shaw, eds., *Social Indicators and Social Policy* (London: Heinemann, 1972), pp. 119–141.

48. Colin Bennett, op. cit., p. 209; italics in the original.

49. Sir Robert Armstrong, in Sydney. Cf. House of Commons, *Debates*, 15 January 1988; Peter Kellner, "Sir Robert Makes a New Move," *The Independent*, 7 December 1987.

CHAPTER IX

Organizing Group Pressures

The unsectional Parliament should know what each section in the nation thought before it gave the national decision.

ORGANIZATION IS NECESSARY to give voice to political views. Without organization, people of the same mind politically have no means of representing their views to government. With organization, there is a spokesperson who can lobby government to act, and government has an organization with whom it can consult about problems of mutual interest. Organization into trade unions greatly increases the influence of millions of formerly unorganized workers. Employers too organize to present their case to government.

The members of a pressure group can be individuals or other organizations. A group such as the Society of Authors will have individual writers as its members, whereas the members of the Publishers Association are firms producing books. A group of individuals may claim to represent voters, but it will find it harder to secure agreement and raise resources than a group that represents a small number of large institutions, such as the Committee of London Clearing Banks. Whatever its form, every pressure group has political problems in securing agreement among its members about its aims, strategy, and tactics. For example, half the members of trade unions affiliated to the Labour Party vote for other parties at a general election.

Both parties and pressure groups present demands to government; they differ in that pressure groups do not contest elections. Because pressure groups do not seek public office, their officials are free to advocate sectional interests without regard to the views of the mass electorate. Pressure groups do not have government's problem of balancing competing claims against each other; they are narrowly concerned with their own members' immediate and specific interests. By contrast a party, especially when in office, must reconcile conflicting demands in ways acceptable to most of the electorate.

Parties and pressure groups are separate institutions, but they are politically interdependent. Both advance political demands in a common policy process. Agreement about particular political issues often leads pressure group officials and party politicians to work together. Conservative politicians and businessmen can find common cause in debates about legislation on industrial relations, and so too can trade union leaders and Labour politicians. A group that is an organization of many organizations, such as the Confederation of British Industry or the Trades Union Congress, sometimes can aggregate varied interests like a political party, and a party may argue that the claims of a particular group close to it represent matters of political principle.

Because the word "group" is broad, it is sometimes argued that all politics is group politics. At the extreme, writers can view "the government and various official agencies as a group actor in the same sense that we view the CBI and TUC as group actors in the policy process." But this assertion is misleading, for it ignores the distinctions between those responsible for exercising the powers of government and groups that stand outside government but seek to influence it.[1]

To analyze pressure groups, we must first of all understand the way in which groups are organized as well as their political resources. Differences in political values are the concern of the second section of this chapter; values affect whether a group can lobby as an insider or an outsider in Whitehall. The chapter next addresses the bargaining process between pressure groups and government. Since pressure groups are only a part of the policy process, they must adapt to changes in policy making. The final section examines the replacement of consensual tripartite bargaining, sometimes described as corporatism, by the arm's-length assertion of authority by the Thatcher government.

DIFFERENCES IN GROUP RESOURCES

While all pressure groups by definition seek to influence government, the thousands of groups that do so differ greatly in their resources. There is little in common between such diverse institutions as the Association of County Councils, the Howard League for Penal Reform, the Distressed Gentlefolks' Aid Association, the Royal Society for the Prevention of Cruelty to Animals, the Transport and General Workers' Union, and the Automobile Association. Pressure groups differ in goals, ability to organize, solidarity, and strategic location.

Interests and Causes as Goals. Some groups promote a permanent sectional interest in society; others seek to achieve a particular cause. A group with a permanent stake in government policy needs continuous representation. Trade unions and business groups expect to be active as long as society has workers or companies. An interest group can simultaneously be involved in discussions with half a dozen Whitehall departments about dozens of specific issues. By contrast, an organized cause usually has a relatively closely focused objective such as the abolition of capital punishment; it is a one-issue organization. Many groups have both immediate and long-term goals, the former capable of achievement in the life of a Parliament and the latter sufficiently ambitious to justify activity for generations.[2]

Cause groups can have an all-or-nothing approach to politics, demanding the total adoption of their demands, whether it be the fluoridation of the water supply or the banning of a chemical preservative in foods. From their perspective, half a loaf is acceptable only as a first installment upon all demands being completely met. By contrast, interest groups, whether their concern is with agricultural subsidies or public-sector wages, try to get more for their members or avoid being given less. They do not expect to get everything; in an endless process of bargaining compromises frequently occur.

Distinctions are sometimes drawn between economic and ideological goals and between groups defending sectional interests and altruistic promotional groups.[3] The difficulty with such distinctions is that what one group describes as a cause or principle another may see as a vested interest. Business groups proclaiming that the profit motive is good for the British economy are attacked as serving the interests of businessmen, and a trade union that campaigns against workers in a declining industry being made unemployed will be accused of trying to protect its own dues income at the expense of the economy as a whole. Members drawing no money income from a group's activities can still gain a reward; campaigning for a cause provides active campaigners with a psychic income.

Ability to Organize. Without organization those who share an interest or a commitment to a cause have no means of lobbying or negotiating with government. Organization converts people who share a common characteristic into a group that can articulate demands and be heard by government. Producer interests are more readily organized than consumer interests because they are specific and immediate. Individuals and companies often derive material benefits from joining producer groups. By contrast, consumer groups are difficult to organize because an individual does not need to belong to a consumer pressure group in order to enjoy the benefits it seeks; these are available to everyone in the marketplace. The Consumers' Association organizes only 3 percent of the nation's consumers, whereas trade unions organize 40 percent of the nation's work force.

The more durable, the more frequent, and the more intense the contacts among individuals, the easier they are to organize for political action. Workers in a one-industry town have many characteristics that encourage organization. They usually work at a large local factory and are likely to be in contact with fellow workers away from the factory. Changes in the organization of work from large factories to many smaller, dispersed workplaces make it harder to organize unions. Increased mobility between jobs and regions is weakening social attachments at the workplace. By contrast, passengers on an air charter flight are almost incapable of organization if they meet only once when waiting at an airport to board an aircraft.

When a person belongs to several groups, there can be conflicts between the goals of different groups that the individual supports. For example, a teacher may belong to a union that campaigns for higher wages in response to inflation and to a consumer group that campaigns for a wage and price freeze to counteract inflation. A business firm may simultaneously belong to a group that protests about taxation and to a trade association asking government to spend more money to help its industry. When competing interests pull an individual in two different directions, the effect of cross-cutting interests is likely to be a moderation in demands.

Solidarity in Action. The more committed members are to a pressure group's goals, the more confident a group's leaders can be that they speak for a united membership. Unity increases a group's influence with government and assures that an agreement reached with it will be accepted by its members. The less committed members are or the more they are cross-pressured by membership in conflicting groups, the more difficulty a group has, for policy makers know that it does not speak with the full backing of its nominal supporters.

It is administratively convenient for Whitehall to deal with pressure groups that have a high degree of solidarity because they are better able to implement an agreement negotiated by their leaders. But decades of attempts to plan the British economy demonstrate that leaders of business and unions cannot guarantee that a bargain they make will be carried out because of a lack of solidarity between leaders and followers. Pressure-group leaders can articulate members' demands but cannot force members to accept a bargain if they deem it against their interests. As one experienced British economist writes:

> Neither the trade unions nor management have systems of private government that can send plenipotentiaries to negotiate on their behalf and commit them to settlement, save on limited issues and particular occasions, when the negotiators can keep in touch with their constituents as the negotiations proceed.[4]

The 1984 coal strike was an extreme example of what happens to a pressure group that lacks solidarity. The leader of the National Union of Mineworkers, Arthur Scargill, called a national strike without a ballot of members and against the wishes of a large portion of the membership, which was prepared to negotiate with the National Coal Board. Divisions within the union were so strong that during the strike miners in some areas remained at work. The result was the formation of a second and rival union, the Union of Democratic Mineworkers. Each group is now more united internally, but coal miners are split in two unions.

The country's major pressure groups—trade unions and business firms—have difficulty maintaining group loyalty. Trade unions are perennially subject to conflicts of interest between members of different unions. From time to time unions dispute which should have jurisdiction over workers in a given industry or factory. They also disagree about wage differentials between different unions, a problem exacerbated by the large number of craft unions dividing workers in a single factory into competing unions. For example, the railways have separate unions for locomotive drivers, ticket clerks, and other workers, each with its own idea of the proper wage differential between them.

The Trades Union Congress (TUC), the coordinating federation of unions, is internally weak because of differences between its largest members. The TUC cannot make a contract with government about wages because the unions that form the federation are not bound to accept whatever agreement it might make. The comparative weakness of the TUC is illustrated by its ratio of headquarters staff to union membership, the lowest of any central labour organization in the Western world.[5]

While many organizations are based upon capital, they nonetheless differ in many ways. Major functional and social differences distinguish banks and financial institutions in the City of London from manufacturers who borrow from banks and retailers who sell consumers goods bought abroad or at home. The name of the Confederation of British Industry implies more unity than exists in fact. Corporate members of the CBI often prefer to rely upon trade associations, and larger firms make direct contacts with government to advance their particular interests. Nationalized industries are owned by government, yet also lobby Whitehall.[6] A review of the creation of pressure groups to represent interests within the City of London concludes that the net effect is that "the modern financial community is much more diverse and less easily manageable."[7] As the City has become an international financial center competing with New York and Tokyo, it is less concerned with what British government does and more concerned with the international economy. This differentiates it further from profit-making organizations primarily concerned with what happens within the British economy.

Strategic Location. An organization occupies a strong strategic position if it commands resources indispensable in society, such as energy, money, or food. Dockers have a much stronger strategic position than cinema owners, for England must import food through the docks to live, but it does not need to import films to amuse itself.

Groups that are a monopoly supplier of an important service, for example unions in the electricity supply industry, are in a strong strategic position. However, very few organizations nowadays enjoy a monopoly; for example, a postal strike can be circumvented by greater reliance upon telephones and telecommunications. Groups representing occupations with a service ethic, such as doctors, nurses, and teachers, have professional norms inhibiting them from refusing their services to clients in need. In the face of economic difficulties these groups now press their claims more actively, sometimes working to rule and refusing all but emergency cases. Politicians do not like to be seen refusing pay claims of valued service workers, but nurses and teachers are equally likely to lose public sympathy if they actually disrupt services by going on strike.

Political perceptions influence a group's bargaining strength. In the 1970s the National Union of Mineworkers believed that the country was so dependent upon coal that the government would have to meet its wage demands on the nationalized industry, even when they were contrary to government policy. In 1984 the Thatcher government was prepared to accept a year-long coal strike, after large stocks of coal were built up and union members split, with some striking and others remaining in work.

Money is a necessity of organization, paying the costs of an office and staff and the preparation of briefs to support the group's demands. But in England money does not buy favors from public officials or parties; it is given openly in recognition of mutual interests. An MP may speak for a pressure group, but party discipline sees to it that the MP votes with the party in the Commons. No pressure group in British politics can confidently claim that its members are so committed to it that they would switch their votes from one party to another at its direction. Trade unions find that their role as primary funder of the Labour Party is a mixed blessing; party politicians need their contributions, but the unions depend upon the electoral success of the party.

Pressure groups with a weak strategic position and few organizational resources may turn to the media for publicity. Publicity gives the appearance of mass support by the multiplier effect of mass circulation. The simplest and cheapest publicity device is to issue a press release or write a letter to *The Times* (London) signed by prominent persons, for names make news. However, publicity can be a sign that the group is unable to advance its claims by quiet negotiations in Whitehall.

PRESSURE GROUPS AND POLITICAL VALUES

Pressure groups do not press in a vacuum; they can only influence government within the parameters of a society's political values. In England, collective action for political ends has been positively valued since before the rise of electoral democracy in the late nineteenth century.[8] Collective action has been accepted in different ways by both Conservative and Labour politicians. But because the goals and values that pressure groups represent are political, they inevitably generate controversy.

Mixing Group and Party Values. The interdependence of pressure-group goals and political values draws the two groups together in pursuit of common ends. The connection is formally recognized in the Labour Party, which regards itself as one wing of the labor movement, complementing trade unions and cooperative societies. The Labour movement is thus two parts pressure group and one part political party. In the picturesque phrase of Ernest Bevin, the party grew out of the bowels of the trade union movement.[9] Today trade unions affiliate more than nine-tenths of the party's membership, elect many members of the party's National Executive Committee, provide more than four-fifths of its income, and sponsor financially more than half of the party's MPs in Parliament.

The link between the Labour Party and trade unions creates substantial difficulties for both sides. At times it can be a means for unions to achieve political goals; for example, the unions were able to veto a 1969 Labour government proposal to amend laws on trade union activity and got the 1975 Labour government to repeal the previous Conservative government's Industrial Relations Act. But party and unions have many different interests. In the winter of 1978 trade unions sought to overturn Labour government guidelines to hold down wage increases. The resulting conflict between the two wings of the movement during what became known as the winter of discontent contributed to Labour's loss of the 1979 election.

As the alternative to Labour, the Conservative Party is inevitably linked with business interests, but the ties are informal. The Conservative Party existed before the Industrial Revolution and before businessmen gained the right to vote. For most of the nineteenth century the Liberal Party was the party of businessmen. The collapse of the Liberals led businessmen into the Conservative Party, but it has never had institutional links with business associations as the Labour Party is linked with unions. Individual wealth, preferably in the hands of landed persons or those who aspire to noble status, has been the historic bulwark of the Conservative Party.[10]

Mrs. Thatcher has identified the leadership of the Conservative Party with the promotion of market values in the abstract. She is fond of telling audiences that the lessons learned as the daughter of a small-town grocer constitute values widely applicable in life. This stands in marked contrast to an alternative and older set of Conservative beliefs about social solidarity, postulating semipaternalist care for all groups within society. Conservatives wishing to avoid identifying the party with business values signify their opposition by speaking about the social responsibilities of Conservatism.

The Liberal Party has suffered because it was not identified with a major economic interest in society. As a party of individuals and nothing but individuals, the Liberals have found it much harder to raise money than have their Conservative and Labour opponents and to appeal to a large bloc of voters as a class. The Liberals' opposition to group ties was maintained by its Alliance formed with the Social Democratic Party; one complaint that the SDP levied against the Labour Party was that it was too closely linked to trade unions. The Social and Liberal Democrats were launched in 1988 as a merger of the Alliance parties independent of large interest groups—and poorer and smaller because of it.

The fortunes of every pressure group are much affected by whether or not its claims are considered partisan. In contemporary England many pressure groups claim to be nonpolitical, that is to say, *multipartisan*; they wish to be on good terms with the government of the day whatever its party.[11] However, the growth of the mixed economy has politicized many issues that pressure-group leaders would prefer to have resolved outside Whitehall.

Parties rather than pressure groups decide whether a group drawing support from across parties (pensioners) is closely linked to one party (business or unions) or appeals to a portion of a single party [the Campaign for Nuclear Disarmament (Labour) or groups favoring capital punishment (Conservative)]. By making a political issue of a group's activities, a party draws it into the arena of party conflict. The Labour Party's tendency to consider most of society's activities the concern of government has led it to initiate partisan debate about everything from secondary education to fox hunting. As the 1964–70 Labour government's reform of education showed, education groups with nonpolitical status found themselves on the sidelines when major decisions about secondary education were made by a party government.[12]

Many pressure groups today face a dilemma. Should they seek multi-partisan status by cooperating with the government of the day, whatever its political color, in hopes that this will secure continuing influence in Whitehall on matters of immediate concern? Or should the group be outspoken in articulating demands, even when this aligns it with the minority party in Parliament, in hopes of greater eventual success through a change of government?

Insiders and Outsiders. The values of a pressure group affect the way in which it advances its claims—and how the government of the day responds. Insider groups frequently advance their views in quiet negotiations with Whitehall. The privacy of government is respected; the group does not leak information obtained from ministries, nor does it make public and embarrassing charges against ministers. The demands advanced by insider groups are deemed reasonable by government, for they do not in principle conflict with the values of the governing party. Requests for money or other resources are carefully calibrated to be within the realm of the politically possible.

By contrast, outsider groups are unable or unwilling to press their cause with government ministers. They may be disqualified because the government of the day believes that the group's demands are unacceptable or because the group does not wish to moderate its claims to bring them within the realm of current political possibilities. Some outsider groups are negatively multipartisan, that is, they are unpopular with the general public and viewed unfavorably by the leaders of all parties and ministries in Whitehall. Outsider groups can fall back upon publicity to state their case because they have no goodwill to lose by going public with demands that the government rejects.

The more consistent pressure-group goals are with general cultural norms, the easier it is to be an insider group, representing a permanent and recognized estate of the realm. The more a group's views are in the minority or in conflict with social values, the more likely a group is to be kept on the outside. At least five different types of pressure groups can thus be identified: three insider groups (permanent, up-and-down, and prisoners) and two outsider groups (aspiring insiders, and complete outsiders).[13]

1. *Permanent Insiders.* When there is harmony between pressure-group demands and general cultural norms, a group reckons that its views will be permanently acceptable in Whitehall, and it adopts behavior appropriate to Whitehall customs. For example, the Royal National Institute for the Blind does not need to run publicity campaigns to mobilize support for its political demands, for they are non-controversial. The role of such a group is to negotiate in Whitehall about details of administration, finance, and the expansion of public policies that directly or indirectly affect the blind. It does this by direct discussion with relevant policy makers in Whitehall.

2. *Up-and-Down Status.* Because politics is about controversy, few major pressure groups can expect to be permanently in harmony with the government of the day. This is most evident in the case of trade unions and business groups, which cannot expect the same treatment from a Conservative and a Labour government. Although society always has some prounion and some proemployer sentiment, the balance fluctuates in response to events, sometimes favoring one party to industrial disputes or refusing sympathy to both. Leaders of pressure groups with fluctuating popular support must be adaptable, pressing claims when support is high and acting defensively when their standing is low. Major pressure groups such as the CBI and the TUC retain the outlook of Whitehall whether they are in favor there or not. They expect continuing collaboration with government to be their best policy in the long run.

3. *Prisoners.* A group that has been created by government and operates subject to government authority or funding is forced to follow an insider strategy, for it lacks the legal and financial ability to go independent. For example, the chairman of a nationalized industry may differ from government policy just as strongly as the chairman of a profit-making company. If the latter attacks the government, the firm's board of directors will cheer, but if the chairman of a nationalized industry does so, he is liable to be sacked. Not-for-profit groups that depend upon the cooperation of Whitehall departments for funds, for access to information, or for status can criticize government policies. But if they do so, this must be done in the discreet language of Whitehall, without aligning an institution with the opposition party.

4. *Aspiring Insiders*. A pressure group cannot negotiate with Whitehall if the demand it is advancing has yet to be adopted as government policy. A group lobbying for equal-opportunity legislation for women can become an insider only by negotiating with government *after* it achieves its aim, the establishment of an Equal Opportunities Commission. It must use publicity, meetings with opinion formers outside government, and the lobbying of backbench MPs to raise its claims higher on the agenda of public policy. A group shows that it is aspiring to be on the inside by preparing draft legislation that carefully takes into account established legislation and government programs.

5. *Complete Outsiders*. Groups may be excluded from Whitehall because the demands they make are unacceptable to all parties or because the group prefers publicity and confrontation through demonstration. The Campaign for Nuclear Disarmament (CND) is a complete outsider because its goal is absolute—Britain's unilateral abandonment of nuclear weapons—and has been rejected by successive Labour and Conservative ministers of Defence. Given a disagreement of principle, there is nothing to negotiate. Deprived of access to government, CND can seek to influence opinion in the press, in the universities, and in the Labour Party in opposition. There are pressures for direct action, ranging from peaceful marches and demonstrations to intentional violations of the law.

Because pressure groups do not need to win majority approval for their views, they can promote policies that are unpopular; parties must pay attention to the values of the electorate. That explains why a Conservative government does not adopt all the right-wing views for which such people as Mrs. Thatcher have sympathy and why a Labour government has not adopted many policies for which left-wing pressure groups lobby. Parties are concerned with aggregating views to secure majority support, whereas pressure groups can stick to minority values.

EXCHANGES BETWEEN WHITEHALL AND PRESSURE GROUPS

The first rule of pressure-group politics is to exert pressure where decisions are made. In England groups concentrate attention upon civil servants and ministers in Whitehall. As Lord Devlin's *Report on Industrial Representation* explained, "All executive policy and most legislation is conceived, drafted and all but enacted in Whitehall."[14]

Pressure groups give most attention to senior civil servants and ministers because the largest number of decisions affecting pressure groups are made in a departmental context. For example, health and safety regulations in the glass industry are unlikely to be discussed in the Cabinet; they can be settled by negotiations between the department and representatives of affected unions and employers. To achieve success in negotiations, group representatives need only convince departmental officials that their position is reasonable, not contrary to Cabinet policy, and not in conflict with other pressure groups.

A direct approach to ministers and civil servants is the normal channel of communication between established pressure groups and Whitehall departments. The channel may be institutionalized by appointing group members to departmental advisory committees. The group spokesmen accept this in order to be able to put their case in Whitehall before decisions are made. Such discussions allow each side to negotiate without acrimonious public exchanges.

Consultation and Exchange. Consultation is a political value of fundamental importance to pressure groups and proof of insider status. Pressure-group officials do not expect that government will meet all their demands, but they do expect that the government of the day will listen to what they have to say before making a firm policy commitment. When consultation does not occur, government invites a criticism that will attract wide sympathy: "We were not consulted." When a government decision about the future of the British Museum was announced without consulting its trustees, the chairman, Lord Radcliffe, denounced this as "almost unbelievable administrative incompetence" and "a grave constitutional impropriety that all these agencies should be ignored and despised."[15]

Communication between pressure groups and government usually involves an exchange of influence. Government seeks to influence pressure groups, and groups press claims upon government. Exchange occurs because each has things that the other wants and needs.

Pressure groups seek four things from government. First, groups seek access to policy makers. To be able to talk with civil servants or ministers whenever problems arise is a great advantage to groups, because they know the power that Whitehall has to affect matters of concern to the group. A second advantage follows from this: groups get information about developments in Whitehall that affect them incidentally or importantly. The information can be used to consult with members and to make representations to a ministry. Thirdly, groups seek the goodwill of Whitehall officials so that officials will interpret their discretionary powers to make decisions satisfactory to the group. Stimulating new legislation is a relatively infrequent concern. Fourth, pressure groups seek status, for example allowing an organization to add the prefix "royal" to its title or having a minister address the group's annual conference. Access, information, goodwill, and status are useful in combination to carry out the everyday tasks that insider pressure groups regard as a primary justification for their existence.

Government seeks four things in return from pressure groups. Information is the first of its needs. Groups accumulate from members much information that does not routinely come to the attention of Whitehall and that is relevant for policy making. For example, exporting firms can advise the Department of Trade & Industry about problems in selling abroad. Second, Whitehall wants advice from pressure groups about what they think ought to be done and how they view alternative policies that a department is considering. The views of insider groups are particularly valued because they appreciate the Whitehall view as well as that of their members. Third, after a decision is made, a department wants pressure groups to support what the government has decided or at least to neutralize opposition. Insider groups may publicly criticize what the government does—but not vociferously or in a way that the department views as unfair. Finally, when a policy has been embodied in an Act of Parliament, government wants pressure groups to cooperate in implementing policies that depend for their success on actions by agencies outside Whitehall. In social policy, other public sector agencies such as local authorities and the health service are particularly important because they deliver services. In economic policy, the cooperation of business and unions is important (cf. Chapter XIII).

Because most wants are complementary, insider pressure groups and government find it easy to negotiate. Negotiations proceed without threats of coercion or bribery because each needs the other. The interdependence of insider groups and government results in an exchange of influence in which policies can be the product of the dialectic rather than the exclusive product of the views of one side or the other.

The Limits of Agreement. Because insider pressure groups and government policy makers are often closeted together, their frequent interaction is sometimes described as if they were identical in outlook and interests. This is a misleading half-truth. The element of truth is that Whitehall ministries and insider pressure groups have a common interest in problems facing government. Furthermore, both partners to negotiations prefer agreement to disagreement. But it is misleading to suggest that because agreement often occurs, the two groups must inevitably agree or are simply two manifestations of a single interest.

Exchange occurs because government and pressure groups differ in what each wants and can command. The influence of a pressure group on government policy depends on the simplicity and scale of the decision. The simpler and smaller a problem, the more likely it is that discussions can be confined to representatives of a few pressure groups and a small number of civil servants within a single department. In such circumstances a small number of people who know each other are expected to come to an agreement in order to avoid escalating a small problem into a big issue.

As an issue increases in complexity and political importance, it becomes more difficult to resolve by agreement between the officials of a single ministry and pressure-group representatives. The more important an issue, the greater the likelihood that a variety of groups will be mobilized. The mobilization of one interest invites the countermobilization of opposing interests. The more strongly one group presses its claims, the greater the incentive for opposing interests to organize. For example, the political success of trade unions has led business groups to strengthen their lobbying activities. When groups are lobbying against each other, success for one side will be a setback for the other. For example, proabortion and antiabortion pressure groups cannot both succeed, for their demands are mutually exclusive. Because demands are varied, many groups can simultaneously achieve some satisfaction. But even when pressure-group politics provides something to every insider group, it does not offer equal satisfaction to all.

Competition between pressure groups limits the influence that any one can exert upon an outcome. When Whitehall officials receive different and often conflicting demands, they realize that a concession to one group, say, commercial broadcasting interests, will be opposed by another, say, newspaper proprietors fearful of losing advertising revenue. Whitehall officials are adept at playing off competing pressure groups against one another in order to achieve an agreement that will be acceptable to the department's own interests as much as or even more than to the groups lobbying it.

The more complex the problem, the greater the likelihood that a number of Whitehall departments will be affected, requiring inter-departmental negotiations in which each department presents the point of view of pressure groups associated with it. A pressure group that is an insider in one department of Whitehall can be con-fronted with opposition from another group that has the inside track in another department. What has initially been a conflict between pressure groups is then translated into a disagreement between Cabinet ministers, where the ideas and political clout of particular ministers are significant in resolving differences.

The more controversial and well publicized an issue, the more certain ministers are to insist upon an outcome consistent with the overall pattern of party policy. Civil servants cannot agree with pressure-group officials to go against the declared position of the government of the day. Moreover, the governing party can insist upon introducing measures with a high priority in the party even though they are opposed by some major pressure groups. Party dis-cipline gives the Cabinet of the day the capacity to impose its pat-tern of policy upon negotiations. A Labour government can start discussions with a business group with the chief agenda item how the group is to be nationalized, not whether nationalization is to occur. A Conservative government can lay down an agenda for dis-cussion with trade unions in which the principal issue is how a new industrial relations act is to be implemented. If the government is prepared to impose legislation against a group's wishes, the group's leaders have the unpleasant choice of negotiating the terms of their defeat or publicly and vainly attacking the government and becom-ing an outsider for an indefinite period.

Once a Cabinet decision has been made, the sponsor department and pressure groups associated with it must accept the result. Pres-sure groups find that the centralized institutions of Whitehall are relatively difficult to influence on major issues of party concern. When unwanted changes in policy loom, insider groups concentrate upon influencing specific details affecting the way in which a mea-sure is to be implemented. A director-general of the Confederation of British Industry writes:

Industry may or may not like the policy; and the CBI will say so on its behalf. But when the issue is decided, it may make a world of difference to industry how the policy is implemented and translated through administration into action.[16]

Confronted with legislation to reform schools by the Thatcher government, the general secretary of the National Association of Head Teachers declared:

> The government must take our objections on board. There is no point in trying to ram through policies without our support. It is our members who actually run the schools.[17]

Government officials do not mechanically weigh the pressure that groups exert, for the assessment of political pressures is a matter of political judgment, not science. Whitehall influences policy by deciding how much influence competing groups should have. The pattern of party policy, when it reflects the views of large numbers of unorganized voters, can put public power in the scales against organized interests. In the relationship between pressure groups and government, it is the government that is of primary importance, for it is responsible for the Acts of Parliament, appropriations of money, and administration that set the limits upon the activities of pressure groups.

PLURALISM AND CORPORATISM

Three different models of pressure-group relations with government are potentially applicable to politics in England. The first is *pluralism*, which emphasizes competition between a multiplicity of groups; government can appear as a relatively weak broker calculating the influence of different group pressures. A second alternative is *corporatism*, a theoretical model generalized from authoritarian and democratic countries that have organized compulsory institutions for bargaining between government, business, and labor. In Britain this is best described as *tripartism*, that is, noncompulsory cooperation between business, trade unions, and government. The third model is called *state-centered* in European countries, emphasizing the durable and binding political authority of the state.

Pluralism and Corporatism. The idea of corporatism was developed in authoritarian regimes to describe the compulsory organization of political interests and their resolution by negotiations involving the authority of the state. In a corporatist system, individuals do not have a choice about whether or not to belong to groups; membership is a condition of work or of doing business. Once a decision is agreed on by representatives of major groups, including government, all groups are bound to deliver the consent of their members. The powers of the state are used to reinforce the authority of capital and labor; in return, interest groups are compelled to accept policies jointly agreed with the government. Corporatism thus rejects the individualism that characterizes much liberal thought in both politics and economics.

Liberal corporatism is a concept developed in an attempt to apply the idea of corporatism to relations between organized groups and government in a democratic political system. It accepts that groups can organize freely and that cooperation cannot be coerced or compelled but is based upon voluntary agreement. Both of these assumptions are important in conventional pluralist models of pressure groups. So too is the assumption that even though government does not have coercive powers, it is an important independent influence upon the outcome of bargaining with groups about public policy.[18]

After systematically examining British pressure groups in terms of both corporatist and pluralist theories, Wyn Grant concludes that pressure-group politics in Britain "look remarkably pluralist."[19] Pressure groups are multiple, and membership is usually voluntary rather than compulsory. The Trades Union Congress cannot issue orders to individual trade unions, nor can business or trade associations enforce orders against particular business firms. Groups are free to organize without interference from government, and British government does not compel people to belong to organizations. Pressure groups have the option of refusing to implement government policies with which they disagree, whereas in a corporate system the state relies upon groups to follow its directions in the public interest. Insofar as British examples of liberal corporatism are cited, the references are usually to small-scale activities such as cooperation between the Milk Marketing Board, a government agency, and the Dairy Trade Federation, designated by government as the official representative of the dairy industry. The limits of corporate action are illustrated by the chronic problems of efforts to secure tripartite management of the economy.

Tripartism in Practice. While British government is politically responsible for the rates of inflation, employment, and economic growth, it can influence but not command the results of the market. Successive governments have sought to reconcile conflicting demands of economic pressure groups by the creation of a host of quasi- and para-governmental institutions involving business and trade unions as well as ministers. Prime Ministers from Harold Macmillan to James Callaghan eagerly sought consultations that could complement (or, their critics have charged, substitute for) Parliament and party. The institutions are best referred to as tripartite because the three separate groups involved—government, business, and unions—are not incorporated in a single organization; each maintains its separate identity and the capacity to act independently. Tripartite institutions are not so like a single stool with three legs; they are like three different animals, each free to be friendly, to fight, or to go its separate way.

Tripartite institutions have rested upon three assumptions. The first is consensus about priorities for inflation, unemployment, and economic growth and about policies appropriate for achieving priority goals. Second, it has been assumed that the representatives in tripartite deliberations could secure the consent of those they represent. Third, tripartite institutions have been seen as supporting stable, long-term policies to deal with the country's economic difficulties and not just ad hoc meetings that will break up under the pressure of economic difficulties. These assumptions have been belied by events.

The contemporary impetus to tripartism came when Conservative Prime Minister Harold Macmillan established the National Economic Development Council (NEDC) in 1961. The intention was for the NEDC to set target rates for economic growth; to develop plans for overcoming obstacles to growth; and to coordinate actions by government, industry, and unions to implement these plans. In the 1970s a series of tripartite executive bodies such as the Manpower Services Commission and the Health and Safety Commission were established to deliver programs of particular relevance to trade union and business interests.

With the deterioration of economic conditions in the late 1960s and 1970s, the focus of tripartite economic bodies gradually shifted from optimistic plans for economic growth to measures for reducing inflationary increases in prices and wages and rising unemployment. As economic growth slowed down, there was no assurance that all participants in tripartite institutions could enjoy benefits. Often the task confronting these organizations was the distribution of economic misery. Both Labour and Conservative governments argued that only by keeping wages from going up as fast as prices could the spiral of inflation be broken and something approximating full employment maintained.[20]

The 1974–79 Labour government sought a social contract with the trade unions as a means of containing conflict about wages in an inflationary period. The theory of the social contract was that publicly financed social benefits for workers and their families would augment limited wage increases agreed by union leaders in tripartite negotiations. In practice the government did not have the money to provide all the benefits demanded. For example, in 1977 a Labour Health and Social Security minister was faced with demands to provide far more benefits than the Treasury could finance. The Department of Health and Social Security (DHSS) called a meeting of pressure groups with an agenda listing each group's proposals and their cost. The total bill was more than twice as much as the DHSS was then spending. Saying yes to each group would have required increasing income tax by almost one-third and thus reducing substantially the take-home pay of workers.[21] The Labour government could not offer trade unions a blank check to finance the social contract.

Voluntary agreements between government and pressure groups have tended to be fragile and short-lived. First of all, tripartite policy making requires consensus on policies and goals, but such consensus tends to be temporary. For example, unions, business, and government agreed that it was in their mutual interest to reduce inflation when the rate was above 20 percent; there was a temporary acceptance of measures to limit wage and price increases. But by 1978 unions were no longer willing to forgo wage claims, since the pay pause had reduced their members' real earnings as well as inflation.

Second, tripartite deliberations are fundamentally weak because participating groups cannot bind their members to accept what their leaders agree. The Cabinet is not committed by agreement between trade unions and business groups. Trade union leaders cannot bind their members, who are divided on many industrial issues, especially ideas about a "proper" wage increase or a "proper" wage differential. The so-called business world is in fact divided into many different nations. As Lord Watkinson, a former Conservative Cabinet minister and President of the Confederation of British Industry, has pointed out, neither the CBI nor the TUC "has effective control over its membership to the extent that it can undertake to deliver a policy by ensuring that all its members will implement it."[22]

The third point follows: tripartite economic institutions have been inherently unstable. Their formation reflects a common desire for collective action in pursuit of immediate and pressing economic goals. But the attempt to carry out policies reveals disagreements between and within each of the three groups. For example, the 1974–79 Labour government entered office boasting of its ability to bargain successfully with unions and deliver industrial peace. It left office after experiencing soaring inflation, rising unemployment, and lower rates of economic growth. The final blow was the 1978 winter of discontent, when rank-and-file trade union members struck for higher wages in the public and private sectors.

The Thatcher Alternative: Dealing at Arm's Length. 'If you can't beat them, don't join them' is the basic assumption of Margaret Thatcher's strategy for dealing with major economic pressure groups. Since 1979 the Conservative government has adopted a strategy of arm's-length dealings with both trade unions and business groups. The reliance of the Thatcher government upon monetary policy to reduce inflation and promote economic growth has not required endless consultations with representatives of unions and businesses. Control of the money supply is within the hands of the government.

A state-centered policy for the economy normally involves the government closely with business and unions in order to make sure that they do what government wants. By contrast, the Thatcher philosophy is better described as *state distancing*, for the institutions of the Crown are not meant to be mixed up in the everyday activities of the marketplace, such as bargaining about wages or making investment decisions. The doctrine is also reflected in the privatization of state-owned industries. By selling industries to the private sector, government further distances itself from the market. Existing tripartite institutions have been reduced in influence; the NEDC is of little importance when the government of the day does not want to hear the views of business and union members.

The state-distancing strategy of the Thatcher government allows it to have an impact upon the economy while insulating itself from the problems and constraints of tripartite bargaining.[23] The introduction of monetarist policies was followed by a big rise in unemployment and a contraction in manufacturing during the recession that marked its first term. This was unpopular with business organizations such as the Confederation of British Industry as well as with the Trades Union Congress. Since monetarist policies, unlike previous tripartite efforts, did not require collaboration of business investors and union wage negotiators, the government could ignore their protests—as long as it retained its majority at a general election. It did this in 1983 and subsequently moderated its economic policies in ways that fit with its own political strategy, independent of demands from unions and many businesses.

Politically, the Thatcher government's distancing first enraged and then weakened trade unions. Unions were enraged by the withdrawal of the "beer and sandwiches" style of consultations that had characterized the previous Labour governments. Secondly, the Thatcher government used its authority as the duly elected government to bring in new industrial relations legislation without consulting the unions. The legislation assumed that union leaders did not necessarily represent their members, giving members more rights within union affairs, including the right to ballot on strike action. It also treated unions as organizations with legal liability, giving employers the right to take legal action against unions that violated the new Acts of Parliament. The effects of high unemployment and changes in the labor force and the political climate have resulted in union membership and dues declining by one-quarter. Less than two-fifths of the labor force are now union members, compared to half when Labour was last in office.

The Thatcher Administration places less reliance upon negotiations with pressure groups and more upon the assertion of the independent authority of the Crown in Parliament. Business and labor are free to carry on as they like—within the pattern of policy imposed by the government's macroeconomic policy and legislation. The pattern of policy of the Thatcher government is not to the liking of trade union leaders or of some businessmen. But the Thatcher government can appear indifferent to their criticisms as long as its actions are more to the liking of the electorate than the tripartite policies that brought the Labour movement to political grief.[24]

NOTES

1. Cf. J. J. Richardson and A. G. Jordan, *Governing under Pressure* (Oxford: Martin Robertson, 1979), p. 17; and comments by Ralf Dahrendorf, "The Politics of Economic Decline," *Political Studies*, 29:2 (1981), p. 290.

2. As the discussion emphasizes, the distinctions are not completely clear-cut. See, e.g., Allen Potter, *Organized Groups in British National Politics* (London: Faber and Faber, 1961), Chapter 1.

3. See David Marsh, ed., *Pressure Politics* (London: Junction Books, 1983), pp. 3ff.

4. E. H. Phelps-Brown, "The National Economic Development Organization," *Public Administration* 41 (Autumn 1963), p. 245.

5. Cf. Bruce W. Headey, "Trade Unions and National Wages Policies," *Journal of Politics* 32:4 (1970), pp. 428ff; Michael Moran, *The Politics of Industrial Relations* (London: Macmillan, 1977); Ben Pimlott and C. Cooke, eds., *Trade Unions in British Politics* (London: Longman, 1982).

6. See Michael Moran, "Finance Capital and Pressure-Group Politics in Britain," *British Journal of Political Science* 11:4 (1981), pp. 381-404; David Steele, "Government and Industry in Britain," *British Journal of Political Science* 12:4 (1982), pp. 449-504; Wyn Grant with Jane Sargent, *Business and Politics in Britain* (London: Macmillan, 1987).

7. M. Moran, "Finance Capital and Pressure-Group Politics," p. 393. More generally, see David Vogel, "Political Science and the Study of Corporate Power," *British Journal of Political Science* 17:4 (1987), pp. 385-408.

8. See J. H. Greenleaf, *The British Political Tradition* Vols. 1 and 2 (London: Methuen, 1983); and Samuel H. Beer, *Modern British Politics: A Study of Parties and Pressure Groups*, 3rd ed. (London: Faber and Faber, 1982).

9. *Labour Party Conference Report, 1935* (London), p. 180. See also William D. Muller, *The Kept Men?* (Brighton: Harvester Press, 1977); Andrew J. Taylor, *The Trade Unions and the Labour Party* (London: Croom Helm, 1987).

10. See Grant with Sargent, *Business and Politics in Britain*, especially Chapter 8.

11. Cf. J. Roland Pennock, "Agricultural Subsidies in Britain and America," *American Political Science Review*, 56:3 (1962); and Robert J. Lieber, "Interest Groups and Political Integration: British Entry into Europe," *ibid.*, 66:1 (1972).

12. See, e.g., Paul E. Peterson, "The Politics of Comprehensive Education in Three British Cities," *Comparative Politics*, 3:3 (1971).

13. This typology, initially developed in previous editions of *Politics in England*, also draws upon distinctions made in Wyn Grant, "Insider and Outsider Pressure Groups," *Social Studies Review* 1:1 (1985), pp. 31-34.

14. Quoted in Wyn Grant and David Marsh, *The Confederation of British Industry* (London: Hodder & Stoughton, 1977).

15. House of Lords, *Debates*, Vol. 287, Cols. 1130ff (13 December 1967).

16. Quoted in Samuel H. Beer, "Pressure Groups and Parties in Britain," *American Political Science Review* 50:1 (1956), p. 8.

17. Quoted in "Heads Signal Revolt against School Reforms," *The Times*, (London) 28 August 1987.

18. Cf. Gerhard Lehmbruch, "Liberal Corporatism and Party Government," *Comparative Political Studies* 10:1 (1977); and Ross M. Martin, "Pluralism and the New Corporatism," *Political Studies* 31:1 (1983).

19. "The Role and Power of Pressure Groups," in R. L. Borthwick and J. E. Spence, eds., *British Politics in Perspective* (Leicester: Leicester University Press, 1984), p. 128. See also Wyn Grant, "Corporatism in Britain," *Social Studies Review* 2:1 (1986), pp. 36ff. Cf. Alan Cawson, *Corporatism and Political Theory* (Oxford: Blackwell, 1986).

20. On the sequence of choices confronting tripartite interests, see Fritz W. Scharpf, "A Game-Theoretical Interpretation of Inflation and Unemployment in Western Europe," *Journal of Public Policy* 7:3 (1987), pp. 227-257.

21. Calculated by the author from an unpublished Department of Health and Social Security briefing paper for a seminar on Social Security priorities, London, 5 July 1977.

22. Lord Watkinson, *Blueprint for Survival* (London: Allen and Unwin, 1976), p. 88.

23. For a more general discussion, see Jim Bulpitt, "The Discipline of the New Democracy: Mrs. Thatcher's Statecraft," *Political Studies* 34:1 (1986), pp. 19-39.

24. Many of the divisions within the Labour Party since 1979, including the swing left through constitutional change and the breakaway of the Social Democrats in 1981, have their origins in conflicts between Labour government policies and trade union leaders and conflicts between union leaders loyal to Labour government policies and militant members who did not want to follow their lead.

CHAPTER X

The Choice of Voters

Party organization is the vital principle of representative government, but that organization is permanently efficient because it is not composed of warm partisans. The body is eager, but the atoms are cool.

BRITISH GOVERNMENT IS PARTY GOVERNMENT. In a general election a voter does not vote for the policies that he or she wishes government to carry out; instead, votes must be cast for a candidate of a party that aggregates the outlooks of millions of citizens. Individuals cannot expect the program of any one party to match their own views exactly. The party system forces voters to choose the alternative that is most representative (or least unrepresentative) of their own political outlook.

Voters do not determine who governs, but which party names the governors. The leader of the party with the most seats in the House of Commons is invited to form a Cabinet. Once in office the Cabinet relies on party discipline to secure parliamentary support for its policies. If no party can secure a working majority, as happened in February 1974, another election is likely to occur shortly, for the conventions of the Constitution assume that there is a majority party in the House of Commons to provide votes of confidence in the actions of the party's leaders in Cabinet.

The way in which votes are counted has a great influence upon which party is declared the election winner. The British electoral system is based on the first-past-the-post principle; the candidate who wins the most votes in a constituency is thereby declared the Member of Parliament. If only two parties compete, then one candidate is sure to win a majority, more than half the votes. But when three parties compete, the candidate with the largest number of votes wins the seat, whether or not it is a majority. Equally important, a party does not need to win half the vote to win a majority in the House of Commons. The first-past-the-post electoral system consistently manufactures a majority of seats in Parliament for a party winning less than half the vote.

Each party is a part of the party system; the term system emphasizes the interdependence of organizations that compete with each other. Parties collectively form a system, for what happens to one affects others. If the governing party loses popularity, then its opponents' support must go up. If one party announces that it favors a policy, such as increasing pensions, the pressure is on its opponents to adopt the same objective or compete by decrying the increased tax revenue needed to finance higher public spending. When one party in a system favors trade unions (Labour), competitors can seek votes by favoring business (the Conservatives) or neither (the Social and Liberal Democrats).

Every democratic party system has more than one party; only if voters are offered a choice between two or more parties is there effective choice. The textbook view is that the British party system involves *minimal* competition between two and only two parties. This judgment is justified by the Westminster practice of assuming that an election is a competition between Ins and Outs. The doctrine of responsible party government is that only the reduction of choice to two parties allows voters a clear-cut opportunity to affirm their support for the party in office or to turn the government out by voting for the Opposition.

In the 1970s more and more voters began to register their dissatisfaction with a party system that restricted their choice to two parties. In the two 1974 general elections, the Liberal Party was the principal beneficiary of a surge in voting for third parties. In the 1980s politicians too registered their dissatisfaction. In 1981 a group of Labour MPs broke off to form the Social Democratic Party, which promptly aligned with the long-established Liberal Party to fight the 1983 and 1987 general elections as the Alliance. Immediately after the 1987 election, the two parties voted to merge into the Social and Liberal Democrats. But Dr. David Owen, leader of the SDP, refused to join the merged group and announced his intention of remaining leader of a fourth party. Hence, since 1974 the electorate has sustained multiparty politics—that is, more than the minimum of two parties.

The British party system is temporarily destabilized by three and sometimes four parties competing for votes and seats in a Parliament built for two. To understand the choices that the party system now offers, the first section of this chapter examines the choice of voters and the way in which the electoral system acts as a device for disproportional representation when translating votes into seats in the House of Commons. Second, we must examine the policy preferences of voters and of parties. To what extent has the multiplication of parties reflected greater divisions in public opinion, or do the views of voters for different parties tend to be similar? To what extent can parties appeal for votes by emphasizing policies that make them distinctive, or do they compete by claiming to be more competent in achieving what a majority of voters want?

ELECTORAL CHOICE

While voters are free to do what they want at a general election, how an individual votes and the election outcome are significantly influenced by actions of parties and by the mechanics of the electoral system. An individual can express his or her choice only within the constraints of the electoral and party system.

Constraints upon Choice. While by law an election must be held once every five years, a decision by one person, the Prime Minister, determines the date on which an election is held. The Prime Minister is free to request the Queen to dissolve Parliament and call a general election at any time the governing party chooses. A Prime Minister tries to arrange government policies so that the results will be popular as the time for calling a general election looms. For example, unpopular economic measures are likely to be taken early in a term of office in hopes that the economy will boom in the run up to a general election. Even with evidence from public opinion polls, by-election results, and local government election results, a Prime Minister often mistimes an election. In the seven elections since the development of sophisticated election analysis in the mid-1960s, the governing party has won four elections and lost three.

The ballot offers a voter a very simple choice. In each parliamentary constituency, a voter receives a sheet of paper giving the name, address, occupation, and party label of three or four people who seek to be its MP. The ideas and arguments of a multiplicity of politicians and party institutions are reduced to a choice of one standard-bearer per party. To discourage frivolous contestants, each candidate is required to post a deposit of £500 with the nomination papers. This deposit is forfeited if the candidate does not secure at least five percent of the vote in the constituency. At the 1987 election, all the Conservative, Labour, and Alliance candidates bar one saved their deposit. Apart from Scottish and Welsh Nationalists, only one other candidate saved a deposit.

Even when only two parties are on the ballot, there is always a third choice: not voting. Because local authorities are responsible for compiling the election register, an individual does not need to make a special effort to qualify to vote.[1] In 1987, 75 percent of the eligible electorate turned out to vote, well above the 55 percent turnout at the 1984 American presidential election but below the normal turnout at a continental European election.

The focus of media attention upon party leaders is mistakenly treated as evidence that party competition has been reduced to competition between the personalities who lead the parties. This is not the case. Voters form their judgments of parties *before* a particular politician becomes its leader. A leader is then evaluated in the light of prior partisan attachments. Conservative supporters tend to like whoever is the Conservative leader, and Labour supporters to like whoever is elected Labour leader. While the leader's personality remains the same, voters' opinions about leaders fluctuate in keeping with their evaluation of the government's record and the performance of the Opposition parties. A party can win an election even when its leader is less popular than the leader of the opposing party, as in 1979, when the Conservatives won even though Margaret Thatcher was much less popular than Labour leader James Callaghan (cf. Table III.2). In America, by contrast, a much larger proportion of the electorate chooses a candidate without regard to party label.[2]

The analysis of political socialization in Chapter VI showed that political principles are the most important single influence upon voting today. Second in importance is the assessment that an individual makes of the performance of parties during the current Parliament. A government or opposition that does well gains support, and if it does badly, it loses support. Such socioeconomic characteristics as housing and such occupational and preadult socialization influences are also of significance. These four sets of influences have been consistently important for decades.[3]

Weakening Party Identification. The concept of party identification is often used to summarize the political inclination of voters to see themselves as long-term supporters of a particular party. A person who says "I'm a Tory" or "We are all Labour in this house" is asserting a psychological identification with a party. By saying this, a person is putting into words the cumulative effect of the socialization influences referred to above. As long as there was a strong sense of long-term identification with the Conservative or Labour Party, then the campaign strategy of the two parties was very simple. They did not have to seek converts from their opponents or appeal to large masses of undecided or apathetic voters. Their task was simply getting to the polls people who were already committed to vote for the party.

In the past two decades, identification with the Conservative and Labour parties has been declining. In the three general elections from 1964 to 1970, an average of 81 percent of the electorate identified with either the Conservative or the Labour Party. At the three general elections of the 1970s, the proportion dropped to an average of 75 percent. In the two elections of the 1980s, an average of 70 percent identify with one of the two largest parties. The decline has been paralleled by an increase in identification with third parties. In the 1960s, an average of 10 percent identified with the Liberals or other third party; in the 1970s, 15 percent, and in the 1980s, 17 percent.[4]

While most individuals continue to identify with a party, their attachment is weakening. In the 1960s an average of 43 percent very strongly identified with a party, but in the 1970s the strongly identified proportion dropped to one-quarter, and it has stayed there since. When a large proportion of the electorate is not strongly identified with a party, the character of electoral competition changes. Parties can no longer rely upon mobilizing battalions of supporters who are unquestioningly loyal. They must appeal to voters who are unsure about what party to vote for.

Moreover, identification with a party is not an exclusive commitment to that party. A 1983 Gallup Poll found that 73 percent of all voters were prepared to vote for more than one party. When asked how they would mark a ballot allowing a voter to express a second as well as a first preference, a system used in Australia, 73 percent were ready to express a second choice. Conservative and Labour voters usually named the Alliance as their second choice: Alliance voters split their preferences more evenly between Labour and Conservatives.[5]

In the past quarter-century there has been a structural change from a closed to an open electorate. In a *closed* electorate, the deci-

sion about how to vote is made long before election day. Firm identification with the Conservative and Labour parties left little room
for a third party to gain support and made party leaders concentrate
upon mobilizing committed supporters. In an *open* electorate, a
large proportion of the electorate is ready to change support from
one election to the next or at the extreme from one day to the next.

The proportion of floating voters has been growing greatly. At
any given general election up to half of the electorate behave differently from at the previous election. The bulk of the movement is
slight, a shift between voting and not voting or a move between
voting for an Alliance party and voting for one of the two established parties. In 1987 only 5 percent of the Conservative vote came
from individuals who said they had voted Labour in 1983, and only
4 percent of the Labour vote came from former Conservative
supporters.[6]

The median British voter today is best described as a *wobbling*
voter; that is, he or she is open-minded about which of several parties to support.[7] In an electoral system in which the effective choice
is reduced to three parties, wobblers may often vote for the same
party at two successive elections, but their vote is not firmly committed, as in a closed system. Wobblers are prepared to alter their
voting intention between elections. This accounts for very big shifts
of votes at many by-elections. It is also registered in fluctuations of
support for parties in monthly opinion polls. In the 1983–87 Parliament, Conservative support ranged between 23 percent and 45 percent; Labour support between 24 percent and 40 percent, and
support for the Alliance parties between 19 percent and 39 percent.[8]

Changing the Party System. While elections have been fought
along party lines for more than a century, the number of parties in
the system has not been constant. There have been four different sets
of parties in the past century, including two since 1945. From 1885
to 1910 there was four-party competition among Conservatives,
Liberals, Irish Nationalists, and Labour. The system is best described
as *multidimensional*. While Labour differed from the Conservatives
along class lines, the religious dimension was important in differen-
tiating Conservatives and Liberals; Irish Nationalists differed on
religious and nationality grounds. Control of government alter-
nated between Conservative and Liberal; sometimes the Irish
Nationalists held the balance when neither party won a majority of
seats in the Commons.

From 1918 until 1945 there was *multiparty* competition among Conservatives, Liberals, and Labour. Repeated splits within the Liberal Party caused it to collapse and accelerated the rise of Labour. Government took three different forms: sixteen years of coalition, eleven years of single-party majority government, and eight years of minority government. The Conservatives were in office for four-fifths of this period, but usually in coalition with other parties.

The *two-party* system described in textbooks only emerged clearly in the 1945 general election. From 1945 to 1970 the Conservative and Labour parties between them took an average of 91 percent of the popular vote and in 1951 as much as 97 percent of the total vote (Figure X.1). The Liberals had difficulty in contesting a majority of seats and even more difficulty in winning seats. Support for the two parties was very evenly balanced: Labour won an average of 46 percent of the vote in this period, and the Conservatives, 45 percent. Labour won four elections, and the Conservatives won four.

A new *multiparty* system of electoral competition began to emerge in 1974. In the February confrontation between Conservatives and Labour the electorate answered with a plague on the houses of both major parties. The Liberals made a breakthrough, winning 19 percent of the popular vote. The combined Conservative plus Labour share of the vote fell to 75 percent and remained there at the October 1974 election. The Liberal vote fell in 1979. The 1980s has affirmed a realignment of electoral competition. The vote for the Alliance and other "third" parties rose to 30 percent of the total in 1983 and remained at one-quarter of the total in 1987. In the present multiparty system the Conservatives have won big majorities in Parliament with little more than two-fifths of the vote, as their two principal opponents have each won less than a third of the vote. By the time of the first general election in the 1990s, all voters below the age of 40 will have known only multiparty electoral competition.

By any measure of electoral competition, Britain has a multiparty (that is, more than two-party) system.[9]

1. *Three Candidates Normally Contest the Majority of Constituencies.* In 1987 the 650 seats in the House of Commons were contested by 2,324 candidates, an average of 3.6 candidates per constituency.

2. *The Popular Vote is Divided Among Three or More Parties.* The Conservative and Labour parties together have won an average

FIGURE X.1 *Votes Cast in General Elections, 1945–1987 (in percentages)*

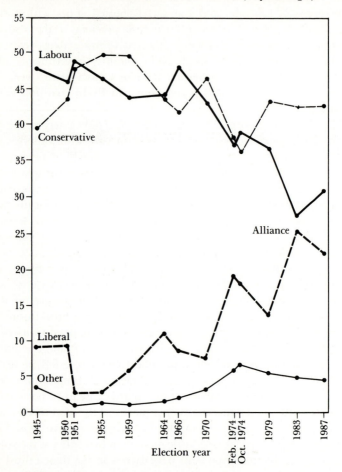

of 75 percent of the vote in the five elections since 1974; they have not won as much as nine-tenths of the vote since 1959.

3. *Competition at Constituency Level Involves More Than Two Parties.* At the 1987 election the Conservatives most often came first, the Alliance parties most often finished second, and Labour candidates finished third where they did not win a seat. Alliance candidates were the chief challengers to MPs representing the Conservative government.

4. *More Than Half a Dozen Parties Consistently Win Seats in the House of Commons.* At each election since 1974 at least seven

different parties have elected MPs: the Conservatives, Labour, Liberal (and Social Democratic allies), the Scottish National Party, the Welsh Nationalist Party Plaid Cymru, and at least two Northern Ireland parties, one Irish Nationalist, and the other Unionist.

5. *Significant Shifts in Votes Involve Changes Between Three Parties.* The concept of swing was defined as the average net shift in votes between the Conservative and Labour parties. Today it is a misleading abstraction, for the Alliance parties have been the chief gainers or losers in votes. A fall in Conservative strength need not register a gain in Labour strength; it has principally benefited the Alliance parties at by-elections. A rise in Labour strength is not so threatening to the Conservatives if it occurs principally at the expense of the Alliance parties. The frequent ups and downs of the Alliance parties thus have a major impact upon the two established parties.[10]

The greater the number of parties, the more likely their popular support is to be unequal, and this is the case in the current multiparty system. In the five general elections since 1974 the Conservatives have averaged 40.5 percent of the vote. Mrs. Thatcher owes victory to the division of votes among the Conservatives' several opponents. Labour has averaged 34.3 percent of the popular vote. The Liberals and Alliance parties have averaged 19.9 percent of the vote.

The party system is aptly described as multiparty rather than three-party because the names and numbers of parties differ from election to election and between the nations of the United Kingdom. In Northern Ireland British parties no longer contest seats. In Scotland the Scottish National Party has polled an average of 19 percent in the five elections since 1974. In Wales Plaid Cymru has averaged just under 10 percent of the vote, making it the fourth party in four-party competition there (cf. Table II.4). The rise of the Liberals and the Alliance parties has generalized a multiparty system throughout Britain. When the Liberals were weak they were often dismissed as a fringe party confined to remote rural constituencies. In the 1980s the Alliance parties actually won a larger proportion of the vote in England than in Scotland and Wales.

Winning Seats. The first-past-the-post electoral system awards seats in the House of Commons to the candidate with a plurality (the largest number) of votes in a constituency. As long as minimal-party competition prevailed, the plurality was also a majority. From

1945 to 1970 about three-quarters of MPs were elected with more than half the vote in their constituency. The rise of multiparty competition has resulted in less than half the Members of Parliament winning their seat with the endorsement of more than half the voters in their constituency. When an MP holds a seat with a minority of the vote, continued success depends upon the continued division of votes between two or more opponents.

The distribution of seats in the House of Commons is determined by where votes are cast as well as by how many votes are cast for a party. A party can elect MPs with a small share of the total vote if it concentrates support in a limited number of constituencies. Ulster parties do this, fighting only the seventeen seats of Northern Ireland; the Scottish Nationalists and Welsh Nationalists also win seats by concentrating their vote in Scottish and Welsh strongholds. The Alliance parties and Liberals have suffered in parliamentary terms because they win about a fifth of the vote in hundreds of constituencies. While this contributes to an impressive total vote, it does not win parliamentary seats. A candidate receiving a fifth of the vote finishes second or third, not first. The Labour Party has concentrated its vote effectively; it usually finishes either first or third. It does not waste lots of votes by finishing a respectable second. In 1987 it won 229 seats, came second in 149 seats, and third or fourth in 255.

The electoral system manufactures a majority in Parliament for a party with a minority of votes. No party has won half the popular vote since the 1935 general election. Yet in eleven of twelve elections since the war, one party has won an absolute majority of seats in the House of Commons. In two-party competition in 1945, Labour needed 48.0 percent of the vote to gain a landslide majority with 393 MPs. In 1951 it lost office even though it won 48.8 percent of the vote. In multiparty competition in 1983, the Conservatives won 397 seats with only 42 percent of the popular vote. In a period of two-party competition, the Conservatives won less than one-third of the seats in the Commons with 39.6 percent of the vote in 1945. In October 1974, a period of multiparty competition, Labour won an absolute majority with a lower share of the popular vote.[11]

The distribution of seats in the House of Commons does not reflect each party's share of the vote. The leading party wins a bigger share of seats than votes, and the second party usually wins much the same share of seats and votes. The number of MPs elected by a party attracting support fairly evenly throughout Britain, such as the Alliance parties, has no relation to its share of the vote. In 1987, the Alliance parties won 22.6 percent of the popular vote and 3.4 percent of the seats in the House of Commons. By contrast, nationalist parties concentrating their appeal won more seats than the Alliance parties with only 3.9 percent of the vote (cf. Table X.1).

Proportional or Disproportional Representation? The British electoral system is a system of disproportional representation. It is not intended to allocate parliamentary seats in proportion to a party's share of the national vote. It is intended to concentrate responsibility for government by giving one party an absolute majority of MPs without an absolute majority of votes. In 1987 the Conservatives won nearly 58 percent of the seats with 42 percent of the vote (Table X.1). Proponents of the first-past-the-post plurality system argue that this difference is a small price to pay in order to vest responsibility for government in the hands of a single party.[12]

Labour politicians have always been prepared to accept the discrepancies of disproportional representation because Labour too has enjoyed majorities manufactured from a minority share of the vote. Even though Labour's share of the vote has fallen to less than a third of the total, the party still enjoys more than a third of the seats in the House of Commons, thanks to the ability to concentrate its vote.

The Alliance parties have been the chief proponents of introducing proportional representation in Britain. The argument has devoted less attention to the details of proportional representation, which comes in many shapes and sizes,[13] than to the basic principle: the first-past-the post electoral system is deemed unfair because the Liberals, alone or in partnership with Social Democrats, have won far fewer seats in Parliament than they would win under propor-

TABLE X.1 *Relationship of Seats to Votes, 1987*

| | Share of | | Seats won | |
	Votes %	Seats %	Actual	Theoretical*
Conservatives	42.3	57.9	376	275
Labour	30.8	35.2	229	200
Alliance	22.6	3.4	22	147
Other parties	4.3	3.5	23	28

*Hypothetical result of pure proportional representation, as calculated by the author.

tional representation. In 1987, for example, the Alliance share of the vote was more than six times that of their share of seats in the House of Commons. In a proportional-representation ballot, the Alliance parties would have won 147 seats; the first-past-the-post system gave the parties twenty-two MPs.[14]

Arguments for proportional representation are sometimes based on self-interest and sometimes on principle. The Social Democratic Party illustrates the importance of self-interest. As long as its founding members were in the Labour Party, arguments for proportional representation were dismissed because the Labour Party was a major beneficiary of disproportional representation. Roy Jenkins and Shirley Williams both served as Labour government ministers in the Home Office, the department responsible for electoral law. While there, neither was prepared to consider the case for proportional representation. Once they decided to form another party, they embraced proportional representation as a basic principle.

Simple arithmetic offers one argument of principle for proportional representation. If a party gets X percent of the popular vote, then it ought to receive X percent of the seats in the House of Commons. The Dutch and the Israelis have electoral systems that provide for this. But in order for this goal to be achieved, the whole of the nation must form a single constituency, thus completely destroying the link between elector and individual representative in Parliament. The Federal Republic of Germany has a compromise system, in which half the members of Parliament are elected by the first-past-the-post system and the other half are allocated by a method designed to make the total number of seats in Parliament accord with their share of the vote won. To avoid the proliferation of a large number of small parties, the German system limits representation in Parliament to parties that have won at least 5 percent of the vote nationwide or have come first in at least three first-past-the-post constituencies. In the Republic of Ireland, within each multi-member constituency a voter has a Single Transferable Vote. Candidates are ranked in order 1,2,3, and so on. Seats are allocated within a constituency by the transfer of preferences as candidates reach the quota needed for election (one-sixth of the vote plus one in a five-member constituency, or one-fourth plus one in a three-member constituency).

Proportional representation would replace single-party government with minority or coalition government. If the electorate divided its vote as at present, the Conservative and Labour parties would finish first and second, but neither would have a majority in the Commons. The Social and Liberal Democrats would decide whether the country had a Conservative or Labour Prime Minister by its choice of coalition partner. Whereas the first-past-the-post system has effectively excluded the Liberals from office, proportional representation holds out the prospect of the Social and Liberal Democrats being permanently in office as a coalition partner. Proponents of proportional representation view coalition government as desirable in principle, avoiding sudden shifts in policy alleged to result from the alternation of office between Conservatives and Labour (cf. Chapter XI). Critics charge that coalition is a prescription for stagnation. Any measure opposed by one of the parties in the coalition would be stalled until all-party agreement could be reached.

The electorate is divided about the merits of coalition government as against government by a single party. When both Conservative and Labour parties are unpopular, coalition appears preferable. But following the Alliance split after the 1987 election, a majority of voters rejected coalition on the grounds that it would accomplish little because it could not provide strong leadership.[15]

POLICY PREFERENCES

The democratic franchise gives the mass of the population a chance to influence the choice of government, but the preferences of individuals do not thereby become the policies of government. One reason is that many members of the public do *not* have opinions about many issues of concern to government. Moreover, the governing party is an organization with members who can develop policies and put them into effect independent of the views of the mass electorate.

The Limits of Public Opinion. Discussion of the role that public opinion ought to play in government usually starts from the assumption that members of the public are full of opinions about politics. In fact, this is not the case. Every survey of public opinion distinguishes between two groups of citizens: those who have an opinion about an issue and those who do not. The proportion of opinioned electors is highest for issues of immediate relevance. When people are asked whether or not they are satisfied with their standard of living, 99 percent usually state a view. When voters are asked to choose between alternative measures for handling an issue of concern to Cabinet ministers, the proportion of "don't-knows" rises to a quarter or a half.[16]

Many voters do not have opinions about government policy because they lack knowledge of government. Most voters lack knowledge of government because they have little interest in politics. Because the ordinary individual can exercise little direct political influence, it is not economical to spend a lot of time and money to obtain political information. The best value-for-money strategy is to delegate responsibility for gathering information to a party.[17] Citizens then need only enough knowledge to choose a party.

The public debate about the United Kingdom's entry to the European Community illustrates the difficulty of trying to relate public opinion to government. The question of entry was not a simple question of in or out; it was also a question of the terms that could be negotiated for British entry. When the issue was first mooted, opinion polls often found that the largest single group of voters were the don't-knows. In the course of a decade of negotiations about entry, public opinion fluctuated widely, sometimes being strongly in favor of entry and sometimes against. When the country entered the European Community, the median Englishman was literally a don't-know; those for and against were almost equal in number. Confusion was not confined to the less well-informed. A survey of university economists found 40 percent favoring entry on economic grounds, 42 percent against, and the median economist undecided.[18] One person was without doubts—the Prime Minister, Edward Heath, who was strongly committed to the European Community. Britain joined.

The first referendum in British history was held in 1975 to test public opinion about membership in the European Community. The referendum was called not because politicians believed that ordinary people knew better than they or had a right to determine major policy issues, but because the Labour government was deeply split on the question, and Prime Minister Harold Wilson reckoned that a referendum might resolve disputes between Cabinet ministers with minimum damage to the governing party.[19] The European Community referendum divided the electorate into three groups: 43 percent voted for entry, 36 percent did not vote, and 21 percent voted against it.

Political leaders want to decide policies in Parliament; they do not want the electorate to decide by a referendum. This has been underscored in the debate about local government finance. In its search for a means of discouraging local councils from setting high property tax rates, a Conservative minister floated the idea of having local referendums, in which voters would ballot for or against a proposed tax increase. Such ballots are often required by law in the United States. However, the idea of letting people vote on their taxes was quickly abandoned as inconsistent with British practice. The Labour opposition attacked the resulting central government curbs on the taxing powers of locally elected councils as an infringement on democracy; it defined this as representative government (that is, decisions by the majority party in a local council) and not as popular choice (that is, decision by referendums).[20]

A general election is the one occasion when the majority of the public speaks its mind. Elections, however, are blunt instruments infrequently used. Counting votes can decide who governs, but it does not tell governors what to do. For propaganda purposes, the winning party speaks of receiving a mandate, as if every voter necessarily read and agreed with its preelection proposals before casting a ballot. But this is not the case. The doctrine of an electoral mandate is a dignified symbol used by the party in office to justify its actions; it is not an authorization that the voters have approved. Election results are only a rough judgment for or against parties.

An Ideological Electorate? If voters have a clear-cut view of what they think government ought to do, then responsibility for dealing with the practicalities of government can be left with ministers and civil servants. All an individual needs is to identify with a party consistent with his or her generalized view of the world.

The term *ideology* is often used to characterize the outlook of parties, and of voters too. An ideology is a set of general ideas that can be used to understand and evaluate political, social, and economic events. A second characteristic is that ideas are logically integrated. Thirdly, an ideology is linked with group interests, such as economic classes. Insofar as interests are in conflict, the views of adherents of different ideologies will be mutually exclusive. Finally, ideology ought to motivate action. As Marx admonished, the task of philosophy is not only to understand the world but also to change it.[21]

If each political party were linked to an ideology, then two ideologies would characterize the electorate in a period of two-party competition, socialism for Labour and capitalism for the Conservatives. The advent of a multiparty system emphasizes that the Liberals have been the heir of a third important philosophical tradition, liberalism, an ideology that supports individual liberty and a market economy. The founders of the Social Democratic Party were sympathetic with both the market economy favored by Conservatives and the social welfare policies of socialism. The post-1987 SDP led by Dr. David Owen is seeking a distinctive ideology to justify the need to organize as a fourth party competing for votes. Concurrently there are many ideologies, such as religious orthodoxy, that are not represented by any party. The attempt to reduce all issues to a choice between the ideology of left or right is, as Samuel Brittan has argued, "a bogus dilemma."[22]

An elaborate survey by Elinor Scarbrough resulted in the identification of six groups according to their political outlooks.[23] The core Tory group is characterized by values stressing Britain's greatness in the world and a respect for authority. The core Socialist group favors advancing to equality by reducing class distinctions and redistributing income. However, these two groups together constitute just under one-third of the total electorate. A liberal group, characterized by individualism and dislike of government rather than by an economic doctrine, constituted an additional seventh of the electorate. Two additional groups are hybrids: a mixed Tory-Liberal category is individualistic but also in favor of government's authority. A Labour-Socialist group is reformist, wanting to improve social conditions without striving for a radically egalitarian society. The residual category of voters is described as confused; they are one-sixth of the electorate, larger than the group of radical socialists.

Every empirical analysis of ideology in the electorate emphasizes the *absence of logical coherence.* While ideologies are logically coherent in the abstract, in empirical reality most voters do not articulate views as expected. Scarbrough found that more than two-thirds of the electorate could not be described as ideologues because their attachment to core beliefs was weak or inconsistent. Other studies have similarly found that many issues of current political controversy are not linked with any ideological coherence.[24]

Cross-Party Agreement Among Voters. Analysis of popular attitudes emphasizes a large measure of agreement among people who vote for different parties. In some cases, the majority of supporters of all the parties can agree upon an issue. In other cases, agreement across party lines is matched by disagreement within the ranks of a party. The extent of agreement is such that it is misleading to view the electorate as divided into mutually exclusive and potentially conflicting camps, as is presupposed by abstract ideological analysis. The Liberals and Social Democrats provide one example of the overlap in outlooks among voters. Notwithstanding separate origins and organizations, the two parties had no difficulty in concluding an electoral alliance to fight the 1983 and 1987 elections on a common platform, nor in subsequently merging to form a single party, the Social and Liberal Democrats, for the supporters of both parties had much in common.[25]

In the discussion of political socialization, four principles were identified—socialism, social welfare, race relations, and morality. Only one of these principles, socialism, divides the electorate along party lines. By contrast, four-fifths or more of supporters of each party endorse a role for government in social welfare. Two-thirds of supporters of each party take a traditional view of morality. Race relations views are consistent in the minds of individuals, but Conservative, Labour, and Alliance voters are each divided on this principle.[26]

If ideology divided voters into mutually exclusive groups, then agreement within one party would be complemented by disagreement with the views of other parties. A majority of Conservative supporters would consistently disagree with a majority of Labour supporters, and both would disagree with supporters of the Alliance parties. Insofar as ideology is weak, we expect a great deal of cross-party similarity in the views of voters about a range of issues.

In fact, there is a high degree of cross-party agreement and similarity on a range of questions about current issues (Table X.2).

1. *Most Conservative, Labour, and Alliance voters agree with each other on three-quarters of issues.*

2. *Most Conservative and Alliance voters agree on nineteen of twenty issues.*

3. *Most Labour and Alliance voters agree on four-fifths of issues.*

On most issues an individual in the majority of public opinion could be a Conservative, Labour, or Alliance voter. Notwithstanding the Labour Party's left-wing image, a majority of Labour voters agreed with supporters of either or both competing parties on four-fifths of issues. Conservative voters were also in the mainstream of the electorate on nineteen of twenty issues. Alliance voters did not

TABLE X.2 *Similarity of Policy Preferences among Partisans*

	Total	Conservative	Alliance	Labour	Conservative-Labour difference
		(% endorsing policy)			
Plurality in all three parties agree					
Spend more against pollution	85	85	84	84	1
Government guide wage, price rises	75	77	74	74	3
Abortion more widely available	43	42	43	45	−3
Equal opportunities for women	75	73	75	78	−5
Spend more on health	95	91	95	97	−6
Send back coloured immigrants	47	52	42	43	9
Reduce sex on TV and in magazines	53	60	50	47	13
Cut spending to reduce inflation	46	54	47	40	14
Spend to reduce unemployment	80	71	82	85	−14
Let council tenants buy their house	76	85	71	70	15
Bring back death penalty	65	76	62	60	16
Give more aid to Africa, Asia	52	42	60	59	−17
Shift power to local government, regions	55	46	56	65	−19
Redistribute wealth to poor	67	50	69	79	−29
Re-establish grammar schools	47	65	45	34	31
Two of three parties agree					
Take Britain out of Common Market	34	27	32	40	−13
Withdraw troops from Northern Ireland	48	40	47	56	−16
Spend as needed to defend Falklands	39	54	42	26	28
Stricter laws on unions	48	68	43	33	35
Give up nuclear weapons	32	11	34	50	−39
Average difference					16

Source: Calculated by the author from Gallup Poll survey, 12–17 November 1986. A plurality need not be 50 percent since on every issue there are always some voters with no opinion.

have their own ideological outlook; instead, they have been like Conservative or Labour voters on particular issues—and often like both.[27] The most common form of disagreement today is *disagreement within parties*. On many issues a third of voters will disagree with their fellow partisans. Intraparty disagreement is the corollary of interparty agreement.

How a person votes is a poor guide to what a person thinks about issues. The link between the political outlooks of electors and how they vote is surprisingly limited. There is a correlation between the views people have about issues and the party for which they vote, but the correlation is weak and accounts for a limited proportion of the variance in the total vote.[28] The party that makes most claim to have an ideology, Labour, has failed to develop a coherent or distinctive outlook among a majority of its own supporters. Nor has the contraction of Labour's vote to less than a third of the electorate made the party more coherent; its supporters are divided between a minority who can be described as consistently socialist in outlook, and a majority who are confused or even Labour-voting conservatives, that is, people who vote Labour because of working-class loyalties but agree with the Conservative Party's position on many major policy issues.[29]

Whether parties should or do stand for different principles is a matter of debate among political scientists.[30] The principles that British parties espouse are few and vague, and many are not specific to a single party. The Conservative Party does not even offer a statement of goals in its constitution. The Liberals' endorsement of peace, prosperity, and liberty, and denunciation of poverty and ignorance could be echoed by almost any party anywhere. Labour does have a statement of principles, but Clause IV, endorsing the "common ownership of the means of production, distribution and exchange" has been treated by proponents and opponents as a commitment to wholesale nationalization. Labour leaders have pragmatically accepted Clause IV as a traditional symbol but have avoided implementing it when in office. As Harold Wilson said in opposing the removal of this symbolic goal: "We were being asked to take Genesis out of the Bible. You don't have to be a fundamentalist in your religious approach to say that Genesis is part of the Bible."[31]

Election Tactics. The one principle that most practicing politicians share is a desire to win elections. Only by winning an election does a party have any chance of putting its policies into effect, and party leaders need election victory to gain office, influence, and status. Any measures necessary to achieve election victory are therefore considered justifiable.

As a general election approaches, party leaders think in terms of tactical principles—how can we win votes?—rather than about ideological principles. Each party commissions opinion polls showing what the electorate favors, the points on which the party is rated high or low, and distinctive characteristics of the floating voters whose support is necessary to win a parliamentary majority. Surveys are sometimes used to test-market the appeal of slogans and campaign themes and also of party personalities. Computer analyses of previous election results are studied avidly to identify distinctive characteristics of marginal seats and to assist in allocating campaign resources to target seats and target groups of electors whose votes can be decisive.

The development of opinion polling has greatly increased the accuracy of the information that party leaders have at hand when planning an election campaign. A generation ago politicians argued among themselves about what the voters thought or wanted without evidence to resolve disputes. Today party leaders have at hand a list of the issues that the voters consider most important, and of those where their own party is trusted or distrusted by the electorate. Parties use this information to emphasize strong points in television and printed appeals for support and to avoid weak points. Poll results do not tell a party leader what to do, for poll data is capable of more than one interpretation. Sometimes the information provided cannot be acted upon. For example, a government told it is unpopular because of high unemployment lacks the means to reduce unemployment in ways that would regain popularity.[32]

Because public opinion polling and psephology (the analysis of election results) are based upon social science methods, the findings are widely available. A party may describe its poll as private, but another pollster asking much the same questions for another party's private poll will arrive at much the same answer. Before a general election published polls in newspapers and academic surveys also publicize the state of public opinion and long-term trends. The election strategists of the parties share a common fund of knowledge about what the electorate thinks. The challenge to each is adopting tactics that increase their appeal, knowing that their opponents are trying to do the same with similar information at hand.

During election campaigns politicians do not compete with each other by discussing political philosophy or by putting forward detailed analyses of the problems and performance of government. There is widespread acceptance in all parties that an election consists of a series of events planned to capture maximum favorable coverage on television and in the press.

All politicians start with evidence showing that the electorate wants peace and prosperity. But the means to these ends remain open. Each party competes by trying to convince the electorate that it is specially capable of doing what the electorate wants. If opinion polls show that a party is trusted as having competent leadership, then a party can stress the personality of leaders. If a party is regarded by most voters as being most competent on the issues that count most, that party can stress the important issues on which it is favored. An election campaign is a discussion in which each party tends to talk past the others, stressing positive themes that the electorate identifies with it. A party that is not clearly identified with any particular theme—the problem of the Liberals—suffers electorally. In the 1980s Labour has lost votes because characteristics with which it has been uniquely identified, for example favoring nuclear disarmament, have been unpopular with the electorate. Neil Kinnock's efforts to rethink socialism require that Labour identify principles that are unique to it—and also popular.

When parties do make positive statements in their election manifestos, these are often general and anodyne. (Table X.3) Many manifesto statements endorse proposals promoted by cross-party pressure groups and favored by all parties.[33] The titles of the

TABLE X.3 *Consensual Titles of Election Manifestos*

	Conservatives	*Labour*
1964	Prosperity with a Purpose	Let's Go with Labour
1966	Action not Words	Time for Decision
1970	A Better Tomorrow	Now Britain's Strong— Let's Make it Great to Live In
1974 (F)	Firm Action for a Fair Britain	Let Us Work Together
1974 (O)	Putting Britain First	Britain Will Win with Labour
1979	The Conservative Manifesto	The Labour Way is the Better Way
1983	The Challenge of Our Times	The New Hope for Britain
1987	The Next Moves Forward	Britain Will Win

Source: Compiled by the author.

manifestos are virtually interchangeable between the Conservative and Labour parties: "Action not Words," "Time for Decision," "A Better Tommorrow," or "The New Hope for Britain." Nor did the Alliance break the mold in its 1983 manifesto, which was entitled "Working Together for Britain." A voter asked to endorse a manifesto captioned "Britain Will Win" would find it difficult to infer the ideology from the label. In 1987 even the party color, red, was missing from the Labour manifesto. The background color was brown, for the yuppie designer Socialists in charge of the party's public relations reckoned that a red manifesto would clash with the ginger hair and freckled face of the party leader, Neil Kinnock.

While parties are free to propose any policies that they choose, the electorate disposes. When the parties study the electorate, they see a mass of voters who have a moderate interest in politics and tend to be nearer the center than well to the left or right (Table X.4). Ideological theories assume a U-shaped distribution of the electorate; that is, most voters are expected to be up on the far left or on the right, and only a few in the center. But empirically we find that the distribution is the opposite. When voters are asked to place them-

TABLE X.4 *Placement of Voters and Parties on Left–Right Scale (in percentage)*

	Places self	Conservatives	Labour	Alliance
Right				
Far/substantially	9	51	4	1
Moderately	27	19	3	10
Slightly right	15	6	2	20
(Total)	(51)	(76)	(9)	(31)
Center				
Middle of road	12	1	2	12
Don't know	12	15	14	32
(Total)	(24)	(16)	(16)	(44)
Left				
Slightly left	12	2	10	15
Moderately	9	2	23	6
Far/substantially	4	3	42	3
(Total)	(25)	(7)	(75)	(24)

Source: *Gallup Political Index* No. 323 (July, 1987), p. 16. Similar but separate results for Liberals and SDP averaged to produce Alliance column.

selves on a left-right scale, they distribute according to a bell-shaped pattern. There is a peak around the center; very few voters place themselves on the far left or the far right. Two-fifths describe themselves as completely middle of the road or only slightly to the left or right. Adding in the people who don't know where they fit on a left-right spectrum increases to more than half the proportion of the electorate with a middle of the road position.

Multipartyism has arisen in the past two decades because the leaders of both the Conservative and Labour parties have not paid close attention to the electorate. In consequence, 70 percent of the voters see the Conservatives as definitely on the right, and 65 percent see Labour as definitely on the left. The Alliance parties were seen in the center by default, for a third of the voters were unable to locate them at all on a left-right scale. The Conservatives won the 1987 election because twice as many voters see themselves on the right as on the left. Labour lost because only a quarter of the electorate now see themselves on the left. Today voters are in the center. To paraphrase Walter Bagehot, even when parties are eager to go hot and heavy at each other, the mass of their voters remain cool.

NOTES

1. The proposed introduction of a community charge or poll tax, which must be paid by every adult in a local authority area, will increase the degree of inaccuracy in the electoral register, as some people will avoid registering to vote in hopes that this will also help them avoid paying the poll tax.

2. See Brian Graetz and Ian McAllister, "Party Leaders and Election Outcomes in Britain, 1974–1983," *Comparative Political Studies* 19:4 (1987), pp. 484–507; and Richard Rose, *The Post-Modern President* (Chatham, NJ: Chatham House, 1988), Chapter 13.

3. See Rose and McAllister, *Voters Begin to Choose* (London: Sage Publications, 1986), Table 7.3. For an overview and further citations to the voluminous literature on British voting studies see Elinor Scarbrough, "The British Electorate Twenty Years On," *British Journal of Political Science* 17:3 (1987); and Ivor Crewe, "On the Death and Resurrection of Class Voting," *Political Studies* 34:4 (1986).

4. Calculations by the author from survey data reported in Ivor Crewe, "The Electorate: Partisan Dealignment Ten Years On," *West European Politics* 6:4 (1983), Table 4; and *Gallup Political Index* No. 323 (1987) p. 25.

5. Richard Rose, *Do Parties Make a Difference?* 2nd edn. (Chatham, N.J.: Chatham House, 1984), Epilogue Table 2.

6. See Ivor Crewe, "Why Mrs. Thatcher Was Returned with a Landslide," *Social Studies Review* 3:1 (1987), Figure 1.

7. For details on floating and wobbling voters, see Rose and McAllister, *Voters Begin to Choose*, pp. 156ff.

8. Cf. Ivor Crewe, "Is Britain's Two Party System Really About to Crumble?" *Electoral Studies* 1:3 (1982), pp. 275–314.

9. For detailed documentation, see Rose and McAllister, *Voters Begin to Choose*, Chapter 2.

10. For a detailed discussion of patterns of constituency competition and swing, see Ian McAllister and Richard Rose, *The Nationwide Competition for Votes*, especially chapter 11.

11. For definitive and detailed statistics on elections, see F.W.S. Craig, *British Electoral Facts, 1832–1980* (Chichester: Parliamentary Research Services, 1980) and related publications by Craig.

12. For a discussion of arguments for and against proportional representation and coalition government, cf. Vernon Bogdanor, *The People and the Party System* (Cambridge: Cambridge University Press, 1981); and V. Bogdanor, *Multi-Party Politics and the Constitution* (Cambridge: Cambridge University Press, 1983); with Philip Norton, *The Constitution in Flux*, Chapter 12. (Oxford: Martin Robertson, 1982).

13. See Richard Rose, "Elections and Electoral Systems: Choices and Alternatives," in V. Bogdanor and D. E. Butler, eds., *Democracy and Elections* (Cambridge: Cambridge University Press, 1983) pp. 20–45.

14. Arguably, the Alliance parties would have won even more votes, and therefore more seats, as proportional representation would have encouraged more people to vote for them, knowing that their votes would not be wasted.

15. See *Gallup Political Index* No. 329 (1988), p. 7.

16. For up-to-date details on public opinion polls, see the monthly *Gallup Political Index*. More generally, see Gordon Heald and Robert J. Wybrow, *The Gallup Survey of Britain* (London: Croom Helm, 1986); and Leslie Watkins and Robert Worcester, *Private Opinions Public Polls* (London: Thames and Hudson, 1986).

17. See Anthony Downs, *An Economic Theory of Democracy* (New York: Harper and Row, 1957).

18. See "The Dons Who Want to Go to Market," *Observer* (London), 24 October 1971; Roger Jowell and J.D. Spence, *The Grudging Europeans* (London: Social & Community Planning Research, 1975), and semiannual *Euro-Barometer* surveys of the European Commission, Brussels.

19. On the referendum and the background to it, see David Butler and Uwe Kitzinger, *The 1975 Referendum;* and Anthony King, *Britain Says Yes: The 1975 Referendum on the Common Market* (Washington, D.C.: American Enterprise Institute, 1977).

20. On the abortive referendum proposal, see Eugene Lee's contribution in Lee and H. Wolman, *Urban Economic Development and Local Democracy* (London: Public Finance Foundation Research Paper No. 11, 1986).

21. For a sophisticated conceptual discussion and empirical evidence about ideologies in Britain, see Elinor Scarbrough, *Political Ideology and Voting* (Oxford: Clarendon Press, 1984).

22. Samuel Brittan, *Left or Right: the Bogus Dilemma* (London: Secker and Warburg, 1968).

23. The following discussion is drawn from evidence in Scarbrough, *Political Ideology and Voting*, Chapter 7.

24. Scarbrough, *Political Ideology and Voting*, p. 160. Rose and McAllister, *Voters Begin to Choose*, pp. 119 and notes, found 46 percent of the variance in attitudes *unexplained* by factor analysis. Moreover, most questions in British Election Surveys do *not* relate to any statistically coherent factor. See also Donley Studlar and Susan Welch, "Mass Attitudes on Political Issues in Britain," *Comparative Political Studies* 14:3 (1981).

25. See John Curtice, "Why Owen is Wrong," *New Society*, 14 August 1987.

26. Rose and McAllister, *Voters Begin to Choose*, p. 124.

27. For a parallel analysis with different data, see Rose and McAllister, *Voters Begin to Choose*, p. 145.

28. The link is even weaker than statistics indicate, since a correlation between party choice and views on issues says nothing about the direction of causation. Views on issues could reflect cues given by the party with which an individual has identified from childhood, or without any ideological awareness. Cf. Scarbrough, *Political Ideology and Voting*, Chapter 10.

29. See Martin Harrop, "Labour-Voting Conservatives," in R.M. Worcester and M. Harrop, eds., *Political Communications* (London: Allen and Unwin, 1982), pp. 152-163; Ivor Crewe and Bo Sarlvik, "Popular Attitudes and Electoral Strategy," in Z. Layton-Henry, ed., *Conservative Party Politics* (London: Macmillan 1980), pp. 244-275; I. Crewe, "The Labour Party and the Electorate," in D. Kavanagh, ed., *The Politics of the Labour Party* (London: Allen and Unwin, 1982), pp. 9-49.

30. For example McKenzie, *British Political Parties,* rules out consideration of party principles in his preface.

31. In a radio interview reprinted in *The Listener* (London) 29 October 1964.

32. See Richard Rose, "Opinion Polls as Feedback Mechanisms: From Cavalry Charge to Electronic Warfare," in Austin Ranney, ed., *The British General Election of 1983* (Durham: Duke University Press, 1985), pp. 108-138.

33. See Rose, *Do Parties Make a Difference?* Chapter 4.

CHAPTER XI

Organizing for Party Government

And the end always is that a middle course is devised which looks as much as possible like what was suggested in opposition but which is as much as possible what patent facts—facts which seem to live in the office, so teasing and unceasing are they—prove ought to be done.

POLITICAL PARTIES ARE COMPLEX organizations with a multiplicity of goals—winning an election, helping people, debating ideology, governing Britain. The diversity of activities within a political party can make it a world within itself: the bounds of the party, rather than the nation as a whole, limit the thinking of many party activists. To become part of government, a party must look outward too: it must organize to compete with other parties and prepare for the challenge of government.

Each party is free to organize as it thinks fit; there are no Acts of Parliament regulating how a party must be organized. The Conservative and Labour parties have had different histories, and this is reflected in their organization. For the Conservatives, formed in Parliament long before the introduction of universal suffrage, the party in Parliament is central; constituency parties belong to a separate organization supporting the party in Parliament. By contrast, the Labour Party was formed as an association of trade unions; lacking any MPs, it was initially a campaigning organization outside Parliament. As the weakest of the traditional parties, the Liberals relied heavily on voluntary activity. The Social Democratic Party was a novel combination of former Labour Cabinet ministers and political novices before it split and a majority of members merged with the Liberals to form the Social and Liberal Democrats, which is seeking to improve upon the parties that it replaces.

The electoral system forces a party to appeal to a broad cross-section of the electorate in order to win an election; it is thus a coalition of individuals and groups with somewhat differing political priorities. By contrast, in a proportional representation system, hard-left politicians can split from soft-left politicians rather than combine into a single Labour Party. Conservatives and free-market liberals are often organized into two separate political parties, whereas in England the Conservative Party combines both. The larger the groups coalescing into a party, the greater its potential electoral appeal. But the more diverse the elements within a party, the greater the likelihood of intraparty conflict and even disruption, as the careers of the Labour and Alliance parties show.

Winning an election presents two major challenges to the successful party. First of all, its leaders must show what they can do in government; governing is much more difficult than making speeches in the House of Commons and at party conferences. Secondly, the entry of party leaders into Cabinet creates a new institution, the party-in-government. The leaders of the party-in-government are the same as when the party was outside Whitehall. But the responsibilities that politicians have as ministers are very different from those of MPs and party members outside government. Ministers are immediately subject to the constraints of government, whereas the political aspirations of other partisans are not. In ideal circumstances the tension can be resolved by the party-in-government achieving successes that satisfy extra-Whitehall partisans. But at some point in a Parliament, party leaders give priority to pressures within Whitehall, and this can produce conflict in the party that they lead.

In order to understand the problems of party government, this chapter looks first at the structure of party organization, and then at the cross-pressures within parties. Conflict can be reduced if different parts of the party are rarely in contact, or if a party fails to win elections, thus avoiding tension with leaders in government. The third section examines the limits of party government, when leaders are confronted with reconciling the aspirations of the party with the constraints that confront ministers regardless of party.

THE STRUCTURE OF PARTIES

Every political party is made up of loosely linked parts. Political parties in England are organized at three major levels: constituency parties, party headquarters, and the party in Parliament. While people active in parties profess allegiance to a common cause, there are great differences in activities, motivations, and consequences for government of what happens at different levels of a party. Because each part is differently composed and differently controlled, much of the effort within a party is concerned with keeping together disparate parts.[1]

Constituency Organization. Local parties are organized according to parliamentary constituencies with an average of about 66,000 voters for each of the 650 areas returning one MP to Parliament. Constituencies are rarely the same size as a city or county; in urban areas they combine a number of wards or several suburbs. Away from the cities, constituencies combine towns and countryside. Very few people who vote in a constituency actually identify with it; they think of themselves as residents of a neighbourhood or a town or village or city. Constituency parties have national significance because they nominate the party's parliamentary candidate. As voluntary organizations provide psychological satisfactions to members, they have social and even emotional significance.

Collectively, constituency parties are significant at Westminster because they select parliamentary candidates, the pool of people who can become MPs and Cabinet ministers. Party headquarters compile lists of hundreds of aspiring candidates, vetoing applicants more for personal reasons (for example, the individual has a criminal record or has very recently been a member of another political party) than on policy grounds. Before choosing a candidate, a constituency party makes up a list of aspiring candidates to interview, some of whom are locally known and some from outside the constituency. A parliamentary candidate is not required to live in the constituency. The final choice of candidate is usually made by a constituency party committee with anything from a dozen up to several hundred members. An aspiring politician cannot seek nomination by appealing to the party's voters in a primary election, as in the United States. Decentralizing the choice of parliamentary candidates and not requiring a candidate to be an elector in the constituency allow an aspiring politician to seek nomination to

Parliament in a number of different places. It also prevents party headquarters from dominating candidate selection.

Because the great majority of constituencies are safe seats for one party, nomination by the dominant party is usually tantamount to election. In most constituencies a local party can rely upon the national campaign broadcast by the media to stimulate supporters to vote. Most MPs can regard their position in the Commons as secure from eviction by dissatisfied voters. A major threat to an MP's position is the redrawing of constituency boundaries in response to population movements. In decaying urban areas the contraction of the population may reduce the number of seats by one, thus denying one Labour MP a seat to represent. In suburban areas, the in-migration of new residents can turn a safe Conservative seat into an unstable marginal. A voter who does not like his or her party's candidate can vote against the party's candidate, abstain, or vote on party lines. Voters faced with a conflict between their allegiance to a party and their dislike of their constituency candidate usually cast their ballot along party lines.[2]

Conservative MPs assume that their constituency association will renominate them as long as they avoid becoming involved in personal scandals, such as arrest for drunken driving or financial irregularities, and are not casual about their limited obligations in the constituency. Every Conservative candidate must endorse Margaret Thatcher as Prime Minister, and the Prime Minister must support every candidate. The formal harmony does not mean that every candidate must endorse everything the Prime Minister says, nor does it bind the Prime Minister to endorse everything that a candidate says. Whatever views a Conservative MP expresses, it is unusual for an MP to be denied renomination by the constituency association on the grounds of political differences of opinion.[3]

In constituency Labour parties, trade union branches and other Labour organizations, as well as ward organizations of individual party members, are affiliated. The distinctive political feature of the Labour selection process is the importance of allegiance to political groups within the Labour Party. An aspiring candidate is asked what kind of a Labour Party he or she favors—hard left, soft left, or moderate—and about his or her views on issues that divide the party, such as nuclear disarmament. A minority of constituencies are dominated by a single faction; supporters of Militant, a hard-left Trotskyite movement, are the best known, but dominance may also be in the hands of a particular trade union, such as the miners, or a strictly local clique. Most constituency selection committees are internally divided, as members occupy different positions on the left. Selectors are concerned with a candidate's ability to get on with people in the party and with canvassing for votes as well as with questions of intraparty debate. There are many different ways in which a candidate can win the votes needed to secure a nomination.[4]

Labour MPs used to be as certain of readoption as Conservative MPs, but left-wing dissatisfaction with the policies of the 1974–79 Labour government has led to each constituency party being required during each Parliament to have a reselection meeting to consider the readoption of their sitting MP. Intermittent efforts to give all party members a vote in the reselection ballot were defeated by left-wing reformers, who argued that active members representing unions and other affiliated groups should have votes as well as representatives of ordinary members at the ward level. Eight Labour MPs failed to win readoption before the 1983 election; others defected to the Social Democrats or announced retirement before their constituency party voted on reselection. Prior to the 1987 election, six MPs were refused renomination, and several more retired. In two cases older left-wing Labour MPs were replaced by successful black candidates, reflecting a change in the racial composition of the constituency.

The Liberals and the Social Democratic parties were handicapped in recruiting candidates because 95 percent or more of their nominees faced almost certain defeat. A candidate who finishes a respectable second cannot hope to be adopted for a safe seat elsewhere, as may happen to a Conservative or Labour candidate. The Liberal Party relied upon locally based nominees; a few particularly assiduous campaigners, experts in the art of "pavement politics" (that is, stressing the need to care for local problems, such as cracked pavements) have thereby won election to Parliament. When the Liberals and SDP fought as an Alliance, the SDP was given the right to nominate candidates for half the parliamentary constituencies; the party was able to attract hundreds of well educated middle-class candidates, the great majority of whom were novices in fighting elections. The Social and Liberal Democratic Party faces a familiar problem: it is easy for active members to become parliamentary candidates but extremely difficult to become an MP.

All parties consider Westminster politics central to politics nationwide. Whereas in a federal system such as the United States the state party is the basic unit, in England it is the national party.

Local parties are organized by constituencies, and not by local government areas. National party headquarters are ambivalent about encouraging local political organization. They welcome having more local authorities in the hands of supporters of their own party. Liberals and Social Democrats have particularly welcomed the opportunity of electing hundreds of councillors, a far easier task than electing MPs.

As voluntary organizations, constituency parties depend upon their members gaining psychological satisfaction from undertaking party work. Only the Conservative Party has a paid party agent in as many as half the constituencies. Most party members locally would rather pay dues than give time to attendance at party meetings. The fewer the number of people regularly participating in local meetings, the easier it is for the party to become introverted and divorced from the party's voters, or ripe for a takeover by an ideologically organized caucus such as Militant, or by supporters of a careerist bent on becoming the leader of the party in local government, or by its MP.

Headquarters and Annual Conference. Party headquarters are apart from the Palace of Westminster. Each party has similar functional divisions: communications, research and organization. The research department is not so much concerned with long-term policy development as it is with preparing briefs for party committees and MPs and for campaign communications. With the rise of television, communication has become more important than constituency-oriented organization, for it is easier to reach voters through public relations efforts that attract television coverage. Moreover, party headquarters can control the content and timing of centralized media efforts, whereas it cannot control the local efforts of volunteers in widely dispersed constituency parties.[5] The size of the staff working for each party differs substantially. The Conservatives have more than twice the staff of Labour, and Labour has a much larger staff than the Social and Liberal Democrats. All parties operate under recurring financial pressures and use the advent of an election or a financial crisis as a reason for a fund-raising drive among their supporters.

Conservative Central Office, the party's headquarters organization, is under the direction of the party leader in Parliament, who appoints the party chairman. The chairman is usually a frontbench MP and often a Cabinet minister. Constituency associations are organized in the National Union of Conservative and Unionist Associations. At the annual conference of the National Union, constituency associations express their views about party policy. Votes at the annual conference are allotted in equal numbers to each constituency association. MPs have no voting rights; the gathering is not their conference. The parliamentary leadership exercises influence informally, by excluding resolutions that could embarrass the leadership and by speaking frequently in conference debates. Because resolutions are usually vague and few delegates wish to vote against their parliamentary leaders, it is rare for a conference debate to conclude with a formal ballot. Whatever the dissatisfaction of the Conservative conference, the views expressed are not a directive to the party in Parliament.

Whereas the Conservative Party insulates the parliamentary party from the extraparliamentary National Union, the Labour Party integrates the two. The constitution of the Labour Party states, "The work of the party shall be under the direction and control of the Party Conference."[6] The Annual Conference debates policy resolutions, which are pressed to a vote when they concern issues divisive within the party. Voters are distributed according to national membership figures; more than nine-tenths of the conference vote is in the hands of trade unions, because they affiliate members wholesale. The vote of each union is cast as a bloc, even though the union's membership may be divided on an issue. Up to a million votes cast in the name of the Transport & General Workers' Union can be swayed by few delegates who hold the balance in deciding how the union delegation will vote. The half-dozen largest affiliated unions together have an absolute majority of the conference vote. The bloc vote thus concentrates far more power in the hands of a few political caucuses than occurs in an American presidential nominating convention.

Between Annual Conferences the National Executive Committee directs the Labour headquarters and issues statements in the name of the Labour Party. Its membership is also dominated by trade union votes. The unions elect twelve of the Committee's twenty-nine members in their own name, and their votes dominate the selection of the five women's representatives and the party's treasurer. The constituency parties elect seven representatives, often back-bench MPs, and the Cooperative Societies and Young Socialists each elect one member. Seats are also reserved for the leader and deputy leader of the Parliamentary Labour Party. Black activists in the Labour Party have voiced an unsuccessful demand for the representation of black sections in the party. The Constitution of the Labour Party states the first objective of the annual conference is "to organize and maintain in Parliament and in the country a political labour party," thus implying that MPs are agents of the party conference, a view that most Labour MPs do not accept.

Parties in Parliament. In terms of governing Britain, the party in Parliament counts most. In constitutional theory and practice, government is accountable to Parliament. This was true long before the organization of parties inside or outside Parliament, and it remains true today. Since MPs are elected by universal suffrage, they can collectively claim to represent the nation as a whole. Organizing the House of Commons along party lines provides the Cabinet with the backing of a disciplined majority in the legislature. As the elected leader of the party and its chief spokesperson in the media, the party leader is inevitably important, defining by his or her actions where the party stands on controversial issues.

The processes for electing the leader in the Conservative and Labour parties reflect differences in their internal structure. The Conservative leader is elected by a ballot of MPs, requiring an absolute majority to win. On the first ballot the candidate with the fewest votes is eliminated, and a fresh compromise candidate may come forward subsequently; balloting continues until by a process of elimination one candidate wins. The system was first used to elect Edward Heath as leader in Opposition in 1965; previously leaders had been chosen by a secret conclave of party elder statesmen. In 1975 Margaret Thatcher won the leadership by challenging the incumbent party leader, former Prime Minister Edward Heath. In theory, any Conservative MP could challenge Margaret Thatcher in a leadership vote at the start of any session of Parliament. In practice, dissatisfaction with a party leader in Downing Street would have to be very high before this was done.

In the Labour Party the leader was elected solely by votes of Labour MPs until the party constitution was changed in 1981. The Labour Party leader is now chosen by an electoral college in which the trade unions collectively have 30 percent of the vote, the constituency parties 30 percent, and the Parliamentary Labour Party 40 percent. In order to be elected leader, a candidate must win support from at least two of the party's three constituent elements. The new system was first used to elect a new leader after Michael Foot resigned following the 1983 election. Neil Kinnock was elected on the first ballot with a majority of votes in all three parts of the electoral college, and Roy Hattersley similarly won election as deputy leader. A Labour leader or deputy leader is more liable to challenge. Given differences in the choice of constituency parties and Labour MPs, the determining vote in the election of a leader rests with the largest trade unions.

The Liberals and Social Democrats have elected their leaders by a vote of the mass membership of the party. When a party has only a few MPs, it is very dependent upon voluntary workers outside Parliament. To make sure that the party leader is in parliamentary politics, candidates for the leadership must be nominated by a group of MPs. In 1988 the members of the new Social and Liberal Democratic Party elected Paddy Ashdown as leader.

A parliamentary leader's position is strongest when in Downing Street. However, only one leader can enjoy the authority and status of Prime Minister at a time. When out of office, the Parliamentary Labour Party elects a Parliamentary committee of twelve to act as its executive committee. The party leader allots shadow ministerial posts to the committee members, and the number is completed by the leader's reward of shadow patronage. In the Conservative Party in opposition the leader selects people for shadow posts; backbenchers also elect a chairman for their own group, the 1922 Committee, named after the year in which it was founded. The dynamics of electoral competition alter the leader's status. The leader of a newly elected government can claim popular justification for authority. Whatever happens to the parties during a Parliament, as another general election approaches, the need to unite a party-in-government or in opposition increases the influence of a leader as the person around whom the party must rally.

The authority appropriate for the parliamentary leadership is disputed between and within the parties. A generation ago Robert T. McKenzie propounded the thesis that constitutional practice required that the leaders of all parties dominate their extraparliamentary party.[7] McKenzie asserted that elected politicians ought to be accountable solely to the electorate and that this was especially true of the Prime Minister and the leader of the Opposition. Within the Conservative Party the McKenzie doctrine was broadly acceptable, for the Conservative leader is independent of the conference of constituency associations and controls the party's central office.

Within the Labour Party the thesis has been a subject of dispute.

No Labour leader has explicitly claimed the authority to dismiss the views of the annual conference, the sovereign (*sic*) body of the extraparliamentary party. The multiplicity of policy-making organs within the Labour Party compels continuing discussion and compromise, especially when the party is in opposition. At the height of one dispute the party's general secretary summarized the practical political moral thus:

> Within the party there are three centers of decision-making: the Annual Conference, the National Executive Committee and the Parliamentary Labour Party. . . . None of these elements can dominate the others. Policy cannot be laid down: it must be agreed.[8]

Neither Clement Attlee nor Harold Wilson, Labour's two long-serving leaders, sought to impose his views on others. Each saw his role as conciliating disparate forces within the Labour movement, and each enjoyed a long period as party leader. Neil Kinnock has sought to assert his personal authority within the party, but as a skilled tactician of the Labour movement, he normally does so only when confident of backing by unions with large bloc votes. Moreover, because he has never had experience of government, when policy issues are in dispute, Kinnock must turn to more knowledgeable and experienced persons for advice.

The Liberal Party organization has been so far from office that it has not been concerned with problems of constitutional accountability. The Liberals have been a loosely organized grass-roots campaign group, ready to seize tactical advantage to win seats in Parliament wherever and whenever practicable.[9] By contrast, the Social Democratic Party was organized from the top by notables, former Labour Cabinet ministers who were suspicious of extraparliamentary influence. It could ballot its members by using a computerized central membership list. At the constituency level, the Alliance parties succeeded in combining efforts in support of either Liberal or SDP candidates. But at the national level there were problems between David Steel and David Owen as leaders of two separate parties. Dr. David Owen's decision to go his own way after a merger creating the new Social and Liberal Democratic Party has left him a senior politician in Parliament, but with only a computerized mailing list of supporters. In the United States this would be sufficient to start the campaign of a candidate running for a Presidential nomination. In England a senior politician must have a party too in order to become Prime Minister.

Is Anyone in Charge? Party organizations are often referred to as machines, but the term is a misnomer. The parties do not have a machine to manufacture votes at election time, nor can party headquarters manufacture support for an unpopular party leader. By the standards of American political parties, British parties are organizations, being formally established with a written constitution, permanent headquarters, routinized committee meetings, and bureaucrats whose careers depend on organizational loyalty rather than loyalty to an individual politician. But by comparison with a participative ideal, the Houghton Committee on Financial Aid to Political Parties concluded: "British political parties frequently operate below the minimum level of efficiency and activity required."[10]

Political parties have an element of *hierarchy* in their structure. Leaders in Parliament can publicly commit the whole of the party, and in a political crisis, such as the Falklands War or a major strike, do so on short notice. Whatever resolutions are adopted by local constituency parties can be ignored if the party's leadership in Parliament wants to do so. A resolution approved by an annual conference can be rejected by the party's leader in Parliament if he or she is confident of having the parliamentary party's support.

The division into a multiplicity of different and loosely linked organizations makes a party a *stratarchy*, that is, an institution in which the different strata of the party—in government, in Parliament, and even more, in annual conference and in the constituencies—each have a large degree of autonomy.[11] Local councillors can follow policies at variance with the party at Westminster and nominate for Parliament a politician known to be unsympathetic to the parliamentary leadership. Neither the Conservative, Labour, nor Liberal headquarters has ever had an accurate record of how many (or who) are party members. The annual conference provides an opportunity for anyone and everyone to voice personal opinions from the rostrum—but for only a few minutes a year. An MP willing to forego a chance of patronage from the party leader (or denied an office for which he or she hoped) can attack the party's elected leader.

The autonomy of different parts of a party is demonstrated by party finance. Money is in principle easy to transfer. Yet none of the parties concentrates the collection and allocation of funds centrally. Parliamentary parties in opposition receive a subsidy from public funds to employ staff for the leadership, thus gaining financial independence from party headquarters. Each constituency party has great discretion in raising and spending funds. While each is expected to make an annual contribution to party headquarters, the latter has no effective sanction to use against a local party delinquent in payment. It must extend credit, for it needs to maintain a party organization in every constituency. Although trade unions raise substantial sums from levies on the dues of their members, little more than half their political fund goes to Labour headquarters or to constituency parties. The unions spend a substantial amount on their own political activities and hoard some in reserve. In the Conservative Party, constituency associations raise more money than the central office and keep the great bulk for their own purposes. The central office raises large sums from corporate contributions solicited by its Central Board of Finance and spends centrally nearly all the money it raises.[12]

The fact that different parts of a party can often go their own way does not mean that they are all equal. National elections give every party member a stake in the success of the party at the center. The pre-eminence of Westminster in British government means that leaders of the parliamentary party will always be important vis-a-vis other parts of their party. Because all parts of a party share a common political identity and unite in the face of electoral competition, *bargaining* is a pervasive characteristic of intraparty politics. A party leader engaged in a winner-take-all struggle to become Prime Minister cannot afford disruptive quarrels within his or her parliamentary party, at the annual conference, or at the constituency level. Equally, other parts of the party recognize that if they attack their leader from behind, this will benefit the opponents that they face.

CROSS-PRESSURES UPON PARTIES

Parties are subject to cross-pressures from within their organization and the electorate. Winning votes is important, but so too is satisfying the aspirations of the party organization. When these goals face in opposing directions, party leaders must decide whether to give greater weight to pressures within the organization or to the electorate. If the conflict between the two becomes too great, a party can split. The history of party politics in England since 1885 has been a history of frequent disruptions reflecting difficulties in resolving conflicting pressures in their organization and electoral coalition.[13]

British parties are specially subject to cross-pressures because they are few in number. Whereas proportional representation makes it easy for politicians to divide into five or more relatively cohesive parties, the first-past-the-post electoral system encourages the maintenance of large coalitions under Conservative and Labour banners. It is also easier to create a larger party in England because of the absence of social differences that multiply party divisions in many countries. British parties are different types of coalitions from American parties because the parliamentary system places a premium upon party discipline. In England the voter chooses between parties, whereas the American primary system allows voters to choose within as well as between parties. The ideological spectrum in America is different, extending further to the right and not so far to the left.

Intraparty Divisions. British parties divide into three distinctive analytic groups: factions, tendencies, and nonaligned partisans.[14] *Factions* are self-consciously organized groups that persistently advance a program for government and have a recognized leader; they can properly be described as a "party within a party." An example is the Bennites, so named after Anthony Wedgwood Benn, leader of the left-wing cause in the Labour Party after the 1979 election; the faction came within 1 percent of electing Benn as the party's deputy leader. Factionalism gives stability to intraparty disputes. It also stimulates controversy, for old factional enemies can transfer their enmities to new issues.

A *tendency* is a stable set of attitudes rather than a stable collection of politicians. MPs adhering to right-wing or left-wing tendencies within a party can vary from issue to issue. To say that there is a "wet" tendency—moderate, as against the "dry" right-wing tendency—in the Conservative Party leaves open which Conservative MPs would publicly challenge the Prime Minister and the issues that would cause this to occur. *Nonaligned MPs* ignore intraparty differences in order to emphasize differences between parties. Factions and tendencies seek to convince nonaligned partisans that their position is most in accord with the party's principles and interests.

The Conservatives have been preeminently a party of tendencies. An analysis of resolutions signed by back-bench Conservatives showed that "such disagreements as arise are struggles between ad hoc groups of members who may be left or right on specific questions; but as new controversies break out, the coherence of the former groups dissolves, and new alignments appear, uniting former enemies and separating old allies."[15] In Margaret Thatcher's period as leader the Conservatives have divided into distinctive tendencies: the so-called wet tendency, which favors social reform and Keynesian economic policies; the dry tendency, which favors free-market and monetarist economic policies; and on many issues there is a substantial number of nonaligned Conservatives who do not want to be caught up in intraparty controversies. Mrs. Thatcher's own position is ambivalent. At the level of rhetoric she is undoubtedly a dry, but her administration has not rolled back the state nearly as much as the dries have wished. In party management Mrs. Thatcher often appears as a faction leader, suspicious of the views of many Conservatives. Her key question about colleagues is: "Is he one of us?" Yet her leadership has also been prudent, incorporating MPs inclined toward different tendencies in order to maintain a broad base of support within the party.[16]

The Labour Party has always had organized factions putting forward competing views as "parties within the party." One reason for frequent disputes is the seriousness of more or less ideological debate within the Labour Party, reflecting the late Lord Samuel's dictum: "There is only one way to sit still, but there are many ways to go forward." Secondly, the relative importance of the extraparliamentary sections of the Labour Party has given opponents of the parliamentary leadership, including dissident MPs, an arena in which to press their views, with the backing of some trade unions and many constituency parties. Thirdly, during Labour's eleven years in office between 1964 and 1979, the Labour government did not do what the left had hoped for. This encouraged the effective organization of left-wing groups against the party's leadership in government. Election defeat in 1979 gave the factions of the left the opportunity to press their views against a leadership weakened in opposition.

Disagreements within the Labour Party reached a peak in 1981, when for the first time since the 1930s the broad left won a majority within the party's annual conference, changing the party constitution in an effort to give the left more influence. While the left had won within the party organization, it lost the party electoral support; in 1983 Labour polled little more than a quarter of the vote. In reaction, Neil Kinnock was elected leader from a position on the soft left. As a campaigner against nuclear weapons he has left-wing credentials, but as a parliamentary party leader he also has ambitions to become Prime Minister. Kinnock's strategy has been to adopt positions that can be supported by a broad coalition of Labour MPs with some experience of government and by soft-left MPs who accept that winning an election is a necessary condition of having a chance to realize their aspirations.

The Alliance of Liberals and Social Democrats was novel in being a coalition between two separately organized parties. The two parties formed an electoral alliance in recognition of broad areas of agreement. After two elections fought as separate parties the great majority of Liberals and Social Democrats concluded that it made neither organizational nor electoral sense to maintain two separate parties. The Social and Liberal Democratic Party was created as a coalition of people who did not agree on every issue; in that they are no different from the leaders of the Conservative and Labour parties.

Cross-Party Links. In times past, cross-pressures have led many major politicians to change parties. A list of party leaders who have switched from one party to another includes such Prime Ministers as Sir Robert Peel, William Gladstone, David Lloyd George, Ramsay MacDonald, Winston Churchill, and the youthful Harold Wilson, a Liberal as an undergraduate but Labour when he stood for Parliament less than a decade later. Dr. David Owen, formerly Labour Foreign Secretary and coleader of the Alliance, would like to see his name added to this list as leader of the Owenite group of Social Democrats.

The debate about British entry to the European Community is the most recent major example of politicians crossing party lines to vote and work together. The parties could not enforce discipline on this issue because the recalcitrant minorities were so large that this would have disrupted both established parties. Those in a minority in their party did not want to form a new party with those with whom they agreed about the Community because they disagreed about much else. The decision was endorsed by Parliament in 1971 by a cross-party coalition consisting of 282 Conservative and sixty-nine Labour MPs; thirty-nine Conservatives and 189 Labour MPs voted against entry. In the 1975 referendum on Community membership, Labour Cabinet ministers and Conservative ex-ministers campaigned together—one group favoring membership and another group opposing it.

The extent to which electoral competition and partisan rhetoric reflect differences about what government should do can be tested by examining votes on government bills in Parliament. When deciding what measures to propose, the Cabinet can be confident that it will have the votes in the House of Commons to carry a measure. If a government proposal differs from what the Opposition wants, then the Opposition can register its disagreement at the second reading debate by dividing the House of Commons against a bill on its principles. However, if the government proposes legislation that is generally popular with the electorate, then opposing parties will not want to court electoral unpopularity by voting against a bill.

Although party discipline requires MPs to vote together, it does not require that the Opposition party whip direct MPs to vote against every measure of the governing party. A vote takes place in the Commons only if an explicit request is made to divide the House. When the object of legislation is likely to be popular, such as providing greater welfare benefits, the Opposition party will hesitate before going on record against a benefit. It will criticize amendments challenging the operation of a bill but not its principles. Refusing to request a division gives tacit consent to the principle of the government's legislation.

The division record of the House of Commons shows that both Conservative and Labour governments have usually put forward bills that will be acceptable to all sides of the House of Commons (Table XI.1). In the decades since 1964, three-quarters of govern-

TABLE XI.1 *Cross-Party Agreement on Government Legislation (in percentage)*

	Official Opposition		Minor
	Accepts	*Opposes*	*Opposition*
Conservative opposition			
1964–70	84	14	2
1974–79	70	20	10
Labour opposition			
1970–74	73	23	4
1979–83	61	37	1
Overall			
1964–83	74	22	4

Source: Adapted from Denis Van Mechelen and Richard Rose, *Patterns of Parliamentary Legislation* (Aldershot: Gower, 1986), Table 5.2. Opposition refers to votes by official Opposition. Minor opposition refers to votes against by small parties, or dissidents in government, or official opposition.

ment bills have gone through the major debate on second reading in Parliament without the Opposition voting against on principle. Even though the procedures and conventions of the House of Commons encourage the Opposition to vote against government legislation, there is sufficient agreement across party lines to ensure that the Parliamentary Labour Party tacitly accepts the principle underlying most measures of a Conservative government, and the Conservatives in opposition give their quiet endorsement to what a Labour government does. The bills that create major controversies in Parliament by emphasizing divisions between parties are newsworthy precisely because they are out of the ordinary; the average government bill is acceptable to all parties in the Commons.

PARTIES-IN-GOVERNMENT

The naive doctrine of democracy is that parties-in-government should give the people what they want. But relating popular preferences to government requires that politicians add a large measure of their own judgment. It is also naive to say that party government is about giving the voters what the party leadership wants. Parties are much more concerned with the advocacy of political goals than they are with devising means to achieve valued ends.

British government is party government, but to be nominally in charge of policy making is insufficient to be the de facto policy maker. "Parties live in a house of power," Max Weber wrote in one of his most gnomic sentences; he did not say whether the party in office resided as master, prisoner, or spectator.[17] To answer this question we must consider what a party needs to do in order to give positive direction to public policies. The basic requirements:

1. *Parties Must Formulate Policy Intentions.* The Conservative and Labour parties are organized to formulate policy intentions in Opposition. As an election approaches, parliamentary leaders and headquarters research staff prepare a detailed statement of policies covering subjects from agriculture to water supplies. The policies are consolidated into an election manifesto that lists upwards of a hundred policy pledges. One of the ways in which Social Democratic Party leaders sought to demonstrate that the Alliance was a serious alternative government was by preparing detailed policy proposals.

2. *A Party's Policy Intentions Must Specify the Programmatic Means to Achieve Desired Ends.* A statement of goals without refer-

ence to means, such as a pledge to seek peace and prosperity, is not a basis for action but a vague and perhaps vain hope. Opposition parties have neither the staff nor the political incentives to draw up programs in detail before an election. Because there is no chance of any of its proposals becoming law, an Opposition party may simply criticize what the government does and seize upon its major mistakes as evidence of the need to throw the governing rascals out. This is convenient, for it absolves the leader of the Opposition from committing himself on issues about which his party may disagree. It also avoids premature commitment to targets that civil servants argue are very difficult or impossible to achieve. Once in office, MPs can be surprised by the difficulties of governing. This view was given classic expression by Emanuel Shinwell, minister responsible for nationalizing the coal mines in the 1945 Labour government:

> We are about to take over the mining industry. That is not as easy as it looks. I have been talking of nationalization for forty years, but the complications of the transfer of property had never occurred to me.[18]

3. *Party Policies Must Be Doable.* Politicians emphasize willpower, that is, what government *ought* to do. But willing a goal is not the same as achieving it. Some policy objectives are intrinsically easier to achieve than others. The most straightforward objectives are those that are complete upon the enactment of an Act of Parliament; for example, permissive legislation of the 1960s simply required the repeal of Acts of Parliament making such things as homosexuality illegal. If a goal involves known technology, for example building a new motorway, it is straightforward to achieve, for civil engineers have the engineering technology to build roads. A goal such as increasing pensions is doable—if the money is available—for the administrative means of paying pensions is at hand. However, many objectives are not so easy to achieve. For example, a party may want to reduce unemployment by a million or to increase exports substantially, but stating this intent does not guarantee success.

4. *Partisans Must Occupy Important Positions in Government and Be Sufficiently Numerous to Dominate the Policy-Making Process.* Within hours of an election result being known, the leader of the winning party takes office as Prime Minister and begins appointing a Cabinet of about twenty colleagues. The constitutional fiction of one minister being personally responsible for the whole of a department inhibits the appointment of partisans to a

French-style *cabinet* assisting the minister as well as the placing of numerous partisans throughout a ministry to give close supervision to civil servants, as happens in Washington. The importance of a Cabinet minister within a department is significantly offset by the limited capacity for influence of a single individual.

5. *Partisans in Office Must Have the Skills Needed to Control Large Bureaucratic Organizations.* The skill that a Cabinet minister is most likely to have is that of managing Parliament. The ability to deal with fellow MPs in the Commons is not the same as the ability to deal with the inherited programs of a ministry. The conventions of a parliamentary career make it difficult for an aspiring minister to acquire experience directing a large organization outside government before becoming a minister. There is a limited likelihood that a new minister will have firsthand knowledge of the substantive social and economic conditions that the ministry is meant to deal with.

6. *Partisans in Office Must Give High Priority to Carrying Out Party Policies.* A politician in office faces many pressures that backbench MPs and partisans outside Parliament do not have to think about. One set of arguments against action is found within the ministry. Civil servants can point out the likely unpopularity of the means needed to achieve a given end or the very high cost in money terms. While many pressure groups can be ignored in Opposition, they must be faced in Whitehall, for example trade unions by a Conservative government and business by a Labour government.

7. *Civil Servants Do Not Identify Major Obstacles to Carrying Out Party Policies.* When out of office, politicians lack access to the views of civil servants; only a limited number of MPs can anticipate the objections that civil servants are likely to make to party proposals, and fewer still will want to bow to the constraints of office while still in opposition. Yet once in office, ministers depend upon civil service expertise for the identification of means to achieve the ends that they will. Expert advisers often cannot find a painless way to achieve what ministers want. Civil servants are concerned with ensuring that their ministers are aware of what Sir William Armstrong, former head of the civil service, has referred to as "ongoing reality," that is, obstacles to what the governing party would like to achieve.[19] Ministers need reminding of these constraints. The Whitehall norm is that the best service that a civil servant can offer is to point out the obstacles facing what a minister wants to do.

Very few ministers, and even fewer Cabinets, are prepared to run the risk of pursuing a policy that is, in the view of civil servants, very risky or almost certain to fail.

If all the above conditions are met, a party in office can make a big difference to the direction of government. But the record of British governments shows that parties make less difference than their leaders and supporters expect. This is most evident in the management of the economy. For more than a generation parties have campaigned with a pledge to make the economy grow faster. Low rates of growth have been normal, and in some periods the economy has actually contracted.[20] At best, a party can make a marginal impact upon the economy; economic models demonstrate that the size of this marginal change is less than voters or politicians would like it to be. For years politicians have unsuccessfully sought an economic growth rate double that actually achieved and unemployment and inflation rates much lower than those actually recorded.

When attention is turned from contesting elections to governing, party leaders must face the fact that there are some things stronger than parties. Entry into office is the first constraint. Commitments inherited from past governments are immediate and palpable. A minister is not asked what he would do if government had no commitments; the task is deciding what to do given the inertia of past commitments on the statute books. Statutory commitments are reinforced by administrative commitments. To make major changes in government is likely to take years when it requires reorganizing established institutions.

The climate of opinion is a second constraint. Ideas that appear attractive in a party conference may not appear attractive when subject to scrutiny by opponents in Parliament, by independent experts writing in the media, or when made the subject of opinion polls. While the governing party has the votes in the House of Commons to carry unpopular measures, it cannot put forward in Parliament a host of unpopular measures without risking the loss of support in the electorate.

A third constraint is that civil servants are at hand pointing out the risk to the reputation of the minister and the governing party if it embarks upon a controversial departure from the inertial course of established programs. Whereas Opposition leaders can confine discussions about policy to pressure groups committed to support the party, such as trade unions or business, a minister is faced with conflicting demands from unfriendly as well as favorably disposed groups. Fiscal constraints also become readily apparent in office, for every measure that costs money must be approved by the Treasury, and the Chancellor of the Exchequer never has enough money to finance all the spending plans of Cabinet colleagues.

International constraints are the ultimate check upon the actions of a party governing Britain today. Even if a governing party can make national institutions respond as it wants, the rest of the world does not have to treat Britain differently simply because a new government has taken office. Foreign countries tend to be neutral about the domestic politics of a country; they are prepared to do business with a government of any party. But this indifference becomes a handicap when the success of a government policy requires other countries to change course because control of British government changes hands. A new government seeking to alter European Community policies or to overcome the effects of a world economic recession will find that the rest of the world is not much interested in the intentions of resolutions passed at annual conferences in Brighton or Blackpool, or in preelection manifesto pledges.

A systematic analysis of what government does from decade to decade rejects the big-bang theory of adversary politics, in which every time control of government changes hands, there is a wholesale reversal of policies. Adversary rhetoric is a luxury of opposition parties. Once in office, a party is confronted by difficulties identified by civil servants, and it has few detailed plans of how to achieve what it would like to do. "Necessity more than ideological consensus is the explanation for similarities in behaviour."[21]

The influence of parties is greatest in the long term. A government that breaks the consensus by introducing a controversial policy can be sure that it will become an Act of Parliament. But if criticisms are borne out in practice, then it may be abandoned by the government that launched it. This often happens with economic policies. However, if a measure is successfully implemented, it is unlikely to be repealed when there is a change in the party in government. Most measures that were originally controversial, such as the abolition of selective secondary schools or entry to the European Community, are carried on by successive governments. Gradually controversial measures are incorporated into a moving consensus. The consensus reflects the large amount of agreement across party lines. Movement reflects the initiatives that parties take when the will of partisans is sufficiently informed by expertise to identify a policy goal that is doable.

NOTES

1. For a full analysis of parties as organizations, see Richard Rose, *The Problem of Party Government* (London: Macmillan, 1976; Penguin, 1976).

2. See Roger Jowell and Colin Airey, *British Social Attitudes: The 1984 Report* (Aldershot: Gower, 1984), p. 17; Bruce Cain, John Ferejohn and Morris Fiorina, *The Personal Vote* (Cambridge, Mass.: Harvard University Press, 1987).

3. Cf. Michael Rush, "The Selectorate Revisited," in Lynton Robins, ed., *Political Institutions in Britain* (London: Longman, 1987), pp. 150-165; and Byron Criddle, "Candidates," in D. E. Butler and Dennis Kavanagh, *The British General Election of 1987*, (London: Macmillan, 1988). 191-210.

4. Cf. John Bochel and David Denver, "Candidate Selection in the Labour Party: What the Selectors Seek," *British Journal of Political Science* 13:1 (1983), pp. 45-70, and an older but still relevant study, Edward G. Janosik, *Constituency Labour Parties in Britain* (New York: Praeger, 1968).

5. See Ivor Crewe and Martin Harrop, eds., *Political Communications: The General Election Campaign of 1983* (Cambridge: Cambridge University Press, 1986); and Richard Rose, *Influencing Voters* (London: Faber and Faber, 1967), Chapter 1.

6. See Lewis Minkin, *The Labour Party Conference*, 2nd ed. (Manchester: Manchester University Press, 1980).

7. R. T. McKenzie, *British Political Parties*, 2d ed., (London: Heinemann, 1963).

8. Morgan Phillips, *Constitution of the Labour Party* (London: Labour Party, 1960), p. 4.

9. For an early organizational study, see Jorgen S. Rasmussen, *The Liberal Party* (London: Constable, 1965). See Vernon Bogdanor, ed., *Liberal Party Politics* (Oxford: Clarendon Press, 1983).

10. *Committee on Financial Aid to Political Parties* (London: HMSO, Cmnd. 6601, 1976), p. 54.

11. Cf. S. J. Eldersveld, *Political Parties: A Behavioral Analysis* (Chicago: Rand McNally, 1964).

12. Cf. Michael Pinto-Duschinsky, *British Political Finance, 1830-1980* (Washington D.C.: American Enterprise Institute, 1981).

13. Richard Rose and Thomas T. Mackie, "Do Parties Persist or Disappear? The Big Tradeoff Facing Organizations," in Kay Lawson and Peter Merkl, eds., *When Parties Fail* (Princeton: Princeton University Press, 1988); and David Butler, ed., *Coalitions in British Politics* (London: Macmillan, 1978).

14. See Richard Rose, "Parties, Factions and Tendencies in Britain," *Political Studies*, 12:1 (1964), pp. 33-46.

15. S. E. Finer, Hugh Berrington, and D. J. Bartholomew, *Backbench Opinion in the House of Commons 1955-59* (Oxford: Pergamon Press, 1961), p. 106. See also Philip Norton and Arthur Aughey, *Conservatives and Conservatism* (London: Temple Smith, 1981).

16. Cf. Dennis Kavanagh, *Thatcherism and British Politics*, and Anthony King, "The Style of a Prime Minister."

17. The following paragraphs summarize ideas dealt with fully in Richard Rose, *The Problem of Party Government*, Chapters 15, 16.

18. Quoted in Alan Watkins, "Labour in Power," in Gerald Kaufman, ed., *The Left* (London: Anthony Blond, 1966), p. 173. For a detailed account of what it feels like to be a Cabinet minister unprepared for government, see the three-volume *Diaries* of R. H. S. Crossman (London: Hamish Hamilton, 1975–77).

19. Sir William Armstrong, "The Role and Character of the Civil Service" (text of a talk to the British Academy, London, 24 June 1970), p. 21. More generally, see Richard Rose, "Steering the Ship of State: One Tiller but Two Pairs of Hands," *British Journal of Political Science* 17:4 (1987).

20. For a more detailed analysis of the lack of party impact upon the economy, see Richard Rose, *Do Parties Make a Difference?*, 2nd ed., Chapter 7.

21. Richard Rose, *Do Parties Make a Difference?*, 2nd ed., p. 146.

CHAPTER XII

Producing Programs

What grows upon the world is a certain matter-of-factness. The test of each century, more than of the century before, is the test of results.

GOVERNMENT POLICIES are statements of intent. A minister's statement in the House of Commons explains what the government would like to do about a problem in society. Such statements usually aggregate a multiplicity of demands from parties and pressure groups, and Whitehall departments too. But an intention is a hypothesis of what might happen; it is not an accomplished fact. The intentions of ministers remain vague generalizations unless and until they are translated into programs that public officials can carry out.

To turn intention into government action Whitehall ministries must produce programs that mobilize resources—laws, money, and public employees. While the existence of a program does not guarantee that a policy will succeed, mobilizing resources is a necessary condition for government advancing toward a political goal.

In order to understand the dynamics of government, we must recognize what government does—produce programs covering everything from agriculture to transportation—as well as what it is, a set of institutions. Government is more than a set of institutions conducted by careful civil servants. It is more than a prize awarded politicians leading the party victorious at a general election. Government is also a set of organizations that produce programs intended to benefit individuals, groups, and the whole of society.

The great growth of government in the twentieth century has not been accompanied by a growth in institutions per se. There is still only one Crown and one Prime Minister. The number of MPs has actually declined since 1900. The great increase in the size of government has come about because of the growth of public programs. Whitehall ministers today are responsible for far more programs than a half century or a century ago. Government is now responsible for a comprehensive national health service, the civil as well as military use of atomic energy, and encouraging the development of new uses of information technology. Government also must mobilize far more money and personnel to maintain programs established long ago, such as national defense and education, which become more complex and more expensive through the years. What we described as the growth of government is in fact the growth of government programs.[1]

Organizations are central in the production of programs, but they are not sufficient (Figure XII.1). Programs are combinations of three resources—laws, money, and personnel—that allocate program responsibilities to particular institutions of government, typically a Whitehall ministry. The ministry is concerned with how these resources can be used to produce public services such as health care or police protection, or goods important in society, whether products of nationalized industries such as electricity, or such col-

FIGURE XII.1 *Mobilizing Resources for Public Policies*

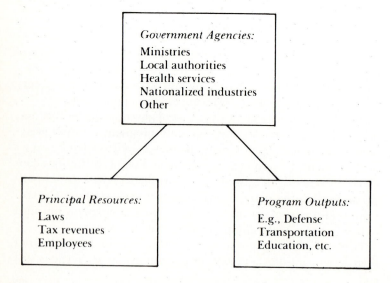

Government Agencies:
Ministries
Local authorities
Health services
Nationalized industries
Other

Principal Resources:
Laws
Tax revenues
Employees

Program Outputs:
E.g., Defense
Transportation
Education, etc.

lective services as defense by the armed forces. Most programs are actually delivered by public sector agencies outside Whitehall (cf. Chapter XIII). But the centralization of authority in the Crown in Parliament makes Cabinet ministers ultimately responsible for all public programs.

To think of government in terms of the programs that it produces concentrates attention upon the purposes of government. To see government solely in terms of the resources that it mobilizes is to see only half the story: what goes into the "black box" of government organizations. Government is not just about passing laws and collecting taxes and employing people. It is also about doing things for public purpose. Even though many people think of the health service, education, social security, or the police as nonpolitical, such programs are the primary evidence that many citizens have of government's activities. Public programs provide the benefits and create the costs of the contemporary mixed-economy welfare state. From a program perspective, the money that government collects is not a burden but a necessary means to the end of financing popular programs for pensions, health, and other social benefits. A quantitative description of government that ignores the purposes for which resources are mobilized risks becoming no more than "recreational mathematics, manipulating statistics in the abstract."[2]

While the purposes of government are important, they are not easily identified, for they are often the object of controversy. The first section of this chapter considers why politicians do *not* necessarily want to make their objectives clear, as is assumed to be the case in many "businesslike" theories of decision making. The second section examines in detail the variety of ways in which resources of laws, tax revenue, and public employment are mobilized, and differences in their uses. In the concluding section the program outputs of government are examined, comparing the relative importance of legal authority, money, and the services of public employees, for public programs concerned with social welfare, the economy, and the central defining concerns of the state: maintaining law and order and national defense.

IN SEARCH OF POLITICAL OBJECTIVES

In pure logic, a program could be designed by politicians first identifying a policy objective and civil servants then identifying efficient means to achieve the given end. But the choice of program ends can depend on the acceptability of means. Ministers and civil servants spend much time discussing the acceptability of measures with groups inside and outside government. A "good" program may even be defined as one that is easily implemented and acceptable to all interested parties. This is sufficient for a minister whose overriding objective is to keep the clients of his ministry satisfied.

Rather than identify precise program objectives, a Prime Minister often enunciates vague themes considered appealing to the ordinary voter. The tendency to keep objectives vague is also found in Acts of Parliament. There is no requirement for government to identify the purposes of a major program in the statute. The Act to end capital punishment contains no statement of its intent, whether it might be designed to encourage the rehabilitation of murderers, reduce the risk of judicial errors, or avoid responsibility for taking human life. The preamble of the landmark 1944 Education Act, making secondary schooling free to everyone, is typical; it simply enunciates a vague intention "to promote the education of the people of England and Wales." The National Health Service Act of 1946 is exceptional in clearly stating objectives: to secure improvement in physical and mental health by the prevention, diagnosis, and treatment of illness—and it specifies means to these ends.

The greater the number of objectives, the more interests that may be satisfied—but the greater the likelihood of confusion or contradiction between objectives. The Coal Industry Nationalization Act of 1946 had as its objectives to get coal from the mines; to secure efficient development of industry; and to sell coal "at such prices as may seem to the directors best calculated to further the public interest in all respects." However, these objectives can conflict. If maximizing the output of coal were the sole goal, then the Coal Board could concentrate upon increasing supplies of this major energy resource, whatever the cost. If efficiency were the sole objective, the amount of coal mined would fall and resources would be concentrated on the most efficient pits. If the miners' interests were identified as tantamount to the public interest, the Coal Board would provide good working conditions and high wages to miners even though this would drive up the cost of coal or of subsidizing the industry from public funds. Determining which objective is primary at any given time is a political choice.

Politicians have reason to avoid stating objectives clearly and succinctly, because measurable objectives provide clear evidence of failure when things do not go as hoped. The language of planning is sometimes used in politics to suggest that policy intentions will be realized according to a clear means-ends logic. But even the best-laid plans of public officials cannot promise the control of future events. A statement of objectives, such as the target for economic growth in the coming year, may be no more than the best estimate of the growth rate that is likely to result in any event.

Politicians have incentives to keep their goals multiple: the more goals enunciated, the more groups may support a program. The vaguer the goals, the easier it is to claim success, and the more difficult it is to prove failure. Multiple and vague goals may be contradictory, but resolving contradictions is part of a politician's stock in trade. Multiple objectives give a politician room for maneuver; a minister can shift the argument in favor of a program as evidence alters or change the interpretation of a program's purpose to suit a particular audience.[3]

The bulk of public programs is carried out without troubling the minister for a definition of objectives. Most of government's resources are devoted to the routine administration of long-established programs, and most public employees are engaged in carrying on programs that were designed and first implemented generations ago. At any given point in time most programs run easily because they are driven by inertial forces ensuring that what government did yesterday will continue to be done today and tomorrow.

From a Whitehall point of view, the immediate objective is to carry out Acts of Parliament with the minimum of difficulty from intended beneficiaries, from MPs, or within the governing party. Bureaucrats are first of all concerned with procedures, not substantive outcomes. From a bureaucratic perspective, doing what the law prescribes and ministers request is sufficient to produce a policy. A Whitehall ministry can regard the health service as satisfactorily run if hospitals are built according to plan and their budgets satisfy the auditors; the condition of the patients in hospitals is not their concern.

From a broader perspective, the money and personnel employed in public programs are not only program outputs: they are also meant to be inputs to social conditions. The programs of the health service are not just ends in themselves; they are also means to the end of maintaining and improving the nation's health. The ultimate objective of a program is to change or maintain conditions in society, e.g. to improve health of individuals. But because many factors influencing health are outside the control of the ministry—for example, diet, exercise, and housing—it is far simpler for public officials to make their objective the proper allocation of the resources for which they are responsible and to be much less concerned with the impact that their efforts have upon society.

Prime Minister Margaret Thatcher has sought to encourage Whitehall departments to go beyond their concern with procedures of programs. An Efficiency Unit has been established under her patronage in the Cabinet office to assess programs in terms of "value for money." The underlying philosophy is that of management accounting; managers are expected to be concerned with what they are buying with what they spend. If a given amount of goods and services can be produced more cheaply than before, this is regarded as desirable because it may improve the company's bottom-line profit.

However, most government programs have no simple pounds-and-pence bottom line, since they are provided free of charge. This is true of collective goods such as defense, for which no charge could be made, since everyone is equally affected by the state of the nation's military. It also includes benefits which are in theory marketable but which, by Act of Parliament, are provided free of charge, such as primary and secondary education. The definition of a good air force or a good school cannot be one that makes a profit, because education and defense are not sold in the marketplace.[4]

The Thatcher Administration's effort to develop performance indicators for public programs has demonstrated how very difficult it is to evaluate programs by the efficiency standards of accountants or production engineers. Departments under pressure to produce quantitative measures have been able to generate many indicators of inputs (that is, sums expended on policies) and of activities (for example, number of patients treated or unemployment benefits paid) and some measures of efficiency (for example, the cost per pupil in different types of universities or studying different subjects). However, the search continues for satisfactory causal models showing that the mobilization of X amount of resources produces Y amount of success in achieving a given political objective. As a proxy objective, Downing Street has been ready to substitute crude measures of money saved: a pound cut from a public program is deemed to reduce waste rather than effectiveness or efficiency,[5] for the overriding (though not always achieved) political objective of the Thatcher Administration is to reduce public expenditure.

MOBILIZING RESOURCES; LAWS, TAXES, PUBLIC EMPLOYEES

The resources that government mobilizes are varied in character. Laws are verbal statements drafted in Whitehall and approved by Parliament to provide statutory authorization for programs. Tax revenues are extracted from individuals, corporations, and other taxpayers; the money thus extracted is used to finance program outputs. Public employees, whether in roles unique to government (submarine captain) or common to many organizations (secretary or clerk), provide services to citizens, but they are first of all servants of government.

Laws. The unique resource of government is legislation. The power to make rules binding upon members of society distinguishes government from other organizations that employ large numbers of people and spend large sums of money. The legitimacy of government makes law a particularly valuable resource for British government. People follow most government directives not because they receive cash benefits for doing so, but because it is the law.

Continuity of government from medieval times results in a vast accumulation of Acts of Parliament through the centuries. The Chronological Table of the Statutes, giving the title of each Act of Parliament, runs to more than 1,300 pages. The earliest statute still in force dates from the thirteenth century. One in ten laws date from before Queen Victoria's accession to the throne in 1837, and more than one-third date from before 1900 (Table XII.1). Every program of government is derived from a succession of laws enacted at different times, without a logical and comprehensive analysis of their cumulative and multiple effects. Every newly elected government inherits responsibility for thousands of Acts of Parliament prepared by its predecessors; this limits its room for maneuver. Any new proposal must be carefully scrutinized for its effect on preexisting legislation; adapting new legislation to old statutes is laborious and often time-consuming.

Drafting a law is a test of the care with which policy makers have thought about their intentions.[6] A law is not like a speech, a form of words that can be as vague as a politician desires. Nor do the consequences of a law disappear at the end of an evening, as often happens with a speech. Legislation requires politicians to tell the draftsmen of parliamentary bills precisely what they intend to do about a problem. It is difficult to transfer attention from drafting

TABLE XII.1 *Persistence of Laws from the Past*

Period	Number of Acts	Percent total in force	Cumulative percent
Before 1760	132	3.9	3.9
1761–1836	215	6.3	10.2
1837–1901	866	25.4	35.6
1902–1918	192	5.6	41.2
1919–1945	479	14.1	55.3
1945–1951	200	5.9	61.2
1951–1964	438	12.8	74.0
1964–1970	284	8.3	82.3
1970–1974	195	5.7	88.0
1974–1979	328	9.6	97.6
1979–1980	81	2.4	100

Source: Denis Van Mechelen and Richard Rose, *Patterns of Parliamentary Legislation* (Aldershot: Gower, 1986), Table 10.5. Up to 1945 reference is to calendar years, from that date reference is to annual sessions of Parliament.

speeches and white papers for ministers to drafting legislative instruments to realize proclaimed intentions. One civil servant experienced in drafting legislation comments: "Very often you don't see the pitfalls and traps until you write your instructions to parliamentary counsel. Having to be so specific, you suddenly realize you have been talking nonsense for months."[7]

Laws are a very different resource from money or personnel; the Whitehall departments that make most use of legislation tend to make less use of money, and big-spending departments with lots of employees tend to make less use of laws. Six departments—the Treasury, the Foreign Office, Trade & Industry, the Home Office, the Scottish Office, and Environment—together have accounted for more than three-fifths of all new government acts in the postwar period. Yet they have claimed less than one-fifth of total expenditure and one-third of public employment. Laws about crime, about the conduct of commerce, and international laws and treaties are important in themselves; they do not require large amounts of money to enforce. By contrast, major spending departments such as Defence and Education rank near the bottom of ministries sponsoring legislation. Their programs are standing commitments that continue without new legislation.[8]

Although law has both authority and sanctions, only one in ten Acts of Parliament invokes compulsion, telling people what they must or must not do. Nine-tenths of laws are guidelines for behavior rather than commands or prohibitions. Rules are promulgated for a lawful marriage; they do not compel people to marry. Company law guarantees a business the protection of the law if it acts within the procedures laid down there, just as road safety acts are designed to protect the motorist in his or her journey, without prescribing where people should drive. Most laws about the everyday activities of citizens are virtually unnoticed, such as laws affecting property rights in a house or the contents of packaged foods. However, the absence of such laws would be noticed.

The liberal idea that legislation is about the rights and obligations of individuals is only half correct. Less than half of all postwar legislation is directed at individuals in their roles as voters, social security claimants, motorists, etc. An additional 11 percent affects both individuals and organizations, for example laws concerning the sale of real estate. Half of all legislation regulates the activities of organizations, including a third that regulates government organizations in relations with citizens, as employing organizations, and in dealings with foreign nations. The high proportion of legislation affecting organizations makes it easier to implement legislation, for organizations are more readily amenable to inspection and enforcement than are individuals—and this is particularly true of organizations that are themselves in the public sector.[9]

Executive decrees can be issued as Orders in Council with the full force of law, and Acts of Parliament can delegate authority to ministers to promulgate statutory instruments, typically rules of relatively minor importance. In practice, civil servants usually negotiate the content of these regulations with pressure groups representing those who are regulated. The Statutory Instruments Committee of the Commons scrutinizes them and can call to the attention of the Commons any measure that it believes goes beyond what is authorized by Act of Parliament. If this is not done, the instrument becomes binding. The number of instruments cited as objectionable is usually less than ten a year, hardly 1 percent of the annual total. Those affected by the regulations have little reason to mobilize MPs in protest, because they have been consulted in advance and accept the rules laid down.

Every program involves some discretionary use of statutory powers. Discretion is particularly great in managing the economy and foreign affairs, both areas of public policy that cannot be controlled by Acts of Parliament. Many discretionary actions are limited in scope, but the result can be of intense significance to a few people, for example, planning permission to add a room to a house. Many decisions involving discretionary use of statutory powers are made by special-purpose administrative tribunals. Industrial tribunals, local valuation courts, national insurance bodies, rent tribunals, supplementary benefit appeal tribunals, and other bodies together hear hundreds of thousands of cases in a year.[10]

While all government programs require statutory authorization, the growth of government does not necessarily require new laws. For example, a new social security act is not needed for more money to be spent on pensions. If more people live to pensionable age, expenditure automatically increases because of existing statutory entitlements. Some seemingly new Acts simply consolidate and update a variety of Acts passed by previous Parliaments. Between 1945 and 1980, a period of great growth in government, the number of Acts of Parliament actually decreased by 38 percent. Successive governments repealed almost twice as many Acts as they approved.[11] Typically, a large number of measures enacted at different times were consolidated into a single omnibus Act, and the consolidated Act was approved without controversy in Parliament.

Tax Revenue. The second major resource of government is money, and taxation is the principal source of government revenue. Tax revenue is first of all determined by laws. Acts of Parliament define the economic activities that constitute the base for taxation. For example, not all income is subject to income tax; the law allows a variety of deductions to be made from gross income for minimum living expenses, children, interest payments on a mortgage, and so forth. Tax is levied only on the net income remaining after the allowances are taken into account. Laws also establish the rate at which tax is to be levied; for example, income tax is currently set at twenty-five pence in the pound for net income up to £19,300 and then at forty pence in the pound. Acts of Parliament also create a legal liability to pay the tax. Usually the obligation is placed upon organizations, which must deduct income tax from the wages of employees and are also liable for paying value-added tax (VAT) on the sale of goods and services. The law is written this way because it is far easier to collect money from incorporated bodies, for example, a whiskey distiller, than from individuals, such as whiskey drinkers.[12]

The total tax revenue of British government is large and continuously growing. In money terms total tax revenue has increased more than 4,000 percent in the postwar era. In 1948 total tax revenue was £4 billion; it is now above £160 billion. The rate of many taxes has actually fallen in this period; for example, the standard rate of income tax has been reduced by more than one-third. Inflation is the principal reason for the nominal increase in public revenue. The growth in the economy has been important too, providing revenue additional to that needed to offset the effects of inflation. When tax revenue is viewed in terms of tax effort—that is, the proportion of the gross domestic product claimed as taxes—then the increase in taxation is very small; taxes claimed 35.5 percent of the national product in 1948 and 38.0 percent in 1985. Hence it is correct to say that taxes have gone up a lot in current money terms. But since the money value of wages has also gone up a lot in the postwar era, it is also correct to say that the tax burden has gone up very little in relation to the national product. By international standards, the tax effort in Britain is average for advanced industrial OECD nations.[13]

Taxes exist in the plural: no one tax provides British government with most of the revenue it needs, and there are dozens of minor taxes producing very small yields. Taxation is highly centralized; more than nine-tenths of tax revenue is raised by the Treasury; the remainder is levied by local authorities, whose tax policies are subject to central government control. The British taxpayer thus has only one major taxing authority to worry about. By contrast, Americans can pay income taxes to federal, state, and local government, and three levels of sales taxes too. Five taxes—income tax, national insurance, VAT, oil taxes, and local authority rates—together account for nearly four-fifths of total tax revenue (Table XII.2).

When income tax was initially introduced as an emergency measure to help finance the wars against Napoleon, it applied only to wealthy people; today the average person in work pays about £1,600 a year in income tax. Income tax is generally considered a fair tax because the amount paid is related to an individual's ability to pay; the more income, the more tax paid. *National insurance contributions* are also a tax on income; a percentage is deducted from the wages of an employee, and the employer must pay a contribution additional to the gross wage. The sums paid are earmarked to finance social security benefits, principally the old-age

Table XII.2 *Principal Sources of Tax Revenue*

Type of tax (billion 1985 revenue)	As percent national tax system	As percent gross domestic product
Income tax (£35.5)	26	10
National insurance (£21.5)	16	6
Value-added tax (VAT) (£21.0)	16	6
Oil taxes (£13.6)[a]	10	4
Local authority rates (£13.6)[b]	10	4
Corporation tax (£9.1)	7	2.5
Tobacco and alcohol (£8.5)	6	2
All other taxes (£12.0)	9	3

[a] Revenue from tax on North Sea oil drilling plus tax on oil consumption.
[b] From 1989 replaced by a community charge head tax on all adults.
Source: Derived from Richard Rose and Terence Karran, *Taxation by Political Inertia* (London: George Allen & Unwin, 1987), Table 2.1.

pension. The contribution is not really an insurance payment because it is compulsory and because the Treasury must contribute money from general revenue in order to finance increases in social security benefits. For the great majority of people in work, the effective marginal rate of tax on income is 34 percent, the combined rate of income tax and national insurance contributions. The take-home pay that an individual receives is thus one-third less than his or her gross wage.

Value-added tax was introduced in 1973 as a condition of Britain joining the European Community; it is a tax upon the sale of goods and services at every stage from production to retailing. It is far broader than a general sales tax, but the base is narrowed by the exemption of food, house sales, and a number of other basic commodities. The rate of VAT is 15 percent, much higher than an American sales tax but lower than the VAT rate in many European countries, such as Sweden, where the rate can go above 20 percent. VAT now accounts for one-sixth of total tax revenue. It is also perceived as a tax that pushes up the cost of living because it is a visible tax on expenditure.

The increase in the number of cars and the use of oil for central heating have greatly boosted oil taxes. The oil price shock of 1973, fortuitously coinciding with the start of oil production in Britain's North Sea oil fields, makes it possible to collect billions by means of a petroleum revenue tax upon oil extraction as well as duties upon the consumption of oil. Oil taxes now raise substantially more money than taxes on tobacco, beer, wines, and spirits and more than general corporation tax. When oil consumption was much lower, in the days of post-war austerity, a much larger share of revenue was raised from taxes on tobacco and beer.

The taxation of property in England dates back many centuries. The rate of taxation is set by each council and has been the primary source of revenue that local government can determine itself. Central government grants have met about half the cost of local government expenditure. Local authority rates rose with inflation in the 1970s and also due to cuts in central government grants in the 1980s, and with decisions by some local authorities to increase spending on the volume of services provided. The Thatcher government therefore has decided to abolish rates on domestic households and set rates on industrial property centrally. The billions of pounds of revenue thus lost are to be paid for by a community charge, that is, a poll or head tax on every person above the age of 18 living in a given local authority area. The change is controversial because the flat-rate tax does not take into account the ability of individuals to pay to the same extent as a tax on the value of a house. The tax will also be much more difficult to administer; property is easy to tax because houses are stationary and visible, whereas the population, especially in inner cities, is mobile, and neither the police nor central government has a register of the address of each citizen.

When the costs of public programs exceed the revenue that government can raise from taxation—because of either an unexpected downturn in the economy or political resistance to increasing taxes—then government turns to borrowing. The amount of borrowing varies with government policy and economic conditions. Borrowing to finance a deficit of public revenue as against expenditure rose in the 1960s and 1970s. In 1961 government borrowed the equivalent of one pound for every twelve it raised in taxes. By 1975 it borrowed one pound for every four raised in taxes. Unlike President Reagan's administration, Mrs. Thatcher's government has made the reduction of public borrowing a major political goal in the belief that this will reduce inflation. In consequence, by 1987 borrowing was reduced to less than one pound for every £25 raised in taxes, and the public-sector borrowing requirement of government is now among the lowest of advanced industrial nations.

The generalization that taxes are always rising is true only in the most trivial sense: the money paid in taxes is sure to go up because of inflation. But in relation to the nation's accounts, it is not true that all taxes rise. In the postwar era, income tax, tobacco, beer, and customs taxes have decreased their contribution to the national tax system, while national insurance and VAT have greatly increased in relative value. When changes in the claims of a tax upon the national product are considered, we find that taxes on income, tobacco, and alcohol and some lesser taxes have decreased their claims, while others now claim a larger share of the national product. The small net increase in total tax effort in postwar Britain is a reflection of some taxes going up, others going down, and yet a third group of taxes remaining much the same in their relative significance.

Changes in taxation principally reflect changes in the economy rather than conscious choices by politicians. The problem facing any government is how to minimize political costs (and increasing tax revenue has costs) while maximizing political benefits (such as increasing public expenditure requiring additional tax revenue). The dilemma can be resolved by relying upon increased revenue from taxes placed on the statute books generations or even centuries ago and kept in force by political inertia. An old tax can generate increased revenue when the economy grows in real terms or through inflation. From one year to the next, an average of 98 percent of tax revenue is collected by laws long in force. The annual budget decisions of the Chancellor of the Exchequer are much publicized in Parliament and the media: it is regarded as news when there is a few pence change in the tax on beer or cigarettes or an alteration in the income tax. But changes in tax rates or in defining the base of a tax have very little effect on total revenue. Moreover, while the Chancellor takes credit for cutting a billion or two off what the Treasury would otherwise claim in taxation, the expansion of the economy places more money in government hands. Thus, total government revenue actually increases, even though annual budget messages make it appear that taxes are being cut. Most so-called cuts only reduce the size of the increase that would otherwise occur.[14]

Public Employees. Labor is the third major resource of government. In the nineteenth century the night-watchman state employed few people, for it had very few programs besides keeping the peace. Today the mixed-economy welfare state employs millions of people. Popular cartoons present the typical public employee as a remote and impersonal bureaucrat, shuffling papers at a desk. This is not the case: the typical public employee delivers a service such as education or health care. Cynical theories postulate that government grows because public officials can thus increase their income, status, and power within public sector organizations. Empirical evidence demonstrates that such theories are ill founded.[15] Whereas a medieval monarch paid people in order to surround himself with loyal retainers, public employees today are hired to deliver particular programs (Table XII.3).[16]

TABLE XII.3 *Program Responsibilities of Public Employees*

	1951	1985	Change
		(× 1,000 employees)	
Social programs			
Health	492	1,538	+1,046
Education	618	1,281	663
Personal social services	116	376	260
Social security, employment, etc.	86	224	138
	1,312	3,419	+2,107
Economic programs			
Transportation	1,017	401	−616
Coal mining	775	221	−554
Steel	292	65	−227
Post office, telephones	340	177	−163
Gas, electricity, water	371	311*	−60
Related economic programs	191	161	−60
Other nationalized industries	3	131*	+128
	2,989	1,467	−1,552
Defining concerns			
Defense (services, civilian)	1,228	521	−707
Police, fire, tax, general admin	755	1,480	725
	1,983	2,001	+ 18
Total number	6,284	6,887	+573
As % work force	26.6	28.2	+1.6

*Scheduled for further reduction by privatization.

Sources: Compiled from Richard Parry, "Britain: Stable Aggregates, Changing Composition," Table 2.3, in Richard Rose et al. *Public Employment in Western Nations* (Cambridge: Cambridge University Press 1985); and Richard Parry, "Public Employment in Britain in the 1980s," Table 3, in Parry and K.D. Schmidt, *Public Employment in Britain and Germany* (Glasgow: U. of Strathclyde Studies in Public Policy No. 157, 1987).

Social programs are the principal cause of public employment today: health and education together account for two-fifths of total public employment and more than one-tenth of all jobs in Britain. Each of these programs provides benefits for millions of individuals entitled by Act of Parliament to receive these benefits. Since the benefits are without charge to recipients, ability to pay does not limit demand. Health service employment has increased by 1,046,000 since 1951 due to the ageing of the population, the provision of health services without charge, and the consequent expansion of demand. Education has added 663,000 to the public payroll due to the baby boom, an increasing number of years of education per pupil, lower pupil-to-teacher ratios, and the addition of ancillary services in schools.

Nationalized industries were central in the 1945 Labour government's plans for the economy; in 1951 *economic programs* accounted for nearly half of public employment in public transport, coal mining, the post office and telephones, electricity, manufacturing industry, and so on. Today, economic programs account for only one-fifth of public employment. Public transportation has contracted most, due to the increased ownership of motor cars. Coal mining has contracted by two-thirds due to a shift of consumer preference to oil and electricity, which are capital-intensive rather than labor-intensive forms of energy. Steel has declined by more than three-quarters as steel production became more capital-intensive, and international competition has depressed world demand for British-made steel. The privatization measures of the Thatcher Administration are added to the decrease in public employment in this sector by turning nationalized industries into companies owned by shareholders.

Defense, the central *defining concern* of government, was the largest single cause of public employment at the height of the cold war in 1951, when military service was compulsory for young men. With changes in world affairs and Britain's role in the world, defense employment has fallen by more than half. The principal expansion has been in hiring police and firemen, more tax officials, and more administrators. Public employees in this category constitute more than one-quarter of all public employees today.

In aggregate, public employment has increased its share of the labor force in the postwar era by only 1.6 percent. In 1951 public employment was 26.6 percent of the work force; in 1985 it was 28.2 percent (Table XII.3). Even this slight increase can be explained as a reflection of private-sector employment having contracted and unemployment having doubled. The British experience contrasts with that of other European nations, which have experienced a big increase in public employment in the postwar era. The contrast is explained by the fact that by 1951 Britain *already* had a big government, created by mobilization for war in 1940 and extended by the 1945–51 Labour government. The United States has been like Britain in having kept total public employment stable as a percentage of the work force, but it has done so at a much lower level—18 percent—because a full range of welfare-state programs have not been adopted in America.[17]

By contrast with the relative stability of total employment, when particular programs are examined, great changes occur. The changes have been in opposite directions: some programs, such as health and education, have increased greatly, while others, such as defense, public transport and coal mining, have contracted greatly. The dynamics of public employment cannot be explained by a general theory of providing benefits to citizens or to employees; they must be explained by examining the causes of change in particular programs, for when government grows, it is programs, not abstract properties of institutions, that are the cause.

PROGRAM OUTPUTS

Analysis separates what government unites. The resources catalogued above—laws, money, and personnel—are brought together in manifold public programs. Laws authorize government to act and create organizations that employ people and spend money to deliver public programs. In education, for example, children are by law compelled to attend school, and citizens must pay taxes to support education even if they do not have children. Millions of youths are taught by hundreds of thousands of teachers in thousands of schools.

When we ask which programs of government are the most important, the answer given depends upon the criterion used. If we think of the programs necessary by definition to maintain an independent state, these are very few. To continue in existence, a government must maintain law and order domestically and protect national security through diplomacy and military force. To meet these obligations it must collect taxes and pay interest on debts from the past.[18] The Crown did this successfully for centuries before the introduction of contemporary programs of the mixed-economy welfare state.

The resources mobilized by British government to meet its minimum defining responsibilities are relatively small (Table XII.4).

TABLE XII.4 *Program Outputs*

Social programs	Money £ bn (billions of pounds)	Employees (× 1,000)	Laws (% total)
Social security	£44.4	224	7.9%
Health	18.8	1,538	7.9%
Personal social services	3.4	376	7.9%
Education	20.1	1,281	2.0
	£86.7	3,419	9.9%
Economic programs			
Agriculture	£2.5	20	5.0%
Trade, industry, energy	3.5	985	13.3
Employment	3.7	54	2.8
Transport	5.7	401	4.4
Housing & environment	8.7	195	8.3
	£24.1	1,655	33.8%
Defining concerns			
Defense	£18.1	521	2.4%
Foreign affairs	3.4	11	9.3
Law and order	6.9	285	17.2
Tax administration	1.3	100	12.3
Debt interest payments	17.8	n.a.	n.a.
	£47.5	917	41.2%
Miscellaneous	3.8	889	15.1%*
	£162.1	6,880	100%

*Includes 9.9 percent of legislation accounted for by Scottish Office, paralleling laws of many Whitehall departments.

Source: Compiled principally from tables in Richard Rose, *Ministers and Ministries* (Oxford: Clarendon Press, 1987) Chapter 3; and *The Government's Expenditure Plans 1988–89 to 1990–91* (London: HMSO, Cm. 288–I), principally Chapter 2. Employment figures differ slightly from Table XII.4 because of minor differences in classification.

The defining programs of government account for little more than one-tenth of the national product, one-quarter of total public expenditure, and less than one-seventh of public employment. Defense claims a large portion of the money and manpower devoted to the fundamental concerns of the state, whereas diplomacy does not. Foreign affairs spending appears significant only because it includes Britain's contribution to the European Community, which spends its revenue principally on such domestic programs as agriculture. Interest payments are the second most costly defining program. Interest is paid on money borrowed to finance programs that the government has been unwilling to finance fully through taxation or to cut back. Maintaining law and order through police, the courts, and prisons is not expensive.

Defining programs tend to be law-intensive, accounting for many more laws than other programs. Government maintains public order by promulgating laws about how citizens ought to behave. Insofar as these standards are met, officials are not needed to patrol the streets or enforce the law through the courts. The great bulk of revenue is paid routinely by organizations obeying their lawful obligation to pay tax; the money spent to pay tax officials for administering the laws is a very small percentage of total revenue collected. Foreign affairs involves a substantial element of international law, for many agreements between nations are registered in Acts of Parliament. This was particularly true during the end of Empire, when Parliament had to enact the terms of independence for ex-colonial countries.

When money and personnel are measures of public programs, a very different profile of public policy emerges. Social programs loom largest: social security, health care, personal social services, and education together account for more than half of public expenditure and for half of all public employment. Public spending on social security is greater than on all the defining concerns of government, and more than twice what is spent on all economic programs. Education ranks second in claims on money and public employment, and health ranks third in cost and first in public employment. While social security spends the most money, it does not have the most employees, because it is a transfer program: the output of social security is money in the hands of a pensioner or a poor person. By contrast, money spent on education and health is used to pay doctors, nurses, teachers, and other employees, and to finance the buildings and supplies required to provide health care and education.

Social programs do not require a spate of new legislation each year; old laws mandate the expenditure of well over half of government revenue. Compulsory education dates to 1870. The first social security and health benefit Acts were introduced before 1914, and their coverage was expanded to cover the whole population four decades ago. The laws entitle citizens as of right to a pension, to health care, and to education. The more people who are eligible to claim these benefits, the more money government must spend, and the more employees it must have. Demographic pressures, such as an increase in the number of children or the elderly, are sufficient to make these programs big or to make them grow bigger still.

Programs directed at particular sectors of the economy, such as industry, agriculture, or transport, mobilize large numbers of public employees but do not account for such a large proportion of public expenditure. The reason is that nationalized industries generate a large portion of their revenue by selling services. This is true of industries that need subsidies because revenue does not cover costs (the railways and the post office) and of industries that have a surplus of revenue (electricity).

In a mixed economy, government does not make train tickets, electricity, and housing available to citizens free of charge, as is done with education, financed from general tax revenue. Instead, government defines its role as providing financial incentives to encourage positive economic developments such as increased exports or new uses of information technology. It also gives subsidies to keep in business industries that are deemed to make a nonmarket contribution to social well-being, such as the railways and agriculture. The economy is regulated by legislation, which is far more important in this field than in social policy. Government seeks to maintain order in the marketplace through legislation about the sale of goods and services, competition, health and safety at work, pollution, and so forth. It also seeks to influence the overall economic climate by decisions taken about taxation, spending on social policies, interest rates, and the money supply (cf. Chapter XIII).

Any attempt to reduce all public programs to a single measuring rod, whether money, public employees or laws, is restrictive, for every government program requires a mix of legal authorization, personnel, and money. To ignore nonmonetary elements in public programs is to dismiss as unimportant the maintenance of law and order and national security. To ignore the role of public employees is to forget the fundamental distinction between programs that put money in people's hands to spend as they like and services that pay public employees to do what they think best to help people. The market too is a resource for public programs, for the programs of government are financed by taxes levied on the resources of the whole of the economy. In terms of nineteenth-century theories of the minimal state, government claims far more than the minimum resources needed for its essential defining programs. Government has grown greatly in this century because the programs it produces such as social security, health care, and education are regarded as "good" goods and services.

NOTES

1. See Richard Rose, "The Programme Approach to the Growth of Government," *British Journal of Political Science*, 15:1 (1985), pp. 1–28.

2. See P. Larkey, C. Stolp, and M. Winer, "Theorizing about the Growth of Government," *Journal of Public Policy*, 1:2 (1981), pp. 157–220.

3. See Richard Rose, *Managing Presidential Objectives* (New York: Free Press, 1976), Chapter 1.

4. For two views of the logic of charging or not charging for public policies, cf. contributions in Ken Judge, ed., *Pricing the Social Services* (London: Macmillan, 1980); and Ralph Harris and Arthur Seldon, *Welfare without the State* (London: Institute of Economic Affairs, Hobart Paperback 26, 1987).

5. Cf. M. S. Levitt and M.A.S. Joyce, *The Growth and Efficiency of Public Spending* (Cambridge: Cambridge University Press, 1987); Christopher Pollitt, "Capturing Quality? The Quality Issue in British and American Health Policies," *Journal of Public Policy* 7:1 (1987), pp. 71–92; Les Metcalfe and Sue Richards, *Improving Public Management* (London: Sage, 1987).

6. See the report of the committee chaired by Sir David Renton, *The Preparation of Legislation* (London: HMSO, Cmnd. 6053, 1975).

7. Quoted in John Clare, "Who Makes the Decisions that Change Our Environment?" *The Times* (London) 9 May 1972. See also G.C. Thornton, *Legislative Drafting*, 2nd ed. (London: Butterworths, 1979).

8. See Denis Van Mechelen and Richard Rose, *Patterns of Parliamentary Legislation* (Farnborough: Gower, 1986), p. 14ff.

9. *Ibid.*, p. 19f.

10. *Social Trends*, Vol. 18 (1988), tables 11.14–11.18.

11. *Ibid.*, chapters 3, 10.

12. See Richard Rose and Terence Karran, *Taxation by Political Inertia* (London: Allen & Unwin, 1987).

13. Data in this and subsequent paragraphs is from Richard Rose and Terence Karran, *Taxation by Political Inertia*, unless otherwise noted.

14. See particularly Rose and Karran, *Taxation by Political Inertia*, Chapter 7.

15. See Christopher Hood, M. Huby, and A. Dunsire, "Bureaucrats and Budgeting Benefits," *Journal of Public Policy* 4:3 (1984), pp. 163–180.

16. See Richard Rose, "The Significance of Public Employment," in Rose et

al., *Public Employment in Western Nations* (Cambridge: Cambridge University Press, 1985); and in the same volume, Richard Parry, "Britain: Stable Aggregates, Changing Composition," pp. 54–96.

17. See Rose, "The Significance of Public Employment."

18. See Richard Rose, "On the Priorities of Government," *European Journal of Political Research* 4 (1976), pp. 247–289.

CHAPTER XIII

Delivering Programs

If we think what a vast information, what a nice discretion, what a consistent will ought to mark the rulers of that empire, we shall be surprised when we see them. We see a changing body of miscellaneous persons, sometimes few, sometimes many, never the same for an hour.

INTENTIONS BECOME ACTIONS only when a policy is delivered. While Westminster has the authority to decide what government ought to do, it does not have its hands on the institutions and employees that deliver most public programs. A distinctive feature of British government is that ministries deliver only a small proportion of the services for which ministers answer in Parliament. Public-sector organizations outside Whitehall deliver the great bulk of programs; education is a local-authority responsibility, health care is in the hands of a separate set of health service institutions, and transport is in the hands of nationalized industries and special-purpose local agencies. Five-sixths of all public employees and about half of total public expenditure is in the hands of organizations outside Whitehall ministries but inside the public sector.[1] In a highly centralized system such as in France, a far higher proportion of expenditure and employment rests with the ministries; education, for example, is organized by the Ministry of Education. In a federal system such as the United States, Cabinet secretaries in Washington are not responsible for many services in the hands of state and local government, such as education.

From the "underall" position of the ordinary citizen, the benefits of government are made evident by the services delivered by teachers at the local primary school, by doctors at a local clinic, by the

315

policeman who answers an emergency call, by a bus conductor, or by the appearance of the rubbish man. None of these persons is a civil servant employed by a Whitehall ministry. Yet the services that they deliver must be authorized by Acts of Parliament; ministers remain answerable to Parliament for them; and ministers have statutory powers or informal means of influencing how programs are delivered nationwide. From an overall Whitehall perspective, public-sector organizations outside the ministries are no more and no less than agencies of government at the center.

Because responsibilities for delivering programs are dispersed among hundreds or thousands of public-sector agencies, the policy process involves a great deal of *interorganizational* politics. To translate a statement of good intentions into a specific program requires running an interorganizational obstacle race involving other ministries in Whitehall, pressure groups and their friends on the back benches of the House of Commons, local authorities, public corporations, and other agencies responsible for implementing policies. Agencies delivering services are particularly well placed to bargain about the terms of implementing programs, for this is in fact their responsibility. However, bargaining between organizations remains *intragovernmental*, because the Cabinet can invoke the authority of the Crown in Parliament, which is final. While accommodating to pressures from other public-sector organizations, as Sharpe notes, "the center almost always has the upper hand if it wants it."[2]

As government has gone "deeper in" to society, undertaking a wider range of programs, the influence of ministries is expanded yet increasingly subject to the constraints of interorganizational politics. Because a minister is identified with the programs delivered by other organizations, he or she will always be happy to take credit for what they do. A minister can sponsor new legislation or fight for more money for a service delivered far from his ministry. But when things go wrong, a minister will have to explain to Parliament why mistakes occurred and declare what the ministry is going to do to improve actions taken by other public-sector agencies. As two students of the politics of administration emphasize: "public management is getting things done through other organizations."[3]

In order to understand the delivery of public policies in England today, we must first of all realize how the growth of government has involved the evolution from a concentration upon government at the center to the delivery of public programs nationwide. The chapter then examines three different ways of delivering services: through locally elected councils; through service organizations that are not directly accountable to the electorate, such as the national health service; and through economic agencies that must adapt to the influence of the market. The chapter concludes by emphasizing the varying extent of the impact of Westminster upon the delivery of programs.

FROM GOVERNMENT AT THE CENTER TO NATIONWIDE GOVERNMENT

Government was created by concentrating authority at the center: Whitehall and the Palace of Westminster have been the seat of government since early medieval times. The Crown was concerned with activities that had to be centrally determined, such as providing a final court of appeal in disputes about laws and determining war and peace. While centralized, the authority of the traditional Crown was largely isolated; its impact did not extend far beyond Westminster.

The growth of government has been the story of the shift from government at the center to government nationwide.[4] Growth added to the necessary small institutions in Whitehall a host of agencies capable of delivering public programs throughout the United Kingdom. The development of the Post Office in the first half of the nineteenth century was an initial landmark in the delivery of services nationwide. Education was the second major nationwide service. The delivery of education emphasizes the interdependence of Westminster and non-Whitehall agencies. Education is authorized by an Act of Parliament, and central government funds are important for finance. However, the actual delivery of education is largely a local government responsibility. Schools are built and owned by local authorities, and teachers are employees of the local authority. Of the 1,281,000 people working in education, only 2,400 are employees of the Whitehall Department of Education & Science. The intentions of Westminster can be carried out only by influencing agencies outside Whitehall.

The center's authority is greatest when exercising its monopoly of laws: Acts of Parliament are the exclusive responsibility of the government at Westminster.[5] Even if a minister does not have the statutory authority to issue a directive to an extra-Whitehall public agency, the minister can issue advice and change the law to make the advice binding if it is not followed. Any organization established outside Whitehall can be abolished by an Act of Parliament, and some are; for example, the old Greater London Council, when left-wing Labour leaders campaigned aggressively against White-hall wishes. Laws can be used to alter the powers and finances of agencies against their wishes, the experience of universities in the 1980s.

The authority of Westminster is much less evident in spending public money and in the services of public employees (Table XIII.1). About two-fifths of money disbursed by public agencies is *not* spent by Whitehall ministries. The Department of Education & Science passes on to local authorities and universities nearly all the money for which it nominally answers to Parliament, and the Health minister passes on money to the national health service. This pattern is so familiar that the Ministry of Defence is unique in being a big-spending ministry that itself spends all the money for which it answers to Parliament. Most ministries operate as pass-through institutions; the money that the Treasury credits to the ministry is passed through to other organizations to disburse.

More than five-sixths of the hands that deliver public services are *not* those of civil servants or members of the armed forces; the great bulk of public officials are employed by local government, by the health service, or by one of a number of nationalized industries. With few exceptions, Whitehall ministries are top-heavy; employ-ment is concentrated among technical experts, administrators, or specialists in looking after the needs of ministers. The Department of Energy, for example, is headed by people who have worked in

TABLE XIII.1 *Organizations Responsible for Legislation, Public Employment, and Expenditure*

	Laws %	Employment (× 1,000)	Spending (billions of pounds)
Whitehall ministries	100	925	81
National health service	0	1,281	18
Local government	0	2,985	38
Nationalized industries	0	1,391	1
Other	0	298	1
	100%	6,880	£139

Sources: As in Table XII.4. Allocation of spending by organization from official figures tends to overestimate Whitehall ministries.

Whitehall rather than in coal, gas, oil, or electricity for most of their lives. The Department of the Environment, which oversees many activities of local government, is staffed by civil servants who have never worked in local government. It is equally important to emphasize that employees of nationalized industries and of local government have not worked in Whitehall and often are dismissive of officials there because they do not understand the problems of delivering programs "at the coal face."

Westminster has the authority to give directions but not the personnel to deliver most public programs. Acts of Parliament fix conditions and set limits upon the actions of other public-sector organizations. Cabinet ministers have supervisory or oversight responsibility for programs. The Treasury allocates money to ministries, which then pass on much of their funds to other agencies to spend. Although Whitehall pays the piper, it does not have its hands on the pipes. It has the legal authority to force any public-sector organization to do whatever it chooses, but this power, as a minister once privately remarked, is "like the atom bomb, so awesome that it is difficult to use."

Many motives lead Whitehall to avoid the responsibility for delivering programs. Ministers do not wish to become bogged down in humdrum daily activities (for example, refuse collection by local authorities). Non-Whitehall agencies can enjoy flexibility to operate as public enterprises (the Post Office); or gain an aura of impartiality in carrying out quasi-judicial activities (the Monopolies Commission). Many agencies have extra-Whitehall origins (the British Standards Institution), and qualified professionals want to regulate their own affairs (Royal College of Physicians and Surgeons). Stationing responsibility outside Whitehall distances controversial matters from Whitehall (the Family Planning Association), and concentrates efforts for a special purpose (a disaster relief fund). The history of a given program is always one of the most important reasons to explain why it is delivered by the means in use today.

LOCAL GOVERNMENT AND CENTRAL ACCOUNTABILITY

Westminster politicians believe that they are justified in exercising authority nationwide because Parliament is elected by the whole of the nation. In the words of a leading lawyer and Labour activist, Professor J. A. G. Griffith, "Councillors are not necessarily political animals. We could manage without them."[6] In the event of a clash between a local council, with an electorate of hundreds of thousands, and Parliament, with an electorate of tens of millions, the latter prevails.

The welfare state's commitment to provide social benefits nationwide has made Westminster very concerned with setting central standards. Whitehall is concerned with *territorial justice*, that wherever citizens live they have access to a reasonable standard of education, health, and other services. In pursuit of this goal, it prescribes standards centrally and uses its taxing and spending powers to redistribute money so that authorities in disadvantaged areas will receive extra money to fund their programs. Where an individual lives is meant to make little difference to the services delivered.[7] The Treasury also uses central standards to impose ceilings on expenditure in an effort to guard against what it regards as unreasonably high spending by some local authorities.

Constitutionally, local government is accountable to Westminster on terms laid down in Acts of Parliament. Local councils are subject to the *ultra vires* (beyond the powers) rule; this gives local councils very little scope to spend money except for programs authorized by an Act of Parliament. The American Constitution starts from the opposite assumption: states have the power to do anything that is not explicitly forbidden by the federal Constitution. When British local authorities wish to spend money, they are normally subject to Treasury guidelines, which do such things as lay down standards for the cost of building local council houses. Central government inspectors examine schools and police services. Auditors examine both small and large expenditures to make sure they are sanctioned by statute. The land-use planning decisions of local authorities may be challenged by an appeal to central government. The salaries and terms of appointment of many local authority employees are also affected by central government decisions. In extreme cases a minister can override decisions made by elected local councils, or even suspend councillors and assume administrative powers directly.

Organization and Politics. The reorganization of local government in the early 1970s created fewer and much more populous local authorities; in effect, it meant that local government is no longer local. The average English shire county now has a population of nearly a million; by contrast, electors usually identify with a small neighborhood, ward, or district within a large local government area.

The structure of local government in England differs with the level of urbanization. Fifty-nine percent of the population lives in shire counties, which combine cities and towns with suburbs and countryside. Shire counties have responsibility for education, strategic land-use planning, roads and transport, and personal social services. Each shire is sub-divided into districts, each with its own elected council, responsible for housing and lesser services. Twenty-five percent live in metropolitan areas, where a two-tier system of metropolitan and district councils was abolished by the Thatcher Administration, concentrating responsibilities in a single tier, the district councils. The process of reallocating responsibilities is meant to be completed by 1993. One-sixth of England lives in Greater London, where service delivery is mostly in the hands of London boroughs, supplemented by a variety of organizations providing transport and other services for a group of boroughs. The Thatcher Administration abolished the Greater London Council, formerly the top tier of a two-tier system of local government.[8]

Because local councillors are elected, councils can claim to be representatives of the people who live in an area and to be "closer" than Westminster. But the claim to representativeness is diminished by the fact that much less than half the electorate turns out for the average local election. Political apathy makes possible the nomination of council candidates whose views are far more extreme than those of their voters. Such candidates can be elected when party identification and national issues determine local election outcomes. Where a local authority is dominated by one party for a period of years, such as shire counties in Conservative hands or cities in Labour hands, a small party caucus has great leeway for doing what it wants, given local apathy. It can also come into conflict with central government when Westminster is controlled by the opposing party.[9]

While partisan politics is no novelty in local government, changes within the Labour Party after 1974 saw some councils swing much further left than the Labour governments of Harold Wilson and James Callaghan. The return of a Conservative government in 1979 stimulated confrontation between Westminster and left-led Labour councils seeking to get around central government restraints on local spending by measures that tested the limits of the law. The changes in local government introduced by the Thatcher Administration have been taken by unilateral central government action. The Conservative government has justified its actions as a response to what it regards as "loony left" activities by Labour-controlled authorities in large cities, especially London. Labour replies that reorganization is motivated by partisan spite.

Even before the Conservatives entered office in 1979, central-local relations were bedeviled by disputes about finance arising from severe cash limits on public expenditure imposed by a Labour government as a condition of its 1976 loan from the International Monetary Fund. The Thatcher Administration has imposed further limitations upon local spending by a series of increasingly restrictive laws placing penalties on local authorities that spend more than central government deems necessary for its services. It has also substantially reduced the central government grant to finance services that local authorities are required to deliver by Act of Parliament. After winning reelection in 1987, the Conservative government has brought in a community charge or poll tax on each adult resident in a local area. It assumes that this will make local authorities more responsive to local electors, because each will be personally liable for a head tax. The great majority of local authorities have opposed the loss of their power to impose a tax on local housing and the rate of tax of industrial property. They claim that the community charge is administratively impractical as well as undesirable on political and social grounds.

Elected councillors are meant to direct the business of each local authority. A majority of councillors are middle class and have had an above-average education; this is true of Labour-controlled local authorities as well as Conservative authorities. Councillors are unpaid but can draw an attendance allowance and claim some payment for income lost due to taking time off work. About half of Labour councillors work in the public sector, as public employees usually find it easier than private to get time off to attend council meetings. The average councillor spends about seventeen hours a week on council business; in larger local authorities there are usually a few leading councillors who are full-time politicians. The first claims on councillors' time are meetings of the full council and its committees and preparation for such meetings. Dealing with the problems of electors comes third.

Each local authority is divided into a number of functional committees that supervise the work of service-delivery departments of the authority. While the committee chair can have substantial importance, the chairperson is part-time and does not have the authority to direct a department: only a committee vote, upheld by the council, can do this. If one party has a council majority, then party discipline strengthens the position of the committee chair. However, if there is no majority because of the division of council seats between Conservative, Labour, Social and Liberal Democrats, and independents, then the influence of the committee chair depends upon coalition politics.

The crucial political relationships within local authorities are between the councillors who chair the most important committees of the council and the professionals who are the chief officers in charge of delivering the programs that the committees supervise. The chief officer for each service is appointed for expertise, merit, and seniority; he or she exercises influence through technical knowledge and commitment to professional values, and by virtue of being a full-time council employee. In major local authorities chief officers are of the same caliber as senior civil servants and can be paid as much, too.

National professional associations of teachers, town planners, architects, social workers, traffic engineers, and so forth are an important vertical link in the making of policy. Chief officers look to their national professional associations for leadership in developing new programs, and Whitehall looks to professional associations to promote change in local authorities in accord with what Whitehall regards as desirable. Each council officer gives priority to the programs of greatest importance in his or her profession. Within a local authority architects, teachers, traffic engineers, and social workers do not have much in common, for each responds to particular national standards set by different Whitehall ministries and professional associations. Even though a council is meant to coordinate policies for a given locality, local authorities are divided internally when delivering programs.

Because central government depends upon local authorities to deliver programs and local authorities depend upon Westminster for legal authority and money, the two sets of organizations cannot operate autonomously. Whitehall has sought a relationship in which reliance upon Treasury directives and professional standards of efficiency would lead to harmony, and Westminster's overriding authority could resolve disputes. Financial and party political pressures of the 1980s have created conflicts between central and local government; in these conflicts the two sides are unequally matched, for the center's power of legislation and of the purse enables it to impose great constraints upon the local authority's delivery of services.[10]

A Paradox. Central authority and decentralized responsibility for services are meant to be complementary but can also be contradictory. The center's power to set minimum standards and maximum costs is balanced by local authorities having their hands on the delivery of services. Lord Hailsham, a minister with experience in many departments, has contrasted being a defence minister in command of the armed forces with being in charge of a ministry whose programs are administered by local authorities.

> In the Admiralty you are a person having authority. You say to one person "come" and he cometh, and another "go" and he goeth. It is not so in the Ministry of Education. You suggest rather than direct. You say to one man "come" and he cometh not, and another "go" and he stays where he is.[11]

Decentralization exists because the central government cannot administer all its services in all parts of the United Kingdom without overloading the center. The desire to push administration out from Whitehall has become a prominent feature of administrative reorganization. While the Thatcher government has been anxious to influence policy at all levels of government, it has been loath to take responsibility for service delivery into its own hands. When challenged to explain why the government did not attack local spending by taking responsibility for delivering education, the single most expensive local government program, Margaret Thatcher replied: "There is no way in which the Department of Education & Science can take over the whole administration of education."[12] Yet simultaneously the Prime Minister has been pushing proposals to increase the influence of the Department of Education & Science over the services that schools deliver.

ACCOUNTABILITY WITHOUT ELECTIONS

The link between the actions of voters and public services is clearest when an election determines responsibility for directing a service-delivery organization. For example, decisions about taxing and spending are the responsibility of the Chancellor of the Exchequer, and the Chancellor holds office by belonging to the party winning a general election. Voters disliking the government's economic policy can vote against the party in office. In local government the delivery of education, housing, and personal social services is the responsibility of an elected council, and a council-house tenant can vote for or against the local council landlord, depending upon attitudes toward rents and services.

However, many public-sector agencies are not directly accountable to the electorate. They are headed by officials who are appointed by ministers. Sometimes directors are chosen by the organization itself; for example, a university head is selected by the university and not appointed by the Education minister. Agencies deriving authority from Acts of Parliament, appointments from ministers, and finance from the Treasury are first of all subject to obligations laid down in laws passed by previous Parliaments. Experts administering these agencies have a strong commitment to professional values that influence what the agencies do. Doctors, teachers, and social workers believe that their expertise should influence the delivery of services whatever the election result, for they, rather than MPs or councillors, are specialists in their field. In agencies headed by officials not immediately accountable to the electorate, direction by laws and expert values is often of primary importance.[13]

National Health Service. The 1946 National Health Service Act entitled everyone to receive a comprehensive range of health services from a local general practitioner, specialist consultancy as needed, hospital treatment, ancillary dental and eye treatment, pharmaceutical supplies, artificial limbs and appliances, ambulances, and community health services. With limited exceptions, the treatment is provided without charge and funded from tax revenue.

From the top the health service resembles a mountain range rather than a pyramid.[14] As the name suggests, the Department of Health & Social Security (DHSS) was created in 1968 by joining together two separate ministries, one responsible for health and the other for social security. The DHSS is responsible for nearly two-fifths of public expenditure and one-third of all public employees. The theory justifying the creation of this megadepartment was that concentrating responsibility in one minister, the Secretary of State for Social Services, would lead to the coordination of the health service, social security, and personal social services. But this mistakenly assumed that having a minister answerable to Parliament for all three services would actually coordinate the delivery of services locally. In fact, the programs are delivered by three completely different organizations. The DHSS itself is responsible for administering social security benefits, albeit from a remote office in Newcastle upon Tyne. Personal social services are delivered by local government employees. The National Health Service (NHS) is an organization without either a Cabinet minister or local councillors at its head. In summer, 1988 the Prime Minister split the OHSS into two ministers again.

The National Health Service employs more than a million people, ranging from surgeons and psychiatrists to hospital orderlies and kitchen staff. Within England the service is organized into fourteen regional health authorities responsible for planning activities and 191 district health authorities. Each district health authority is meant to devolve responsibilities to particular operational units, such as a hospital or clinic. In addition, the Health Service maintains units concerned with community care nationwide, such as the elderly and mentally ill, and special programs for drug abuse and AIDS.[15]

Because a hospital is a large organization, it can be subject to a number of standard bureaucratic procedures. The initial decision about whether or not to build a new hospital in an area is analogous to a decision about building a school. Questions of staffing levels, recruitment, and personnel are similar to those facing a local authority or a Whitehall department. Decisions about expanding some hospital services and reducing others are common to most fields of budgeting. The need for expensive new equipment is faced in universities too. In many respects a hospital is a village, with people doing many different things from making meals or handling hospital laundry to providing front-line services directly to patients.

Health care outside hospitals, often called primary health care, is much harder to subject to bureaucratic controls; it is the responsibility of doctors, dentists, and ophthalmic specialists. These professionally qualified groups normally are self-employed or work in partnership with professional colleagues; they are not civil servants or salaried employees of local authorities or the health service. When the NHS was set up, pressure groups representing medical doctors were adamant that they wished to remain self-employed rather than become civil servants or local government employees. The National Health Service pays doctors on a formula basis that affects conditions of medical practice. But the responsibility for providing care rests first of all with the doctor.

From the bottom-up view of an individual patient, the doctor's office is the place where medical services are usually delivered. The doctor is chosen by the patient, and the doctor is, as the German term puts it, a free professional. Instead of being paid for each treatment, doctors are principally remunerated according to the number of persons who have chosen to register as their patients. This gives a doctor an economic interest in keeping patients in good health, for income is not increased by patients receiving more frequent treatment. The importance of doctors is not derived from their numbers, for they constitute less than 5 percent of health service personnel, and the payment of doctors accounts for less than one-sixth of total health service spending.

Doctors are important because their professional values and judgments are of major importance in the operation of the national health service. Because the great majority of patients are rank amateurs in health matters, doctors are important as gatekeepers, recommending whether a patient requires admission to a hospital or a variety of specialist services. Cabinet ministers and civil servants overseeing health care are also amateurs in medical matters. Many senior staff in the health service are professional administrators, and they too must defer to the professional expertise of medically qualified advisors. Doctors can make their views effective collectively through pressure-group representation by such bodies as the British Medical Association and by participation in many NHS committees. Doctors also make important judgments as individual practitioners, deciding whether or not to recommend a patient for an operation or treatment in hospital. The National Health Service and Acts of Parliament entitle citizens to receive medical treatment. However, doctors prescribe what that treatment is.

While the goals of the health service are consensual, the operation and financing of the health service is a perennial issue of debate at Westminster.[16] The scale of the health service is very great, whether judged by the Treasury or by an ordinary family. Every year one-third of all families have at least one member receiving medical treatment, and more than one-quarter receive hospital treatment. Public spending on the health service accounts for almost one-eighth of total public spending on programs. If the health service were not funded from tax revenues, the average family would have to pay about £1,500 a year in insurance premiums to purchase health insurance—and problems would arise in treating the health of the elderly and those who did not have an employer or earnings that could meet the cost of health insurance.

Health care is usually provided without charge to individuals, but services must be paid for. Central government pays for more than 90 percent of the bills for hospitals and medical treatment. As the number of elderly and very elderly persons increases, so too does the demand for intensive medical and hospital care. As new equipment and drugs provide new health benefits to people with temporary or chronic problems, the cost of treating patients increases. The effective limit on what is provided is set by the Treasury. Treasury decisions determine the number of hospital beds and the number of doctors trained and employed in Britain. The British Treasury has succeeded in keeping costs of the health service low by European standards, and even more by comparison with the United States.

Queuing is the basic mechanism by which the health service controls the use of medical and hospital facilities. Access free of charge does not mean instant access. A patient wanting to see a doctor must wait in a queue. If the queue gets long, the doctor can either speed up the treatment of each individual, or some individuals will drop out, deciding that their pains are not worth the trouble of a long wait to see a doctor. Patients requiring hospitalization will be admitted immediately if there is an emergency, such as a heart attack or a leg broken in a car accident. But many people must wait weeks or months in a queue for operations for which facilities are not immediately available. Some patients in queues for hospital treatment require nonurgent treatment for such things as varicose veins; others are waiting for such things as a heart bypass operation. Since less than 10 percent of the population is covered by private health insurance, waiting in a queue or doing without treatment are the only alternatives for the great mass of the British people.

Inevitably there is tension between medical doctors and nurses, who want more and better-financed services, and the Treasury, which determines the cash limit of spending on the health service. Following the 1987 election, the annual debate about how much money should be spent on the health service took a new turn, as MPs of all parties and public opinion polls registered a demand for improved and more extensive services. Margaret Thatcher was averse to spending more on the health service as currently organized; her first thought has been to provide more services for the same amount of money by increasing efficiency. However, the greater the degree of inefficiency believed to exist, the more this implies a need for a major structural change in the health service. The popularity of free access to the health service makes it politically risky for a government to convert the existing system into a European- or American-type insurance system. The inertia of past political decisions faces a government favoring market principles with the political responsibility of administering a health service run according to non-market principles.

Fringe Organizations. The number and form of public-sector organizations today is not the product of a plan applying principles logically and consistently. It is the cumulative effect of political inertia. The character of each public-sector organization is influenced by its distinctive history. A host of organizations ranging from the universities, the Red Deer Commission, the Gaming Board for Britain, the College of Arms, and the Women's Royal Voluntary Service cannot be fitted into standard categories of ministries or local government agencies. Sometimes these agencies are described as quangos (that is, quasi-non-governmental organizations). So heterogeneous are the institutions thus lumped together that the originator of the term quango has concluded: "As a means of describing anything, however, the word is useless."[17] The term fringe organization is used here to categorize agencies that are not headed by elected officials, nor are they trading in the market, as are nationalized industries. The National Health Service has been separately described, since its size is so great.

Fringe organizations that are *executive,* that is, concerned with service delivery, collectively account for little more than 2 percent of total public employment. Particular agencies can be significant to the nation as a whole, for example the British Broadcasting Corporation, whose radio and television programs are heard everywhere. Most fringe organizations provide services of special concern to a narrower constituency, for example the universities, the Forestry Commission, or the Commission for Racial Equality. Because these agencies are financially dependent upon central government, Whitehall ministries can exert influence. But because they are independently organized, their own directors have powers to make decisions about what is done, and their staffs are often professionals with a strong commitment to expert values.

Many fringe bodies are *advisory* rather than executive; their membership typically offers comments to a minister or an executive agency. Members of advisory bodies usually represent the interests affected by a Whitehall ministry or service-delivery agency. One study found that Whitehall departments named more than 23,000 people to unpaid advisory appointments, about 6,000 to part-time appointments for which a fee is paid, and 1,600 to more or less full-time salaried posts.[18] The total cost of fees and salaries for members of advisory bodies is trivial in relation to the value of the budgets on which they comment.

Advisory bodies are politically significant because they have privileged access to Whitehall without the justification of popular election. They exist because Whitehall ministries find it politically helpful to receive advice from committees that provide inputs of information and evaluation on behalf of clients and that may mobilize support from those most concerned with particular services. While election legitimates the claim of ministers and local councillors to represent the people, it does not give them expertise in the delivery of public programs.

STATE AND MARKET

While it is customary to speak of British government managing the economy, this is misleading, for the economy is not an organization in which there are thousands of low-ranking officials ready to follow directives issued by ministers. The economy is a market; the total of goods and services that it delivers is the sum of activities by hundreds of thousands of organizations and tens of millions of producers and consumers. Public-sector institutions influence the output of the economic system, but in no sense do they determine it. The gross national product reflects private-sector as well as public-sector activities and actions abroad as well as at home. While the Chancellor of the Exchequer answers to Parliament for the state of the economy, the many difficulties of the postwar era are a reminder that the Treasury's influence upon what happens is limited.

The British economy is a mixed economy. There is a substantial private sector, organized into profit-making firms and trade unions bargaining for higher wages and millions of relatively unorganized consumers and workers. Employment in the private sector affects public revenue from taxes levied upon income, sales and profits. It also influences spending on policies compensating for unemployment and recession. Public-sector organizations employ more than a quarter of the labor force and allocate more than two-fifths of the national product. Major Treasury decisions about taxing and spending and Bank of England decisions about monetary policy have a pervasive effect upon the economy, influencing wages, prices, and total output.

Nationalization and Privatization. Nationalized industries are an extreme example of the mixed economy, for they are hybrid organizations, owned by the state yet selling their products in the market. To an economist a nationalized industry appears as no more than a trading enterprise. But the justification for public ownership is that the industry has nonmarket purposes as well. The initial impetus for nationalization came from convictions of the Labour Party, which has been more in favor of state-owned industries than Labour and Socialist parties in Continental Europe. The 1945 Labour government nationalized a large number of industries, such as coal, the railways, electricity, and gas. One argument in favor was that this gave government more influence upon the economy, and government was deemed better than private-sector firms in making decisions about investment, production, and pricing. A second justification was that profit from major industries should not remain in private hands. A third justification was social: government was regarded as a more humane and considerate employer than profit-seeking companies. Finally, major unions within the Labour Party represented workers in industries that had suffered unemployment in the interwar depression and expected nationalization to produce job security and high wages.

In the 1970s nationalization was extended as the result of the weakness, not the strength, of major manufacturing firms; it was a policy for dealing with lame ducks. Neither the Conservative government of Edward Heath nor its successor Labour government wanted to face the political embarrassment of witnessing the closure of a major British-owned motor car manufacturer, Rolls-Royce, which had run into financial difficulties in manufacturing airplane engines. By 1979, nationalized industries were responsible for rail, air, and local bus services; telephones and postal services; coal, gas, electricity, and a substantial portion of oil production; steel; shipbuilding; waterways; aircraft manufacturing; a significant part of motor car manufacturing; and a miscellany of other firms.

Nationalized industries are public corporations; their directors are not elected, but appointed by ministers. They are meant to be nonpolitical (in the sense of nonparty) yet to have a public purpose. They are exempt from many forms of parliamentary scrutiny applicable to Whitehall ministries. Their employees are not civil servants, and most are industrial workers rather than office workers, as in Whitehall. Nationalization did not change the way in which industries delivered their products: they are still sold in the market.

However, nationalized industries are not conventional trading enterprises, for they are not solely dependent upon the market for revenue. For years British Rail and the National Coal Board have had large operating losses; in 1986 British Rail reported a loss of £926 million, and British Coal, £546 million. These losses are met by grants from the Treasury.

Some nationalized industries have been making substantial profits, while others have registered substantial losses, thus rejecting glib generalizations about the virtues or vices of the market or of socialism.[19] The industries differ greatly in whether they are capital-intensive (for example, electricity) or labor-intensive (for example, the post office), which affects the ability to increase efficiency. Some nationalized industries have a steadily increasing demand (electricity), whereas others are in a contracting market (the railways). Industry-specific characteristics are important determinants of the financial results of nationalized firms.

Every nationalized industry has had a common problem: a lack of clear and consistent political priorities. A House of Commons committee offered the following vague guidance:

> The nationalized industries cannot be regarded only as very large commercial concerns which may be judged mainly on their commercial results; all have, although in varying degrees, wider obligations than commercial concerns in the private sector.[20]

Each industry is immediately responsible to its own board and full-time executive directors, but its board can be called to account by the minister who oversees and appoints it. A minister has vaguely specified statutory authority to give direction about matters that the minister deems affecting the public interest.

The Conservative government of Margaret Thatcher has claimed to have found a clear standard for assessing nationalized industries: "effectiveness and efficiency as commercial concerns." The intended goal is "to strengthen them to the point where they can be transferred to the private sector or, where necessary, remain as successful businesses within the public sector."[21] Where an industry has already been successful in commercial terms, privatization—that is, the sale of government shares in the market—is possible. In some instances public corporations that had been running at a loss were turned into profit-making organizations, a necessary condition for a successful sale of shares. Nationalized industries producing losses of hundreds of millions of pounds a year have been subject to severe financial scrutiny. Losses, employment, and output in coal, the railways and shipbuilding have been held constant or reduced, and British Steel has registered operating profits in place of losses. Industries sold or scheduled for sale after the 1987 election include British Telecommunications, responsible for telephones; gas, electricity; major oil producers; British Airways; British airports; Jaguar and Austin Rover Motor Cars; British Aerospace; and the water authorities.

The Thatcher government has had ideological and practical motives for privatization. The ideological objective has been to reduce the scope and size of government. Selling off government-owned public corporations immediately reduces the number of public-sector organizations and employees and removes from public-sector accounts finance provided for investment or occasional losses—as well as any profit that an industry has made. The practical incentive is that the revenue received from the sale of these assets can be substituted for tax revenue or borrowing to finance current public expenditure. In 1986 the sale of nationalized industries produced £4.4 billion.[22]

The Labour Party has opposed privatization with very different arguments. Traditional defenses of the presumed virtues of public ownership have been unsuccessful against a government committed to the market and unconvincing to experts familiar with the vague goals assigned nationalized industries by both Labour and Conservative governments. A second set of Labour criticisms is financial. The government has been said to be unwise in selling off corporations that were consistently making a profit for the Treasury, such as telephones and electricity. It is said to be spendthrift in using the sale of assets to finance current expenditure, thus threatening a crisis when it runs out of assets to sell. The fact that the shares of most firms have risen after their sale has been cited as evidence that the government did not sell assets at a high enough price. Thirdly, privatization can be criticized as insufficiently market-oriented, for in some cases transfer of ownership has not encouraged competition. The government's dilemma is that the greater the degree of competition, the lower the likely profit of a public corporation and thus the price at which it can be sold.

The Thatcher Administration has succeeded in its political objective, reducing the role of publicly owned corporations in the economy, and it is doing so on a scale so great that a subsequent Labour government would find it difficult to raise the money to buy back every corporation that has been privatized. The Thatcher Administration has also succeeded in greatly expanding the number of shareowners in Britain. While the typical shareowner has very little capital invested in the firms sold, more than one-sixth of the population are now shareowners, double what was previously the case.

Privatization still leaves questions about the extent of public interest in companies now in the private sector. The sale of firms to the private sector has not released them from government regulation. The Act of Parliament that authorized the sale of British Telecommunications also established a new regulatory authority, OFTEL (the Office of Telecommunications) to promote competition and regulate prices in the newly privatized industry. Where privately owned corporations are public utilities with an element of monopoly, the Thatcher Administration continues to regulate prices and/or competition, as in the case of the airways. In a mixed economy, the particular role of government and of private sector firms can alter, while the two continue to be interdependent.

The Treasury Balancing Act. As the Whitehall ministry concerned with the economy, the Treasury has a multiplicity of objectives that it must balance or trade off against each other. Within government the Treasury is concerned with taxing and spending and with the size of any budget deficit. In the domestic economy, the Treasury seeks desirable levels of economic growth, inflation, and employment. Internationally, the Treasury is concerned with a satisfactory exchange rate for the pound and a balance of payments in trade between the sterling area and other parts of the world. While all areas of economic policy are in principle interrelated, the pursuit of one goal can often be in conflict with another. For example, policies intended to reduce inflation may also increase unemployment; measures intended to boost economic growth may also increase imports and the balance of payments deficits.

The Treasury's involvement in balancing the economy is part of the political strategy of the government. The Thatcher Administration has had two very high political priorities: to cut inflation and to cut taxation. Given these broad goals, the Treasury has been concerned with keeping down spending and borrowing in order to limit the risk of prices rising quickly, and to lower the deficit sufficient to make significant cuts in income tax and other taxes. The Thatcher government has been prepared to accept a substantial rise in unemployment and slow initial rates of growth as part of the cost of achieving its higher priorities. The 1964 and 1974 Labour governments gave priority to economic growth and full employment, even when its actions resulted in a higher rate of inflation. In unfavorable international economic climates, both Conservative and Labour governments have been responsible for far more economic costs and far fewer benefits than they would like.[23]

The Treasury exerts substantial influence within government for three reasons. First of all, the Chancellor of the Exchequer is a senior politician in the governing party; this gives him the power to overrule spending requests from many lesser ministers, and in certain circumstances, to disagree with the Prime Minister as well. Secondly, Treasury officials are among the best and the brightest of all higher civil servants. Working in the Treasury is regarded as an asset for the career of an ambitious civil servant; former Treasury officials can be found in leading positions in Downing Street and elsewhere. Thirdly, the problems of concern to the Treasury are also of central political importance to the government of the day. The Treasury view is not always popular, but it often carries the day. A former Treasury official, Sir Leo Pliatzky, argues:

> A lot of people, including some Prime Ministers, don't like the force of circumstances, they don't like the force of reality. They think: "If only somehow I could get a different sort of Treasury." Okay, why don't they abolish the Treasury instead of trying to set up a counterpoint? Well, they can't, because the Treasury stands for reality.[24]

The annual public expenditure cycle makes manifest the influence of the Treasury upon spending departments. Each year it prepares an economic forecast the Cabinet approves, stating the likely total sum available for public expenditure and tax revenue and the estimated size of any resulting deficit. The budget is based upon Treasury calculations of the growth rate of the economy and the rate of growth of established public programs, taking into account expanding demand for such entitlements as health care and unemployment benefit as well as public-sector wage increases. If a new program is proposed to Cabinet, the Treasury must first be consulted about costs, and the costs must have Treasury approval before a proposal is considered in Parliament.

The annual public expenditure review is necessary whether the government is seeking to increase or cut back spending, for the spending plans put forward by ministers inevitably add up to more than the total that the Treasury reckons is available. The disparity is not a function of party politics. In a Conservative government pledged to cut government spending, there remain ministers who want to see the programs for which they are responsible grow. In a Labour government nominally dedicated to increased expenditure, the Treasury will want to prevent spending, from forcing big tax increases or inflationary deficits. The differences between the bids of spending departments and Treasury views are first dealt with in a series of bargaining sessions between the Chief Secretary of the Treasury, its Treasury's second Cabinet minister, and the head of each spending department. The Treasury must concede some increases in order to avoid alienating all spending ministers, but each spending minister must accept some reduction in departmental bids so that the government's overall target can be reached. If initial differences cannot be resolved by bilateral bargaining, then a special committee of the Cabinet, the Star Chamber, seeks to adjudicate, with a nondepartmental minister in the chair. An appeal to full Cabinet is possible but rare.[25]

Traditionally, Treasury control was meant to be about "saving candle ends," in Mr. Gladstone's picturesque Victorian phrase equating economics with parsimony. Uniquely among postwar Prime Ministers, Margaret Thatcher has sought to revive the idea that a major priority of the Treasury is to cut public spending, equating expenditure cuts with efficiency. But the spending commitments of government are so great that the millions that have been saved by cuts are very small in proportion to the billions spent on continuing public programs.

The Treasury is also important in continuously representing British interests in international relations. In London Treasury officials monitor closely the movement in sterling's value in exchange for foreign currencies; fluctuations in interest rates in international markets; and international trade. Computerized econometric models are used to relate changes in international markets to the British economy and to draw out implications for changes in government economic policy. The Treasury has officials stationed in Washington, Tokyo, Paris, and other centers of economic policy, and it represents the British government in a variety of international and intergovernmental organizations such as the International Monetary Fund meetings and OECD.

The Bank of England is separate from the Treasury, but it is not remote from government. The governor of the Bank of England is appointed for a five-year term by the Prime Minister. Normally, the governor comes from a private-sector financial institution in the City of London. The Bank acts as the government's banker, managing the enormous cash flow of funds for taxing and spending and borrowing money on the government's behalf. Government borrowing has a short-term element, reflecting fluctuations in the flow of tax receipts and spending claims; it also has a medium-term policy role, influencing domestic interest rates, investment, demand, and prices. The Bank of England is very active in international markets, managing the country's gold and foreign-currency reserves and intervening in international markets to influence the foreign exchange rate of the pound. It also regulates private sector banking firms.[26]

The relationships between the Bank of England and the government of the day are close but sometimes strained. They are close because the Bank's activities in national and international financial markets inevitably reflect and influence Treasury policies. They can be strained because the Bank's priorities are first and last financial; it gives foremost attention to money, whereas the Chancellor of the Exchequer and his Cabinet colleagues are also concerned with economic growth, unemployment, British industry, and election outcomes. In a mixed economy, the Bank cannot ignore what government does, but it pointedly reminds government that the private sector, abroad even more than at home, can act against the government's interest at Westminster. When their interests and priorities diverge, each can use the other as a whipping boy, privately or publicly. The Bank of England cannot work in fundamental opposition to the government, just as Westminster cannot ignore the pressures that national and international markets place upon the Bank.

Every Chancellor has an explicit or implicit idea about cause and effect relationships in the economy. Economic models make explicit and public the assumptions and implications of differing assumptions of cause and effect and of changes that might result from government action or action elsewhere that affects the British economy. In the postwar era Britain was in the forefront in relying upon a simple model of macro-economic policy derived from the work of John Maynard Keynes, who was a Treasury adviser and critic for two generations and a world-class economic theorist. The Keynesian model prescribed ways in which the Treasury could act when confronted with the threat of recession or inflation. Until the mid-1970s the broad outlines of Keynesianism were accepted by Chancellors in both parties. Even while disagreeing about how much inflation should be traded off for how much economic growth, they believed that Keynesian models provided the means of effectively influencing the economy.

Confidence in the ability of economic models to provide a good guide for managing the economy was undermined by events in the world economy in the 1970s, which did not fit simple assumptions. The accumulation of experience with models showed that many of their cause-and-effect prescriptions often were not borne out by events. A Bank of England economist, C. A. E. Goodhart, concludes:

> Looking at exactly the same economy and even using on occasions very similar structural equations, different modelers come to totally different policy conclusions because of their fundamental perceptions about the working of the economy. Econometrics has not, at least so far, provided any alternative for basic judgment, only some quantitative dressing and support for such judgments.[27]

When economists disagree, politicians are offered advice from competing and conflicting sources, and thus are free (or even forced) to choose between alternative policy prescriptions, each supported by some professional economists, and scoffed at by others.[28] The severe difficulties of the British economy under Edward Heath, Harold Wilson, and James Callaghan led Margaret Thatcher to embrace monetarist theories propounded by Nobel-Prize-winning economist Milton Friedman and others. Monetarism appealed to the Conservative leader because it promised a way to reduce inflation and in the long run led to an economy with a sounder structure of employment and investment. In the short run, it imposed high costs in terms of rising interest rates and unemployment. After entering office in 1979, the Thatcher Administration sought to apply monetarist economics. The government immediately ran into substantial technical problems in efforts to control the money supply, which was not easy to do in an open international economy. It also ran into severe political criticism as the short-term costs of its policies produced a deep recession. In response it demonstrated flexibility in adapting policies to boost the economy and reduce objections. The immediate result was a demonstration of the immediate limitations in applying monetarist theories. The upswing in the British economy in the mid-1980s has been cited by the Thatcher government as evidence of the long-term wisdom of its approach.[29]

Internationalization. While central government's influence on the economy has increased substantially by comparison with before World War II, the influence of world economic conditions on the economy is very strong too. A Chancellor of the Exchequer cannot expect to reduce inflation when inflation is rising throughout the world. Nor can a Cabinet wanting to reduce unemployment expect to achieve its aspirations if unemployment is rising worldwide. While Britain is a relatively large nation, it cannot dominate the world economy, for it accounts for a small proportion of the total product of advanced industrial nations; it does not have the displacement of the mammoth American economy or of the Japanese economy. What happens in the rest of the world has a big displacement in the British economy, given London's role as a world financial center and the importance of imports and exports (cf. Table II.2). The government of the day answers to Parliament for the state of the economy, but the actual condition of the British economy often reflects international trends outside the control of Westminster.

Insofar as international trends are dominant, an improvement in international economic conditions should be paralleled by an upswing in British conditions—and a downturn in world markets matched by a downturn in Britain. Whether or not the overall performance of all advanced industrial OECD nations is better than Britain, the national economy and the international economy should move in the same direction and to a similar extent. Alternatively, if the course of the British economy is largely a consequence of what is done at Westminster, there should be no correlation between what happens in the international economy

and what happens in OECD nations. The relationship between the
international economy and in the British economy can be tested in
three different ways: the overall rate of growth, the rate of inflation,
and unemployment.[30]

For a quarter century all parties have made the growth of the
economy a major issue, and each has claimed that it can do better
than its opponents. Implicit in the argument, and in the prescriptions of most analysts, is the assumption that the power to make the
economy grow faster or slow down is at Westminster. This is only
half true. Comparing the annual growth rate of the real national
product of Britain with the average for OECD nations shows that in
fact the two tend to move together and the correlation is statistically
significant (Figure XIII.1). When economies have boomed worldwide, British growth rates have tended to go up. When there is a
world recession, the British growth rate has gone down. The rise in
the British economy in the early 1970s and mid-1980s was in accord

FIGURE XIII.1   *Economic Growth in the United Kingdom and OECD Nations
Compared, 1964–1985*

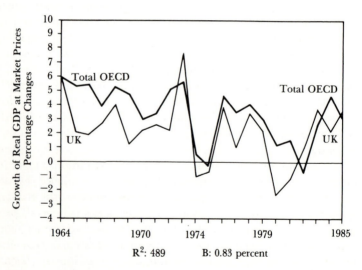

R^2: 489   B: 0.83 percent

Sources 1964–65: *OECD Economic Outlook,* Vol. 22, December 1977, p. 124;
1966–85: *OECD Economic Outlook,* Vol. 40, December 1986, Table R1, p. 156.

with world trends. When the British economy contracted in 1975, it was in keeping with a worldwide recession. In the election year of 1983 the Thatcher Administration took credit for a 2.6 percent increased in economic growth from the previous year; the average in OECD nations was a 3.2 percent increase.

On both occasions when the British economy differed from international trends, it did so by suffering a worse recession than the international average. In the mid-1960s the Wilson government experienced a low rate of growth while other OECD nations were still booming. After the 1979 election the Thatcher government actually saw the economy contract while in other countries the rate of growth was simply slowing down. The so-called English disease has not been a failure to grow; it has been a failure to grow as fast as other economies in good times. For every 1 percent increase in growth internationally, the British economy has expanded 0.83 percent. In the course of more than two decades, seemingly small differences in annual growth rates can cumulatively become big.

When inflation became a problem of major concern in Britain in the mid-1970s, it was simultaneously becoming a big problem worldwide. In the 1960s, when inflation was of lesser concern in Britain, it was also of less concern internationally. The two shock increases in oil prices engineered by OPEC seriously disrupted relative prices globally. The economic policies adopted in reaction by most major governments, including the British, had the incidental effect of fueling inflation further. In the mid-1970s the Labour government of Harold Wilson pushed inflation up well above the international average. Following a 1979 election victory Margaret Thatcher also saw British inflation rise well above the international average increase in response to the second OPEC oil shock. The fall in British inflation since has been very much in line with the trend downward internationally. The Thatcher government has been happy to take credit for this (Figure XIII.2).

A total of 78 percent of the variance in the annual inflation rate in Britain since 1964 can be accounted for by trends in international price levels. The ups and downs of inflation in Britain have been consistent with movements in international price levels. The distinctive feature of British inflation is not its direction but its magnitude. For every 1 percent increase in prices in the average OECD nation, the consumer price index in Britain has risen by 1.5 percent.

FIGURE XIII.2 *Inflation Rates in the United Kingdom and OECD Nations*
Compared, 1964–1985

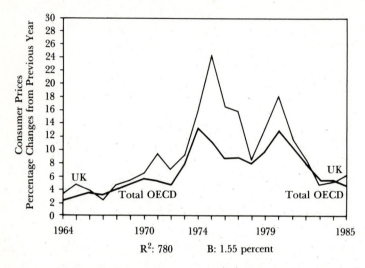

R^2: 780   B: 1.55 percent

Source; 1964–65: *OECD Economic Outlook*, Vol. 22, December 1977, p. 125;
1966–85: *OECD Economic Outlook*, Vol. 40, December 1986, Table R10, p. 165.

Since price levels in Britain have tended to rise faster than the international average for most of the past quarter century, the net effect
is that cumulatively British prices have risen by as much as 100
percent in a five-period and tripled in a decade. For that, both
governing parties can take a share of the blame.

Unemployment has been the third main concern of national
governments, and since the onset of a world recession in the mid-
1970s, virtually all advanced industrial nations have experienced
substantial increases in the national level of unemployment. In Britain the increase, especially since 1979, has been attributed exclusively to the policies of Margaret Thatcher. In fact, unemployment
rates have been rising throughout the OECD world. Moreover, British unemployment has been above the average level of unemployment in OECD nations for more than a decade. This holds true
even when figures are standardized to control for the effect of differences in national statistical methods (Figure XIII.3).

FIGURE XIII.3 *Unemployment in the United Kingdom and OECD Nations Compared, 1974–1986*

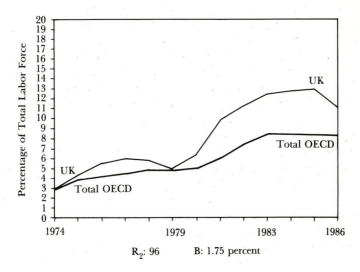

R_2: 96   B: 1.75 percent

Note: Graph uses OECD-standardized unemployment rates.
Source: *OECD Economic Outlook*, Vol. 40, December 1986, Table R12, p. 167.

Increases in British unemployment have almost exactly paralleled increases in national levels of unemployment throughout the OECD world. The long-term problems of the British economy are shown by the fact that while unemployment was at virtually the same level as the average for OECD nations in 1974, since then it has been rising faster than in other nations. For each 1 percent increase in the level of unemployment in OECD nations generally, unemployment in Britain has on average gone up 1.75 percent. In 1986 a downward trend in unemployment began, and the total fell below 9 percent by mid 1988.

The influence of the international economy upon the British economy is clearly demonstrated by the above figures. When conditions are improving in the world economy, they improve in Britain too. When the world economy is heading toward recession, the British economy also has difficulties. In managing the economy, the government of the day is more likely to influence the degree of change than the direction. By comparison with other nations, the distinctive feature of the British economy is that the desirable increase in economic growth is less than average, while inflation and unemployment increase at an above-average rate.

THE CONTINGENCY OF INFLUENCE

Programs are the outcome of a process that begins with the articulation of intentions by political parties. The process continues through the formulation of alternatives for action by Whitehall ministries, bargaining with pressure groups, formal approval by Parliament, and the allocation of resources by the Treasury. It ends with the delivery of services by public agencies. Given the number of different stages in this process, Whitehall cannot control everything; the influence of ministers is contingent, depending on the problem at hand.

Neither Fixed Nor Few. As the Bagehot quotation at the start of this chapter emphasizes, a country's rulers are neither fixed nor few. Policies are made in a variety of ways, and the groups involved in one policy arena, for example teachers' salaries, need not be involved in another, such as national defense. To test the extent to which the policy process involves the same few people or many different persons, C. J. Hewitt analyzed twenty different cases of domestic and foreign policy covering a variety of fields of government concern.[31] The results emphasize the contingency of influence: six different models were appropriate for at least one area of public policy.

A *ruling clique* model usually describes the making of foreign policy in Britain. Major decisions about diplomacy and defense are consistently made by a small group of people around the Prime Minister, the Foreign Office, the Ministry of Defence, and when financial considerations are significant, the Treasury. While participants are few in number, they are not so homogeneous as to be sure to agree, for the organizations represented are likely to reflect different approaches to problems diplomatic, military, and economic. The group is a clique because it is relatively isolated from influences outside its narrow circle, and it is ruling because decisions made by the Prime Minister and Foreign Secretary are binding on British government. But decisions of British government are not final: in foreign policy they are subject to decisions taken in other national capitals.

Balance-of-power pluralism involves a few groups consistently competing in the same policy arena with each winning some of the time; this characterizes the making of domestic economic policy. Typically, business and financial interests are arrayed on one side and unions on the other, with the government's senior economic officials representing a third point of view. The weight of each group in the balance varies with changing economic and political circumstances. For example, in the course of three decades the British steel industry was nationalized, denationalized, renationalized, and then drastically reduced in size, depending upon the balance of power between proponents of nationalized industries as against market forces.

Social policies are usually resolved through *segmented pluralism*; the participants differ from issue to issue, but within a given issue they are usually stable. For example, the cluster of groups involved with education are consistent and few, as in the balance-of-power model, but they are unconnected with those concerned with health. Teachers and doctors have different professional associations, assuring each a continuing role within their own segment of public policy.

Amorphous pluralism describes policy arenas in which participants are constantly changing; controversies about land-use planning are an example. Each controversy involves a specific plot of land. Whereas planners expect consistency of principles from case to case, most participants only care about land that may literally be in their own back yard. The personalities and groups in planning controversies are thus *ad hoc* and transitory, depending on the particular site in dispute.

Policy making is *populist* when a large mass of people directly influence the outcome. Nationalized industries are particularly subject to populist pressures, for a shift in consumer demand is a signal to produce more or less of a product. The decision of many people to buy cars and rely less on railways and buses influences transportation policy. Central government has built more roads to accommodate increased car traffic, and it has cut public transport in response to falling popular demand.

A *veto* model describes the frustration of government policy by extra-governmental groups. Occasionally policy proposals are vetoed by public opposition from strategic pressure groups. More often, the veto power of a group prevents an issue from being put on the political agenda. Until the advent of the Thatcher Administration, the Trades Union Congress successfully prevented Conservative as well as Labour governments from legislating about industrial relations. Today, the capacity of multi-national corporations and investors to move their resources from nation to nation can veto government proposals that are so resented that a flight of capital investment and jobs would result.

For any given issue policy making is oligopolistic, for only a relatively small number of groups are involved. But across twenty different issues the total number of groups involved is very large. More than 300 different extragovernmental organizations were involved in at least one case examined by Hewitt; only 6 percent were involved in three or more issues. Five-sixths of organizations were involved in only one case. When there was clear evidence of popular preferences from public-opinion poll data, the decision was almost always consistent with popular views.[32]

The contingent and limited involvement of many groups gives special advantage to those most consistently involved in the policy process, public officials. Ministers and civil servants must be involved in matters that require government action. Ministers do not dominate all areas of policy, but they can take initiatives to which others must react. Governors are more than experienced players in the policy process; they are also the referees who at the end of the day arbitrate between group demands and deliver public services.

The making of policy by nominally sovereign governments is constrained by the fact that the public-sector is a cluster of organizations, not a unitary monolith. There is almost always competition between public-sector organizations to define what government will do. Different Whitehall departments have separate identities and distinctive ideas about what should be the policy of the Crown in Parliament. Questions of public policy are as likely to pit different Whitehall departments (or Whitehall and extra-Whitehall institutions) against each other as they are to involve major differences between political parties. While conflict is interorganizational, because of the centralization of authority in Cabinet, the conflict remains intragovernmental.

The nature of intragovernmental conflict is illustrated by disputes in land-use planning. A nationalized industry may claim that the industrial use of a plot of land is in the public interest, but a local authority may wish to keep the land free of industry because it feels green spaces are even more important for the common good. Central government hears arguments and after a lengthy delay determines which of the competing public-sector organizations has the most persuasive notion of the public interest. As government has grown from a small group clustered in Westminster to a nationwide congeries of public agencies delivering a wide range of services, the possibility of pursuing conflicting interests increases. The greater the scope of government's concerns, the more likely public-sector organizations are to contain within themselves most of the political conflicts and contradictions found in English society.

NOTES

1. See Richard Rose, *Ministers and Ministries* (Oxford: Oxford University Press, 1986), Tables 3.2, 3.4.

2. "Central Coordination and the Policy Network," *Political Studies*, 33:3 (1985), p. 374.

3. Les Metcalfe and Sue Richards, *Improving Public Management* (London: Sage Publications, 1987), p. 220.

4. See Richard Rose, "From Government at the Centre to Government Nationwide," in Yves Meny and Vincent Wright, eds., *Centre-Periphery Relations in Western Europe* (London: George Allen & Unwin, 1985), pp. 13–32; and Richard Parry, "Territory and Public Employment: A General Model and British Evidence," *Journal of Public Policy* 1:2 (1981), pp. 221–250.

5. Cf. Edward C. Page, "Laws as an Instrument of Policy: A Study in Central-Local Government Relations," *Journal of Public Policy* 5:2 (1985), pp. 241–267.

6. J. A. G. Griffith, *Central Departments and Local Authorities* (London: Allen and Unwin, 1966), p. 542.

7. For a discussion of territorial justice, see David Heald, *Public Expenditure* (Oxford: Martin Robertson, 1983), Chapter 10.

8. For an overview of local government institutions, see Tony Byrne, *Local Government in Britain*, 4th ed. (Harmondsworth: Penguin, 1986).

9. See John Gyford and Mari James, *National Parties and Local Politics* (London: Allen and Unwin, 1983).

10. Cf. Gyford and James, *National Parties and Local Politics*, Chapter 7; George Jones and John D. Stewart, *The Case for Local Government* (London: Allen and Unwin, 1983); and R. A. W. Rhodes, "Power Dependence," in M. Goldsmith, ed., *New Research in Central-Local Relations* (Farnborough: Aldershot, 1986).

11. Quoted in Maurice Kogan, *The Politics of Education* (Harmondsworth: Penguin, 1971), p. 31.

12. "Thatcher Rejects Poll Tax Pay Move," *The Times* (London), 8 July 1987. On historic divisions between "high" politics (Westminster concerns) and "low" (local government services), see Jim Bulpitt, *Territory and Power in the United Kingdom: An Interpretation* (Manchester: Manchester University Press, 1983).

13. See Richard Rose, "Giving Direction to Permanent Officials: Signals from the Electorate, the Market, Laws and Expertise," in Jan-Erik Lane, ed., *Bureaucracy and Public Choice* (London: Sage, 1987), pp. 210–230.

14. For an overview see Rudolf Klein, *The Politics of the National Health Service* (London: Longman, 1983); and on the territorial dimension, D. J. Hunter, "Organizing for Health: The National Health Service in the United Kingdom," *Journal of Public Policy*, 2:3 (1982), pp. 263–300.

15. For detailed statistics, see *The Government's Expenditure Plans 1988–89 to 1990–91* (London: HMSO, Cm. 228-II), Chapter 14.

16. See debates in the House of Commons following the 1987 election about what changes are appropriate within the terms of reference of the existing service or by altering public provision.

17. Anthony Barker, ed., *Quangos in Britain* (London: Macmillan, 1982), p. 1.

18. Cf. *A Directory of Paid Public Appointments Made by Ministers 1978* (London: HMSO, 1978); and P. Holland and M. Falleon, *The Quango Explosion* (London: Conservative Political Centre, 1978).

19. See, e.g., Robert Millward and D. M. Parker, "Public and Private Enterprise: Comparative Behaviour and Relative Efficiency," in R. Millward et al., *Public Sector Economics* (London: Longman, 1983), pp. 199–274.

20. *Financial and Economic Obligations of the Nationalized Industries* (London: HMSO, Cmnd. 1337, 1961). More generally, see Richard Pryke, *The Nationalized Industries: Policies and Performance since 1968* (Oxford: Martin Robertson, 1981).

21. *The Government's Expenditure Plans, 1988–89*, Cm 288-I, p. 80; it also provides financial details of nationalized industries.

22. For overviews, see D. Steel and D. Heald, eds., *Privatizing Public Enterprise: Options and Dilemmas* (London: Royal Institute for Public Administration, 1984); and J. A. Kay, C. P. Mayer, and D. A. Thompson, eds., *Privatization and Regulation—the UK Experience* (Oxford: Oxford University Press, 1986).

23. Cf. Richard Rose, *Do Parties Make a Difference?* 2nd ed., Chapter 7; Paul Mosley, *The Making of Economic Policy* (Brighton: Wheatsheaf, 1984); Peter Browning, *Economic Policy 1964–1985* (London: Longman, 1986).

24. Quoted in Peter Hennessy, "The Guilt of the Treasury 1,000," *New Statesman*, 23 January 1987.

25. For varied approaches, see e.g. Hugh Heclo and Aaron Wildavsky, *The Public Government of Private Money*, 2d. ed. (London: Macmillan, 1981); Joel Barnett, *Inside the Treasury* (London: Andre Deutsch, 1982); Hugo Young and Anne Sloman, *But Chancellor* (London: BBC, 1964); and David Heald and Richard Rose, eds., *The Public Expenditure Process: Learning by Doing* (London: Public Finance Foundation and Price Waterhouse, 1987).

26. For an overview, see Michael Moran, *The Politics of Banking*, 2nd ed. (London: Macmillan, 1986).

27. C. A. E. Goodhart, "Monetary Policy," in Michael Posner, ed., *Demand Management* (London: Heinemann for National Institute of Economic and Social Research, 1978), p. 188.

28. See Richard Rose, "The Political Appraisal of Employment Policies," *Journal of Public Policy*, 7:3 (1987), pp. 283–303.

29. For the view of the Prime Minister's economic adviser, see Sir Alan Walters, *Britain's Economic Renaissance* (Oxford: Oxford University Press, 1986); for criticisms, see David Smith, *The Rise and Fall of Monetarism* (Harmondsworth: Penguin, 1987). For the importance of ideas in institutions, see Wyn Grant and Shiv Nath, *The Politics of Economic Policymaking*, and Peter A. Hall, *Governing the Economy* (London: Polity Press, 1986).

30. Different years are used for these tests, as follows. Economic growth and inflation are examined from 1964, when the Labour government began to give priority to growth. Unemployment is measured from 1974, for internationally comparable unemployment rates are not available for the 1960s, and 1974 was at the start of a massive world recession.

31. The first statistic is the r2 value from a multiple regression; the relative rate of change in the two economies is the b value from this equation. All relationships reported here are statistically significant.

32. See C. J. Hewitt, "Elites and the Distribution of Power in British Society," in P. Stanworth and A. Giddens, eds., *Elites and Power in British Society* (Cambridge: Cambridge University Press, 1974); and Hewitt's "Policy-making in Postwar Britain," *British Journal of Political Science*, 4:2 (1974).

33. Hewitt, "Elites and the Distribution of Power," p. 57.

CHAPTER XIV

Evaluating Change

It is needful to keep the ancient show while we secretly interpolate the new reality.

IN ORDER TO EVALUATE political change, we must first ask: What changes when politics changes? A historian focusing upon the English Constitution might argue that no fundamental change has occurred since the Glorious Revolution of 1688. Yet a new Prime Minister can take office within a few hours after the result of a general election is declared, and journalists then write about the dawn of a new era. However, changing the name of the Prime Minister does not guarantee a transformation of government: the constraints of office can change ministers more than they alter government. Yet leaving a name unchanged is the characteristic English way in which ancient appearances can be maintained while interpolating the new reality into Westminster.

Political changes differ in extent; the biggest changes are nominal changes in kind. A change in kind occurs when a country shifts from being at peace to being at war. The introduction of a small proportion of New Commonwealth immigrants into England since the 1950s is another change in kind, turning England from an all-white to a multiracial society. Some nominal changes occur at precise times, such as the approval of an Act of Parliament. But many changes that produce a discontinuity—for example, the process of moving from a two-party system to a three-party system—can take a decade or more to accomplish.

Everyday policy alterations usually concern changes in degree, small increments of movement along a continuum of choice. Changes in public spending typically involve altering the budget by a few percent up or down; the base of expenditure remains untouched. The annual rate of economic growth is measured in tenths of one percent. However, seemingly small changes in degree can compound into big changes: the long-term increase in spending on social security and health illustrates how changes in degree can cumulatively compound into a change in magnitude. Occasionally, a small percentage shift is a change in kind. For example, the increase in unemployment in Britain from under 3 percent in the early 1970s to above 10 percent in the 1980s was a nominal change from a low to a high level of unemployment.

Facts and figures are necessary but not sufficient to evaluate change. We also need criteria for judging whether changes are desirable. Criteria are often a matter of dispute; for example, ecologists will regard the decrease in British industry as desirable, whereas trade unionists see it as an erosion of the nation's economic base. Values can be confused when the nominally Conservative Party is led by a Prime Minister who asserts a desire for radical change, while the Labour Party anxiously seeks to conserve its traditional place as the alternative government in a two-party system. The Social and Liberal Democrats proclaim that they are a "new" party, but their chief resources are those of the two parties that merged to form the Democrats.

This chapter looks first at change in government, in order to distinguish relatively short-term and cyclical changes from long-term and irreversible alterations. Popular evaluations are important, because mass support for the status quo can be an obstacle to change, just as mass dissatisfaction is a pressure for government to act. The concluding section considers the ways in which parties evaluate the present and the changes that they would like to see in future. After a decade of a Conservative government under Margaret Thatcher, we must begin to think about the Thatcher legacy.

THE PROCESS OF CHANGE

The Constitution of the Crown is not so much a machine for resolving problems as a device for coping with or adapting to them. Whitehall officials talk about the machinery of government, but they do not believe that government can manufacture solutions to pressing problems or be treated as if it were made of electronic hardware. Reflecting upon a decade as a very senior minister in Whitehall, including five years at the Treasury, Denis Healey commented: "Running the economy is more like gardening than operating a computer."[1] Within the year there is a familiar cycle of planting, cultivating, and reaping, which results in Acts of Parliament, white papers, and the death of proposals that could have spread like weeds. Cumulatively, big changes can occur, for example, with the passing of generations.

Demographic Change. Changes in the electorate affect public policies and can affect political values too. Major social programs are particularly sensitive to changes in the age structure. Because most of these programs provide benefits for individuals, the more people of an age to be entitled to a benefit, the more government must spend to make sure that everyone receives it. Everything else being equal, it costs twice as much to provide secondary education to a million youths as to half a million young people.

Young people and old people make the biggest demands upon the services of the welfare state. An Act of Parliament makes schooling compulsory for everyone between the age of 5 and 16. When the number of young people in the population increases, more schools are needed. The immediate postwar baby boom led to a great expansion in primary education in the 1950s and in higher education in the 1960s and 1970s. When the birth rate falls, there is no longer a need to hire so many new teachers or build new schools. Social security is another program driven by demographic pressures. The more people born 65 years ago (or 62 for women), the more pensions must be paid today; the longer that people live in retirement, the greater is total expenditure on pensions. Demand for health services comes specially from the elderly and very elderly and from infants. The lower the proportion of the population of working age, the greater the taxes required from each worker to finance services for a larger proportion of dependent people.

Changes in the structure of the population force changes in the nature of public policies. Until the members of the postwar baby boom reached university entrance age, there were very few universities and thus few graduates. Most employers did not expect a bright young person to be a graduate, and a degree was not necessary to become a lawyer, an accountant, or a teacher. Population pressures led to the creation of dozens of new universities to provide for greatly expanded demand, and then to a raising of standards by employers and professions, so that a degree is now a normal qualification for many better-paid jobs. The explosion in the number of elderly and very elderly people has affected the health service, which is now concerned about the provision of services for the elderly outside hospitals, to prevent hospitals from filling up with elderly people who could be better off in their own home, in sheltered housing, or in a nursing home.

Even if the structure of the population remains constant, the composition will inexorably change, for millions of elderly die each decade, and millions of youths mature into adults. The passing of the elderly is rapidly removing from the electorate the few who have a first-hand recollection of England's role as a world power prior to the First World War and diminishes the proportion who recall the Depression years up to 1939. At the 1945 general election the median voter was born about 1900 and had been socialized into awareness of Empire, wars, and the Depression. Today, anyone old enough to have been unemployed before World War II is now retired. The median voter at the next general election will have started work in the 1960s, the age of the Beatles, and cast his or her first ballot in 1970 or 1974.

The impact of generational change upon politics is gradual. Young people are one among many minorities and cannot dominate politics by their numbers. If the young are defined as persons age eighteen to twenty-five, then 85 percent of the electorate is *not young*. If all voters under the age of 35 are regarded as young, the nonyoung still constitute two-thirds of the electorate. The median voter is neither young nor old; she is middle-aged. It takes a quarter-century for formative experiences of a youthful generation to be shared by a majority of voters. Changes in political values occur only insofar as young people think differently about the world. However, the process of political socialization is very much about maintaining continuity in values from generation to generation. The views of young people are shaped not only by their own experiences but also by what is learned from parents, institutions such as schools, and older friends.

Insofar as generational differences are more important than party loyalties, young people should differ from old people in their political views more than Conservatives differ from Labour voters. This hypothesis is particularly appropriate in the 1980s, as party loyalties have been in decline and differences between the young and elderly are said to be increasing. However, the hypothesis is inconsistent with the evidence.

Comparing the views of young people born between 1952 and 1968 with those of people born in the early 1920s or before shows that policy preferences are not much influenced by age; across a range of twenty different issues, young and old differ by an average of only 9 percent (Table XIV.1). For at least half the issues, the difference between young and old are statistically insignificant. The greatest difference—a 40 percent gap between young and old in attitudes towards sex on TV and in magazines—is remote from party politics. On only one other issue—the repatriation of colored immigrants—is there a difference of as much as 20 percent between the generations. Young and old people have much the same policy preferences about most political issues, ranging from unemployment and council housing to equal opportunities for women and spending on the national health service.

Although the differences between Conservative and Labour partisans are not large, they average seven percent more than those between young and old. Differences between partisans are greater than differences between the generations on twelve of twenty issues. Moreover, the differences between partisans tend to be greatest on matters of major dispute in Parliament, such as nuclear weapons and the regulation of trade unions. By contrast, generational differences tend to relate to issues that parties often treat as conscience matters outside their responsibility, such as the death penalty and the repatriation of colored immigrants.

Tempo of Change. In time almost everything can be changed. The insular position of Britain has been eroded by the development of the airplane and after generations of discussion, by the commencement of work on a tunnel under the English Channel. To politicians involved with immediate events, actions that only promise long-term results are often unappealing, for current office-holders must absorb the political costs without reaping long-term benefits. To those working for future generations, the need to invest years in preparing for change is an argument for commencing action now so that posterity may sooner enjoy the benefits.

There is always one good political argument for maintaining the status quo: the fact that it is there. The introduction of decimal coinage illustrates how slow and cautious government can be before acting upon a proposed policy. The abandonment of the old £sd (pounds-shillings-pence) system of coinage was first debated in Parliament in 1817. Two decades later, Charles Babbage, Cambridge professor and pioneer of ideas basic to modern computing, offered a detailed scheme for converting the currency into decimal coinage, and in 1855 a government report recognized the advantages of decimal coinage. But it was not until 1971, 154 years after the topic

TABLE XIV.1 *Comparing the Effect of Age and Party on Policy Preferences*

	Total	Young	Old	Difference Age	Difference Party
		(% endorsing policy)			
Party more important than age (12)					
Give up nuclear weapons	32	40	30	10	39
Stricter laws on unions	48	43	53	10	35
Re-establish grammar schools	47	38	49	11	31
Redistribute wealth to poor	67	71	66	5	29
Spend as needed to defend Falklands	39	37	39	2	28
Shift power to local govt., regions	55	55	54	1	19
Give more aid to Africa, Asia	52	62	48	14	17
Withdraw troops from Northern Ireland	48	47	46	1	16
Let council tenants buy their houses	76	77	76	1	15
Spend to reduce unemployment	80	82	80	2	14
Cut spending to reduce inflation	46	47	41	6	14
Equal opportunities for women	75	77	76	1	5
Age more important than party (7)					
Reduce sex on TV, in magazines	53	33	73	40	13
Send back colored immigrants	47	34	60	26	9
Bring back death penalty	65	55	74	19	16
Take Britain out of Common Market	34	27	41	14	13
Government guide wage/price increases	75	71	78	7	3
Make abortion more widely available	43	44	38	6	3
Spend more on health	95	96	93	3	2
No difference (1)					
Spend more against pollution	85	85	84	1	1
Average difference				9	16

Source: Calculated by the author from 1986 Gallup Poll survey. Young: age 18–34; old: age 65 plus; for party, see Table X.2.

was first raised in Parliament, that a system of decimal currency along lines recommended by early nineteenth-century reformers was adopted.

Many changes that can be accomplished quickly involve cyclical fluctuations. This is particularly true in the management of the economy. Interest rates, inflation rates, and unemployment rates each go up and go down. Policy makers watch closely to see whether the latest change is moving in the desired direction or signals the reversal of a trend. A 1 percent change is treated as politically significant whether a change for the better or a change for the worse. If unemployment is up, the Opposition will demand fresh government measures. If it is down, the government will take credit for this movement in the cycle.

The public esteem of political leaders and parties fluctuates at a much faster rate than substantive changes in parties or in the basic personalities of politicians. Party leaders can dismiss a single unfavorable opinion poll as a "rogue" reflecting sampling fluctuations, but a decline in the government's lead over the Opposition is threatening if sustained for several months. The 1970 British general election provided an especially vivid demonstration of the speed with which electoral favor can shift. In January the Labour Party trailed the Conservatives badly in all opinion polls, but it was ahead in all the polls in May. Labour Prime Minister Harold Wilson called a snap general election to cash in on what he thought was a trend in favor of the government, only to see opinions reverse and Labour lose office at the election in mid-June.

An Act of Parliament normally takes several years to accomplish from the time a minister decides that a bill should be prepared to formal enactment and delivery by public agencies remote from Whitehall. If a government does not begin preparing a bill within a year or two of winning office, it is unlikely to have time to see a measure through before it once again faces the electorate. Because the Thatcher Administration has won three successive elections, it has had the unusual opportunity of making its influence felt by planning measures during one Parliament and enacting them in the next.

Many major policies require more than a five-year Parliament to plan and implement. A particularly long lead time is required by major capital investment programs for school buildings, hospitals, or roads. For example, to help meet the rising demand for university education, seven completely new universities were founded in

England between 1961 and 1965. Because each literally commenced on a green-field site, growth came slowly. By 1988 the seven universities, each more than two decades old, have a total enrollment of less than 30,000 students, 40 percent fewer than the enrollment accumulated by the University of London in a century and a half of gradual growth.

Past choices limit present policies. A newly elected government will find itself committed to many decisions that it is too late to stop or reverse except at a very high political or monetary cost. For example, the roads and highways policy of any newly elected government must start from the fact that in the lifetime of a Parliament more than 95 percent of traffic will be traveling on roads planned or built under previous governments.

Present choices constrain future actions. A newly elected government can make major decisions that its successors will have to carry on. The great bulk of its legislation will not be repealed by its successors. While political inertia can make it difficult to put new programs into effect, once a new program is established, inertia can carry it forward for decades after its sponsors have left office. For example, the 1964 Labour government abolished segregation by academic ability in secondary schools; by the time the Conservatives regained office in 1970, this policy was treated as an accomplished fact, and it remains in effect today. Labour's decision was not, however, taken on the spur of the moment. The 1945 Labour government actually helped implement the construction of many selective secondary schools. Only in its 1955 election manifesto did the Labour Party begin to argue for a policy of comprehensive schools.

Coping with Change. A newly elected government need not regard the persistence of public programs as a justification for doing nothing. As former Prime Minister James Callaghan once said pointedly to a Downing Street adviser: "I do not need to be told how difficult things are. I want to know the way through." Ministers want to make a mark by introducing new measures that will subsequently be carried forward as routine by their successors; they also want to make selective alterations in programs inherited from their predecessors.

In an era of big government, the replacement of an established program by a completely new program is usually the most difficult thing to accomplish, for it means overcoming the ongoing force of political inertia. Even if the pressures to maintain a program are not great, a minister rarely has a green-field site on which to build a new program. A minister is usually confronted with an inheritance of programs that imply commitments to groups of beneficiaries and establish procedures and institutions that must be taken into account in framing a policy in succession to it. The more complex and well institutionalized an established program (for example, pensions) the greater the force needed to alter the direction in which inertia is carrying it. What a minister presents as a new policy is usually an amendment of existing programs.[2]

The standard operating procedures of Whitehall concentrate on difficulties already at hand. The Fulton report on the civil service described how Whitehall routinely copes with problems:

> The operation of existing policies and the detailed preparation of legislation, with the associated negotiations and discussions, frequently crowd out demands that appear less immediate. Civil servants, particularly members of the Administrative Class, have to spend a great deal of their time preparing explanatory briefs, answers to parliamentary questions and ministers' cases. Generally, this work involves the assembly of information to explain to others (civil servants, outside bodies and so on) the policies of the department, how they are operating and how they apply in particular cases. Almost invariably, there are urgent deadlines to be met in this kind of work. In this press of daily business, long-term policy planning and research tend to take second place.[3]

The most frequent justification for standard governmental practices is given by the doctrine of muddling through, or as it is known in its most elaborate form, the theory of serial disjointed incrementalism.[4] Politicians are expected to make decisions one at a time, responding empirically to problems immediately before them. They are not expected to worry about the further consequences of what they do, because these consequences cannot be completely known; they are problems to be dealt with tomorrow. If the consequences of today's decisions are bad, they should be reversed tomorrow, and if they are satisfactory, then they can be sustained. In this model of coping with change, a policy is not so much a statement of intent; it is the after-the-fact description of decisions made over a significant length of time.

Muddling through is an ambiguous phrase; one can emphasize the muddle or winning through. Those caught in the muddle are likely to be less satisfied than analysts at a distance. By a process of trial and error, muddling through can lead policy makers to hit upon an acceptable and durable policy. A decade of trying first one policy then another can also result in muddling around in circles. Since there is no "hidden hand" ensuring that every muddle will sooner or later be resolved, the shortcomings of one government are sometimes reinforced by the next. Margaret Thatcher has attracted support because she argues that ad hoc policy making in the style of her predecessors is less effective and desirable than consistency in the pursuit of longer-term principles.[5]

POPULAR EVALUATION

People evaluate the impact of government in the light of established values about what government ought (and ought not) to do; these beliefs are grounded in their experience of what government can realistically be expected to achieve. After 1945 there was good reason to expect popular evaluations of government to be positive, for Britain had emerged victorious from the Second World War after a heroic struggle. By contrast, in the 1970s a spate of writings assumed that the world recession threatened to make Britain "ungovernable," because popular consent was assumed to depend upon the provision of a high (or rising) level of material benefits to its citizens. An economist and former adviser to the Labour government wrote:

> The performance of the economy since 1964 had been worse than most observers would have thought possible; and the situation in 1976 was so bad that it was reasonable to wonder whether the sacrifices, needed to get the economy back into internal and external balance, could really be exacted by a government which had to rule by consent.[6]

Expecting economic difficulties to cause political collapse was false to history. In the interwar years, when depression was widespread, politics in England avoided the extremism that was widespread on the European continent. The mentality that defines economic problems as the worst problems that could face a government ignores what television shows: the place violently challenging Westminster is Northern Ireland, where disturbances reflect centuries-old differences of religion and nationality.[7] Within England for generations, independent of fluctuations in the economy, there has been respect for the liberty of the individual, freedom of speech, and the right of the electorate to dismiss the government of the day.

Expectations Negative, Reaction Positive. Frustration with the shortcomings of government presupposes a prior expectation of success. In fact, most English people usually do not expect government to succeed in dealing with the problems of the economy. Each year since 1957 the Gallup Poll has asked about expectations for the economy in the year ahead. For a generation most English people have normally expected the coming year to be worse than the year before. Taxes are expected to rise, and it is usually assumed that prices and unemployment will rise too, and the economy will be in difficulty (Table XIV.2). A government responsible for a deteriorating economy would therefore be fulfilling popular expectations!

The negative expectations that the public has about the British economy are partially justified. Prices have risen annually, albeit by very different amounts, sometimes more and sometimes less than the price increase of the previous year. As a consequence of inflation, the amount of money paid in taxes rises even if tax rates are cut. Unemployment rates have tended to fluctuate up and down. Popular expectations of economic difficulties have tended to be overly pessimistic. The economy has grown in the great majority of years since 1957. Even if it has not grown as much as MPs would like, the trend is upward.

When people expect the economy to be in trouble, shortcomings are not likely to trigger frustration because problems have already been anticipated. Frustration occurs only when people do not get what they expect. If the economy deteriorates less than expected, this may even be regarded as a sign of positive progress. For example, once an inflation rate rises above 20 percent, as it did under

TABLE XIV.2 *Popular Expectations of Economic Conditions in the Year Ahead, 1957–1988*

| | | Number of Years in Which Largest Group Expects | |
	Increase	No change	Fall
Taxes	28	2	1
Prices	25	3	3
Unemployment	25	1	5
Economic difficulties*			

*Question asked for 28 years.

Source: *Gallup Political Index No. 329* (London: Gallup Poll, January 1988), pp. 26–28.

the Wilson government, then a reduction to 10 percent can be heralded as a big fall in inflation, and once unemployment goes into double digits, a reduction to less than 10 percent can be described as progress.

The extent of economic difficulties in the 1970s created the circumstances for a politics of reprieve.[8] As economic conditions worsened, expectations declined. The government of the day claimed credit for economic conditions that were not so bad as anticipated. A small amount of economic growth could be hailed as positive progress and any increase in mass living standards as evidence that things were better than expected. Ordinary voters are adaptable and can learn from government's past shortcomings not to expect much in future. The result was not protest politics but what James Alt described as "a politics of quiet disillusion, in which lack of involvement or indifference to organized party politics was the most important feature."[9]

While the media highlight the problems of the unemployed and the disadvantaged, the great majority of English people report that they are getting by with what they have. When the Gallup Poll asks people whether they are able to save a little of what they earn, just managing to make ends meet, or have to draw on savings or run into debt, five-sixths normally report that they are making ends meet or saving. Less than a sixth report having to draw on savings or temporarily running into debt. Insofar as households feel a pinch, it is rarely because people are short of food or shelter. Typically, economic difficulties are reflected in a problem in maintaining a second-hand car or meeting the costs of central heating; a quarter century ago both cars and central heating were considered luxuries.

Most people do not evaluate their personal circumstances in the same terms that they use for evaluating the national economy. Each year the Gallup Poll asks people: "As far as you are concerned, do you think that next year will be better or worse than this year?" Nine-tenths of the time a majority say that they expect the coming year to be all right for themselves or improving, even though economic difficulties are normally anticipated. Economic prosperity is desirable, but it is not a condition of personal well-being.[10]

Evaluating Democracy. Since 1973 surveys by the European Commission have included a question asking British people to say how satisfied they are with the way that democracy works. Since the surveys commenced just before the onset of major economic difficulties in Britain, they can help in evaluating whether or not major problems of the mid-1970s have caused dissatisfaction with democracy, or whether the Thatcher Administration has created a reaction against representative institutions among those who voted against the Conservative government.

The British public's attitude toward democracy is both moderate and stable. Less than one-eighth normally say that they are very satisfied with democracy or that they are not at all satisfied. The average English person is fairly satisfied with democracy; this group includes almost half the electorate (Table XIV.3). A second striking feature of public opinion is consistency: in the past fourteen years the average person has always been fairly satisfied. The proportion expressing great dissatisfaction has been consistently small, notwithstanding major difficulties of government in the period.

The great majority of English people are also generally satisfied with the life they lead. In 1973, shortly before a decade of economic difficulties began, 85 percent reported themselves satisfied with their lives. In 1987, after a period of political uncertainties and economic difficulties, 85 percent again reported themselves as satisfied with their life; the percentage has remained virtually consistent throughout the period. Moreover, those saying that they are very satisfied with life outnumber those saying they are very dissatisfied by a margin of three to one.[11]

The contrast between unfavorable economic expectations, qualified assessments of the system of government, and a high level of satisfaction with life overall emphasizes how the most important concerns of the great majority of people are insulated from the major political controversies of society. Time and again, when sur-

TABLE XIV.3 *Popular Views of Democracy in Britain*

	1973	1977	1979	1981	1983	1985	1987
			(% replying)				
Very satisfied	7	10	7	6	12	7	9
Fairly satisfied	37	49	46	42	52	44	49
Not very satisfied	34	24	27	29	23	30	26
Not at all satisfied	20	12	13	13	7	13	11
Don't know	2	5	7	10	6	6	5

Source: *Eurobarometer* (Brussels: Commission of the European Community No. 28, December 1987), p. B-22.

veys ask people to evaluate their lives, the same pattern recurs: people are most satisfied with their family, friends, home, and job and least satisfied with major institutions of society. Individuals generalize their view of life primarily from face-to-face experiences, not from actions of distant political institutions.

THE THATCHER LEGACY

The assumption that there will always be an England is not a guide to the character of the England to be. Once the meaning of politics alters, much else changes in consequence. Value changes cannot be predicted by computer simulations or extrapolating a line on a graph. The values of politicians reflect diverse influences: political socialization within a party, judgments about what the electorate wants or will not stand for, experience of government, and principles revealed in response to events.

Attempts to forecast the direction of change are inevitably affected by value assumptions of forecasters. A traditional conservative can stress the need to protect achievements from the past, not least the fully legitimate authority of government. Socialists think less about forms of government and more about the redistribution of wealth, status, and political power. Economists assert that all talk of change is meaningless unless there are the material resources to pay for what citizens want to do. Some social theorists argue that the next major development in English society should assist the handicapped and deprived rather than productive groups in society. Environmentalists foresee the need to reduce rather than increase material change. Libertarians argue for removal of all kinds of government constraints on behavior.

Neither Direction Nor Consensus. In the dynamics of party competition, yesterday's disputed issues are often buried in today's consensus; they are succeeded by new issues that excite passionate disagreement until they too are incorporated in an interparty consensus. An observer may emphasize the extent of interparty agreement, evident in the views of voters and often in votes in the House of Commons (cf. chapters X and XI). But from the point of view of party leaders, it is the areas of disagreement that are most important. Party competition requires politicians to stress the differences between parties.

Deciding the direction of party policy is difficult. If all parties simply reflected the views of the median voter, they would all recommend the same policies. This does not happen. Each party has a different set of traditional values and interests, and this is especially so in the long-established Conservative and Labour parties. The governing party maintains at least a minimum of consensus: whatever the government does is desirable or is defended as the best that is possible in a difficult world. Writing during the Labour government of Harold Wilson two decades ago, I described this as the practice of "directionless consensus."[12]

Today, Opposition parties suffer from a lack of both direction and consensus. Because the Labour Party and the Social and Liberal Democrats are out of office, they cannot claim that their views reflect a consensus of the electorate. Even though the Conservatives failed to win half the vote, each of their opponents has failed to win even one-third of the vote. Election defeats and reorganizations have caused confusion within both Opposition parties about the direction in which politicians ought to lead. Devoid of the authority of office and humbled by successive electoral failures, party leaders cannot impose a sense of direction upon supporters who disagree among themselves. Disagreements in the alliance led some social democrats to refuse joining the Social and Liberal democrats. The Labour Party is a coalition of factions and tendencies.

From 1945 until 1979 Labour saw itself as a party of government, holding office for half this period. Direction came from the defense of what Labour ministers were doing in office and when out of office from unfavorably comparing the actions of Conservative ministers with what Labour ministers had done or would again do. When supporters asked for an articulation of Socialist values, the answer could be summed up in the phrase of Herbert Morrison, a leading Labour parliamentarian: "Socialism is what the Labour government does."[13] The domestic achievements of the 1945-51 Labour government, promoting full employment, social welfare policies, and nationalization of basic industries, were consistent with traditional Labour principles. But the 1964-70 Labour government failed to move the economy in the direction that Harold Wilson had indicated; a group of his advisers concluded that this was because of "the constraints on economic policy and the fact that the problems are always much more difficult than they appear to be from the outside." The conclusion of a sympathetic Fabian review of the 1974–79 Labour government's record described it as "intensely disappointing."[14]

Since 1979 Labour has headed in two opposite directions. In reaction against the record of Labour governments, the party veered left with a program very different from that of previous Labour governments and under Michael Foot nearly dropped to third place in popular support in the 1983 general election. The events were described by one Labour MP in a book entitled *Four Years in the Death of the Labour Party*.[15] By autumn 1983 Labour had a new leader, Neil Kinnock, who helped the party recover morale but not votes. The 1987 Labour electoral defeat has left the leadership without a clear sense of direction. Disputes about the record of past Labour governments are receding into the past. But the path leading the Labour Party to electoral victory has yet to be identified or agreed within the party.

During half a century in the political wilderness, the Liberal Party could claim that it could identify major new directions in policy. The proponents of archetypal programs of the postwar mixed-economy welfare state—John Maynard Keynes and Lord Beveridge—were Liberals. The Liberal Party was the first to advocate Britain's membership in the European Community, and it campaigned for the repeal of restrictive laws on abortion and sexual morality. Market-oriented economics is derived from a liberal philosophy of individualism. The weakness of the Liberals was that the party could not win sufficient votes to give it a big voice in the House of Commons. The surge of popular support for the Liberals in the 1960s and 1970s showed how formidably great a barrier the first-past-the-post electoral system is to the advance of a third party in Parliament.

The cooperation of the Liberals and the Social Democratic Party in fighting as the Alliance in the 1983 and 1987 elections reflected electoral necessity. It also reflected a large amount of agreement between the two parties on policy. The leaders of the SDP, Roy Jenkins and David Owen, found it easier to compose differences with Liberals than with Labour Party colleagues with whom they had previously served in Cabinet. However, merging the two parties into the Social and Liberal Democrats revealed a lack of consensus, for David Owen announced that he and his personal followers would refuse to join. The merger process also revealed a lack of direction about policy. Initially, Liberals wanted no detailed policy statement, arguing that it would be outdated by the next general election, whereas SDP members wanted to commit the new party to details of policy. When Robert Maclennan, SDP leader, insisted upon a detailed statement, this was accepted without thought by

Liberal leader David Steel, only to have it rejected by Liberal MPs as "Thatcherite." The vacuum was filled by forms of words that only highlight the uncertainties about whether the Democrats are leaning to the left or right of center.

Direction without Consensus. For three decades after the Second World War the Conservative Party gloried in being a consensual party, even if this sometimes caused confusion about the direction in which it was heading. Traditional Tories described their party as the national party and criticized Labour for dividing the nation by bringing politics into discussions about how the country should be governed. Direction was meant to be imparted by events, when a Conservative government would do whatever it deemed necessary and desirable in the national interest.

Labour's landslide victory at the 1945 election led to the emergence of a group of One Nation Tories, who described themselves by invoking a phrase by Benjamin Disraeli about the importance of the party drawing support across all social classes. Conservative leaders were afraid that if the party favored only the interest of capitalists and the middle class, electoral defeat would follow, because these groups are a minority of the electorate. By accepting most of Labour's achievements while disputing its proposals, Conservative leaders reckoned that they would be successful in steering a vaguely defined middle way between the extremes of socialism and of laissez-faire capitalism. Harold Macmillan was the epitome of this style of leadership. In 1961 he noted in his diary that his Cabinet was an amalgam of people reflecting "a quite deep divergence of views between ministers, really corresponding to whether they had old Whig, Liberal laissez-faire tradition, or Tory opinions, paternalist, and not afraid of a little *dirigisme*."[16]

Like a Marxist, Margaret Thatcher believes in a cause and has the confidence to assert that her beliefs are right, thus giving direction to the Conservative Party. From the beginning Margaret Thatcher's views have not represented a consensus within the Conservative Party. They were notably out of harmony with Edward Heath's period as Prime Minister, a period that one of his colleagues and her supporters described as Socialist government, that is, a government that did not reflect the principles of the market. Nor have her views been consensus views within the Cabinets that she has led since 1979. Conservative proponents of a vague One Nation philosophy, collectively known as wets, have gradually been replaced by younger, more malleable Cabinet ministers. But when they think she is pushing in a direction that will doom their ministry to unpopularity or failure, ministers can argue against their patron, the Prime Minister.

A decade in office has given Margaret Thatcher an opportunity unprecedented in this century to leave a stamp upon the direction of the government of the day and the party that she leads. Previous chapters have indicated the extent to which she has been able to carry out distinctive policies and to win electoral support. The record is incidentally an account of the limits of one individual's influence. Many measures have remained in place notwithstanding the Prime Minister's known disapproval. For example, while the Prime Minister speaks of Victorian morality, her government has not repealed permissive legislation that made abortion and homosexuality legal and gave broadcasters and publishers the right to publish virtually anything without fear of prosecution for pornography or obscenity. The Thatcher Administration has made some difference in the way that Britain has been governed, but it has not transformed completely the commitments of government carried forward by the force of political inertia. Unlike her postwar predecessors, years in office have not dissipated Margaret Thatcher's zeal for fresh initiatives. It was characteristic that she fought the 1987 general election with a manifesto that offered a new cycle of initiatives in social policy.

The Thatcher legacy will be the imprint that remains upon government when she eventually leaves office. What happens when Thatcherism becomes a "wasm"? One test of an innovating leader is whether or not a person institutionalizes changes introduced while in office. By this standard, General de Gaulle truly qualified as a charismatic leader, for the force of his ideas and personality were important in leading to the breakdown of the Fourth Republic of France in 1958 and its replacement by the Gaullist Constitution for the Fifth Republic. Although General de Gaulle left office two decades ago, the institutions that he established have endured.

As the person responsible for deciding who is in Cabinet, Margaret Thatcher is assured of many loyal supporters—as long as she is the source of government patronage. But her readiness to speak first and to concentrate discussion upon *her* ideas, reducing Cabinet colleagues to the status of *her* ministers, means that after she leaves office the direction that she gives is gone. The course that the next Conservative leader takes is up to him and will reflect the political circumstances of the moment—including the possibility that the party's electoral fortunes will best be served by appealing to groups that have been put off voting Conservative by Mrs. Thatcher's style and policies.

Public opinion surveys document that Margaret Thatcher has only half succeeded in winning popular support for her views. Victory at three successive elections has owed much to the division of votes among opponents. While most voters find something to admire in the Prime Minister, they also find lots to disagree with. Voters continue to endorse more spending on the National Health Service, government action to find jobs for the unemployed, and a host of other measures that the Prime Minister dismisses as inconsistent with her market philosophy. The Prime Minister's distinctive style of leadership—articulating a strong sense of direction without regard to consensus or compromise—is rejected by a majority of voters.[17]

The Prime Minister is distinctive among British politicians in giving her name to a philosophy of government. We speak of Thatcherism but not of Churchillism or of Wilsonism. The Prime Minister encourages talk of a Thatcher revolution, expressing her aspiration for a wholesale change in the outlook of the British people. There is one major obstacle to success: fewer than one-third of British people like the idea of the Thatcher revolution (Table XIV.4). The firmness, even abrasiveness with which Margaret Thatcher has argued her case has created, in reaction, a cadre of counterrevolutionaries. The strength of her legacy will be assured only if other parties adopt her views too, so that what was once thought of as distinctive to one Conservative Prime Minister

TABLE XIV.4 *Popular Views of the Thatcher Revolution (in percentage)*

	Total	Con.	Alc.	Labour
Favorable	28	38	22	20
Unfavorable	49	42	55	57
Neutral; don't know	22	20	23	23

(Question: When you hear people talking about the Thatcher revolution, do you think they are taking a favorable or an unfavorable view of how things are going in Britain?)

Source: *Gallup Political Index* No. 328 (December 1987), p. 8.

becomes part of a moving consensus. As journalist Geoffrey Smith notes:

> If Mrs. Thatcher is to change British life as profoundly as she hopes, either the Conservatives will have to rule forever or her principal reforms will have to become part of the common ground.[18]

The force of political inertia will ensure that Margaret Thatcher's legacy is still felt up to the year 2000. Even if her successors are anxious to repeal or reverse many of her programs, they will find that altering the work of a decade is not a task that can be accomplished overnight. Reinstating a tax that has been repealed is more difficult than repealing it, and reestablishing employment in manufacturing firms that have been closed is more difficult still. To reverse policies that have placed in the hands of citizens title to houses formerly owned by the local council or shares in formerly nationalized industries would require government taking away what is now owned by millions of people. The actions that the Opposition would have taken had they been in office after 1979 will be irrelevant in the 1990s. The challenges that they will face will be different: the legacy of achievements and problems left by Margaret Thatcher. Paradoxically, the best guarantee of the legacy of this self-styled radical remaining in place is conservatism, that is, the tendency for a program once in place to remain in place due to the force of political inertia.

NOTES

1. Quoted in Paul Mosley, *The Making of Economic Policy* (Brighton: Wheatsheaf, 1984).

2. See Brian Hogwood and B. Guy Peters, *Policy Succession* (Brighton: Wheatsheaf, 1983).

3. The Fulton Committee, *Report*, Vol. 1, p. 57.

4. David Braybrooke and C. E. Lindblom, *A Strategy of Decision* (New York: Free Press, 1963).

5. For a careful questioning of Margaret Thatcher's consistency, see Anthony King, "Margaret Thatcher: The Style of a Prime Minister," in King, ed., *The British Prime Minister*, 2nd ed. (London: Macmillan, 1985), pp. 96–140.

6. Michael Stewart, *The Jekyll and Hyde Years* (London: Dent, 1977), p. 234, quoted approvingly in the doom-laden last chapter of Keith Middlemas, *Politics in Industrial Society* (London: Weidenfeld and Nicolson, 1979), p. 447.

7. These challenges have political, not economic, roots. See Richard Rose, *Governing without Consensus*, especially chapters 14 and 15.

8. See Richard Rose, "Misperceiving Public Expenditure—Feelings about 'Cuts,'" in Charles H. Levine and Irene Rubin, eds., *Fiscal Stress and Public Policy* (Beverly Hills and London: Sage Publications, 1980), p. 228.

9. James Alt, *The Politics of Economic Decline* (Cambridge: Cambridge

University Press, 1979), p. 270. On reprieve, see Richard Rose, "Misperceiving Public Expenditure—Feelings about 'Cuts,' " p. 228.

10. See *Gallup Political Index* No. 329 (London, January 1988), p. 24.

11. *Ibid.*, p. B–10.

12. Richard Rose, "The Variability of Party Government," *Political Studies* 17:4 (1969).

13. Quoted in Peter Jenkins, *The Battle of Downing Street*, p. 101. For a critique of this philosophy from a Marxist standpoint, see Ralph Miliband, *Parliamentary Socialism* (London: George Allen & Unwin, 1961); and Alan Warde, *Consensus and Beyond* (Manchester: Manchester University Press, 1983).

14. See (a) the preface of Wilfred Beckerman, ed., *The Labour Government's Economic Record 1964-1970* (London: Duckworth, 1972); and (b) the preface of Nick Bosanquet and Peter Townsend, eds., *Labour and Equality: A Fabian Study of Labour in Power 1974-79* (London: Heinemann, 1980).

15. Austin Mitchell, (London: Methuen, 1983).

16. Harold Macmillan, *At the End of the Day, 1961-63* (London: Macmillan, 1973), p. 37; see also Richard Rose, "Tensions in Conservative Philosophy," *Political Quarterly* 32:3 (1961), pp. 275-283.

17. For opinion poll data, see Rose and McAllister, *Voters Begin to Choose*, 147ff.

18. Geoffrey Smith, "Commentary," *The Times* (London), 22 July 1987.

Index

371